AIRMAN'S INFORMATION MANUAL

1980

by

the Aeronautical Staff of Aero Publishers, Inc.

AERO PUBLISHERS, INC.

329 West Aviation Road, Fallbrook, CA 92028

FEDERAL AVIATION ADMINISTRATION

The Federal Aviation Administration is responsible for insuring the safe and efficient use of the Nation's airspace, by military as well as civil aviation, for fostering civil aeronautics and air commerce in the United States and abroad, and for supporting the requirements of national defense.

The activities required to carry out these responsibilities include: safety regulation; airspace management and the establishment, operation, and maintenance of a civil-military common system of air traffic control and navigation facilities; research and development in support of the fostering of a national system of airports, promulgation of standards and specifications for civil airports, and administration of Federal grants-in-aid for developing public airports; various joint and cooperative activities with the Department of Defense; and technical assistance (under State Department auspices) to other countries.

FOREWORD

This manual is designed to provide airmen with basic flight information and ATC procedures for use in the National Airspace System (NAS) of the U.S. The information contained parallels the U.S. Aeronautical Information Publication (AIP) distributed internationally.

This manual contains the fundamentals required in order to fly in the U.S. NAS. It also contains items of interest to pilots concerning health and medical facts, factors affecting flight safety, a pilot/controller glossary of terms used in the Air Traffic Control System, and information on safety, accident and hazard reporting.

This manual is complemented by other operational publications which are available upon separate subscription. These publications are:

Graphic Notices and Supplemental Data—A publication containing a tabulation of Parachute Jump Areas; Special Notice Area Graphics; Terminal Area Graphics; Terminal Radar Service Area (TRSA) Graphics; Olive Branch Routes; and other data, as required, not subject to frequent change. This publication is issued quarterly and is available through subscription from the Superintendent of Documents.

Notices to Airmen (Class-II)—A publication containing current Notices to Airmen (NOTAMs) which are considered essential to the safety of flight as well as supplemental data affecting the other operational publications listed here. It also includes current FDC NOTAMs, which are regulatory in nature, issued to establish restrictions to flight or amend charts or published Instrument Approach Procedures. This publication is issued every 14 days and is available through subscription from the Superintendent of Documents.

Airport/Facility Directory, Alaska Supplement, Pacific Supplement— These publications contain information on airports, communications, navigational aids, instrument landing systems, VOR receiver check points, preferred routes, FSS/Weather Service telephone numbers, Air Route Traffic Control Center (ARTCC) frequencies, part-time control zones, and various other pertinent, special notices essential to air navigation. These publications are available upon subscription from the National Ocean Survey (NOS), Distribution Division (C–44), Riverdale, Maryland 20840.

NOTES FROM THE EDITORS

This 1980 **AIRMAN'S INFORMATION MANUAL** should be a part of every pilot's Flight Planning Kit for study and reference purposes and is required by the FAA for proper flight planning procedures. The FAA written examinations for pilots require a basic knowledge and understanding of the AIM.

The AIM is issued by the FAA on an annual subscription basis. Aero Publisher's reprint of the AIM includes the complete "Basic Flight Information and ATC Procedures" as well as excerpts of "Notices to Airmen (Class Two)" and "Graphic Notices and Supplemental Data." These last two FAA publications are provided, in excerpt form, to complement the AIM and to familiarize the student and pilot with these types of data and their presentation. Consult them in their entirety prior to completion of Flight Planning, utilizing FAA Flight Service Stations (FSS) or subscriptions through the "Superintendent of Documents."

AIRMAN'S INFORMATION MANUAL
TABLE OF CONTENTS

Basic Flight Information and ATC Procedures Section
COMPLETE IN THIS BOOK

EXCERPTS

Notices to Airmen (Class Two NOTAMS)

Graphic Notices and Supplemental Data

TABLE OF CONTENTS

Chapter 1. NAVIGATION AIDS

Chapter 2. AIRPORT, AIR NAVIGATION LIGHTING AND MARKING AIDS

TABLE OF CONTENTS—Continued

TABLE OF CONTENTS—Continued

TABLE OF CONTENTS—Continued

TABLE OF CONTENTS—Continued

TABLE OF CONTENTS—*Continued*

TABLE OF CONTENTS—Continued

Chapter 1.   NAVIGATION AIDS

Section 1.   AIR NAVIGATION RADIO AIDS

1. GENERAL

a. Various types of air navigation aids are in use today, each serving a special purpose in our system of air navigation. These aids have varied owners and operators namely: the Federal Aviation Administration, the military services, private organizations; and individual states and foreign governments. The Federal Aviation Administration has the statutory authority to establish, operate, and maintain air navigation facilities and to prescribe standards for the operation of any of these aids which are used by both civil and military aircraft for instrument flight in federally controlled airspace. These aids are tabulated in the Airport/Facility Directory.

2. NON-DIRECTIONAL RADIO BEACON (NDB)

a. A low or medium-frequency radio beacon transmits nondirectional signals whereby the pilot of an aircraft properly equipped can determine his bearing and "home" on the station. These facilities normally operate in the frequency band of 200 to 415 kHz and transmit a continuous carrier with either 400 Hz or 1020 Hz modulation keyed to provide identification except during voice transmission.

b. When a radio beacon is used in conjunction with the Instrument Landing System markers, it is called a Compass Locator.

c. All radio beacons except the compass locators transmit a continuous three-letter identification in code except during voice transmissions. Compass locators transmit a continuous two-letter identification in code. The first and second letters of the three-letter location identifier are assigned to the front course outer marker compass locator (LOM), and the second and third letters are assigned to the front course middle marker compass locator (LMM).

Example:

ATLANTA, ATL, LOM-AT, LMM-TL.

d. Voice transmissions are made on radio beacons unless the letter "W" (without voice) is included in the class designator (HW).

e. Radio beacons are subject to disturbances that result in ADF needle deviations, signal fades and interference from distant station during night operations. Pilots are cautioned to be on the alert for these vagaries.

3. VHF OMNI-DIRECTIONAL RANGE (VOR)

a. VOR's operate within the 108.0–117.95 MHz frequency band and have a power output necessary to provide coverage within their assigned operational service volume. The equipment is VHF, thus, it is subject to line-of-sight restriction, and its range varies proportionally to the altitude of the receiving equipment. There is some "spill over," however, and reception at an altitude of 1000 feet is about 40 to 45 miles. This distance increases with altitude.

b. Most VOR's are equipped for voice transmission on the VOR frequency.

c. The effectiveness of the VOR depends upon proper use and adjustment of both ground and airborne equipment.

(1) **Accuracy:** The accuracy of course alignment of the VOR is excellent, being generally plus or minus 1°.

(2) **Roughness:** On some VORs, minor course roughness may be observed, evidenced by course needle or brief flag alarm activity (some receivers are more subject to these irregularities than others). At a few stations, usually in mountainous terrain, the pilot may occasionally observe a brief course needle oscillation, similar to the indication of "approaching station." Pilots flying over unfamiliar routes are cautioned to be on the alert for these vagaries, and in particular, to use the "to-from" indicator to determine positive station passage.

(a) Certain propeller RPM settings can cause the VOR Course Deviation Indicator to fluctuate as much as ±6°. Slight changes to the RPM setting will normally smooth out this roughness. Helicopter rotor speeds may also cause VOR course disturbances. Pilots are urged to check for this propeller modulation phenomenon prior to reporting a VOR station or aircraft equipment for unsatisfactory operation.

d. The only positive method of identifying a VOR is by its Morse Code identification or by the recorded automatic voice identification which is always indicated by use of the word "VOR" following the range's name. Reliance on determining the identification of an omnirange should never be placed on listening to voice transmissions by the Flight Service Station (FSS) (or approach control facility) involved. Many FSS remotely operate several omniranges which have different names from each other and in some cases none have the name of the "parent" FSS. (During periods of maintenance the coded identification is removed.)

e. Voice identification has been added to numerous VHF omniranges. The transmission consists of a voice announcement, "AIRVILLE VOR" alternating with the usual Morse Code identification.

4. VOR RECEIVER CHECK

a. Periodic VOR receiver calibration is most important. If a receiver's Automatic Gain Control or modulation circuit deteriorates, it is possible for it to display acceptable accuracy and sensitivity close in to the VOR or VOT and display out-of-tolerance readings when located at greater distances where weaker signal areas exist. The likelihood of this deterioration varies between receivers, and is generally considered a function of time. The best assurance of having an accurate receiver is periodic calibration. Yearly intervals are recommended at which time an authorized repair facility should recalibrate the receiver to the manufacturer's specifications.

b. Part 91.25 of the Federal Aviation Regulations provides for certain VOR equipment accuracy checks prior to flight under instrument flight rules. To comply with this requirement and to ensure satisfactory operation of the airborne system, the FAA has provided pilots with the following means of checking VOR receiver accuracy: (1) FAA VOR test facility (VOT) or a radiated test signal from an appropriately rated radio repair station, (2) certified airborne check points, and (3) certified check points on the airport surface.

(1) The FAA VOR test facility (VOT) transmits a test signal for VOR receivers which provides users of VOR a convenient and accurate means to determine the operational status of their receivers. The facility is designed to provide a means of checking the accuracy of a VOR receiver while the aircraft is on the ground. The radiated test signal is used by tuning the receiver to the published frequency of the test facility. With the Course Deviation Indicator (CDI) centered the omnibearing selector should read 0° with the to-from indication being "from" or the omnibearing selector should read 180° with the to-from indication reading "to". Should the VOR receiver operate an RMI (Radio Magnetic Indicator), it will indicate 180° on any OBS setting when using the VOT. Two means of identification are used with the VOR radiated test signal. In some cases a continuous series of dots is used while in others a continuous 1020 hertz tone will identify the test signal. Information concerning an individual test signal can be obtained from the local Flight Service Station.

(2) A radiated VOR test signal from an appropriately rated radio repair station serves the same purpose as an FAA VOR signal and the check is made in much the same manner with the following differences: (1) the frequency normally approved by the FCC is 108.0 MHz the repair stations are not permitted to radiate the VOR test signal continuously, consequently the owner/operator must make arrangements with the repair station to have the test signal transmitted. This service is not provided by all radio repair stations, the aircraft owner/operator must determine which repair station in his local area does provide this service. A representative of the repair station must make an entry into the aircraft logbook or other permanent record certifying to the radial accuracy which was transmitted and the date of transmission. The owner/operator or representative of the repair station may accomplish the necessary checks in the aircraft and make a logbook entry stating the results of such checks. It will be necessary to verify with the appropriate repair station

the test radial being transmitted and whether you should get a "to" or "from" indication.

(3) Airborne and ground check points consist of certified radials that should be received at specific points on the airport surface, or over specific landmarks while airborne in the immediate vicinity of the airport.

(4) Should an error in excess of ±4° be indicated through use of a ground check, or ±6° using the airborne check, IFR flight shall not be attempted without first correcting the source of the error. CAUTION: no correction other than the "correction card" figures supplied by the manufacturer should be applied in making these VOR receiver checks.

(5) Airborne check points, ground check points and VOTs are included in the Airport/Facility Directory.

(6) If dual system VOR (units independent of each other except for the antenna) is installed in the aircraft, the person checking the equipment may check one system against the other. He shall turn both systems to the same VOR ground facility and note the indicated bearing to that station. The maximum permissible variations between the two indicated bearings is 4°.

5. TATICAL AIR NAVIGATION (TACAN)

a. For reasons peculiar to military or naval operations (unusual siting conditions, the pitching and rolling of a naval vessel, etc.) the civil VOR–DME system of air navigation was considered unsuitable for military or naval use. A new navigational system, Tactical Air Navigation (TACAN), was therefore developed by the military and naval forces to more readily lend itself to military and naval requirements. As a result, the FAA has been in the process of integrating TACAN facilities with the civil VOR–DME program. Although the theoretical, or technical principles of operation of TACAN equipment are quite different from those of VOR–DME facilities, the end result, as far as the navigating pilot is concerned, is the same. These integrated facilities are called VORTAC's.

b. TACAN ground equipment consists of either a fixed or mobile transmitting unit. The airborne unit in conjunction with the ground unit reduces the transmitted signal to a visual presentation of both azimuth and distance information. TACAN is a pulse system and operates in the UHF band of frequencies. Its use requires TACAN airborne equipment and does not operate through conventional VOR equipment.

6. VHF OMNIDIRECTIONAL RANGE/TACTICAL AIR NAVIGATION (VORTAC)

a. VORTAC is a facility consisting of two components, VOR and TACAN, which provides three individual services: VOR azimuth, TACAN azimuth and TACAN distance (DME) at one site. Although consisting of more than one component, incorporating more than one operating frequency, and using more than one antenna system, a VORTAC is considered to be a unified navigational aid. Both components of a VORTAC are envisioned as operating simultaneously and providing the three services at all times.

b. Transmitted signals of VOR and TACAN are each identified by three-letter code transmission and are interlocked so that pilots using VOR azimuth with TACAN distance can be assured that both signals being received are definitely from the same ground station. The frequency channels of the VOR and the TACAN at each VORTAC facility are "paired" in accordance with a national plan to simplify airborne operation.

7. DISTANCE MEASURING EQUIPMENT (DME)

a. In the operation of DME, paired pulses at a specific spacing are sent out from the aircraft (this is the interrogation) and are received at the ground station. The ground station (transponder) then transmits paired pulses back to the aircraft at the same pulse spacing but on a different frequency. The time required for the round trip of this signal exchange is measured in the airborne DME unit and is translated into distance (Nautical Miles) from the aircraft to the ground station.

b. Operating on the line-of-sight principle, DME furnishes distance information with a very high degree of accuracy. Reliable signals may be received at distances up to 199 NM at line-of-sight altitude with an accuracy of better than ½ mile or 3% of the distance, whichever is greater. Distance information received from DME equipment is SLANT RANGE distance and not actual horizontal distance.

c. DME operates on frequencies in the UHF spectrum between 962 MHz and 1213 MHz. Aircraft equipped with TACAN equipment will receive distance information from a VORTAC automatically, while aircraft equipped with VOR must have a separate DME airborne unit.

d. VOR/DME, VORTAC, ILS/DME, and LOC/DME navigation facilities established by the FAA provide course and distance information from colocated components under a frequency pairing plan. Aircraft receiving equipment which provides for automatic DME selection assures reception of azimuth and distance information from a common source whenever designated VOR/DME, VORTAC, ILS/DME, and LOC/DME are selected.

e. Due to the limited number of available frequencies, assignment of paired frequencies has been required for certain military noncolocated VOR and TACAN facilities which serve the same area but which may be separated by distances up to a few miles. The military is presently undergoing a program to colocate VOR and TACAN facilities or to assign nonpaired frequencies to those facilities that cannot be colocated.

f. VOR/DME, VORTAC, ILS/DME, and LOC/DME facilities are identified by synchronized identifications which are transmitted on a time share basis. The VOR or localizer portion of the facility is identified by a coded tone modulated at 1020 Hz or by a combination of code and voice. The TACAN or DME is identified by a coded tone modulated at 1350 Hz. The DME or TACAN coded identification is transmitted one time for each three or four times that the VOR or localizer coded identification is transmitted. When either the VOR or the DME is inoperative, it is important to recognize which identifier is retained for the operative facility. A single coded identification with a repetition interval of approximately 30 seconds indicates that the DME is operative.

g. Aircraft receiving equipment which provides for automatic DME selection assures reception of azimuth and distance information from a common source whenever designated VOR/DME, VORTAC and ILS/DME navigation facilities are selected. Pilots are cautioned to disregard any distance displays from automatically selected DME equipment whenever VOR or ILS facilities, which do not have the DME feature installed, are being used for position determination.

8-9. RESERVED

10. CLASS OF NAVAIDS

a. VOR, VORTAC, and TACAN aids are classed according to their operational use. There are three classes.

T (Terminal)
L (Low altitude)
H (High altitude)

b. The normal service range for the T, L, and H class aids is included in the following table. Certain operational requirements make it necessary to use some of these aids at greater service ranges than are listed in the table. Extended range is made possible through flight inspection determinations. Some aids also have lesser service range due to location, terrain, frequency protection, etc. Actual restrictions to service range are listed with the navaid in the Airport/Facility Directory.

c. VOR/VORTAC/TACAN NAVAIDS
Normal Usable Altitudes and Radius Distances

Class	Altitudes	Distance (nautical miles)
T	12,000' and below	25
L	Below 18,000'	40
H	Below 18,000'	40
H	Within the conterminous 48 states only, between 14,500' and 17,999'	100
H	18,000' — FL 450	130
H	Above FL 450	100

d. NON-DIRECTIONAL RADIO BEACON (NDB)
Usable Radius Distances for all Altitudes

Class	Power (watts)	Distance (nautical miles)
Compass Locator	Under 25	15
MH	Under 50	25
H	50 — 1999	*50
HH	2000 or more	75

* Service range of individual facilities may be less than 50 nautical miles. Restrictions to service range are listed with the navaid in the Airport/Facility Directory.

11. MARKER BEACON

a. Marker beacons serve to identify a particular location in space along an airway or on the approach to an instrument runway. This is done by means of a 75-MHz transmitter which transmits a directional signal to be received by aircraft flying overhead. These markers are generally used in conjunction with enroute navaids and the Instrument Landing Systems as point designators.

b. The class FM fan markers are used to provide a positive identification of positions at definite points along the airways. The transmitters have a power output of approximately 100 watts. Two types of antenna array are used with class FM fan markers. The first type used, and generally referred to as the standard type, produces an elliptical-shaped pattern, which at an elevation of 1000 feet above the station is about four nautical miles wide and 12 nautical miles long. At 10,000 feet the pattern widens to about 12 nautical miles wide and 35 nautical miles long.

c. The second array produces a dumbell or bone-shaped pattern, which, at the "handle" is about three miles wide at 1000 feet. The boneshaped marker is preferred at approach control locations where "timed" approaches are used.

d. The class LFM or low-powered fan markers have a rated power output of 5 watts. The antenna array produces a circular pattern which appears elongated at right angles to the airway due to the directional characteristics of the aircraft receiving antenna.

e. The Station Location, or Z-Marker, was developed to meet the need for a positive position indicator for aircraft operating under instrument flying conditions to show the pilot when he was passing directly over a Low Frequency navigational aid. The marker consists of a 5-watt transmitter and a directional antenna array which is located on the range plot between the towers or the loop antennas.

f. ILS marker beacon information is included under "ILS."

12. INSTRUMENT LANDING SYSTEM (ILS)

a. GENERAL

(1) The instrument landing system is designed to provide an approach path for exact alignment and descent of an aircraft on final approach to a runway.

(2) The ground equipment consists of two highly directional transmitting systems and, along the approach, three (or fewer) marker beacons. The directional transmitters are known as the localizer and glide slope transmitters.

(3) The system may be divided functionally into three parts:

Guidance information—localizer, glide slope
Range information—marker beacons
Visual information—approach lights, touchdown and centerline lights, runway lights

(4) Compass locators located at the outer marker or middle marker may be substituted for these marker beacons. DME when specified in the procedure may be substituted for the outer marker.

(5) At some locations a complete ILS system has been installed on each end of a runway; on the approach end of runway 4 and the approach end of runway 22 for example. When such is the case, the ILS systems are not inservice simultaneously.

b. LOCALIZER

(1) The localizer transmitter, operating on one of the forty ILS channels within the frequency range of 108.10 MHz to 111.95 MHz, emits signals which provide the pilot with course guidance to the runway centerline.

(2) The approach course of the localizer, which is used with other functional parts, e.g., glide slope, marker beacons, etc., is called the front course. The localizer signal emitted from the transmitter at the far end of the runway is adjusted to produce an angular width between 3° and 6°, as necessary, to provide a linear width of approximately 700' at the runway approach threshold.

(3) The course line along the extended centerline of a runway, in the opposite direction to the front course is called the back course. **CAUTION**—unless your aircraft's ILS equipment includes reverse sensing capability, when flying inbound on the back course it is necessary to steer the aircraft in the direction opposite of the needle deflection on the airborne instrument when making corrections from off-course to on-course. This "flying away from the needle" is also required when flying outbound on the front course of the localizer. DO NOT UTILIZE BACK COURSE SIGNALS for approach unless a BACK COURSE APPROACH PROCEDURE has been published for the particular runway and is authorized by ATC.

(4) Identification is in International Morse Code and consists of a three-letter identifier preceded by the letter I (● ●) transmitted on the localizer frequency (Example: I–DIA).

(5) The localizer provides course guidance throughout the descent path to the runway threshold from a distance of 18 NM from the antenna between an altitude of 1000' above the highest terrain along the course line and 4500' above the elevation of the antenna site. Proper off-course indications are provided throughout the following angular areas of the operational service volume: (1) To 10° either side of the course along a radius of 18 NM from the antenna, and (2) From 10°–35° either side of the course along a radius of 10 NM.

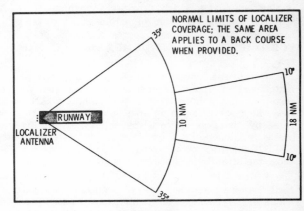

NORMAL LIMITS OF LOCALIZER COVERAGE; THE SAME AREA APPLIES TO A BACK COURSE WHEN PROVIDED.

Figure 1–1

(6) Proper off-course indications are generally not provided between 35–90° either side of the localizer course. Therefore, instrument indications of possible courses in the area from 35° to 90° off-course should be disregarded. All unrestricted localizer facilities provide reliable course guidance information within the areas described above.

(7) The Atlantic City, Atlanta, and San Francisco Category III localizers include a far field monitor which

will automatically remove the localizer from service when the course signal is displayed 10 microamperes (approximately 20 feet at the runway threshold) or more from the runway centerline for a period of approximately 70 seconds or longer. The 70 second delay is necessary to prevent unnecessary localizer shutdowns for temporary conditions. These temporary conditions may be caused by taxiing aircraft, by aircraft overflight or other conditions between the localizer antenna and the far field monitor (normally located at the middle marker).

(a) Approximately 65 seconds after the far field monitor detects a continuing 10 microamperes or more displacement of the course it will transmit simultaneous 1900 and 2100 Hz audible alert tones on the localizer frequency. This feature is to advise pilots that the localizer will shutdown 5 seconds after the alert tones are first transmitted. Out of tolerance signals detected by the main internal monitor at the localizer will shutdown the facility immediately without warning.

(8) The Localizer-type Directional Aid (LDA) is of comparable utility and accuracy to a localizer but is not part of a complete ILS. The LDA course usually provides a more precise approach course than the similar Simplified Directional Facility (SDF) installation, which may have a course width of 6° or 12°. The LDA is not aligned with the runway. Straight-in minima may be published where alignment does not exceed 30 degrees between the course and runway. Circling minima only are published where this alignment exceeds 30 degrees.

c. GLIDE SLOPE

(1) The UHF glide slope transmitter, operating on one of the forty ILS channels within the frequency range 329.15 MHz, to 335.00 MHz radiates its signals primarily in the direction of the localizer front course. Normally, a glide slope transmitter is not installed with the intent of radiating signals toward the localizer back course; however, there are a few runways at which an additional glide slope transmitter is installed to radiate signals primarily directed toward the localizer back course to provide vertical guidance. The two glide slope transmitters will operate on the same channel but are interlocked to avoid simultaneous radiation to support either the front course or the back course, but not both at the same time. Approach and landing charts for the runways which have glide slopes on the localizer back course will be depicted accordingly.

Caution: Spurious glide slope signals may exist in the area of the localizer back course approach which can cause the glide slope flag alarm to disappear and present unreliable glide slope information. Disregard all glide slope signal indications when making a localizer back course approach unless a glide slope is specified on the approach and landing chart.

(2) The glide slope transmitter is located between 750′ and 1250′ from the approach end of the runway (down the runway) and offset 400–600′ from the runway centerline. It transmits a glide path beam 1.4° wide. The term "glide path" means that portion of the glide slope that intersects the localizer.

(3) The glide path projection angle is normally adjusted to 3 degrees above horizontal so that it intersects the middle marker at about 200 feet and the outer marker at about 1400 feet above the runway elevation. The glide slope is normally usuable to the distance of 10 NM. However, at some locations, the glide slope has been certified for an extended service volume which exceeds 10 NM.

(4) In addition to the desired glide path, false course and reversal in sensing will occur at vertical angles considerably greater than the usable path. The proper use of the glide slope requires that the pilot maintain alertness as the glide path interception is approached and interpret correctly the "fly-up" and "fly-down" instrument indications to avoid the possibility of attempting to follow one of the higher angle courses. Provided that procedures are correctly followed and pilots are properly indoctrinated in glide path instrumentation, the fact that these high angle courses exist should cause no difficulty in the glide path navigation.

(5) Every effort should be made to remain on the indicated glide path (reference: FAR 91.87(d)(2)). Extreme caution should be exercised to avoid deviations below the glide path so that the predetermined obstacle/terrain clearance provided by an ILS instrument approach procedure is maintained.

(6) A glide path facility provides a path which flares from 18–27 feet above the runway. Therefore, the glide path should not be expected to provide guidance completely to a touchdown point on the runway.

d. MARKER BEACON

(1) ILS marker beacons have a rated power output of 3 watts or less and an antenna array designed to produce an elliptical pattern with dimensions, at 1000 feet above the antenna, of approximately 2400 feet in width and 4200 feet in length. Airborne marker beacon receivers with a selective sensitivity feature should always be operated in the "low" sensitivity position for proper reception of ILS marker beacons.

(2) Ordinarily, there are two marker beacons associated with an instrument landing system; the outer marker and middle marker. However, some locations may employ a third marker beacon to indicate the point at which the decision height should occur when used with a Category II ILS.

(3) The outer marker (OM) normally indicates a position at which an aircraft at the appropriate altitude on the localizer course will intercept the ILS glide path. The OM is modulated at 400 Hz and identified with continuous dashes at the rate of two dashes per second.

(4) The middle marker (MM) indicates a poistion at which an aircraft is approximately 3500 feet from the landing threshold. This will also be the position at which an aircraft on the glide path will be at an altitude of approximately 200 feet above the elevation of the touchdown zone. The MM is modulated at 1300 Hz and identified with alternate dots and dashes keyed at the rate of 95 dot/dash combinations per minute.

(5) The inner marker (IM), where installed, will indicate a point at which an aircraft is at a designated decision height (DH) on the glide path between the middle marker and landing threshold. The IM is modulated at 3000 Hz and identified with continuous dots

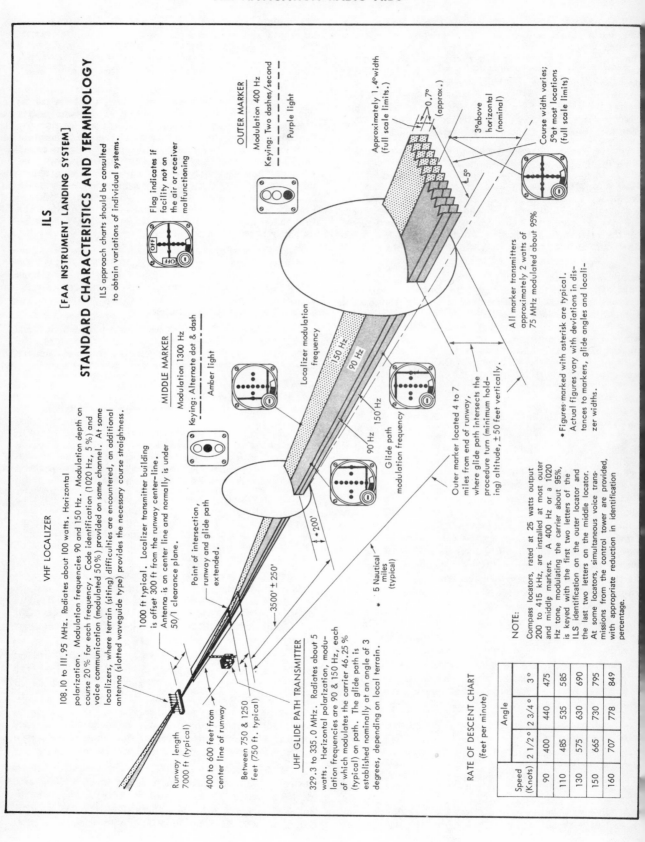

keyed at the rate of six dots per second and a white marker beacon light.

(6) A back course marker, where installed, normally indicates the ILS back course final approach fix where approach descent is commenced. The back course marker is modulated at 3000 Hz and identified with two dots at a rate of 72 to 95 two-dot combinations per minute and a white marker beacon light.

e. COMPASS LOCATOR

(1) Compass locator transmitters are often situated at the middle and outer marker sites. The transmitters have a power of less than 25 watts, a range of at least 15 miles and operate between 200 and 415 kHz. At some locations, higher-powered radio beacons, up to 400 watts, are used as outer marker compass locators. These generally carry Transcribed Weather Broadcast (TWEB) information.

(2) Compass locators transmit two-letter identification groups. The outer locator transmits the first two letters of the localizer identification group, and the middle locator transmits the last two letters of the localizer identification group.

f. ILS FREQUENCY

The following frequency pairs have been allocated for ILS. Although all of these forty frequency pairs are not being utilized, they will be in the future.

ILS

Localizer MHz	Glide Slope MHz	Localizer MHz	Glide Slope MHz
108.10	334.70	110.1	334.40
108.15	334.55	110.15	334.25
108.3	334.10	110.3	335.00
108.35	333.95	110.35	334.85
108.5	329.90	110.5	329.60
108.55	329.75	110.55	329.45
108.7	330.50	110.70	330.20
108.75	330.35	110.75	330.05
108.9	329.30	110.90	330.80
108.95	329.15	110.95	330.65
109.1	331.40	111.10	331.70
109.15	331.25	111.15	331.55
109.3	332.00	111.30	332.30
109.35	331.85	111.35	332.15
109.50	332.60	111.50	332.9
109.55	332.45	111.55	332.75
109.70	333.20	111.70	333.5
109.75	333.05	111.75	333.35
109.90	333.80	111.90	331.1
109.95	333.65	111.95	330.95

g. ILS MINIMUMS

(1) ILS Minimums with all components operative normally establish a DH (Decision Height MSL) with a HAT (Height Above Touchdown) of 200 feet, and a visibility of one-half statute mile. Refer to Inoperative Component Table for adjustment to minimums when airborne equipment is inoperative or not used or when a component of the ILS is reported out of service.

h. ILS COURSE DISTORTION

(1) All pilots should be aware that disturbance to ILS localizer/glide slope courses may occur when surface vehicles/aircraft are operated near the localizer/glide slope antennas. Antenna locations are such that few ILS installations are not subject to signal interference by either surface vehicles, aircraft or both. ILS "CRITICAL AREAS" are established on the surface about each localizer and glide slope antenna. Air traffic control (ATC) procedures exist to control the operation of vehicle/aircraft traffic on the portions of taxiways and runways that lie within the critical areas and to adjust the flow of arrival/departure traffic so that the proximity of one aircraft to an ILS antenna does not cause interference to the ILS course signals being used by another when the weather/visibility conditions are below specific values.

(2) Air traffic control issues control instructions to avoid interfering operations within ILS critical areas at controlled airports during the hours the airport traffic control tower is in operation as follows:

(a) Weather Conditions—At or above ceiling 800 feet and/or visibility 2 miles.

1. No critical area protective action is provided.

2. If an aircraft advises the TOWER that an "AUTOLAND"/"COUPLED" approach will be conducted, an advisory will be promptly issued if a vehicle/aircraft will be in or over a critical area when the arriving aircraft is inside the ILS middle marker.

Example:
GLIDE SLOPE SIGNAL NOT PROTECTED.

(b) Weather Conditions—Less than ceiling 800 feet and/or visibility 2 miles.

1. GLIDE SLOPE CRITICAL AREA—Vehicles/aircraft are not authorized in the area when an arriving aircraft is between the ILS final approach fix and the airport unless the aircraft has reported the airport in sight or is circling/side stepping to land on other than the ILS runway.

2. LOCALIZER CRITICAL AREA—Except for aircraft that may operate in or over the area when landing or exiting a runway or for departures or missed approaches, vehicles/aircraft are not authorized in or over the area when an arriving aircraft is between the ILS final approach fix and the airport. Additionally, when the ceiling is less than 200 feet and/or the visibility is RVR 2,000 or less, vehicle/aircraft operations in or over the area are not authorized when an arriving aircraft is inside the ILS middle marker.

(3) While a "critical area" is not specifically established outward from the airport to the final approach fix, an aircraft holding below 5,000 feet AGL inbound toward an airport between the ILS final approach fix and the airport can cause reception of unwanted localizer signal reflections by aircraft conducting an ILS approach. Accordingly, such holding is not authorized when weather/visibility conditions are less than ceiling 800 feet and/or visibility 2 miles.

(4) Pilots are cautioned that vehicular traffic not subject to control by ATC may cause momentary deviation to ILS course/glide slope signals. Also, no active protection of "critical areas" exists at airports without an operational airport traffic control tower or at airports with an operational control tower when weather/visi-

bility conditions are above those requiring protective measures. Aircraft conducting "coupled" or "autoland" operations should be especially alert in monitoring automatic flight control systems.

13. SIMPLIFIED DIRECTIONAL FACILITY (SDF)

a. The Simplified Directional Facility provides a final approach course which is similar to that of the ILS localizer described in this chapter. A clear understanding of the ILS localizer and the additional factors listed below completely describe the operational characteristics and use of the SDF.

b. The SDF transmits signals within the range of 108.10 MHz to 111.95 MHz. It provides no glide slope information.

c. For the pilot, the approach techniques and procedures used in the performance of an SDF instrument approach are essentially identical to those employed in executing a standard no-glide-slope localizer approach except that the SDF course may not be aligned with the runway and the course may be wider, resulting in less precision.

d. Usable off-course indications are limited to 35° either side of the course centerline. Instrument indications in the areas between 35° and 90° are not controlled and should be disregarded.

e. The SDF antenna may be offset from the runway centerline. Because of this, the angle of convergence between the final approach course and the runway bearing should be determined by reference to the instrument approach procedure chart. This angle is generally not more than 3°. However, it should be noted that inasmuch as the approach course originates at the antenna site, an approach which is continued beyond the runway threshold will lead the aircraft to the SDF offset position rather than along the runway centerline.

f. The SDF signal emitted from the transmitter is fixed at either 6° or 12° as necessary to provide maximum flyability and optimum course quality.

g. Identification consists of a three letter identifier transmitted on the SDF frequency (e.g., SAN, ETT, etc.). The appropriate instrument approach chart will indicate the identifier used at a particular airport.

14. INTERIM STANDARD MICROWAVE LANDING SYSTEM (ISMLS)

a. The ISMLS is designed to provide approach information similar to the ILS for an aircraft on final approach to a runway. The system provides both lateral and vertical guidance which is displayed on a conventional course deviation indicator or approach horizon. Operational performance and coverage areas are also similar to the ILS as defined above.

b. ISMLS operates in the C-band microwave frequency range (about 5000 MHz) so the signal will not be received by unmodified VHF/UHF ILS receivers. Aircraft utilizing ISMLS must be equipped with a C-band receiving antenna in addition to other special equipment mentioned below. The receiving aperture of the C-band antenna limits reception of the signal to signal until flying a magnetic heading within 50° either side of the inbound course. Because of this, ISMLS

an angle of about 50° from the inbound course. Therefore, an aircraft so equipped will not receive the ISMLS procedures are designed to preclude use of the ISMLS signal until the aircraft is in position for the final approach. Transition to the ISMLS, holding and procedure turns at the ISMLS facility must be predicated on other navigation aids such as NDB, VOR, etc. Once established on the approach course inbound, the system can be flown identical to ILS. No back course is provided.

c. The Interim Standard Microwave Landing System consists of the following basic components:

　(1) C-Band (5000 MHz–5030 MHz) localizer.

　(2) C-Band (5220 MHz–5250 MHz) glide path.

　(3) VHF marker beacons (75 MHz).

　(4) A VHF/UHF ILS receiver modified to be capable of receiving the ISMLS signals.

　(5) C-Band antenna.

　(6) Converter unit.

　(7) A Microwave/ILS Mode Control.

d. The identification consists of a three letter Morse Code identifier preceded by the Morse Code for "M" (– –). (e.g., M–STP.) The "M" will distinguish this system from ILS which is preceded by the Morse Code for "I" (● ●). (e.g., I–STP.)

e. Approaches published in conjunction with the ISMLS will be identified as "MLS Rwy —— (Interim)." The frequency displayed on the ISMLS approach chart will be a VHF frequency. ISMLS frequencies are tuned by setting the receiver to the listed VHF frequencies. When the ISMLS mode is selected, receivers modified to accept ISMLS signals will not receive the VHF/UHF frequency but a paired LOC/GS C-Band frequency that will be processed by the receiver.

CAUTION: Aircraft not equipped for ISMLS operation should not attempt to fly ISMLS procedures.

15. MAINTENANCE OF FAA NAVAIDS

a. During periods of routine or emergency maintenance, the coded identification (or code and voice, where applicable) will be removed from certain FAA navaids; namely, ILS localizers, VHF ranges, NDB's, compass locators and 75 MHz marker beacons. The removal of identification serves as warning to pilots that the facility has been officially taken over by "Maintenance" for tune-up or repair and may be unreliable even though on the air intermittently or constantly.

16. NAVAIDS WITH VOICE

a. Voice equipped en route radio navigational aids are under the operational control of an FAA Flight Service Station (FSS), or an approach control facility. Most are remotely operated.

b. Unless otherwise noted on the chart, all radio navigation aids operate continuously except during interruptions for voice transmissions on the same frequencies where simultaneous transmission is not available, and during shutdowns for maintenance purposes. Hours of operation of those facilities not operating continuously are annotated on the charts.

17–18. RESERVED

19. USER REPORTS ON NAVAID PERFORMANCE

a. Users of the National Airspace System can render valuable assistance in the early correction of navaid malfunctions by reporting their observations of undesirable performance. Although the navaid is monitored by electronic detectors within the equipment or in the field of radiation near the antenna, adverse effects of electronic interference, new obstructions or changes in terrain near the navaid can exist without detection by the ground monitors. Some of the characteristics of malfunction or deteriorating performance which should be reported are: Erratic course or bearing indications; intermittent, or full, flag alarm; garbled, missing or obviously improper coded identification; poor quality communications reception; or, in the case of frequency interference, an audible hum or tone accompanying radio communications or navaid identification.

b. Reports should identify the navaid, location of the aircraft, time of the observation and type of aircraft and describe the condition observed; the type of receivers in use will also be useful information. The FAA has established procedures to respond to user reports which can be made in any of the following ways:

(1) Report by radio communication to the controlling Air Route Traffic Control Center, Control Tower, or Flight Service Station. This method will provide the most timely resolution of the reported condition.

(2) Report by telephone to the nearest FAA facility.

(3) Report by FAA Form 8000-7, Safety Improvement Report, a self addressed, postage-paid card designed with this purpose in mind. A supply of these cards may be found at FAA Flight Service Stations, General Aviation District Offices and General Aviation Fixed Base Operations.

c. In complex aircraft radio installations involving more than one receiver, there are many combinations of possible interference between units. This interference can cause either erroneous navigation indications, or complete or partial blanking out of the communications. Pilots should be familiar enough with the radio installation of particular airplanes they fly to recognize this type of interference.

20. LORAN

a. Loran-C has been selected by the Federal Government as the radio-navigation system for the Coastal Confluence Region. Harbors and Estuaries of the United States. Loran-C, with its high accuracy and availability, will meet the requirements of all users in the Coastal Confluence Region while providing the nation the capability of wider system application, including over-land use, in the future. Loran-C is a companion to the Omega system, which is being implemented for long-range, worldwide usage beyond the U.S. Coastal Confluence Region.

b. During the major transition while the Loran-C system is being constructed, a primary concern is the future of our present Loran-A system. To alleviate much of the difficulty in this major shift of systems, the U.S. Coast Guard will continue operation of the Loran-A system for a period of two years subsequent to completion of each phase of the Loran-C system. Thus the schedule for Loran-A termination in the Coastal Confluence Region is:

Area	Date of Termination
Hawaiian Islands	1 July 1979
Aleutian Islands	1 July 1979
Gulf of Alaska	31 December 1979
U.S. West Coast	31 December 1979
Gulf of Mexico	31 December 1980
U.S. East Coast	31 December 1980
Caribbean	31 December 1980

c. A prerecorded telephone answering service to provide information pertaining to LORAN-C operations is available from the LORAN station in Seneca, New York (telephone 607-869-5395) and Malone, Florida (904-569-5241). The service provides the user of LORAN-C with the current operational status of all LORAN-C stations within the 9960, 9930, and 7980 chains. If additional information pertaining to chain operation is required, contact point is the coordinator of chain operations at the LORAN station in Seneca, New York for LORAN-C Chain 9960 or coordinator of chain operations at the LORAN station in Malone, Florida for Chains 7980 and 9930.

21. OMEGA AND OMEGA/VLF NAVIGATION SYSTEMS

a. Omega

(1) Omega is a network of eight transmitting stations located throughout the world to provide worldwide signal coverage. These stations transmit a phase stable 10 kW signal in the Very Low Frequency (VLF) band. Because of the low frequency, the signals are receivable to ranges of thousands of miles. The eight stations are located in Norway, Liberia, Hawaii, North Dakota (USA), La Reunion, Argentina, *Trinidad, and Japan.

> NOTE.—Trinidad is operating temporarily at one kw rated power in the time slot to be occupied by Australia. It is anticipated that the Australian station, approximate site location 38°29′S 146°56′E will be operational in 1980. The Trinidad station may or may not remain operation until that time.

(2) Presently each station transmits on four basic navigational frequencies: 10.2 kHz, 11.05 kHz, 11.3 kHz, and 13.6 kHz, in sequenced format. This time sequenced format prevents inter-station signal interference. The pattern is arranged so that during each transmission interval only three stations are radiating, each at a different frequency. With eight stations and a silent .2-second interval between each transmission, the entire cycle repeats every 10 seconds.

(3) In addition to the four basic navigational frequencies, each station transmits a unique navigation frequency. An Omega station is said to be operating in full format when the station is transmitting on the basic frequencies plus the unique frequency. Unique frequencies are presently assigned as follows:

Station A	Norway	12.1 kHz
Station B	Liberia	12.0 kHz
Station C	Hawaii	11.8 kHz
Station D	North Dakota	13.1 kHz
Station E	La Reunion	12.3 kHz
Station H	Japan	12.8 kHz

> NOTE.—Station F Argentina and Temporary Station G Trinidad do not have an assigned unique navigational frequency and, therefore, are not operating in full format.

b. VLF

(1) The U.S. Navy operates a communications system in the VLF band. The transmitting stations are located worldwide and transmit at powers of 500–1000 kW. Some airborne Omega receivers have the capability to receive and process these VLF signals for navigation in addition to Omega signals. The VLF stations generally used for navigation are located in Australia, Japan, England, Hawaii, and, in the U.S., in Maine, Washington and Maryland (Annapolis).

(2) Although the Navy does not object to the use of VLF communications signals for navigation, the system is not dedicated to navigation. Signal format, transmission, and other parameters of the VLF system are subject to change at the Navy's discretion. The VLF communications stations are individually shut down for scheduled maintenance for a few hours each week. Regular NOTAM service regarding the VLF system or station status is not available. However, the Naval Research Laboratory provides a taped message concerning phase differences, phase values, and shutdown information for both the VLF communications network and the Omega system (phone 202–254–4662).

c. Operational Use of Omega and Omega/VLF

(1) Experience has shown that the Omega navigation network is capable of providing consistent fixing information to an accuracy of ±2 NM depending upon the level of sophistication of the receiver/processing system. Omega signals are affected by propagation variables which may degrade fix accuracy. These variables include diurnal variation of phase velocity, polar cap absorption, and sudden ionospheric disturbances (solar activity). Although the diurnal variation can be compensated for within the receiver/processor, occasional excessive solar activity and its effect on Omega cannot be completely forecast or anticipated. If an unusual amount of solar activity disturbs the Omega signal propagation paths to any extent, the U.S. Coast Guard advises the FAA and an appropriate NOTAM is promulgated.

(2) At 16 minutes past each hours, WWV (Fort Collins, Colorado) broadcasts a message concerning the status of each Omega station, signal anomalies, and other information concerning Omega. At 47 minutes past each hour, WWVH (Hawaii) broadcasts similar information. The U.S. Coast Guard provides a taped Omega status report (202–245–0298). NOTAMS concerning Omega are available through any Flight Service Station. It is recommended that Omega NOTAMs be requested by Omega station name.

(3) The FAA has recognized Omega and Omega/VLF systems as an additional, but not the sole, means of enroute IFR navigation in the conterminous United States and Alaska when approved in accordance with FAA guidance information. Use of Omega or Omega/VLF requires that all navigation equipment otherwise required by the Federal Aviation Regulations be installed and operating. When flying RNAV routes, VOR and DME are required to be installed.

(4) The FAA does not recognize the use of the Naval VLF communications system as a sole means of navigation. VLF communications signals may be used to supplement Omega navigation if the equipment is capable of reverting to Omega only for navigation.

22. VHF DIRECTION FINDER

a. The VHF Direction Finder (VHF/DF) is one of the Common System equipments that helps the pilot without his being aware of its operation. The VHF/DF is a ground-based radio receiver used by the operator of the ground station where it is located.

b. The equipment consists of a directional antenna system and a VHF radio receiver. At a radar-equipped tower or center, the cathode-ray tube indications may be superimposed on the radarscope.

c. The VHF/DF display indicates the magnetic direction of the aircraft from the station each time the aircraft transmits. Where DF equipment is tied into radar, a strobe of light is flashed from the center of the radarscope in the direction of the transmitting aircraft.

d. DF equipment is of particular value in locating lost aircraft and in helping to identify aircraft on radar. (See **462—DIRECTION FINDING INSTRUMENT APPROACH PROCEDURE.**)

23–29. RESERVED

Section 2.   RADAR SERVICES AND PROCEDURES

30.   RADAR

a. Capabilities

(1) Radar is a method whereby radio waves are transmitted into the air and are then received when they have been reflected by an object in the path of the beam. *Range* is determined by measuring the time it takes (at the speed of light) for the radio wave to go out to the object and then return to the receiving antenna. The *direction* of a detected object from a radar site is determined by the position of the rotating antenna when the reflected portion of the radio wave is received.

(2) More reliable maintenance and improved equipment have reduced radar system failures to a negligible factor. Most facilities actually have some components duplicated—one operating and another which immediately takes over when a malfunction occurs to the primary component.

b. Limitations

(1) It is very important for the aviation community to recognize the fact that there are limitations to radar service and that ATC controllers may not always be able to issue traffic advisories concerning aircraft which are not under ATC control and cannot be seen on radar.

(a) The characteristics of radio waves are such that they normally travel in a continuous straight line unless they are:

(1) "Bent" by abnormal atmospheric phenomena such as temperature inversions;

(2) Reflected or attenuated by dense objects such as heavy clouds, precipitation, ground obstacles, mountains, etc.; or

(3) Screened by high terrain features.

(b) The bending of radar pulses, often called anomalous propagation or ducting, may cause many extraneous blips to appear on the radar operator's display if the beam has been bent toward the ground or may decrease the detection range if the wave is bent upward. It is difficult to solve the effects of anomalous propagation, but using beacon radar and electronically eliminating stationary and slow moving targets by a method called moving target indicator (MTI) usually negate the problem.

(c) Radar energy that strikes dense objects will be reflected and displayed on the operator's scope thereby blocking out aircraft at the same range and greatly weakening or completely eliminating the display of targets at a greater range. Again, radar beacon and MTI are very effectively used to combat ground clutter and weather phenomena, and a method of circularly polarizing the radar beam will eliminate some weather returns. A negative characteristic of MTI is that an aircraft flying a speed that coincides with the canceling signal of the MTI (tangential or "blind" speed) may not be displayed to the radar controller.

(d) Relatively low altitude aircraft will not be seen if they are screened by mountains or are below the radar beam due to earth curvature. The only solution to screening is the installation of strategically placed multiple radars which has been done in some areas.

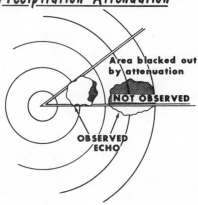

The nearby target absorbs and scatters so much of the out-going and returning energy that the radar does not detect the distant target.

Figure 1—3

(e) There are several other factors which affect radar control. The amount of reflective surface of an aircraft will determine the size of the radar return. Therefore, a small light airplane or a sleek jet fighter will be more difficult to see on radar than a large commercial jet or military bomber. Here again, the use of radar beacon is invaluable if the aircraft is equipped with an airborne transponder. All ARTCC radars in the conterminous U.S. and many airport surveillance radars have the capability to interrogate Mode C and display altitude information to the controller from appropriately equipped aircraft. However, there are a number of airport surveillance radars that are still two dimensional (range and azimuth) only and altitude information must be obtained from the pilot.

(f) At some locations within the ATC en route environment, secondary-radar-only (no primary radar) gap filler radar systems are used to give lower altitude radar coverage between two larger radar systems, each of which provides both primary and secondary radar coverage. In those geographical areas served by secondary-radar only, aircraft without transponders cannot be provided with radar service. Additionally, transponder equipped aircraft cannot be provided with radar advisories concerning primary targets and weather. (See RADAR/RADIO DETECTION AND RANGING in the Pilot/Controller Glossary.)

(g) The controllers' ability to advise a pilot flying on instruments or in visual conditions of his proximity to another aircraft will be limited if the unknown aircraft is not observed on radar, if no flight plan information is available, or if the volume of traffic and workload prevent his issuing traffic information. First priority is given to establishing vertical, lateral, or longitudinal separation between aircraft flying IFR under the control of ATC.

c. FAA radar units operate continuously at the locations shown in the Airport/Facility Directory, and their services are available to all pilots, both civil and military. Contact the associated FAA control tower or ARTCC on any frequency guarded for initial instructions, or in an emergency, any FAA facility for information on the nearest radar service.

31. AIR TRAFFIC CONTROL RADAR BEACON SYSTEM (ATCRBS)

a. The Air Traffic Control Radar Beacon System (ATCRBS), sometimes referred to as secondary surveillance radar, consists of three main components:

(1) **Interrogator.** Primary radar relies on a signal being transmitted from the radar antenna site and for this signal to be reflected or "bounced back" from an object (such as an aircraft). This reflected signal is then displayed as a "target" on the controller's radarscope. In the ATCRBS, the *Interrogator*, a ground based radar beacon transmitter-receiver, scans in synchronism with the primary radar and transmits discrete radio signals which repetitiously requests all transponders, on the mode being used, to reply. The replies received are then mixed with the primary returns and both are displayed on the same radarscope.

(2) **Transponder.** This airborne radar beacon transmitter-receiver automatically receives the signals from the interrogator and selectively replies with a specific pulse group (code) only to those interrogations being received on the mode to which it is set. These replies are independent of, and much stronger than a primary radar return.

(3) **Radarscope.** The radarscope used by the controller displays returns from both the primary radar system and the ATCRBS. These returns, called targets, are what the controller refers to in the control and separation of traffic.

b. The job of identifying and maintaining identification of primary radar targets is a long and tedious task for the controller. Some of the advantages of ATCRBS over primary radar are:

(1) **Reinforcement of radar targets.**

(2) Rapid target identification.

(3) Unique display of selected codes.

c. A part of the ATCRBS ground equipment is the decoder. This equipment enables the controller to assign discrete transponder codes to each aircraft under his control. Normally only one code will be assigned for the entire flight. Assignments are made by the ARTCC computer on the basis of the National Beacon Code Allocation Plan. The equipment is also designed to receive Mode C altitude information from the aircraft. Refer to figures 1–4 and 1–5 with explanatory legend for an illustration of the target symbology depicted on radar scopes in the NAS Stage A (enroute), the ARTS III (terminal) systems, and other non-automated (broad band) radar systems.

d. It should be emphasized that aircraft transponder greatly improve the effectiveness of radar systems. (See 171—TRANSPONDER OPERATIONS.)

32. SURVEILLANCE RADAR

a. Surveillance radars are divided into two general categories: Airport Surveillance Radar (ASR) and Air Route Surveillance Radar (ARSR). (1) Airport Surveillance Radar (ASR) is designed to provide relatively short range coverage in the general vicinity of an airport and to serve as an expeditious means of handling terminal area traffic through observation of precise aircraft locations on a radarscope. The ASR can also be used as an instrument approach aid. (2) Air Route Surveillance Radar (ARSR) is a long-range radar system designed primarily to provide a display of aircraft locations over large areas.

b. Surveillance radars scan through 360° of azimuth and present target information on a radar display located in a tower or center. This information is used independently or in conjunction with other navigational aids in the control of air traffic.

33. PRECISION APPROACH RADAR (PAR)

a. Precision approach radar is designed to be used as a *landing aid*, rather than an aid for sequencing and spacing aircraft. PAR equipment may be used as a primary landing aid, or it may be used to monitor other types of approaches. It is designed to display *range* *azimuth* and *elevation* information.

b. Two antennnas are used in the PAR array, one scanning a vertical plane, and the other scanning horizontally. Since the range is limited to 10 miles, azimuth to 20 degrees, and elevation to 7 degrees, only the final approach area is covered. Each scope is divided into two parts. The upper half presents altitude and distance information, and the lower half presents azimuth and distance.

34–39. RESERVED

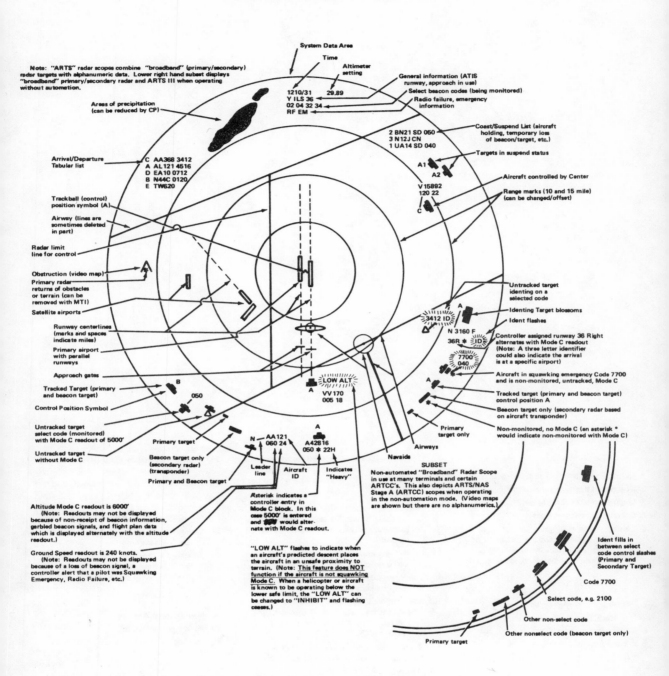

Note: "ARTS" radar scopes combine "broadband" (primary/secondary) radar targets with alphanumeric data. Lower right hand subset displays "broadband" primary/secondary radar and ARTS III when operating without automation.

Areas of precipitation (can be reduced by CP)

System Data Area

Time

Altimeter setting

1210/31   29.89
Y ILS 36
02 04 32 34
RF EM

General information (ATIS runway, approach in use)

Select beacon codes (being monitored)

Radio failure, emergency information

2 BN21 SD 050
3 N12J CN
1 UA14 SD 040

Coast/Suspend List (aircraft holding, temporary loss of beacon/target, etc.)

Targets in suspend status

A1
A2

Aircraft controlled by Center

V 15892
120 22
C

Range marks (10 and 15 mile) (can be changed/offset)

Arrival/Departure Tabular list

C AA368 3412
A AL121 4516
D EA10 0712
B N44C 0120
E TW620

Trackball (control) position symbol (A).

Airway (lines are sometimes deleted in part).

Radar limit line for control

Obstruction (video map)

Primary radar returns of obstacles or terrain (can be removed with MTI)

Satellite airports

Runway centerlines (marks and spaces indicate miles)

Primary airport with parallel runways

Approach gates

Tracked Target (primary and beacon target)

Control Position Symbol

Untracked target select code (monitored) with Mode C readout of 5000'

Untracked target without Mode C

Primary target

Beacon target only (secondary radar) (transponder)

Primary and Beacon target

Leader line

Aircraft ID

B

050

N   AA121
     060 24

A
A42816
050 ✱ 22H

LOW ALT
VV 170
005 18
A

Indicates "Heavy"

Airways

Navaids

Untracked target identing on a selected code

Identing Target blossoms

Ident flashes

3412 ID
A

N 3160 F

36R ✱ ID

7700
040

Controller assigned runway 36 Right alternates with Mode C readout (Note: A three letter identifier could also indicate the arrival is at a specific airport)

Aircraft in squawking emergency Code 7700 and is non-monitored, untracked, Mode C

Tracked target (primary and beacon target) control position A

Beacon target only (secondary radar based on aircraft transponder)

Non-monitored, no Mode C (an asterisk ✱ would indicate non-monitored with Mode C)

A

Primary target only

SUBSET
Non-automated "Broadband" Radar Scope in use at many terminals and certain ARTCC's. This also depicts ARTS/NAS Stage A (ARTCC) scopes when operating in the non-automation mode. (Video maps are shown but there are no alphanumerics.)

Altitude Mode C readout is 6000' (Note: Readouts may not be displayed because of non-receipt of beacon information, garbled beacon signals, and flight plan data which is displayed alternately with the altitude readout.)

Ground Speed readout is 240 knots. (Note: Readouts may not be displayed because of a loss of beacon signal, a controller alert that a pilot was Squawking Emergency, Radio Failure, etc.)

Asterisk indicates a controller entry in Mode C block. In this case 5000' is entered and ▪▪▪▪ would alternate with Mode C readout.

"LOW ALT" flashes to indicate when an aircraft's predicted descent places the aircraft in an unsafe proximity to terrain. (Note: This feature does NOT function if the aircraft is not squawking Mode C. When a helicopter or aircraft is known to be operating below the lower safe limit, the "LOW ALT" can be changed to "INHIBIT" and flashing ceases.)

Ident fills in between select code control slashes (Primary and Secondary Target)

Code 7700

Select code, e.g. 2100

Other non-select code

Other nonselect code (beacon target only)

Primary target

ARTS III Radar Scope with Alphanumeric Data. Note: A number of radar terminals do not have ARTS equipment. Those facilities and certain ARTCC's outside the contiguous US would have radar displays similar to the lower right hand subset. ARTS facilities and NAS Stage A ARTCC's, when operating in the non-automation mode would also have similar displays and certain services based on automation may not be available.

Figure 1—4

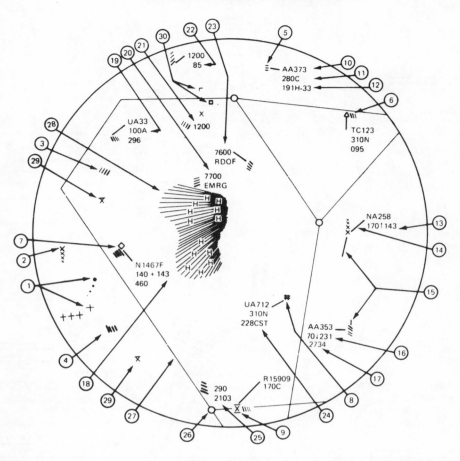

Target Symbols

1 Uncorrelated primary radar target   + ●
2 *Correlated primary radar target   X
3 Uncorrelated beacon target   /
4 Correlated beacon target   \
5 Identing beacon target   ≡
    (*Correlated means the association
    of radar data with the computer pro-
    jected track of an identified aircraft)

Position Symbols

6 Free track (No flight plan tracking) △
7 Flat track (flight plan tracking) ◊
8 Coast (Beacon target lost) ⧣
9 Present Position Hold ⊠

Data Block Information

10 *Aircraft Identification
11 *Assigned Altitude FL280, mode C altitude
    same or within ±200' of asgnd altitude

12 *Computer ID #191, Handoff is to Sector 33
    (0-33 would mean handoff accepted)
    (*Nr's 10, 11, 12 constitute a "full data
    block")
13 Assigned altitude 17,000', aircraft is
    climbing, mode C readout was 14,300
    when last beacon interrogation was
    received
14 Leader line connecting target symbol
    and data block
15 Track velocity and direction vector
    line (Projected ahead of target)
16 Assigned altitude 7000, aircraft is
    descending, last mode C readout (or
    last reported altitude was 100'
    above FL230
17 Transponder code shows in full data block
    only when different than assigned code
18 Aircraft is 300' above assigned
    altitude
19 Reported altitude (No mode C readout)
    same as assigned. An "N" would indi-
    cate no reported altitude)
20 Transponder set on emergency code 7700
    (EMRG flashes to attract attention)

21 Transponder code 1200 (VFR) with no
    mode C
22 Code 1200 (VFR) with mode C and last
    altitude readout
23 Transponder set on Radio Failure code
    7600, (RDOF flashes)
24 Computer ID #228, CST indicates target is
    in Coast status
25 Assigned altitude FL290, transponder
    code (These two items constitute a
    "limited data block")

Other symbols

26 Navigational Aid
27 Airway or jet route
28 Outline of weather returns based on
    primary radar (See Chapter 4, ARTCC
    Radar Weather Display. H's represent
    areas of high density precipitation
    which might be thunderstorms. Radial
    lines indicate lower density precipi-
    tation)
29 Obstruction
30 Airports   Major: □   Small: ⌐

     NAS Stage A Controllers Plan View Display. This figure illustrates the controller's radar scope (PVD) when operating
in the full automation (RDP) mode, which is normally 20 hours per day. (Note: When not in automation mode, the display is
similar to the broadband mode shown in Figure 1-5. Certain ARTCC's outside the contiguous U.S. also operate in "broadband"
mode.)

Figure 1—5

Chapter 2. AIRPORT, AIR NAVIGATION LIGHTING AND MARKING AIDS

Section 1. AIRPORT LIGHTING AIDS

40. INSTRUMENT APPROACH LIGHT SYSTEMS (ALS)

a. Instrument approach light systems provide the basic means for transition from instrument flight using electronic approach aids to visual flight and landing. Operational requirements dictate the sophistication and configuration of the approach light system for a particular airport.

b. Condenser-Discharge Sequenced Flashing Light Systems (SFL) are installed in conjunction with the instrument approach light system at some airports which have U.S. Standard "A" approach lights as a further aid to pilots making instrument approaches. The system consists of a series of brilliant blue-white bursts of light flashing in sequence along the approach lights. It gives the effect of a ball of light traveling towards the runway. An impression of the system as a pilot first observes the flashing lights when making an approach is that of large tracer shells rapidly fired from a point in space toward the runway.

c. Omnidirectional flashing light lead-in approach and runway end identifier light systems are now being installed at several airports. This system consists of five flashing lights located on the extended runway centerline and two located on either side of the runway threshold. The lights flash toward the threshold in sequence.

41. VISUAL APPROACH SLOPE INDICATOR (VASI)

a. The VASI is a system of lights so arranged to provide visual descent guidance information during the approach to a runway. These lights are visible from 3–5 miles during the day and up to 20 miles or more at night. The visual glide path of the VASI provides safe obstruction clearance within ±10 degrees of the extended runway centerline and to 4 nautical miles from the runway threshold. Descent, using the VASI, should not be initiated until the aircraft is visually aligned with the runway. Lateral course guidance is provided by the runway or runway lights.

b. VASI installations may consist of either 2, 4, 6, 12, or 16 lights units arranged in bars referred to as near, middle, and far bars. Most VASI installations consist of two bars, near and far, and may consist of 2, 4, or 12 light units. Some airports have VASI's consisting of three bars, near, middle, and far, which provide an additional visual glide path for use by high cockpit aircraft. This installation may consist of either 6 or 16 light units. VASI installations consisting of 2, 4, or 6 light units are located on one side of the runway, usually the left. Where the installation con-

sists of 12 or 16 light units, the light units are located on both sides of the runway.

c. Two bar VASI installations provide one visual glide path which is normally set at 3 degrees. Three bar VASI installations provide two visual glide paths. The lower glide path is provided by the near and middle bars and is normally set at 3 degrees while the upper glide path, provided by the middle and far bars, is normally ¼ degree higher. This higher glide path is intended for use only by high cockpit aircraft to provide a sufficient threshold crossing height. Although normal glide path angles are three degrees, angles at some locations may be as high as 4.5 degrees to give proper obstacle clearance. Pilots of high performance aircraft are cautioned that use of VASI angles in excess of 3.5 degrees may cause an increase in runway length required for landing and rollout.

d. The following information is provided for pilots as yet unfamiliar with the principles and operation of this system and pilot technique required. The basic principle of the VASI is that of color differentiation between red and white. Each light unit projects a beam of light having a white segment in the upper part of the beam and red segment in the lower part of the beam. The light units are arranged so that the pilot using the VASIs during an approach will see the combination of lights listed below.

e.

2–BAR VASI	Light Bar	Color
(1) Below glide path	Far	Red
	Near	Red
(2) On glide path	Far	Red
	Near	White
(3) Above glide path	Far	White
	Near	White

f.

3–BAR VASI		
(1) Below both glide paths	Far	Red
	Middle	Red
	Near	Red
(2) On lower glide path	Far	Red
	Middle	Red
	Near	White
(3) On upper glide path	Far	Red
	Middle	White
	Near	White
(4) Above both glide paths	Far	White
	Middle	White
	Near	White

g. When on the proper glide path of a 2–bar VASI, the pilot will see the near bar as white and the far bar as red. From a position below the glide path, the pilot will see both bars as red. In moving up to the glide path, the pilot will see the color of the near bar change from red to pink to white. From a position above the glide slope the pilot will see both bars as white. In moving down to the glide path, the pilot will see the color of the far bar change from white to pink to red. When the pilot is below the glide path the red bars tend to merge into one distinct red signal and a safe obstruction clearance may not exist under this condition.

h. When using a 3–bar VASI it is not necessary to use all three bars. The near and middle bars constitute a two bar VASI for using the lower glide path. Also, the middle and far bars constitute a 2–bar VASI for using the upper glide path. A simple rule of thumb when using a two-bar VASI is:

All Red _____ Too Low
All White _____ Too High
Red & White __ On Glide Path

i. In haze or dust conditions or when the approach is made into the sun, the white lights may appear yellowish. This is also true at night when the VASI is operated at a low intensity. Certain atmospheric debris may give the white lights an orange or brownish tint; however, the red lights are not affected and the principle of color differentiation is still applicable.

42. TRI-COLOR VISUAL APPROACH SLOPE INDICATOR

a. Tri-color Visual Approach Indicators have been installed at general aviation and air carrier airports. The Tri-color Approach Slope Indicator normally consists of a single light unit, projecting a three-color visual approach path into the final approach area of the runway upon which the system is installed. In all of these systems, a below glide path indication is red, the above glide path indication is amber and the on path indication is green.

b. Presently installed Tri-color Visual Approach Slope Indicators are low candlepower projector-type systems. Research tests indicate that these systems generally have a daytime useful range of approximately ½ to 1 mile. Nighttime useful range, depending upon visibility conditions, varies from 1 to 5 miles. Projector-type Visual Approach Slope Indicators may be initially difficult to locate in flight due to their small light source. Once the light source is acquired, however, it will provide accurate vertical guidance to the runway. Pilots should be aware that this yellow-green-red configuration produces a yellow-green transition light beam between the yellow and green primary light segments and an anomalous yellow transition light beam between the green and red primary light segments. This anomalous yellow signal could cause confusion with the primary yellow too-high signal.

43. RUNWAY END IDENTIFIER LIGHTS (REIL)

a. Runway End Identifier Lights are installed at many airfields to provide rapid and positive identification of the approach end of a particular runway. The system consists of a pair of synchronized flashing lights, one of which is located laterally on each side of the runway threshold facing the approach area. REILs may be located longitudinally 200 feet either upwind or downwind from the runway threshold. They are effective for:

(1) Identification of a runway surrounded by a preponderance of other lighting.

(2) Identification of a runway which lacks contrast with surrounding terrain.

(3) Identification of a runway during reduced visibility.

44. RUNWAY EDGE LIGHT SYSTEMS

a. Runway edge lights used to outline the edges of runways during periods of darkness and restricted visibility conditions. These light systems are classified according to the intensity or brightness they are capable of producing; they are the High Intensity Runway Lights (HIRL), Medium Intensity Runway Lights (MIRL), and the Low Intensity Runway Lights (LIRL). The HIRL and MIRL systems have variable intensity controls, whereas the LIRL's normally have one intensity setting.

b. The runway edge lights are white except that on instrument runways aviation yellow replaces white on the last 2,000 feet or half the runway length, whichever is less, to form a caution zone for landings. The lights marking the longitudinal limits of the runway emit red light toward the runway to indicate the end of runway to a departing aircraft and emit green outward from the runway end to indicate the threshold to landing aircraft.

45. IN-RUNWAY LIGHTING

a. Touchdown zone lighting and runway centerline lighting are installed on some precision approach runways to facilitate landing under adverse visibility conditions. Taxiway turnoff lights may be added to expedite movement of aircraft from the runway.

(1) **Touchdown Zone Lghting (TDZL)**—two rows of transverse light bars disposed symmetrically about the runway centerline in the runway touchdown zone. The system starts 100 feet from the landing threshold and extends to 3000 feet from the threshold or the midpoint of the runway, whichever is the lesser.

(2) **Runway Centerline Lighting (RCLS)**—flush centerline lights spaced at 50-foot intervals beginning 75 feet from the landing threshold and extending to within 75 feet of opposite end of the runway.

(3) **Runway Remaining Lighting**—is applied to centerline lighting systems in the final 3,000 feet as viewed from the takeoff or approach position. Alternate red and white lights are seen from the 3,000 foot points to the 1,000 foot points, and all red lights are seen for the last 1,000 feet of the runway. From the opposite direction, these lights are seen as white lights.

(4) **Taxiway turnoff lights**—flush lights spaced at 50-foot intervals, defining the curved path of aircraft travel from the runway centerline to a point on the taxiway.

46. CONTROL OF LIGHTING SYSTEMS

a. Operation of approach light systems and runway lighting is controlled by the control tower. At some locations the FSS may control the lights where there is no control tower in operation.

b. Pilots may request that lights be turned on or off. Runway edge lights, in-pavement lights and approach lights also have intensity controls which may be varied to meet the pilots request. Sequenced flashing lights (SFL) may be turned on and off. Some sequenced flashing light systems also have intensity control.

c. The Medium Intensity Approach Lighting System with Runway Alignment Indicators (MALSR) has been installed at many airports. The control of MALSR is now being transferred from the runway light circuits to Air Traffic Control Towers and/or radio control from approaching aircraft. As soon as the transfer becomes effective, operational procedures for control from aircraft will be published. In the interim, with few exceptions, MALSR will operate only when runway edge lights are turned on and its intensity will vary directly as the runway edge light intensity is varied.

47. PILOT CONTROL OF AIRPORT LIGHTING

a. The Federal Aviation Administration is installing controls on selected airport lights to provide pilots with the ability to control lights by keying the microphone. These controls will be available at all times at selected locations that do not have a tower or flight service station. Airports served by part-time towers or stations will have the control system activated when the tower or station is not operating. Control of the lights will be possible when aircraft are within 15 miles of the airport. Only one lighting system per runway may be operated by a pilot control system. Where a single runway is served by both approach lights and runway edge lights, priority for pilot control will be given to the approach light system. If no approach lights are installed, priority will be given to runway edge lights over other lighting systems such as REIL and VASI.

b. FAA approved control systems provide for the installation of three types of radio controls. These types are: a three step system that provides low, medium, or high intensity; a two step system that provides medium or high intensity; and a control to turn on a light system without regard to intensity. Each activation or change of intensity will start a timer to maintain the selected light intensity step of 15 minutes (which should be adequate time to complete an approach, landing, and necessary taxiing.) A new 15 minute period may be obtained by repeating the (desired) microphone keying to the appropriate step.

(1) The two step control must be activated to the highest intensity setting (key mike 5 times) before low intensity may be selected.

(2) The three step control may be activated to provide either low, medium or high intensity initially.

c. Suggested useage would be to always activate the control by keying the mike 5 times to ensure the lights are activated. All controls, regardless of the system can be activated by keying the mike 5 times. Adjustment can then be made to high or low intensity as appropriate or desired at a later time. Each microphone keying resets the timer to maintain the lights for an additional 15 minutes from each keying.

LEGEND FOR LIGHT CONTROLS

Radio Control System	Key Mike	Intensity
3 step light system	7 times in 5 seconds	High
	5 times in 5 seconds	Medium
	3 times in 5 seconds	Low
*2 step light systems	5 times in 5 seconds	High
	3 times in 5 seconds	Medium
ACTIVATE (Rwy lights, REIL, or VASI)	5 times in 5 seconds	Lights on

*Must be activated to High intensity before MEDIUM may be selected.

d. Where the airport is not served by an instrument approach procedure, it may have either the standard FAA approved control system or an independent type system of different specification installed by the airport sponsor. The airport directory contains descriptions of pilot controlled lighting systems for each airport having these systems and explains the type lights, method of control, and operating frequency in clear text.

e. Where the airport is served by one or more instrument approach procedures, the instrument approach chart will include sufficient data to identify the control device, light system, and the control frequency(s). For example: a three step control for a MALSR installed on runway 25 that is controlled on frequency 122.8 MHz would be noted on the instrument approach chart as follows: 3 step MALSR Rwy 25—122.8. To turn on Runway 25 edge lights using 122.3 or 281.6 with a control that does not have the intensity steps, the instrument approach chart would be annotated: Activate Runway 25 MIRL 122.3/281.6.

48—49. RESERVED

Section 2. AIRPORT AIR NAVIGATION LIGHTING

50. AERONAUTICAL LIGHT BEACONS

a. An aeronautical light beacon is a visual NAVAID displaying flashes of white and/or colored light to indicate the location of an airport, a heliport, a landmark, a certain point of a Federal airway in mountainous terrain, or a hazard. The light used may be a rotating beacon or one or more flashing lights. The flashing lights may be supplemented by steady burning lights of lesser intensity.

b. The color or color combination displayed by a particular beacon and/or its auxiliary lights tell whether the beacon is indicating a landing place, landmark, point of the Federal airways, or hazard. Coded flashes of the auxiliary lights, if employed, further identify the beacon site.

51. AUXILIARY LIGHTS

a. The auxiliary lights are of two general kinds: code beacons and course lights. The code beacon, which can be seen from all directions, is used to identify airports and landmarks and to mark hazards. The number of code beacon flashes are:

(1) **Green coded flashes** not exceeding 40 flashes or character elements per minute, or constant flashes 12 to 15 per minute, for identifying land airports.

(2) **Yellow coded flashes** not exceeding 40 flashes or character elements per minute, or constant flashes 12 to 15 per minute, for identifying water airports.

(3) **Red flashes**, constant rate, 12 to 40 flashes per minute, for marking hazards.

b. The course light, which can be seen clearly from only one direction, is used only with rotating beacons of the Federal Airway System; two course lights, back to back, direct coded flashing beams of light in either direction along the course of airway. (See **54—AIRWAY BEACONS**.)

52. ROTATING BEACON

a. The rotating beacon has a vertical light distribution such as to make it most effective at angles of one to three degrees above the horizontal from its site; however, it can be seen well above and below this peak spread. Rotation is in clockwise direction when viewed from above. It is always rotated at a constant speed which produces the visual effect of flashes at regular intervals. Flashes may be one or two colors alternately. The total number of flashes are:

(1) 12 to 30 per minute for beacons marking airports, landmarks, and points on Federal airways.

(2) 30 to 60 per minute for beacons marking heliports.

(3) 12 to 60 per minute for hazard beacons.

b. The colors and color combinations of rotating beacons and auxiliary lights are basically:

White and Green ___	Lighted land airport
*Green alone _____	Lighted land airport
White and Yellow __	Lighted water airport
*Yellow alone _____	Lighted water airport
White and Red _____	Landmark or navigational point
White alone _____	Unlighted land airport (rare installation)
Red alone _____	Hazard
Green, Yellow, and White _____	Lighted heliport
White _____	Hazard

*Green alone or yellow alone is used only in connection with a not far distant white-and-green or white-and-yellow beacon display, respectively.

c. Military airport beacons flash alternately white and green, but are differentiated from civil beacons by dual-peaked (two quick) white flashes between the green flashes.

d. In control zones, operation of the rotating beacon during the hours of daylight may indicate that the ground visibility is less than 3 miles and/or the ceiling is less than 1,000 feet. ATC clearance in accordance with FAR Part 91 would be required for landing, takeoff and flight in the traffic pattern. Pilots should not rely solely on the operation of the rotating beacon to indicate weather conditions, IFR versus VFR. At locations with control towers and if controls are provided, ATC personnel turn the beacon on. However, at many airports throughout the country, the rotating beacon is turned on by a photoelectric cell or time clocks and ATC personnel have no control as to when it shall be turned on. Also, there is no regulatory requirement for daylight operation and pilots are reminded that it remains their responsibility for complying with proper pre-flight planning in accordance with FAR Part 91.5.

53. OBSTRUCTION LIGHTS

a. Obstructions are marked/lighted to warn airmen of its presence during daytime and nighttime conditions. They may be marked/lighted in any of the following combinations:

(1) **Aviation Red Obstruction Lights.** Flashing aviation red beacons and steady burning aviation red lights during nighttime operation. Aviation orange and white paint is used for daytime marking.

(2) **High Intensity White Obstruction Lights.** Flashing high intensity white lights during daytime with reduced intensity for twilight and nighttime operation. When this type system is used, the marking of structures with red obstruction lights and aviation orange and white paint may be omitted.

(3) **Dual Lighting.** A combination of flashing aviation red beacons and steady burning aviation red lights for nighttime operation and flashing high intensity white lights for daytime operation. Aviation orange and white paint may be omitted.

b. High intensity flashing white lights are being used to identify some supporting structures of overhead transmission lines located across rivers, chasms, gorges, etc. These lights flash in a middle, top, lower light sequence at approximately 60 flashes per minute. The top light is normally installed near the top of the supporting structure, while the lower light indicates the approximate lower portion of the wire span. The lights are beamed towards the companion structure and identify the area of the wire span.

c. High intensity, flashing white lights are also employed to identify tall structures, such as chimneys and towers, as obstructions to air navigation. The lights provide a 360 degree coverage about the structure at 40 flashes per minute and consist of from one to seven levels of lights depending upon the height of the structure. Where more than one level is used the vertical banks flash simultaneously.

54. AIRWAY BEACONS

Airway beacons are remnants of the "lighted" airways which antedated the present electronically equipped Federal Airways System. Only a few of these beacons exist today to mark airway segments in remote mountain areas. Flashes in Morse Code identify the beacon site.

55–59. RESERVED

Section 3. AIRPORT MARKING AIDS

60. AIRPORT MARKING AIDS

a. In the interest of safety, regularity, or efficiency of aircraft operations, the FAA has recommended for the guidance of the public the following airport marking. (Runway numbers and letters are determined from the approach direction. The number is the whole number nearest one-tenth the magnetic azimuth of the centerline of the runway, measured clockwise from the magnetic north.) The letter or letters differentiate between parallel runways:

For two parallel runways "L" "R"

For three parallel runways "L" "C" "R"

b. Basic Runway Marking—markings used for operations under Visual Flight Rules: centerline marking and runway direction numbers.

Figure 2–1—BASIC RUNWAY

c. Non-Precision Instrument Runway Marking—markings on runways served by a nonvisual navigation aid and intended for landings under instrument weather conditions: basic runway markings plus threshold marking.

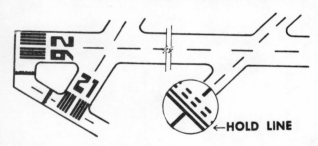

Figure 2–2—NON-PRECISION INSTRUMENT RUNWAY

d. Precision Instrument Runway Marking—markings on runway served by non-visual precision approach aids and on runways having special operational requirements, non-precision instrument runway marking, touchdown zone marking, fixed distance marking, plus side stripes.

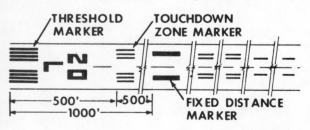

Figure 2–3—PRECISION INSTRUMENT RUNWAY

e. Threshold—A line perpendicular to the runway centerline designating the beginning of that portion of a runway usable for landing.

f. Displaced Threshold—A threshold that is not at the beginning of the full strength runway pavement. The paved area behind the displaced runway threshold is available for taxiing, the landing rollout, and the takeoff of aircraft.

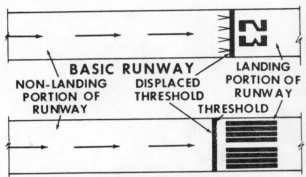

Figure 2–4—PRECISION/NON-PRECISION RUNWAY

g. Closed or Overrun/Stopway Areas—Any surface or area which appears usable but which, due to the nature of its structure, is unusable.

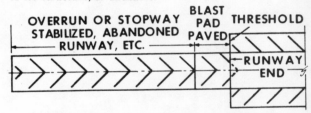

Figure 2–5—OVERRUN/STOPWAY AND BLAST PAD AREA

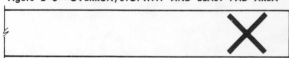

Figure 2–6—CLOSED RUNWAY OR TAXIWAY

h. Fixed Distance Marker—To provide a fixed distance marker for landing of turbojet aircraft on other than a precision instrument runway. This marking is similar to the fixed distance marking on a precision instrument runway and located 1,000 feet from the threshold.

i. STOL (Short Take Off and Landing) Runway—In addition to the normal runway number marking, the letters STOL are painted on the approach end of the runway and a touchdown aim point is shown.

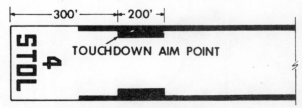

Figure 2–7—STOL RUNWAY

j. Taxiway Marking — The taxiway centerline is marked with a continuous yellow line. The taxiway edge may be marked with two continuous yellow lines six inches apart. Taxiway HOLDING LINES consist of two continuous and two dashed lines, spaced six inches between lines, perpendicular to the centerline. When

HELICOPTER LANDING AREA

Recommended Marking for
Civil Heliports

Some Civil and Military Heliports May
Be Marked With This Symbol

Recommended Marking for
Closed Heliports

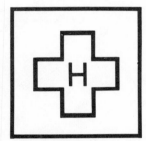

Recommended Marking for
Hospital Heliports

Figure 2–8—HELICOPER LANDING AREAS

instructed by ATC "HOLD SHORT OF (runway, ILS critical area, etc.)," the pilot should stop so no part of the aircraft extends beyond the holding line. When approaching the holding line from the side with the continuous lines, a pilot should not cross the holding line without ATC clearance at a controlled airport or without making sure of adequate separation from other aircraft at uncontrolled airports. An aircraft exiting the runway is not clear until all parts of the aircraft have crossed the holding line.

k. Detailed airport marking information is published in FAA Advisory Circular 150/5340–1D, Marking of Paved Areas On Airports.

l. Helicopter Landing Areas—Details on heliport markings can be found in FAA Advisory Circular 150/5390–1B, Heliport Design Guide. See Figure 2–8.

61. AIRCRAFT ARRESTING DEVICES

a. Certain airports are equipped with a means of rapidly stopping military aircraft on a runway. This equipment, normally referred to as EMERGENCY ARRESTING GEAR, generally consists of pendant cables supported over the runway surface by rubber "donuts". Although most devices are located in the overrun areas, a few of these arresting systems have cables stretched over the operational areas near the ends of a runway. Arresting cables which cross over a runway require special markings on the runway to identify the cable location. These markings consist of 10 feet diameter solid circles painted "identification yellow", 30 feet on center, perpendicular to the runway centerline across the entire runway width. Details are contained in FAA Advisory Circular 150/5220–9, Aircraft Arresting Systems for Joint/Civil Military Airports. Aircraft operations on the runway are NOT restricted by such installations.

62.–69. RESERVED

Chapter 3.   AIRSPACE

Section 1.   GENERAL

70. GENERAL

Airspace users' operations and needs are varied. must be placed upon others for safety reasons. The complexity or density of aircraft movements in other airspace areas may result in additional aircraft and pilot requirements for operation within such airspace. It is of the utmost importance that pilots be familiar with the operational requirements for the various airspace segments.

Section 2.   UNCONTROLLED AIRSPACE

71. GENERAL

Uncontrolled airspace is that portion of the airspace that has not been designated as continental control area, control area, control zone, terminal control area, or transition area.

72. VFR REQUIREMENTS

Rules governing VFR flight have been adopted to assist the pilot in meeting his responsibility to see and avoid other aircraft. Minimum weather conditions and distance from clouds required for VFR flight are contained in these rules.   (FAR 91.105.)

73. IFR REQUIREMENTS

Federal Aviation Regulations specify the pilot and aircraft equipment requirements for IFR flight. Pilots are reminded that in addition to the altitude/flight level indicated in the table, FAR 91.119 includes a requirement to remain at least 1,000 feet (2,000 feet in designated mountainous terrain) above the highest obstacle within a horizontal distance of 5 statute miles from the course to be flown.

74. MINIMUM VISIBILITY AND DISTANCE FROM CLOUDS—VFR

ALTITUDE	UNCONTROLLED AIRSPACE		CONTROLLED AIRSPACE	
	Flight Visibility	Distance From Clouds	** Flight Visibility	** Distance From Clouds
1200' or less above the surface, regardless of MSL Altitude	*1 statute mile	Clear of clouds	3 statute miles	500' below 1000' above 2000' horizontal
More than 1200' above the surface, but less than 10,000' MSL	1 statute mile	500' below 1000' above 2000' horizontal	3 statute miles	500' below 1000' above 2000' horizontal
More than 1200' above the surface and at or above 10,000' MSL	5 statute miles	1000' below 1000' above 1 statute mile horizontal	5 statute miles	1000' below 1000' above 1 statute mile horizontal

* Helicopters may operate with less than 1 mile visibility, outside controlled airspace at 1200 feet or less above the surface, provided they are operated at a speed that allows the pilot adequate opportunity to see any air traffic or obstructions in time to avoid collisions.

** In addition, when operating within a control zone beneath a ceiling, the ceiling must not be less than 1000'. If the pilot intends to land or takeoff or enter a traffic pattern within a control zone, the ground visibility must be at least 3 miles at that airport. If ground visibility is not reported at the airport, 3 miles flight visibility is required. (FAR 91.105)

75. ALTITUDES AND FLIGHT LEVELS

CONTROLLED AND UNCONTROLLED AIRSPACE VFR ALTITUDES AND FLIGHT LEVELS			
If your magnetic course (ground track) is	More than 3000' above the surface but below 18,000' MSL fly	Above 18,000' MSL to FL 290 (except within Positive Control Area, FAR 71.193) fly	Above FL 290 (except within Positive Control Area, FAR 71.193) fly 4000' intervals
0° to 179°	Odd thousands, MSL, plus 500' (3500, 5500, 7500, etc)	Odd Flight Levels plus 500' (FL 195, 215, 235, etc)	Beginning at FL 300 (FL 300, 340, 380, etc)
180° to 359°	Even thousands, MSL, plus 500' (4500, 6500, 8500, etc)	Even Flight Levels plus 500' (FL 185, FL 205, 225, etc)	Beginning at FL 320 (FL 320, 360, 400, etc)

UNCONTROLLED AIRSPACE — IFR ALTITUDES AND FLIGHT LEVELS			
If your magnetic course (ground track) is	Below 18,000' MSL, fly	At or above 18,000' MSL but below FL 290, fly	At or above FL 290, fly 4000' intervals
0° to 179°	Odd thousands, MSL, (3000, 5000, 7000, etc)	Odd Flight Levels, FL 190, 210, 230, etc)	Beginning at FL 290, (FL 290, 330, 370, etc)
180° to 359°	Even thousands, MSL, (2000, 4000, 6000, etc)	Even Flight Levels (FL 180, 200, 220, etc)	Beginning at FL 310, (FL 310, 350, 390, etc)

76–89. RESERVED

Section 3   CONTROLLED AIRSPACE

90. GENERAL

Controlled airspace consists of those areas designated as Continental Control Area, Control Area, Control Zones, Terminal Control Areas and Transition Areas, within which some or all aircraft may be subject to Air Traffic Control. Safety, users' needs, and volume of flight operations are some of the factors considered in the designation of controlled airspace. When so designated, the airspace is supported by ground/air communications, navigation aids, and air traffic services.

91. CONTINENTAL CONTROL AREA

The continental control area consists of the airspace of the 48 contiguous States, the District of Columbia and Alaska, excluding the Alaska peninsula west of Longitude 160°00'00''W, at and above 14,500 feet MSL, but does not include:

a. The airspace less than 1,500 feet above the surface of the earth; or

b. Prohibited and restricted areas, other than the restricted areas listed in FAR Part 71 Subpart D.

92. CONTROL AREAS

Control areas consist of the airspace designated as Colored Federal airways, VOR Federal airways, Additional Control Areas, and Control Area Extensions, but do not include the Continental Control Area. Unless otherwise designated, control areas also include the airspace between a segment of a main VOR airway and its associated alternate segments. The vertical extent of the various categories of airspace contained in control area is defined in FAR Part 71.

93. POSITIVE CONTROL AREA

Positive control area is airspace so designated in Part 71.193 of the Federal Aviation Regulations. This area includes specified airspace within the conterminous United States from 18,000 feet to and including FL600, excluding Santa Barbara Island, Farallon Island, and that portion south of latitude 25°04'N. In Alaska, it includes the airspace over the State of Alaska from 18,000 feet to and including FL600, but not including the airspace less than 1,500 feet above the surface of the earth and the Alaskan Peninsula west of longitude 160°00'W. Rules for operating in positive control area are found in FARs 91.97 and 91.24.

94. TRANSITION AREAS

a. Transition areas are designated to contain IFR operations in controlled airspace during portions of the terminal operation and while transitioning between the terminal and en route environment.

b. Transition areas are controlled airspace extending upward from 700 feet or more above the surface when designated in conjunction with an airport for which an instrument approach procedure has been prescribed; or from 1,200 feet or more above the surface when designated in conjunction with airway route structures or segments. Unless specified otherwise, transition areas terminate at the base of overlying controlled airspace

95. CONTROL ZONES

a. Control zones are controlled airspace which extend upward from the surface and terminate at the base of the continental control area. Control zones that do not underlie the continental control area have no upper limit. A control zone may include one or more airports and is normally a circular area within a radius of 5 statute miles and any extensions necessary to include instrument departure and arrival paths.

b. Control zones are depicted on charts (for example— on the sectional charts the zone is outlined by a broken blue line) and if a control zone is effective only during certain hours of the day, this fact will also be noted on the charts. A typical control zone is depicted in paragraph 134. (See **264**—SPECIAL VFR CLEAR-ANCES.)

96. TERMINAL CONTROL AREA

a. A Terminal Control Area (TCA) consists of controlled airspace extending upward from the surface or higher to specified altitudes, within which *all aircraft* are subject to operating rules and pilot and equipment requirements specified in Part 91 of the FAR's. TCA's are described in Part 71 of the FAR's. Each such location is designated as a Group I or Group II terminal control area, and includes at least one primary airport around which the TCA is located. (See FAR 71.12)

(1) Group I terminal control areas represent some of the busiest locations in terms of aircraft operations and passengers carried, and it is necessary for safety reasons to have more strict requirements for operation within Group I TCA's. (See FAR 91.70(c) and 91.90)

(2) Group II terminal control areas represent less busy locations, and though safety dictates some pilot and equipment requirements, they are not as stringent as those for Group I locations. (See FAR 91.70(c) and FAR 91.90)

b. Terminal Control Areas are charted on Sectional, World Aeronautical, En Route Low Altitude, DOD Flip and TCA charts.

(1) The following areas have been designated as Group I Terminal Control Areas and are depicted on VFR Terminal Area Charts.

Atlanta	Miami
Boston	New York
Chicago	San Francisco
Dallas	Washington, D.C.
Los Angeles	

(2) The following areas have been designated as Group II Terminal Control Areas and are depicted on VFR Terminal Area Charts.

Cleveland	Minneapolis
Denver	New Orleans
Detroit	Philadelphia
Houston	Pittsburgh
Kansas City	Seattle
Las Vegas	St. Louis

97. IFR ALTITUDES/FLIGHT LEVELS

Pilots operating IFR within controlled airspace will fly at an altitude/flight level assigned by ATC. When operating IFR within controlled airspace with an altitude assignment of "VFR-ON-TOP", flight is to be conducted at an appropriate VFR altitude which is not below the minimum IFR altitude for the route. (See paragraph 74) VFR-ON-TOP is not permitted in certain airspace such as positive control airspace, certain Restricted Areas, etc. Consequently, IFR flights operating VFR-ON-TOP will avoid such airspace.

98. VFR REQUIREMENTS

a. Minimum flight visibility and distance from clouds have been prescribed for VFR operation in controlled airspace. (See paragraph 74) In addition, appropriate altitudes/flight levels for VFR flight in controlled, as well as in uncontrolled airspace have been prescribed in FAR 91.109. (See paragraph 75) The ever increasing speeds of aircraft result in increasing closure rates for opposite direction aircraft. This means that there is less time for pilots to see each other and react to avoid each other. By adhering to the altitude/flight level appropriate for the direction of flight, a "built-in" vertical separation is available for the pilots.

99–109. RESERVED

Section 4. SPECIAL USE AIRSPACE

110. GENERAL

Special use airspace consists of that airspace wherein activities must be confined because of their nature, or wherein limitations are imposed upon aircraft operations that are not a part of those activities, or both. Except for controlled firing areas, special use airspace areas are depicted on aeronautical charts.

111. PROHIBITED AREA

a. Prohibited areas contain airspace of defined dimensions identified by an area on the surface of the earth within which the flight of aircraft is prohibited. Such areas are established for security or other reasons associated with the national welfare. These areas are published in the Federal Register and depicted on aeronautical charts.

112. RESTRICTED AREA

a. Restricted areas contain airspace identified by an area on the surface of the earth within which the flight of aircraft, while not wholly prohibited, is subject to restrictions. Activities within these areas must be confined because of their nature or limitations imposed upon aircraft operations that are not a part of those activities or both. Restricted areas denote the existence of unusual often invisible, hazards to aircraft such as artillery firing, aerial gunnery, or guided missiles. Penetration of restricted areas without authorization from the using or controlling agency may be extremely hazardous to the aircraft and its occupants. Restricted areas are published in the Federal Register and constitute Part 73 of the Federal Aviation Regulations. (See **346**—OPERATION IN RESTRICTED AIRSPACE.)

113. WARNING AREA

a. Warning areas are airspace which may contain hazards to nonparticipating aircraft in international airspace. Warning areas are established beyond the 3 mile limit. Though the activities conducted within warning areas may be as hazardous as those in Restricted areas, Warning areas cannot be legally designated because they are over international waters. Penetration of Warning areas during periods of activity may be hazardous to the aircraft and its occupants. Official descriptions of Warning areas may be obtained on request to the FAA, Washington, D.C.

114. MILITARY OPERATIONS AREAS (MOA)

a. Military Operations Areas consist of airspace of defined vertical and lateral limits established for the purpose of separating certain military training activities from IFR traffic. Whenever an MOA is being used, nonparticipating IFR traffic may be cleared through an MOA if IFR separation can be provided by ATC. Otherwise, ATC will reroute or restrict nonparticipating IFR traffic.

b. Some training activities may necessitate acrobatic maneuvers, and the USAF is exempted from the regulation prohibiting acrobatic flight on airways within MOAs.

c. Pilots operating under VFR should exercise extreme caution while flying within an MOA when military activity is being conducted. Information regarding activity in MOA's may be obtained from any FSS within 200 miles of the area.

d. These areas will be depicted on Sectional, VFR Terminal and Low Altitude En Route Charts.

115. ALERT AREA

a. Alert areas are depicted on aeronautical charts to inform nonparticipating pilots of areas that may contain a high volume of pilot training or an unusual type of aerial activity. Pilots should be particularly alert when flying in these areas. All activity with an Alert Area shall be conducted in accordance with Federal Aviation Regulations, without waiver, and pilots of participating aircraft as well as pilots transiting the area shall be equally responsible for collision avoidance. Information concerning these areas may be obtained upon request to the FAA, Washington, D.C.

116. CONTROLLED FIRING AREAS

a. Controlled firing areas contain activities which, if not conducted in a controlled environment, could be hazardous to non-participating aircraft. The distinguishing feature of the controlled firing area, as compared to other special use airspace, is that its activities are suspended immediately when spotter aircraft, radar, or ground lookout positions indicate an aircraft might be approaching the area. There is no need to chart controlled firing areas since they do not cause a non-participating aircraft to change its flight path.

117–129. RESERVED

Section 5.   OTHER AIRSPACE AREAS

130. AIRPORT TRAFFIC AREAS

a. Unless otherwise specifically designated (FAR Part 93), that airspace within a horizontal radius of five statute miles from the geographical center of any airport at which a control tower is operating, extending from the surface up to, but not including, an altitude of 3,000 feet above the elevation of the airport.

b. The rules prescribed for airport traffic areas are established in FAR 91.70, 91.85 and 91.87. They require, in effect, that unless a pilot is landing or taking off from an airport within the airport traffic area, he must avoid the area unless otherwise authorized by ATC (either directly from the ATC facility responsible for the Airport Traffic Area, or from a facility from which the pilot is receiving radar services). If operating to, from or on the airport served by the control tower, he must also establish and maintain radio communications with the tower. Maximum indicated airspeeds are prescribed. Airport traffic areas are indicated on sectional charts by the blue airport symbol, but the actual boundary is not depicted. (See paragraph 134)

131. AIRPORT ADVISORY AREA

a. The area within five statute miles of an airport where a control tower is not operating but where a Flight Service Station is located. At such locations, the FSS provides advisory service to arriving and departing aircraft. (See 155—AIRPORT ADVISORY PRACTICES AT NONTOWER AIRPORTS.)

b. It is not mandatory that pilots participate in the airport advisory service program, but it is strongly recommended that they do.

132. MILITARY TRAINING ROUTES (MTR)

a. National security depends largely on the deterrent effect of our airborne military forces. To be proficient, the military services must train in a wide range of airborne tactics. One phase of this training involves "low level" combat tactics. The required maneuvers and high speeds are such that they may occasionally make the see-and-avoid aspect of VFR flight more difficult without increased vigilance in areas containing such operations. In an effort to ensure the greatest practical level of safety for all flight operations—the military training route program was conceived.

b. The Military Training Routes (MTRs) program is a joint venture by the Federal Aviation Administration (FAA) and the Department of Defense (DOD) in that the routes are mutually developed for use by the military for the purpose of conducting low-altitude, high-speed training. The routes above 1,500 feet above ground level (AGL) are developed to be flown, to the maximum extent possible, under instrument flight rules. The routes at 1,500 feet AGL and below are generally developed to be flown under visual flight rules.

c. Generally, MTRs are established below 10,000 feet MSL for operations at speeds in excess of 250 KTS. However, route segments may be defined at higher altitudes for purposes of route continuity. For example, route segments may be defined for descent, climbout, and mountainous terrain. There are IFR and VFR routes as follows:

(1) IFR Military Training Routes—IR

Operations on these routes are conducted in accordance with instrument flight rules regardless of weather conditions.

(2) VFR Military Training Routes—VR

Operations on these routes are conducted in accordance with visual flight rules.

d. Military training routes will be identified and charted as follows:

(1) Route identification.

(a) *IRs/VRs at or below 1,500 feet AGL* (with no segment above 1,500) will be identified by four digit numbers; e.g., IR 1006, VR 1007, etc.

(b) *IRs/VRs above 1,500 feet AGL* (segments of these routes may be below 1,500) will be identified by three digit numbers; e.g., IR 008, VR 009, etc.

(2) Route charting.

(a) IFR Low Altitude En Route Chart—This chart will depict all IR routes and all VR routes that accommodate operations above 1,500 feet AGL.

(b) VFR Planning Chart—This chart will depict routes (military training activities such as IR and VR regardless of altitude), Military Operations Areas (MOA), and restrcited, warning and alert areas.

(c) AP/1B Chart (DOD Flight Information Publication—FLIP). This chart is published by the Department of Defense primarily for military users and contains detailed information on both IRS and VRs.

e. The FLIP contains charts and narrative descriptions of these routes. This publication is available to the general public by single copy or annual subscription from the National Ocean Survey, Distribution Division, C–44, Riverdale, Maryland 20849. This DOD FLIP is available for pilot briefings at FSS and many airports.

f. Current information concerning MOAs and MTRs is available upon request from FSSs within 200 NM of the route.

133. TEMPORARY FLIGHT RESTRICTIONS

a. Temporary flight restrictions may be put into effect in the vicinity of any incident or event which by its nature may generate such a high degree of public interest that the likelihood of a hazardous congestion of air traffic exists. FAR 91.91, as amended 1 March, 1971, prohibits the operation of nonessential aircraft in airspace that has been designated in a NOTAM as an area within which temporary flight restrictions apply. The revised rule will continue to be implemented in the case of disasters of substantial magnitude. It will also be implemented as necessary in the case of demonstrations, riots, and other civil disturbances, as well as major sporting events, parades, pageants, and similar functions which are likely to attract large crowds and encouraging viewing from the air.

b. NOTAM's implementing temporary flight restrictions will contain a description of the area in which the restrictions apply. Normally the area will include the airspace below 2,000 feet above the surface within 5 miles of the site of the incident. However, the exact dimensions will be included in the NOTAM.

c. Pilots are not to operate aircraft within such an area described in the NOTAM unless they are one of the following:

(1) That aircraft is participating in disaster relief activities and is being operated under the direction of the agency responsible for relief activities;

(2) They are operating to or from an airport within the area and such operation will not hamper or endanger relief activities;

(3) Their operation is authorized under an IFR ATC clearance;

(4) Flight around the area is impracticable because of weather or other considerations and advance notice is given to the Air Traffic facility specified in the NOTAM, and enroute flight through the area will not hamper or endanger relief activities; or

(5) They are carrying accredited news representatives or persons on official business concerning the incident, and the flight is conducted in accordance with FAR 91.76 and a flight plan is filed with the Air Traffic facility specified in the NOTAM.

AIRSPACE

134. GENERAL DIMENSIONS OF CONTROL ZONES, AIRPORT TRAFFIC AREAS, AND THE VERTICAL EXTENT OF AIRSPACE SEGMENTS

Refer to FARs or specific dimensions, exceptions, geographical areas covered, exclusions, specific transponder/equipment requirements, and flight operations. Arrows ending near but not touching reference lines mean "up to/down to" but not including the referenced altitude.

* Federal airways in Hawaii have no vertical limits.

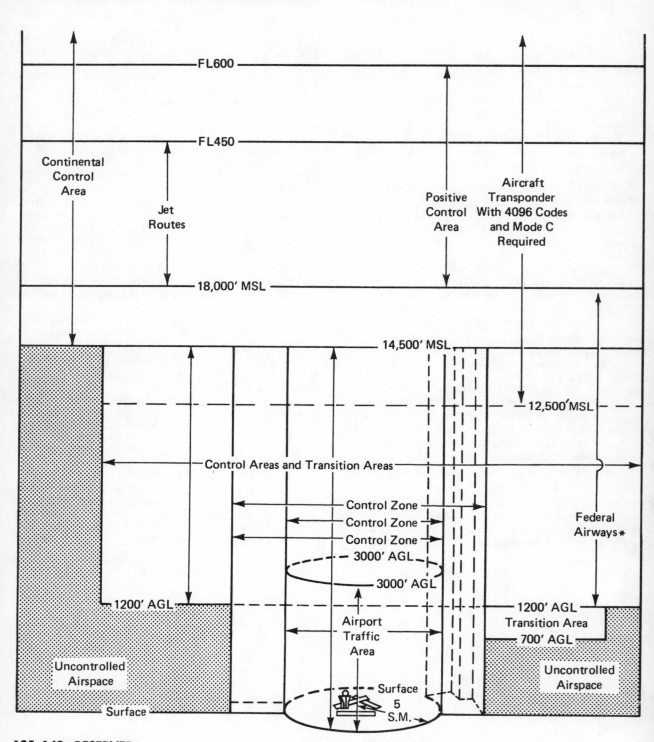

135–149. RESERVED

Chapter 4. AIR TRAFFIC CONTROL

Section 1. SERVICES AVAILABLE TO PILOTS

150. AIR ROUTE TRAFFIC CONTROL CENTERS

a. Centers are established primarily to provide air traffic service to aircraft operating on IFR flight plans within controlled airspace, and principally during the enroute phase of flight.

151. CONTROL TOWERS

Towers have been established to provide for a safe, orderly and expeditious flow of traffic on and in the vicinity of an airport. When the responsibility has been so delegated, towers also provide for the separation of IFR aircraft in the terminal areas. (See 362—APPROACH CONTROL.)

152. FLIGHT SERVICE STATIONS

Flight Service Stations are the Air Traffic Service facilities within the National Airspace System which have the prime responsibility for preflight pilot briefing, en route communications with VFR flights, assisting lost VFR aircraft, originating NOTAMS, broadcasting aviation weather information, accepting and closing flight plans, monitoring radio NAVAIDS, participating with search and rescue units in locating missing VFR aircraft, and operating the national weather teletypewriter systems. In addition, at selected locations, FSSs take weather observations, issue airport advisories, administer airman written examinations, and advise Customs and Immigration of transborder flight.

153. PILOT VISITS TO AIR TRAFFIC FACILITIES

Pilots are encouraged to visit air traffic facilities—Towers, Centers and Flight Service Stations and participate in "Operation Raincheck". Operation Raincheck is conducted at these facilities and is designed to familiarize pilots with the ATC system, its functions, responsibilities and benefits. On rare occasions, facilities may not be able to approve a visit because of workload or other reasons. It is therefore requested that pilots contact the facility prior to the visit—give the number of persons in the group, the time and date of the proposed visit, the primary interest of the group. With this information avaialble, the facility can prepare an itinerary and have someone available to guide the group through the facility.

154. VFR ADVISORY SERVICE

a. VFR advisory service is provided by numerous nonradar *Approach Control* facilities to those pilots intending to land at an airport served by an approach control tower. This service includes: wind, runway, traffic and NOTAM information, unless this information is contained in the ATIS broadcast and the pilot indicates he has received the ATIS information.

b. Such information will be furnished upon initial contact with concerned approach control facility. The pilot will be requested to change to the *tower* frequency at a predetermined time or point, to receive further landing information.

c. Where available, use of this procedure will not hinder the operation of VFR flights by requiring excessive spacing between aircraft or devious routing. Radio contact points will be based on time or distance rather than on landmarks.

d. Compliance with this procedure is not mandatory but pilot participation is encouraged.

155. AIRPORT ADVISORY PRACTICES AT NONTOWER AIRPORTS

a. There is no substitute for alertness while in the vicinity of an airport. An airport may have a flight service station, UNICOM operator, or no facility at all. Pilots should predetermine what, if any, service is available at a particular airport. Combining an aural/visual alertness and complying with the following recommended practices will enhance safety of flight into and out of uncontrolled airports.

b. Recommended Traffic Adivsory Practices—As standard operating practice all inbound traffic should continuously monitor the appropriate field facility frequency from 15 miles to landing. Departure aircraft should monitor the appropriate frequency either prior to or when ready to taxi. (See appropriate Airport/Facility Directory or Enroute Supplement for UNICOM frequencies in use.)

(1) Inbound Aircraft

Airport	Frequency	Broadcast Position, Altitude, Intentions	Broadcast Position
–Part-Time Tower (when closed)	Tower Local Control	5 Miles	Downwind, Base, Final
–Part-Time Tower (closed) but Full-Time FSS	Tower Local Control	*15 Miles	*5 Miles
–Part-Time Tower/ Part-Time FSS (both closed)	Tower Local Control	5 Miles	Downwind, Base, Final
–Part-Time FSS (closed)	123.6	5 Miles	Downwind, Base, Final
–Full-Time or Part-Time FSS (open)	123.6	*15 Miles	*5 Miles
–UNICOM	122.7, 122.8, 123.0	*5 Miles	
–UNICOM (if able establish contact)	122.7, 122.8, 123.0	5 Miles	Downwind, Base, Final

Airport	Frequency	Position
–No Facility on Airport	122.9	5 Miles Downwind, Base, Final

(2) Outbound Aircraft

Airport	Frequency	Broadcast Position And Intentions
–Part-Time Tower (closed)	Tower Local Control	When ready to taxi; and before taking runway for takeoff
–Part-Time Tower (closed) but Full-Time FSS	Tower Local Control	*When ready to taxi; and before taking runway for takeoff
–Part-Time Tower Part-Time FSS (both closed)	Tower Local Control	When ready to taxi; and before taking runway for takeoff
–Part-Time FSS (closed)	123.6	When ready to taxi; and before taking runway for takeoff
–Full-Time or Part-Time FSS (open)	123.6	*When ready to taxi; and before taking runway for takeoff
–UNICOM	122.7, 122.8, 123.0	*When ready to taxi; and before taking runway for takeoff
–UNICOM (if unable establish contact)	122.7, 122.8, 123.0	When ready to taxi; and before taking runway for takeoff
–No facility on airport	122.9	When ready to taxi; and before taking runway for takeoff

*Contact appropriate facility first; e.g., "Zanesville Radio, this is Cessna 12345, Over," before announcing arrival/departure intentions. Except for scheduled air carriers and other civil operators having authorized company call signs, departure aircraft should state the aircraft type, identification number, type of flight planned, i.e., VFR or IFR, and the planned destination.

Note.—FSS at part-time non-FAA tower locations do not have tower local control frequency. Use 123.6.

c. Information Furnished by FSS or UNICOM

FSSs provide airport advisory service at airports where there is no control tower or when the tower is not in operation (part-time tower location). Advisories provide: wind direction and velocity, favored or designated runway, altimeter setting, known traffic (caution: all aircraft in the airport vicinity may not be communicating with the FSS), notices to airmen, airport taxi routes, airport traffic patterns, and instrument approach procedures. These elements are varied so as to best serve the current traffic situation. Some airport managers have specified that under certain wind or other conditions, designated runways are to be used. Pilots using other than the favored or designated runways should advise the FSS immediately.

Note.—Airport Advisory Service is offered to enhance safety: TRAFFIC CONTROL IS NOT EXERCISED.

d. Recommended Phraseologies
(1) Departures

Example:

Aircraft: JOHNSON RADIO, COMANCHE SIX ONE THREE EIGHT, ON TERMINAL BUILDING RAMP, READY TO TAXI, VFR TO DULUTH, OVER

FSS: COMANCHE SIX ONE THREE EIGHT, JOHNSON RADIO, ROGER, WIND THREE TWO ZERO AT TWO FIVE, FAVORING RUNWAY THREE ONE ALTIMETER THREE ZERO ZERO ONE, CESSNA ONE-SEVENTY ON DOWNLEG MAKING TOUCH AND GO LANDINGS ON RUNWAY THREE ONE

Note.—The takeoff time should be reported to the FSS as soon as practicable. If the aircraft has limited equipment and it is necessary to use the navigational feature of the radio aid immediately after takeoff, advise the FSS of this before changing frequency to the range. In such cases, advisories will be transmitted over 123.6 or the tower local control frequency, as appropriate, and the aid frequency.

(2) Arrivals

Example:

Aircraft: JOHNSON RADIO, TRIPACER ONE SIX EIGHT NINER, OVER KEY WEST, TWO THOUSAND, LANDING GRAND FORKS, OVER

FSS: TRIPACER ONE SIX EIGHT NINER, JOHNSON RADIO, OVER KEY WEST AT TWO THOUSAND, WIND ONE FIVE ZERO AT FOUR, DESIGNATED RUNWAY FIVE, ALTIMETER THREE ZERO ZERO ONE, DC–3 TAKING OFF RUNWAY FIVE, BONANZA ON DOWNWIND LEG RUNWAY FIVE MAKING TOUCH AND GO LANDINGS, COMANCHE DEPARTED RUNWAY ONE SEVEN AT ONE SIX PROCEEDING EASTBOUND, OVER

Note.—Pilots should guard 123.6 or the tower local control frequency, as appropriate, until clear of the runway after landing and report leaving the runway to the FSS.

(3) Transmissions (blind broadcasts) When Not Communicating With an FSS or UNICOM Operator
(a) Inbound

Example:

THIS IS APACHE TWO TWO FIVE ZULU, FIVE MILES EAST OF STRAWN AIRPORT, TWO THOUSAND DESCENDING TO ENTER DOWNWIND FOR RUNWAY ONE SEVEN STRAWN

(b) Outbound

Example:

THIS IS QUEENAIRE SEVEN ONE FIVE FIVE BRAVO, AT STRAWN AIRPORT TAXIING ONTO RUNWAY TWO SIX FOR TAKEOFF

156. AERONAUTICAL ADVISORY STATIONS (UNICOM)

a. UNICOM is a non-government air/ground radio communication facility which may provide airport advisory service at certain airports. Locations and frequencies of UNICOMs are shown on aeronautical charts and publications.

b. THIS SERVICE SHALL NOT BE USED FOR AIR TRAFFIC CONTROL PURPOSES, except for the verbatim relay of ATC information limited to the following:

(1) Revision of proposed departure time.

(2) Takeoff, arrival, or flight plan cancellation time.

(3) ATC clearance *provided* arrangements are made between the ATC facility and UNICOM licensee to handle such messages.

c. The following listing depicts the frequencies which are currently designated by the Federal Communications Commission (FCC) for use as Aeronautical Advisory Stations (UNICOM).

Frequency	Use
122.700	uncontrolled fields
122.725	private airports (not open to public)
122.750	private airports (not open to public) and air-to-air communications
122.800	uncontrolled airports
122.950	airports with a control tower
122.975	high altitude
123.000	uncontrolled airports
123.050	heliports
123.075	heliports

157–159. RESERVED

160. AERONAUTICAL MULTICOM SERVICE

a. This is a mobile service used to provide communications essential to conduct of activities being performed by or directed from private aircraft. For example it may include ground/air communications pertaining to agriculture, ranching, conservation activities, forest fire fighting, aerial advertising and parachute jumping.

b. THIS SERVICE SHALL NOT BE USED FOR AIR TRAFFIC CONTROL PURPOSES, except for the verbatim relay of ATC information limited to the following:

(1) Revision of proposed departure time.

(2) Takeoff, arrival, or flight plan cancellation time.

(3) ATC clearances *provided* arrangements are made between the ATC facility and UNICOM licensee to handle such messages.

c. The following listing depicts the frequencies which are currently designated by the Federal Communications Commission (FCC) for use as Aeronautical Multicom Service.

Frequency

122.850 122.900 122.925

161. AUTOMATIC TERMINAL INFORMATION SERVICE (ATIS)

Automatic Terminal Information Service (ATIS) is the continuous broadcast of recorded noncontrol information in selected high activity terminal areas. Its purpose is to improve controller effectiveness and to relieve frequency congestion by automating the repetitive transmission of essential but routine information. Pilots are urged to cooperate in the ATIS program as it relieves frequency congestion on approach control, ground control, and local control frequencies. The Airport Facility/Directory indicates airports for which ATIS is provided.

a. Information to include the time of the latest weather sequence, ceiling, visibility (sky conditions/ceilings below 5000 feet and visibility less than 5 miles will be broadcast; if conditions are at or better than 5000 and 5, sky condition/ceiling and visibility may be omitted) obstructions to visibility, temperature, wind direction (magnetic) and velocity, altimeter, other pertinent remarks, instrument approach and runways in use is continuously broadcast on the voice feature of a TVOR/VOR/VORTAC located on or near the airport, or in a discrete UHF/VHF frequency. The departure runway/s will only be given if different from the landing runway/s except at locations having a separate ATIS for departure. Where VFR arrival aircraft are expected to make initial contact with approach control, this fact and the appropriate frequencies may be broadcast on ATIS. Pilots of aircraft arriving or departing the terminal area can receive the continuous ATIS broadcasts at times when cockpit duties are least pressing and listen to as many repeats as desired. ATIS broadcasts shall be updated upon the receipt of any official weather, regardless of content change and reported values. A new recording will also be made when there is a change in other pertinent data such as runway change, instrument approach in use, etc.

Sample Broadcast:

DULLES INTERNATIONAL INFORMATION SIERRA. 1300 GREENWICH WEATHER. MEASURED CEILING THREE THOUSAND OVERCAST. VISIBILITY THREE, SMOKE. TEMPERATURE SIX EIGHT. WIND THREE FIVE ZERO AT EIGHT. ALTIMETER TWO NINER NINER TWO. ILS RUNWAY ONE RIGHT APPROACH IN USE. LANDING RUNWAY ONE RIGHT AND LEFT. DEPARTURE RUNWAY THREE ZERO. ARMEL VORTAC OUT OF SERVICE. ADVISE YOU HAVE SIERRA.

b. Pilots should listen to ATIS broadcasts whenever ATIS is in operation.

c. Pilots should notify controllers that they have received the ATIS broadcast by repeating the alphabetical code word appended to the broadcast.

EXAMPLES: "INFORMATION SIERRA RECEIVED."

d. When the pilot acknowledges that he has received the ATIS broadcast, controllers may omit those items contained in the broadcast if they are current. Rapidly changing conditions will be issued by Air Traffic Control and the ATIS will contain words as follows:

"LATEST CEILING / VISIBILITY / ALTIMETER / WIND/(OTHER CONDITIONS) WILL BE ISSUED BY APPROACH CONTROL/TOWER."

The absence of a sky condition/ceiling and/or visibility on ATIS indicates a sky condition/ceiling of 5000 feet or above and visibility of 5 miles or more. A remark may be made on the broadcast, "The weather is better than 5000 and 5," or the existing weather may be broadcast.

e. Controllers will issue pertinent information to pilots who do not acknowledge receipt of a broadcast or who acknowledge receipt of a broadcast which is not current.

f. To serve frequency-limited aircraft, Flight Service Stations (FSS) are equipped to transmit on the omnirange frequency at most en route VORs used as ATIS voice outlets. Such communication interrupts the ATIS broadcast. Pilots of aircraft equipped to receive on other FSS frequencies are encouraged to do so in order that these override transmissions may be kept to an absolute minimum.

g. While it is a good operating practice for pilots to make use of the ATIS broadcast where it is available, some pilots use the phrase "Have Numbers" in communications with the control tower. Use of this phrase means that the pilot has received wind, runway and altimeter information ONLY and the tower does not have to repeat this information. It does indicate receipt of the ATIS broadcast and should never be used for this purpose.

162. RADAR TRAFFIC INFORMATION SERVICE

A service provided by radar air traffic control facilities. Pilots receiving this service are advised of any radar target observed on the radar display which may be in such proximity to the position of their aircraft or its intended route of flight that it warrants their attention. This service is not intended to relieve the pilot of his responsibility for continual vigilance to see and avoid other aircraft.

a. Purpose of the Service—

(1) The issuance of traffic information as observed on a radar display is based on the principle of assisting and advising a pilot that a particular radar target's position and track indicates it may intersect or pass in such proximity to his intended flight path that it warrants his attention. This is to alert the pilot to the traffic so that he can be on the lookout for it and thereby be in a better position to take appropriate action should the need arise.

(2) Pilots are reminded that the surveillance radar used by ATC does not provide altitude information unless the aircraft is equipped with Mode C and the Radar Facility is capable of displaying altitude information.

b. Provisions of the Service—

(1) Many factors, such as limitations of the radar, volume of traffic, controller workload and communications frequency congestion, could prevent the controller from providing this service. The controller possesses complete discretion for determining whether he is able to provide or continue to provide this service in a specific case. His reason against providing or continuing to provide the service in a particular case is not subject to question nor need it be communicated to the pilot. In other words, the provision of this service is entirely dependent upon whether the controller believes he is in a position to provide it. Traffic information is routinely provided to all aircraft operating on IFR Flight Plans except when the pilot advises he does not desire the service, or the pilot is operating within positive controlled airspace. Traffic information may be provided to flights not operating on IFR Flight Plans when requested by pilots of such flight.

(2) When receiving VFR radar advisory service, pilots should monitor the assigned frequency at all times, This is to preclude controllers' concern for radio failure or emergency assistance to aircraft under his jurisdiction. VFR radar advisory service does not include vectors away from conflicting traffic unless requested by the pilot. When advisory service is no longer desired, advise the controller before changing frequencies then change your transponder code to 1200 if applicable.

Except in programs where radar service is automatically terminated, the controller will advise the aircraft when radar is terminated.

NOTE.—Participation by VFR pilots in formal programs implemented at certain terminal locations constitutes pilot request. This also applies to participating pilots at those locations where arriving VFR flights are encouraged to make their first contact with the tower on the approach control frequency.

c. Issuance of Traffic Information—Traffic information will include the following concerning a target which may constitute traffic for an aircraft that is:

(1) Radar identified:
(a) Azimuth from the aircraft in terms of the twelve hour clock;
(b) Distance from the aircraft in nautical miles;
(c) Direction in which the target is proceeding; and
(d) Type of aircraft and altitude if known.

Example:

Traffic 10 o'clock, 3 miles, west-bound (type aircraft and altitude, if known, of the observed traffic). The pilot may, upon receipt of traffic information, request a vector (heading) to avoid such traffic. The vector will be provided to the extent possible as determined by the controller provided the aircraft to be vectored is within the airspace under the jurisdiction of the controller.

(2) Not radar identified:
(a) Distance and direction with respect to a fix;
(b) Direction in which the target is proceeding; and
(c) Type of aircraft and altitude if known.

Example:

Traffic 8 miles south of the airport northeast-bound, (type aircraft and altitude if known).

d. The examples depicted in the figures below point out the possible error in the position of this traffic when it is necessary for a pilot to apply drift correction to maintain this track. This error could also occur in the event a change in course is made at the time radar traffic information is issued.

(1) In this figure traffic information would be issued to the pilot of aircraft "A" as 12 o'clock. The actual position of the traffic as seen by the pilot of aircraft "A" would be one o'clock. Traffic information issued to aircraft "B" would also be given as 12 o'clock, but in this case, the pilot of "B" would see his traffic at 11 o'clock.

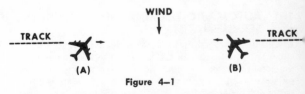

Figure 4-1

(2) In this figure traffic information would be issued to the pilot of aircraft "C" as two o'clock. The actual position of the traffic as seen by the pilot of aircraft "C" would be three o'clock. Traffic information issued to aircraft "D" would be at an 11 o'clock position. Since it is not necessary for the pilot of aircraft "D" to apply wind

correction (crab) to make good his track, the actual position of the traffic issued would be correct. Since the radar controller can only observe aircraft track (course) on his radar display, he must issue traffic advisories accordingly, and pilots should give due consideration to this fact when looking for reported traffic.

Figure 4–2

163. SAFETY ADVISORY

a. A safety advisory will be issued to pilots of aircraft being controlled by ATC if the controller is aware the aircraft is at an altitude which, in the controller's judgment, places the aircraft in unsafe proximity to terrain, obstructions or other aircraft. The provision of this service is contingent upon the capability of the controller to have an awareness of situation(s) involving unsafe proximity to terrain, obstructions and uncontrolled aircraft. The issuance of a safety advisory cannot be mandated, but it can be expected on a reasonable, though intermittent basis. Once the advisory is issued, it is solely the pilot's prerogative to determine what course of action, if any, he will take. This procedure is intended for use in time critical situations where aircraft safety is in question. Noncritical situations should be handled via the normal traffic advisory procedures.

b. Terrain/Obstruction Advisory

(1) The controller will immediately issue an advisory to the pilot of an aircraft under this control if he is aware the aircraft is at an altitude which, in the controller's judgment, places the aircraft in unsafe proximity to terrain/obstructions. The primary method of detecting unsafe proximity is through Mode C.

Example:

LOW ALTITUDE ALERT, CHECK YOUR ALTITUDE IMMEDIATELY. THE (MEA, MVA, MOCA, etc., as appropriate) IN YOUR AREA IS (altitude).

(2) Some automated terminal facilities (ARTS III) are equipped with a computer function which, if operating, generates an alert to the controller when a tracked Mode C equipped aircraft under his control is below or is predicted, by the computer, to go below a predetermined minimum safe altitude. This function is called Minimum Safe Altitude Warning (MSAW). It is designed solely to aid the controller in detecting tracked aircraft with an operating Mode C transponder which may be in unsafe proximity to terrain/obstructions. The automated facility (ARTS III) which is equipped with this function will, when it is operating, process:

(a) All IFR aircraft, with an operating transponder and altitude encoder, which are being tracked.

(b) All VFR aircraft, with an operating transponder and altitude encoder, which are being tracked and have requested MSAW.

NOTE.—Pilots operating on VFR flight plans may request MSAW processing by the ARTS III computer if their aircraft has an operating transponder with altitude encoding. (Mode C)

Example:

APACHE THREE THREE PAPA REQUEST MSAW.

c. Aircraft Conflict Advisory

(1) The controller will immediately issue an advisory to the pilot of an aircraft under his control if he is aware of an aircraft that is not under his control at an altitude which, in the controller's judgment, places both aircraft in unsafe proximity to each other. With the alert the controller will offer the pilot an alternate course(s) of action when feasible. Any alternate course(s) of action the controller may recommend to the pilot will be predicated only on other traffic under his control.

Example:

AMERICAN THREE, TRAFFIC ALERT, ADVISE YOU TURN RIGHT/LEFT HEADING (DEGREES) AND/OR CLIMB/DESCEND TO (ALTITUDE) IMMEDIATELY.

164. RADAR ASSISTANCE TO VFR AIRCRAFT

a. Radar equipped FAA Air Traffic Control facilities provide radar assistance and navigation service (vectors) to VFR aircraft provided the aircraft can communicate with the facility, are within radar coverage, and can be radar identified.

b. Pilots should clearly understand that authorization to proceed in accordance with such radar navigational assistance does not constitute authorization for the pilot to violate Federal Aviation Regulations. In effect, assistance provided is on the basis that navigational guidance information issued is advisory in nature and the job of flying the aircraft safely, remains with the pilot.

c. In many cases, the controller will be unable to determine if flight into instrument conditions will result from his instructions. To avoid possible hazards resulting from being vectored into IFR conditions, pilots should keep the controller advised of the weather conditions in which he is operating and along the course ahead.

d. Radar navigation assistance (vectors) may be initiated by the controller when one of the following conditions exist:

(1) The controller suggests the vector and the pilot concurs.

(2) A special program has been established and vectoring service has been advertised.

(3) In the controller's judgment the vector is necessary for air safety.

e. Radar navigation assistance (vectors) and other radar derived information may be provided in response to pilot requests. Many factors, such as limitations of radar, volume of traffic, communications frequency, congestion, and controller workload could prevent the controller from providing it. The controller has complete discretion for determining if he is able to provide the service in a particular case. His decison not to provide the service in a particular case is not subject to question.

165. TERMINAL RADAR PROGRAMS FOR VFR AIRCRAFT

a. STAGE I SERVICE (Radar Advisory Service for VFR Aircraft)

(1) In addition to the use of radar for the control of IFR aircraft, Stage I facilities provide traffic information and limited vectoring to VFR aircraft on a workload permitting basis.

(2) Vectoring service may be provided when requested by the pilot or with pilot concurrence when suggested by ATC.

(3) Pilots of arriving aircraft should contact approach control on the publicized frequency and give their position, altitude, radar beacon code (if transponder equipped), destination, and request traffic information.

(4) Approach control will issue wind and runway, except when the pilot states 'HAVE NUMBERS' or this information is contained in the ATIS broadcast and the pilot indicates he has received the ATIS information. Traffic information is provided on a workload permitting basis. Approach control will specify the time or place at which the pilot is to contact the tower on local control frequency for further landing information. Upon being told to contact the tower, radar service is automatically terminated.

b. Stage II Service Radar Advisory and Sequencing for VFR Aircraft).

(1) This service has been implemented at certain terminal locations (See locations listed in the Airport/Facility Directory). The purpose of the service is to adjust the flow of arriving VFR and IFR aircraft into the traffic pattern in a safe and orderly manner and to provide radar traffic information to departing VFR aircraft. Pilot participation is urged but it is not mandatory.

(2) Pilots of arriving VFR aircraft should initiate radio contact on the publicized frequency with approach control when approximately 25 miles from the airport at which Stage II services are being provided. On initial contact by VFR aircraft, approach control will assume that Stage II service is requested. Approach control will provide the pilot with wind and runway (except when the pilot states "Have Numbers" or that he has received the ATIS information), routings, etc., as necessary for proper sequencing with other participating VFR and IFR traffic en route to the airport. Traffic information will be provided on a workload permitting basis. If an arriving aircraft does not want the service, the pilot should state NEGATIVE STAGE II, or make a similar comment, on initial contact with approach control.

(3) After radar contact is established, the pilot may navigate on his own into the traffic pattern or, depending on traffic conditions, he may be directed to fly specific headings to position the flight behind a preceding aircraft in the approach sequence. When a flight is positioned behind the preceding aircraft and the pilot reports having that aircraft in sight, he will be directed to follow it. If other "non-participating" or "local" aircraft are in the traffic pattern, the tower will issue a landing sequence. Upon being told to contact the tower, radar service is automatically terminated.

(4) Standard radar separation will be provided between IFR aircraft until such time as the aircraft is sequenced and the pilot sees the traffic he is to follow. Standard radar separation between VFR or between VFR and IFR aircraft will not be provided.

(5) Pilots of departing VFR aircraft are encouraged to request radar traffic information by notifying ground control on initial contact with their request and proposed direction of flight.

Example:

"XRAY GROUND CONTROL, N18 AT HANGAR 6, READY TO TAXI, VFR SOUTHBOUND, HAVE INFORMATION BRAVO AND REQUEST RADAR TRAFFIC INFORMATION."

Following takeoff, the tower will advise when to contact departure control.

(6) Pilots of aircraft transiting the area and in radar contact/communication with approach control will receive traffic information on a controller workload permitting basis. Pilots of such aircraft should give their position, altitude, radar beacon code (if transponder equipped), destination, and/or route of flight.

c. Stage III Service (Radar Sequencing and Separation Service for VFR Aircraft).

(1) This service has been implemented at certain terminal locations. The service is advertised in the Airport/Facility Directory and the publication Graphic Notices and Supplemental Data. The purpose of this service is to provide separation between all participating VFR aircraft and all IFR aircraft operating within the airspace defined as the Terminal Radar Service Area (TRSA). Pilot participation is urged but it is not mandatory.

(2) If any aircraft does not want the service, the pilot should state NEGATIVE STAGE III, or make a similar comment, on initial contact with approach control or ground control, as appropriate.

(3) TRSA charts and a further description of the Services Provided, Flight Procedures, and ATC Procedures are contained in the publication Graphic Notices and Supplemental Data.

(4) While operating within a TRSA, pilots are provided Stage III service and separation as prescribed in this chapter. In the event of a radar outage, separation and sequencing of VFR aircraft will be suspended as this service is dependent on radar. The pilot will be advised that the service is not available and issued wind, runway information, and the time or place to contact the tower. Traffic information will be provided on a workload permitting basis.

(5) Visual separation is used when prevailing conditions permit and it will be applied as follows:

(a) When a VFR flight is positioned behind the preceding aircraft and the pilot reports having that aircraft in sight, he will be directed to follow it. Upon being told to contact the tower, radar service is automatically terminated.

(b) When IFR flights are being sequenced with other traffic and the pilot reports the aircraft he is to follow in sight, the pilot may be directed to follow it and will be cleared for a "visual approach."

(c) If other "non-participating" or "local" aircraft are in the traffic pattern, the tower will issue a landing sequence.

(d) Departing VFR aircraft may be asked if they can visually follow a preceding departure out of the TRSA. If the pilot concurs, he will be directed to follow it until leaving the TRSA.

(6) Until visual separation is obtained, standard vertical or radar separation will be provided.

(a) 1000 feet vertical separation may be used between IFR aircraft.

(b) 500 feet vertical separation may be used between VFR aircraft, or between a VFR and an IFR aircraft.

(c) Radar separation varies depending on size of aircraft and aircraft distance from the radar antenna. The minimum separation used will be 1½ miles for most VFR aircraft under 12,500 pounds GWT. If being separated from larger aircraft, the minimum is increased appropriately.

(7) Pilots operating VFR under Stage III in a TRSA—

(a) Must maintain an altitude when assigned by ATC unless the altitude assignment is to maintain at or below a specified altitude. ATC may assign altitudes for separation that do not conform to FAR 91.109. When the altitude assignment is no longer needed for separation or when leaving the TRSA, the instruction will be broadcast, "Resume Appropriate VFR Altitudes." Pilots must then return to an altitude that conforms to FAR 91.109 as soon as practicable.

(b) When not assigned an altitude should coordinate with ATC prior to any altitude change.

(8) Within the TRSA, traffic information on observed but unidentified targets will, to the extent possible, be provided all IFR and participating VFR aircraft. At the request of the pilot, he will be vectored to avoid the observed traffic, insofar as possible, provided the aircraft to be vectored is within the airspace under the jurisdiction of the controller.

(9) Departing aircraft should inform ATC of their intended destinaton and/or route of flight and proposed cruising altitude.

d. PILOTS RESPONSIBILITY: THESE PROGRAMS ARE NOT TO BE INTERPRETED AS RELIEVING PILOTS OF THEIR RESPONSIBILITIES TO SEE AND AVOID OTHER TRAFFIC OPERATING IN BASIC VFR WEATHER CONDITIONS, TO MAINTAIN APPROPRIATE TERRAIN AND OBSTRUCTION CLEARANCE, OR TO REMAIN IN WEATHER CONDITIONS EQUAL TO OR BETTER THAN THE MINIMA REQUIRED BY FAR 91.105. WHENEVER COMPLIANCE WITH AN ASSIGNED ROUTE, HEADING AND/OR ALTITUDE IS LIKELY TO COMPROMISE SAID PILOT RESPONSIBILITY RESPECTING TERRAIN AND OBSTRUCTION CLEARANCE AND WEATHER MINIMA, APPROACH CONTROL SHOULD BE SO ADVISED AND A REVISED CLEARANCE OR INSTRUCTION OBTAINED.

166. TERMINAL CONTROL AREA OPERATION

a. Operating Rules and Equipment Requirements. Regardless of weather conditions, ATC authorization is required prior to operating within a TCA. Pilots should not request such authorization unless the requirements of FAR 91.24 and 91.90 are met. Included among these requirements are:

(1) Group I TCAs

(a) A two-way radio capable of communicating with ATC on appropriate frequencies.

(b) A VOR or TACAN receiver, except for helicopters.

(c) A 4096 code transponder with Mode C automatic altitude reporting equipment, except for helicopters operating at or below 1,000 feet AGL under a Letter of Agreement. (ATC may authorize a deviation from the altitude reporting equipment requirement immediately; however, request for a deviation from the 4096 transponder equipment requirement must be submitted to the controlling ATC facility at least 4 hours before the proposed operation.)

(d) A private pilot certificate or better in order to land or takeoff from an airport within the TCA.

(e) Unless otherwise authorized by ATC, each person operating a large turbine engine powered airplane to or from a primary airport shall operate at or above the designated floors while within the lateral limits of the terminal control area.

(f) No person may operate an aircraft in the airspace underlying a terminal control area, at an indicated airspeed of more than 200 knots (230 m.p.h.) (FAR 91.70).

(2) Group II TCAs

(a) A two-way radio capable of communicating with ATC on appropriate frequencies.

(b) A VOR or TACAN receiver, except for helicopters.

(c) A 4096 code transponder, except for helicopters operating at or below 1,000 feet under a letter of agreement, or for IFR flights operating to or from an airport outside of but in close proximity to the TCA when the commonly used transition, approach, or departure procedures to such airport require flight within the TCA. (ATC may authorize deviations from the transponder requirements. Requests for deviation should be submitted to the controlling ATC facility at least four hours before the proposed operation.)

(d) Unless otherwise authorized by ATC, large turbine-powered aircraft must operate at or above the floor of the TCA while operating to or from the primary airport.

(e) No person may operate an aircraft in the airspace underlying a Terminal Control Area, at an indicated airspeed of more than 200 knots (230 m.p.h.) (FAR 91.70).

b. Flight Procedures

(1) *IFR Flights.* Aircraft operating within the TCA shall be operated in accordance with current IFR procedures. A clearance for a visual approach is not authorization for an aircraft to operate below the designated floors of the TCA.

(2) *VFR Flights.*

(a) Arriving VFR flights should contact ATC on the appropriate frequency and in relation to geographical fixes shown on local charts. Although a pilot may be operating beneath the floor of the TCA on initial contact, communications with ATC should be established in relation to the points indicated for spacing and sequencing purposes.

(b) Departing VFR aircraft should advise the ground controller of the intended altitude and route of flight to depart the TCA.

(c) Aircraft not landing/departing the primary airport may obtain ATC clearance to transit the TCA when traffic conditions permit and provided the requirements of FAR 91.90 are met. Such VFR transiting aircraft are encouraged, to the extent possible, to transit through VFR corridors or above or below the TCA.

(d) VFR non-TCA aircraft are cautioned from operating too close to TCA boundaries, especially where the floor of TCA is 3,000 feet or less or where normal VFR cruise altitudes coincide with the floor at higher levels. Pilot observance of this precaution will reduce the potential for a civil jet operating at TCA floor altitudes from encountering uncontrolled traffic and vice versa.

c. **ATC Clearances and Separation.** While operating within a TCA, pilots are provided the service and separation as in the Stage III, Terminal Radar Programs For VFR Aircraft in this chapter. In the event of a radar outage, separation and sequencing of VFR aircraft will be suspended as this service is dependent on radar. The pilot will be advised that the service is not available and issued wind, runway information and the time or place to contact the tower. Traffic information will be provided on a workload permitting basis.

(1) Assignment of radar headings and/or altitudes are based on the provision that a pilot operating in accordance with visual flight rules is expected to advise ATC if compliance with an assigned route, radar heading or altitude will cause the pilot to violate such rules.

(2) ATC may assign altitudes to VFR aircraft that do not conform to FAR 91.109. When the altitude assignment is no longer needed for separation or when leaving the TCA, the instruction will be broadcast, "Resume Appropriate VFR Altitudes." Pilots must return to an altitude that conforms to FAR 91.109 as soon as practicable.

167–169. RESERVED

170. RADAR SERVICE FOR VFR AIRCRAFT IN DIFFICULTY

a. Radar equipped FAA Air Traffic Control facilities provide radar assistance and navigation service (vectors) to VFR aircraft in difficulty provided the aircraft can communicate with the facility, are within radar coverage, and can be radar identified. Pilots should clearly understand that authorization to proceed in accordance with such radar navigational assistance does not constitute authorization for the pilot to violate Federal Aviation Regulations. In effect, assistance provided is on the basis that navigational guidance information issued is advisory in nature and the job of flying the aircraft safely, remains with the pilot.

b. Experience has shown that many pilots who are not qualified for instrument flight cannot maintain control of their aircraft when clouds or other reduced visibility conditions are encountered. In many cases, the controller will be unable to determine if flight into instrument conditions will result from his instructions. To avoid possible hazards resulting from being vectored into IFR conditions, a pilot in difficulty should keep the controller advised of the weather conditions in which he is operating and along the course ahead; and should observe the following:

(1) If an alternative course of action is available which will permit flight in VFR weather conditions, noninstrument rated pilots should choose the alternative

rather than requesting a vector or approach into IFR weather conditions; or,

(2) If no alternative course of action is available, the noninstrument rated pilot should so advise the controller and 'declare an emergency.'

(3) If the pilot is instrument rated and the aircraft is instrument equipped, the pilot should so indicate by filing an IFR flight plan. Assistance will be provided on the basis that the flight can operate safely in IFR weather conditions.

c. Some 'DO's' and 'DONT's :'

(1) DO let ATC know of your difficulty immediately. DON'T wait until the situation becomes an emergency.

(2) DO give as much information as possible on initial contact with ATC-nature of difficulty, position (in relation to a navaid if possible), altitude, radar beacon code (if transponder equipped), weather conditions, if instrument rated or not, destination, service requested.

(3) DON'T chage radio frequency without informing the controller.

(4) DO adhere to ATC instructions or information or if not possible, DO advise ATC immediately that you cannot comply.

171. TRANSPONDER OPERATION

a. **GENERAL**

(1) Air Traffic Control Radar Beacon System (ATC-RBS) is similar to and compatible with military coded radar beacon equipment. Civil Mode A is identical to military Mode 3.

(2) Civil and military transponders should be adjusted to the "on" or normal operating position as late as practicable prior to takeoff and to "off" or "standby" as soon as practicable after completing landing roll unless the change to "standby" has been accomplished previously at the request of ATC. IN ALL CASES, WHETHER VFR OR IFR, THE TRANSPONDER SHOULD BE OPERATING WHILE AIRBORNE UNLESS OTHERWISE REQUESTED BY ATC.

(3) If entering a U.S. domestic control area from outside the U.S., the pilot should advise on first radio contact with a U.S. radar air traffic control facility that such equipment is available by adding "transponder" to the aircraft identification.

(4) It should be noted by all users of the ATC Transponders that the coverage they can expect is limited to "line of sight." Low altitude or aircraft antenna shielding by the aircraft itself may result in reduced range. Range can be improved by climbing to a higher altitude. It may be possible to minimize antenna shielding by locating the antenna where dead spots are only noticed during abnormal flight attitudes.

(5) For ATC to utilize one or a combination of the 4096 discrete codes FOUR DIGIT CODE DESIGNATION will be used, e.g., code 2100 will be expressed as TWO ONE ZERO ZERO.

(6) Pilots should be particularly sure to abide by the provisions of subparagraph b above. Additionally, due to the operational characteristics of the rapidly expanding automated air traffic control system, THE LAST TWO DIGITS OF THE SELECTED TRANSPONDER CODE SHOULD ALWAYS READ '00' UNLESS SPECIFICALLY REQUESTED BY ATC TO BE OTHERWISE.

(7) Some transponders are equipped with a Mode C automatic altitude reporting capability. This system converts aircraft altitude in 100 foot increments, to coded digital information which is transmitted together with MODE C framing pulses to the interrogating radar facility. The manner in which transponder panels are designed differs, therefore, a pilot should be thoroughly familiar with the operation of his transponder so that ATC may realize its full capabilities.

(8) Adjust transponder to reply on the Mode A/3 code specified by ATC and, if equipped, to reply on Mode C with altitude reporting *capability activated* unless deactivation is directed by ATC or unless the installed aircraft equipment has not been tested and calibrated as required by FAR 91.36. If deactivation is required by ATC, turn off the altitude reporting feature of your transponder. An instruction by ATC to "STOP ALTITUDE SQUAWK, ALTITUDE DIFFERS (number of feet) FEET," may be an indication that your transponder is transmitting incorrect altitude information or that you have an incorrect altimeter setting. While an incorrect altimeter setting has no effect on the Mode C altitude information transmitted by your transponder (transponders are preset at 29.92), it would cause you to fly at an actual altitude different from your assigned altitude. When a controller indicates that an altitude readout is invalid, the pilot should initiate a check to verify that the aircraft altimeter is set correctly.

(9) Pilots of aircraft with operating Mode C altitude reporting transponders should report exact altitude/flight level to the nearest hundred foot increment when establishing initial contact with an air traffic control facility. Exact altitude/flight level reports on initial contact provide air traffic control with information that is required prior to using Mode C altitude information for separation purposes. This will significantly reduce altitude verification requests.

(10) The transponder shall be operated only as specified by ATC. Activate the "IDENT" feature only upon request of the ATC controller.

(11) Under no circumstances should a pilot of a civil aircraft operate the transponder on Code 0000. This code is reserved for military interceptor operations.

(12) Military pilots operating VFR or IFR within restricted/warning areas should adjust their transponders to code 4000 unless another code has been assigned by ATC.

(13) When making routine code changes, pilots should avoid inadvertent selection of codes 7500, 7600 or 7700 thereby causing momentary false alarms at automated ground facilities. For example when switching from code 2700 to code 7200, switch first to 2200 then 7200, NOT to 7700 and then 7200. This procedure applies to nondiscrete code 7500 and all discrete codes in the 7600 and 7700 series (i.e., 7600–7677, 7700–7777) which will trigger special indicators in automated facilities. Only nondiscrete code 7500 will be decoded as the hijack code.

(14) Specific details concerning requirements, exceptions and ATC authorized deviations for transponder and Mode C operation above 12,500' and below 18,000' MSL are found in FAR 91.24. In general, the FAR requires aircraft to be equipped with Mode A/3 (4096 codes) and Mode C altitude reporting capability when operating in controlled airspace of the 48 contiguous States and the District of Columbia above 12,500 MSL, excluding airspace at and below 2500' AGL. Pilots should insure that their aircraft transponder is operating on an appropriate or ATC assigned VFR/IFR code and Mode C when operating in such airspace. If in doubt about the operational status of either feature of your transponder while airborne, contact the nearest ATC facility or Flight Service Station and they will advise you what facility you should contact for determining the status of your equipment. In-fight requests for "immediate" deviation may be approved by controllers only when the flight will continue IFR or when weather conditions prevent VFR descent and continued VFR flight in airspace not affected by the FAR. All other requests for deviation should be made by contacting the nearest Flight Service/Air Traffic facility in person or by telephone. The nearest ARTC Center will normally be the controlling agency and is responsible for coordinating requests involving deviations in other ARTCC areas.

(15) Pilots should be aware that proper application of these procedures will provide both VFR and IFR aircraft with a higher degree of safety in the environment where high-speed closure rates are possible. Transponders substantially increase the capability of radar to see an aircraft and the Mode C feature enables the controller to quickly determine where potential traffic conflicts may exist. Even VFR pilots who are not in contact with ATC will be afforded greater protection from IFR aircraft and VFR aircraft which are receiving traffic advisories. Nevertheless, pilots should never relax their visual scanning vigilance for other aircraft.

b. INSTRUMENT FLIGHT RULES (IFR) FLIGHT PLAN

(1) If the pilot cancels his IFR flight plan prior to reaching the terminal area of destination, the transponder should be adjusted according to the instructions below for VFR flight.

(2) The transponder shall be operated only as specified by ATC. Activate the "IDENT" feature only upon request of the ATC controller.

c. VISUAL FLIGHT RULES (VFR)

(1) Unless otherwise instructed by an Air Traffic Control Facility, adjust Transponder to reply on Mode 3/A code 1200 regardless of altitude.

(2) Adjust transponder to reply on Mode C, with altitude reporting *capability activated* if the aircraft is so equipped, unless deactivation is directed by ATC or unless the installed equipment has not been tested and calibrated as required by FAR 91.36. If deactivation is required and your transponder is so designed, turn off the altitude reporting switch and continue to transmit MODE C framing pulses. If this capability does not exist, turn off MODE C.

d. EMERGENCY OPERATION

(1) When an emergency occurs, the pilot of an aircraft equipped with a coded radar beacon transponder, who desires to alert a ground radar facility to an emergency condition and who cannot establish communications without delay with an air traffic control facility may adjust the transponder to reply on Mode A/3, Code 7700.

(2) Pilots should understand that they may not be within a radar coverage area and that, even if they are certain radar facilities are not yet equipped to auto-

matically recognize Code 7700 as an emergency signal. Therefore, they should establish radio communications with an air traffic control facility as soon as possible.

e. RADIO FAILURE

(1) Should the pilot of an aircraft equipped with a coded radar beacon transponder experience a loss of two-way radio capability the pilot should:

(a) Adjust his transponder to reply on Mode A/3, code 7700 for a period of 1 minute,

(b) then change to code 7600 and remain on 7600 for a period of 15 minutes or the remainder of the flight, whichever occurs first.

(c) repeat steps, as practicable.

(2) Pilots should understand that they may not be in an area of radar coverage. Also many radar facilities are not presently equipped to automatically display code 7600 and will interrogate 7600 only when the aircraft is under direct radar control at the time of radio failure. However, replying on code 7700 first increases the probability of early detection of a radio failure condition.

f. RADAR BEACON PHRASEOLOGY

Air traffic controllers, both civil and military, will use the following phraseology when referring to operation of the Air Traffic Control Radar Beacon System (ATCRBS) Instructions by air traffic control refer only to Mode A/3 or Mode C operation and do not affect the operation of the transponder on other Modes.

(1) SQUAWK (number)—Operate radar beacon transponder on designated code in Mode A/3.

(2) IDENT—Engage the "IDENT" feature (military I/P of the transponder.

(3) SQUAWK (number) and IDENT—Operate transponder on specified code in Mode A/3 and engage the "IDENT" (military I/P) feature.

(4) SQUAWK STANDBY—Switch transponder to standby position.

(5) SQUAWK LOW/NORMAL—Operate transponder on low or normal sensitivity as specified. Transponder is operated in "NORMAL" position unless ATC specified "LOW" ("ON is used instead of "NORMAL" as a master control label on some types of transponders.)

(6) SQUAWK ALTITUDE—Activate MODE C with automatic altitude reporting.

(7) STOP ALTITUDE SQUAWK—Turn off altitude reporting switch and continue transmitting MODE C framing pulses. If your equipment does not have this capability, turn off MODE C.

(8) STOP SQUAWK (mode in use)—Switch off specified mode. (Use for military aircraft when the controller is unaware if a military service requires the aircraft to continue operating on another MODE.)

(9) STOP SQUAWK—Switch off transponder.

(10) SQUAWK MAYDAY—Operate transponder in the emergency position. (Mode A Code 7700 for civil transponder. Mode 3 Code 7700 and emergency feature for military transponder.)

172. HAZARDOUS AREA REPORTING SERVICE

a. Selected Flight Service Stations provide flight monitoring where regularly traveled VFR routes cross large bodies of water, swamps, and mountains, for the purpose of expeditiously alerting Search and Rescue facilities when required.

(1) When requesting the service either in person, by telephone or by radio, pilots should ask for the service desired and be prepared to give the following information—type of aircraft, altitude, indicated airspeed, present position, route of flight, heading.

(2) Radio contacts are desired at least every 10 minutes. If an aircraft does not report within 15 minutes after an estimated checkpoint, Search and Rescue will be alerted. Pilots are responsible for cancelling their request for service when they are outside the service area boundary. Pilots experiencing two-way radio failure are expected to land as soon as practicable and cancel their request for the service. The following illustration includes the areas and the FSS facilities involved in this program.

b. LONG ISLAND SOUND REPORTING SERVICE (LIRS)—The New York and Windsor Locks FSSs provide Long Island Sound Reporting service on request for aircraft traversing Long Island Sound.

(1) When requesting the service pilots should ask for SOUND REPORTING SERVICE and should be prepared to provide the following appropriate information: (1) Type and color of aircraft, (2) The specific route and altitude across the sound including the shore crossing point, (3) The overwater crossing time, (4) Number of persons on board, (5) True air speed.

(2) Radio contacts are desired at least every 10 minutes, however, for flights of shorter duration a mid-sound report is requested. If the aircraft does not report within 15 minutes after an estimated checkpoint, "Search and Rescue" will be alerted in accordance with the National Search and Rescue Plan. Pilots are responsible for cancelling their request for the Long Island Sound Reporting Service when outside the service area boundary. Aircraft experiencing radio failure will be expected to land as soon as practicable and cancel their request for the service.

(3) COMMUNICATIONS: Primary communications—pilot trans 122.1 MHz and listen on VOR freq.

(a) NEW YORK FSS CONTROLS:

Hampton VORTAC _____T113.6/R122.1 MHz
Riverhead VORTAC _____T117.2 MHz
Kennedy VORTAC _____T115.9/R122.1 MHz

(b) WINDSOR LOCKS FSS CONTROLS:

Madison VORTAC _____T110.4/R122.1 MHz
Trumbull VOR _____T111.8/R122.1 MHz
Bridgeport VOR _____T108.8/R122.1 MHz

c. BLOCK ISLAND REPORTING SERVICE (BIRS)—Within the Long Island Reporting Service, the New York FSS/IFSS also provides an additional service for aircraft operating between Montauk Point and Block Island. When requesting this service, pilots should ask for BLOCK ISLAND REPORTING SERVICE and should be prepared to provide the same flight information as that required for the Long Island Sound Reporting Service.

(1) A minimum of three position reports are mandatory for this service; these are:

(a) Report leaving Montauk Point or Block Island.

(b) Midway report.

(c) Report when over Montauk Point or Block Island at which time the pilot cancels the overwater service.

(2) COMMUNICATIONS: Pilot transmits on 122.1 MHz and listens to the Hampton VORTAC (HTO) frequency 113.6 MHz.

(3) Pilots are advised that 122.1 MHz is a remote receiver located at the Hampton VORTAC site and designed to provide radio coverage between Hampton and Block Island. Flights proceeding beyond Block Island may contact the Boston FSS on 122.7 MHz (transmit and receive) or by transmitting on 122.1 MHz and listening to Martha's Vineyard VORTAC (MVY) frequency 108.2 MHz.

d. CAPE COD AND ISLANDS RADAR OVERWATER FLIGHT FOLLOWING—In addition to normal VFR radar advisory services, traffic permitting, Otis Approach Control provides a radar overwater flight following service for aircraft traversing the Cape Cod and adjacent Island area. Pilots desiring this service may contact Otis RAPCON on 118.2 MHz.

(1) Pilots requesting this service should be prepared to give the following information: (1) type and color of aircraft, (2) altitude, (3) position and heading, (4) route of flight, and (5) true airspeed.

(2) For best radar coverage, pilots are encouraged to fly at 1500' MSL or above.

(3) Pilots are responsible for cancelling their request for overwater flight following when they are over the mainland and/or outside the service area boundary.

173–189. RESERVED

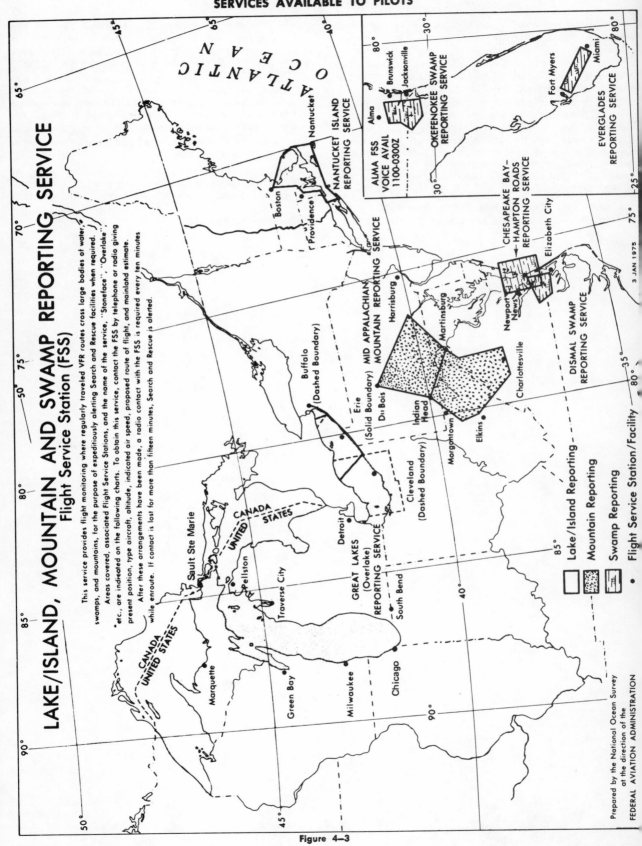

LAKE/ISLAND, MOUNTAIN AND SWAMP REPORTING SERVICE
Flight Service Station (FSS)

This service provides flight monitoring where regularly traveled VFR routes cross large bodies of water, swamps, and mountains, for the purpose of expeditiously alerting Search and Rescue facilities when required. Areas covered, associated Flight Service Stations, and the name of the service, "Stoneface", "Overlake", "etc., are indicated on the following charts. To obtain this service, contact the FSS by telephone or radio giving present position, type aircraft, altitude, indicated air speed, proposed route of flight, and mainland estimate.

After these arrangements have been made, a radio contact with the FSS is required every ten minutes while enroute. If contact is lost for more than fifteen minutes, Search and Rescue is alerted.

Lake/Island Reporting

Mountain Reporting

Swamp Reporting

● Flight Service Station/Facility

Prepared by the National Ocean Survey
at the direction of the
FEDERAL AVIATION ADMINISTRATION

3 JAN 1975

Figure 4–3

52

Section 2. RADIO COMMUNICATIONS PHRASEOLOGY AND TECHNIQUES

190. GENERAL

a. Radio communications are a critical link in the ATC system. The link can be a strong bond between pilot and controller—or it can be broken with surprising speed and disastrous results. Discussion herein provides basic procedures for new pilots and also highlights safe operating concepts for all pilots.

b. The single, most important thought in pilot-controller communications is understanding. Brevity is important, and contacts should be kept as brief, as possible, but the controller must know what you want to do before he can properly carry out his control duties. And you, the pilot, must know exactly what he wants you to do. Since concise phraseology may not always be adequate, use whatever words are necessary to get your message across.

c. All pilots will find the Pilot/Controller Glossary very helpful in learning what certain words or phrases mean. Good phraseology enhances safety and is the mark of a professional pilot. Jargon, chatter and "CB" slang have no place in ATC communications. The Pilot/Controller Glossary is the same glossary used in the ATC controller's handbook. We recommend that it be studied and reviewed from time to time to sharpen your communication skills.

191. RADIO TECHNIQUE

a. *Listen* before you transmit. Many times you can get the information you want through ATIS or by monitoring the frequency. Except for a few situations where some frequency overlap occurs, if you hear someone else talking, the keying of your transmitter will be futile and you will probably jam their receivers causing them to repeat their call. If you have just changed frequencies, pause for your receiver to tune, listen and make sure the frequency is clear.

b. *Think before* keying your transmitter. Know what you want to say and if it is lengthy, e.g., a flight plan or IFR position report, jot it down. (But do not lock your head in the cockpit).

c. The microphone should be very close to your lips and after pressing the mike button, a slight pause may be necessary to be sure the first word is transmitted. Speak in a normal conversational tone.

d. When you release the button, wait a few seconds before calling again. The controller or FSS specialist may be jotting down your number, looking for your flight plan, transmitting on a different frequency, or selecting his transmitter to your frequency.

e. Be alert to the sounds *or lack of sounds* in your receiver. Check your volume, recheck your frequency and *make sure that your microphone is not stuck* in the transmit position. Frequency blockage can, and has, occurred for extended periods of time due to unintentional transmitter operation. This type of interference is commonly referred to as a "stuck mike," and controllers may refer to it in this manner when attempting to assign an alternate frequency. If the assigned frequency is completely blocked by this type of interference, use the procedures described in Chapter 3, En Route IFR, Radio Frequency Outage, to establish/reestablish communications with ATC.

f. Be sure that you are within the performance range of your radio equipment and the ground station equipment. Remote radio sites do not always transmit and receive on all of a facilities available frequencies, particularly with regard to VOR sites where you can hear but not reach a ground station's receiver. Remember that higher altitude increases the range of VHF "line of sight" communications.

g. Except for emergencies, avoid calling FSS stations at 15 minutes past the hour because you may interfere with scheduled weather broadcasts.

192. CONTACT PROCEDURES

a. *Initial Contact.*

(1) The term "initial contact" or "initial callup" means the first radio call you make to a given facility, or the first call to a different controller/FSS specialist within a facility. *Use are following format:* (a) name of facility being called, (b) your *full* aircraft identification as filed in the flight plan or as discussed under Aircraft Call Signs below, (c) type of message to follow or your request if it is short, and (d) the word "Over."

Examples:

"NEW YORK RADIO, MOONEY THREE ONE ONE ECHO, OVER." "COLUMBIA GROUND CONTROL, CESSNA THREE ONE SIX ZERO FOXTROT, IFR MEMPHIS, OVER."

(2) If radio reception is reasonably assured, inclusion of your request, your position or altiutde, the phrase "Have numbers" or "Information Charlie received" (for ATIS) in the initial contact helps decrease radio frequency congestion. Use discretion and do not overload the controller with information he does not need. When you do not get a response from the ground station, recheck your radios or use another transmitter and keep the next contact short.

b. *Initial contact when your transmitting and receiving frequencies are different.*

(1) If you are attempting to establish contact with a ground station and you are receiving on a different frequency than that transmitted, indicate the VOR name or the frequency on which you expect a reply. Most FSSs and control facilities can transmit on several VOR stations in the area. Use the appropriate FSS call sign as indicated on charts.

Example:

New York FSS transmits on the Kennedy, Hampton and Riverhead VORTACs. If you are in the Riverhead area, your callup should be "New York Radio, Cessna Three One Six Zero Foxtrot, Receiving Riverhead VOR, Over."

(2) If the chart indicates FSS frequencies above the VORTAC or in FSS communications boxes, transmit or receive on those frequencies nearest your location.

(3) When unable to establish contact and you wish to call *any* ground station, use the phrase "any radio (tower) (station), give Cessna Three One Six Zero Foxtrot a call on (frequency) or (VOR)." If an emergency exists or you need assistance, so state.

c. *Subsequent Contacts and Responses to Callup from a Ground Facility.* Use the same format as used for initial contact except you should state your message or request with the callup in one transmission. The ground station name and the word "Over" may be omitted if the message requires an obvious reply and there is no possibility for misunderstandings. *You should acknowledge all callups or clearances* unless the controller or FSS specialist advises otherwise. There are some occasions when the controller must issue time-critical instructions to other aircraft and he may be in a position to observe your response, either visually or on radar. If the situation demands your response, take appropriate action or immediately advise the facility of any problem. Acknowledgement is made with one of the words "Wilco, Roger, Affirmative, Negative" or other appropriate remarks; e.g., "Piper Two One Four Lima, Roger." If you have been receiving services, e.g., VFR traffic advisories and you are leaving the area or changing frequencies, advise the ATC facility and terminate contact.

d. *Acknowledgement of Frequency Changes.* When advised by ATC to change frequencies, acknowledge the instruction. If you select the new frequency without an acknowledgement, the controller's workload is increased because he has no way of knowing whether you received the instruction or lost your radios.

193. AIRCRAFT CALL SIGNS

a. *Precautions in the Use of Call Signs.* Improper use of call signs can result in pilots executing a clearance intended for another aircraft. Call signs should *never be abbreviated on an initial contact or at any time when other aircraft call signs have similar numbers/ sounds or identical letters/numbers,* (e.g., Cessna 6132F, Cessna 1622F, Baron 123F, Cherokee 7732F, etc.). As an example, assume that a controller issues an approach clearance to an aircraft at the bottom of a holding stack and an aircraft with a similar call sign (at the top of the stack) acknowledges the clearance with the last two or three numbers of his call sign. If the aircraft at the bottom of the stack did not hear the clearance and intervene, flight safety would be affected, and there would be no reason for either the controller or pilot to suspect that anything is wrong. This kind of "human factors" error can strike swiftly and is extremely difficult to rectify. *Pilot's therefore, must be certain that aircraft identification is complete and clearly identified before taking action on an ATC clearance.* FAA personnel will not abbreviate call signs of air carrier or other civil aircraft having authorized call signs. *FAA may initiate abbreviated call signs of other aircraft by using the prefix and the last three digits/letters of the aircraft identification after communications are established.* Controllers, when aware of similar/identical call signs, will take action to minimize errors by emphasizing certain numbers/letters, by repeating the entire call sign, repeating the prefix, or by asking pilots to use a different call sign temporarily. Pilots should use the phrase "Verify clearance for (your complete call sign)" if doubt exists concerning proper identity.

b. Civil aircraft pilots should state the aircraft type, model or manufacturer's name followed by the digits/ letters of the registration number. When the aircraft manufacturer's name or model is stated, the prefix "N" is dropped.

"BONANZA SIX FIVE FIVE GOLF," "DOUGLAS ONE ONE ZERO," "BREEZY SIX ONE THREE ROMEO EXPERIMENTAL" (Omit "Experimental" after initial contact).

c. Air Taxi or other commercial operators *not* having FAA authorized call signs should prefix their normal identification with the phonetic word "Tango." (e.g., Tango Aztec Two Four Six Four Alpha.)

d. Air carriers and commuter air carriers having FAA authorized call signs should identify themselves by stating the complete call sign, using group form for the numbers and the word 'heavy" if appropriate.

Examples:

UNITED TWENTY-FIVE HEAVY, MIDWEST COMMUTER SEVEN ELEVEN.

e. Military aircraft use a variety of systems including serial numbers, word call signs and combinations of letters/numbers. Examples include Army Copter 48931, Air Force 61782, MAC 31792, Pat 157, Air Evac 17652, Navy Golf Alfa Kilo 21, Marine 4 Charlie 36, etc.

f. Civilian air ambulance flights responding to medical emergencies (carrying patients, organ donors, organs, or other urgently needed lifesaving medical material) will be expedited by ATC when necessary. When expeditious handling is required, add the word "lifeguard" in the remarks of the flight plan. In radio communication use the call sign "lifeguard" followed by the aircraft type and registration letters/numbers. When requested by the pilot, necessary notification to expedite ground handling of patients, etc., is provided by ATC; however, when possible, this information should be passed in advance through non-ATC communications systems. Extreme discretion is necessary in using the term "lifeguard." It is intended only for those missions of an urgent medical nature and for use only for that portion of the flight requiring expedited handling. Similar provisions have been made for the use of "Air Evac" and "Med Evac" by military air ambulance flights, except that these military flights will receive priority handling only when specifically requested.

Example:

LIFEGUARD CESSNA TWO SIX FOUR SIX.

g. *Student Pilots Radio Identification.* The FAA desires to help the student pilot in acquiring sufficient practical experience in the environment in which he will be required to operate. To receive additional assistance while operating in areas of concentrated air traffic, a student pilot need only identify himself as a student pilot during his initial call to an FAA radio facility. For instance, "Dayton Tower, this is Fleetwing 1234, Student Pilot, over." This special identification will alert FAA air traffic control personnel and enable them to provide the student pilot with such extra assistance and consideration as he may need. This procedure is not mandatory.

194. GROUND STATION CALL SIGNS

Pilots, when calling a ground station, should begin with the name of the facility being called followed by the type of the facility being called, as indicated in the following examples.

Examples are self-explanatory:

Airport Unicom _____	"Shannon Unicom"
FAA Flight Service Station _____	"Shannon Radio"
FAA Flight Service Station (En Route Flight Adivsory Service (Weather) _____	"Seattle Flight Watch"
Airport Traffic Control Tower _____	"Augusta Tower"
Clearance Delivery Position (IFR) _____	"Dallas Clearance Delivery"
Ground Control Position in Tower _____	"Miami Ground"
Radar or Nonradar Approach Control Position _____	"Oklahoma City Approach"
Radar Departure Control Position _____	"St. Louis Departure"
FAA Air Route Traffic Control Center _____	"Washington Center"

195. PHONETIC ALPHABET

a. The International Civil Aviation Organization (ICAO) phonetic alphabet is used by FAA personnel when communications conditions are such that the information cannot be readily received without their use. Air traffic control facilities may also request pilots to use phonetic letter equivalents when aircraft with similar sounding identifications are receiving communications on the same frequency. Pilots should use the phonetic alphabet when identifying their aircraft during initial contact with air traffic control facilities. Additionally use the phonetic equivalents for single letters and to spell out groups of letters or difficult words during adverse communications conditions.

Letter	Morse	Word	Pronunciation
A	•■	Alfa	(AL-FAH)
B	■•••	Bravo	(BRAH-VOH)
C	■•■•	Charlie	(CHAR-LEE) or (SHAR LEE)
D	■••	Delta	(DELL-TAH)
E	•	Echo	(ECK-OH)
F	••■•	Foxtrot	(FOKS-TROT)
G	■■•	Golf	(GOLF)
H	••••	Hotel	(HOH-TEL)
I	••	India	(IN-DEE-AH)
J	•■■■	Juliett	(JEW-LEE-ETT)
K	■•■	Kilo	(KEY-LOH)
L	•■••	Lima	(LEE-MAH)
M	■■	Mike	(MIKE)
N	■•	November	(NO-VEM-BER)
O	■■■	Oscar	(OSS-CAH)
P	•■■•	Papa	(PAH-PAH)
Q	■■•■	Quebec	(KEH-BECK)
R	•■•	Romeo	(ROW-ME-OH)
S	•••	Sierra	(SEE-AIR-RAH)
T	■	Tango	(TANG-GO)
U	••■	Uniform	(YOU-NEE-FORM) or (OO-NEE-FORM)
V	•••■	Victor	(VIK-TAH)
W	•■■	Whiskey	(WISS-KEY)
X	■••■	Xray	(ECKS-RAY)
Y	■•■■	Yankee	(YANG-KEY)
Z	■■••	Zulu	(ZOO-LOO)

	Morse	Word	Pronunciation
1	•■■■■	One	(WUN)
2	••■■■	Two	(TOO)
3	•••■■	Three	(TREE)
4	••••■	Four	(FOW-ER)
5	•••••	Five	(FIFE)
6	■••••	Six	(SIX)
7	■■•••	Seven	(SEV-EN)
8	■■■•◠	Eight	(AIT)
9	■■■■•	Nine	(NINE-ER)
0	■■■■■	Zero	(ZEE-RO)

Figure 4—4—PHONETIC ALPHABET AND MORSE CODE

196–199. RESERVED

200. FIGURES

a. Figures indicating hundred and thousands in round number, as for ceiling heights, and upper wind levels up to 9900 shall be spoken in accordance with the following examples:

500	FIVE HUNDRED
4500	FOUR THOUSAND FIVE HUNDRED

b. Numbers above 9900 shall be spoken by separating the digits preceding the word "thousand." Examples:

10000	ONE ZERO THOUSAND
13500	ONE THREE THOUSAND FIVE HUNDRED

c. Transmit airway or jet route numbers as follows:

Examples:

V12	VICTOR TWELVE
J533	J FIVE THIRTY THREE

d. All other numbers shall be transmitted by pronouncing each digit.

Example:

10	ONE ZERO

e. When a radio frequency contains a decimal point, the decimal point is spoken as "POINT."

Examples:

122.1	ONE TWO TWO POINT ONE

(ICAO Procedures require the decimal point be spoken as "DECIMAL" and FAA will honor such usage by military aircraft and all other aircraft required to use ICAO Procedures.)

201. ALTITUDES AND FLIGHT LEVELS

a. Up to but not including 18,000' MSL—by stating the separate digits of the thousands, plus the hundreds, if appropriate.

Examples:

12,000	ONE TWO THOUSAND
12,500	ONE TWO THOUSAND FIVE HUNDRED

b. At and above 18,000' MSL (FL 180) by stating the words "flight level" followed by the separate digits of the flight level.

Example:

190	FLIGHT LEVEL ONE NINER ZERO

202. DIRECTIONS

The three digits of bearing, course, heading or wind direction should always be magnetic. The word "true" must be added when it applies.

Examples:

(magnetic course) 005	ZERO ZERO FIVE
(true course) 050	ZERO FIVE ZERO TRUE
(magnetic bearing) 360	THREE SIX ZERO
(magnetic heading) 100	ONE ZERO ZERO
(wind direction) 220	TWO TWO ZERO

203. SPEEDS

The separate digits of the speed followed by the word 'knots'. The controller may omit the word "knots" when using speed adjustment procedures, "Reduce/Increase Speed To One Five Zero."

Examples:

250	TWO FIVE ZERO KNOTS
185	ONE EIGHT FIVE KNOTS
95	NINER FIVE KNOTS

204. TIME

a. FAA uses Greenwich Mean Time (GMT) (or "Z") for all operations.

To Convert From:	To Greenwich Mean Time:
Eastern Standard Time	Add 5 hours*
Central Standard Time	Add 6 hours*
Mountain Standard Time	Add 7 hours*
Pacific Standard Time	Add 8 hours*

* For Daylight Time subtract 1 hour.

b. The 24-hour clock system is used in radiotelephone transmissions. The hour is indicated by the first two figures and the minutes by the last two figures.

Examples:

0000	ZERO ZERO ZERO ZERO
0920	ZERO NINER TWO ZERO

c. Time may be stated in minutes only (two figures) in radio telephone communications when no misunderstanding is likely to occur.

d. Current time in use at a station is stated in the nearest quarter minute in order that pilots may use this information for time checks. Fractions of a quarter minute less than eight seconds are stated as the preceding quarter minute; fractions of a quarter minute of eight seconds or more are stated as the succeeding quarter minute.

Examples:

Time

0929:05	TIME, ZERO NINER TWO NINER
0929:10	TIME, ZERO NINER TWO NINER AND ONE-QUARTER

205. COMMUNICATIONS WITH TOWER WHEN AIRCRAFT TRANSMITTER/RECEIVER OR BOTH ARE INOPERATIVE (See FAR 91.87 and 91.77)

a. Arriving Aircraft

(1) Receiver inoperative—If you have reason to believe your receiver is inoperative, remain outside or above the airport traffic area until the direction and flow of traffic has been determined, then advise the tower of your type aircraft, position, altitude, intention to land and request that you be controlled with light signals. (See paragraph 233) When you are approximately 3 to 5 miles from the airport, advise the tower of your position and join the airport traffic pattern. From this point on, watch the tower for light signals. Thereafter, if a complete pattern is made, transmit your position downwind and/or turning base leg.

(2) Transmitter inoperative—Remain outside or above the airport traffic area until the direction and flow of traffic has been determined, then join the airport traffic pattern. Monitor the primary local control frequency as depicted on Sectional Charts for landing or traffic information, and look for a light signal which may be addressed to your aircraft. During hours of daylight, acknowledge tower transmissions or light signals by rocking your wings. At night, acknowledge by blinking the landing or navigation lights.

(3) Transmitter and receiver inoperative—Remain outside or above the airport traffic area until the direction and flow of traffic has been determined, then join the airport traffic pattern and maintain visual contact with the tower to receive light signals. Acknowledge light signals as noted above.

b. Departing Aircraft

(1) If you experience radio failure prior to leaving the parking area, make every effort to have the equipment repaired. If you are unable to have the malfunction repaired, call the tower by telephone and request authorization to depart without two-way radio communications. If tower authorization is granted, you will be given departure information and requested to monitor the tower frequency or watch for light signals, as appropriate. During daylight hours, acknowledge tower transmissions or light signals by moving the ailerons or rudder. At night, acknowledge by blinking the landing or navigation lights. If radio malfunction occurs after departing the parking area, watch the tower for light signals or monitor tower frequency.

206. COMMUNICATIONS FOR VFR FLIGHTS

a. On VFR flights, guard the voice channel of VORs for broadcasts and calls from FAA Flight Service Stations (FSS). Where the VOR voice channel is being utilized for ATIS broadcasts, pilots of VFR flights are urged to guard the voice channel of an adjacent VOR. When in contact with a control facility, notify the controller if you plan to leave the frequency. This could save the controller time by not trying to call you on that frequency.

207–219. RESERVED

Section 3. AIRPORT OPERATIONS

220. GENERAL

a. Increased traffic congestion, aircraft in climb and descent altitudes, and pilots preoccupation with cockpit duties are some factors that increase the hazardous accident potential near the airport. The situation is further compounded when the weather is marginal—that is, just meeting VFR requirements. Pilots must be particularly alert when operating in the vicinity of an airport. This section defines some rules, practices and procedures that pilots should be familiar with, and adhere to, for safe airport operations.

221. TOWER—CONTROLLED AIRPORTS

a. When operating to an airport where traffic control is being exercised by a control tower, pilots are required to maintain two-way radio contact with the tower while operating within the airport traffic area unless the tower authorizes otherwise. Initial call-up should be made about 15 miles from the airport.

b. When necessary, the tower controller will issue clearances or other information for aircraft to generally follow the desired flight path (traffic patterns) when flying in the airport traffic area/control zone, and the proper taxi routes when operating on the ground. If not otherwise authorized or directed by the tower, pilots approaching to land in an airplane must circle the airport to the left, and pilots approaching to land in a helicopter must avoid the flow of fixed wing traffic. However, an appropriate clearance must be received from the tower before landing.

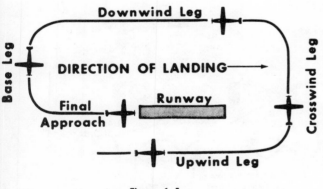

Figure 4—5

NOTE.—This diagram is intended only to illustrate terminology used in identifying various components of a traffic pattern. It should not be used as a reference or guide on how to enter a traffic pattern.

c. The following terminology for the various components of a traffic pattern has been adopted as standard for use by control towers and pilots:

(1) **Upwind leg**—A flight path parallel to the landing runway in the direction of landing.

(2) **Crosswind leg**—A flight path at right angles to the landing runway off its takeoff end.

(3) **Downwind leg**—A flight path parallel to the landing runway in the opposite direction of landing.

(4) **Base leg**—A flight path at right angles to the landing runway off its approach end and extending from the downwind leg to the intersection of the extended runway center line.

(5) **Final approach**—A flight path in the direction of landing along the extended runway center line from the base leg to the runway.

d. The tower controller will consider that pilots of turbine powered aircraft are ready for takeoff when they reach the runway/warm-up block unless they advise otherwise.

222. NON—TOWER AIRPORTS

a. Preparatory to landing at an airport without an operating control tower, *but at which either an FSS or a UNICOM* is located, pilots should contact the FSS or UNICOM for traffic advisories, wind, runway in use, and traffic flow information. CAUTION—ALL AIRCRAFT MAY NOT BE COMMUNICATING WITH THE FSS OR UNICOM. THEY CAN ONLY ISSUE TRAFFIC ADVISORIES ON THOSE THEY ARE AWARE OF. (See **155**—AIRPORT ADVISORY PRACTICES AT NONTOWER AIRPORTS.)

b. At those airports *not having a tower, FSS or UNICOM* (See **155**—ADVISORY PRACTICES AT NONTOWER AIRPORTS), visual indicators, if installed, provides the following information:

(1) The segmented circle system is designed to provide traffic pattern information at airports without operating control towers. The system consists of the following components:

(a) **The segmented circle**—Located in a position affording maximum visibility to pilots in the air and on the ground and providing a centralized location for other elements of the system.

(b) **The Wind Direction Indicator**—A wind cone, wind sock, or wind tee installed near the operational runway to indicate wind direction and velocity. The large end of the wind cone/wind sock points into the wind as does the large end (cross bar) of the wind tee. FAA directives require that the wind tee be free swinging and not tied down or locked to indicate landing direction. These signaling devices may be located in the center of the segmented circle and may be lighted for night use. Pilots are cautioned against using a tetrahedron to indicate wind direction and velocity.

(c) **The Landing Direction Indicator**—A tetrahedron is installed when conditions at the airport warrant its use. It may be used to indicate the direction of landings and takeoffs. A tetrahedron may be located at the center of a segmented circle and may be lighted for night operations. The small end of the tetrahedron points in the direction of landing. Pilots are cautioned against using a tetrahedron for any purpose other than as an indicator of landing direction, and to disregard the tetrahedron at an airport with an operating tower. Tower instructions supersede tetrahedron indications.

(d) Landing strip indicators—Installed in pairs as shown in the segmented circle diagram and used to shown the alignment of landing strips.

(e) Traffic pattern indicators—Arranged in pairs in conjunction with landing strip indicators and used to indicate the direction of turns when theer is a variation from the normal left traffic pattern. (If there is no segmented cricle installed at the airport, traffic pattern indicators may be installed on or near the end of the runway.)

(2) Where installed, a flashing amber light near the center of the segmented circle (or on top of the control tower or adjoining building) indicates that a right traffic pattern is in effect at the time.

c. Preparatory to landing at an airport without a control tower, or when the control tower is not in operation, the pilot should concern himself with the indicator for the approach end of the runway to be used. When approaching for landing, all turns must be made to the left unless a light signal or traffic pattern indicator indicates that turns should be made to the right. If the pilot will mentally enlarge the indicator for the runway to be used, the base and final approach legs of the traffic pattern to be flown immediately become apparent. Similar treatment of the indicator at the departure end of the runway will clearly indicate the direction of turn after takeoff.

d. When two or more aircraft are approaching an airport for the purpose of landing, the aircraft at the lower altitude has the right of way, but it shall not take advantage of this rule to cut in front of another which is on final approach to land, or to overtake that aircraft. (Ref: FAR 91.67(f))

223. TRAFFIC PATTERNS

a. At most airports and military air bases, traffic pattern altitudes for propeller driven aircraft generally extend from 600 feet to as high as 1500 feet above the ground. Also traffic pattern altitudes for military turbojet aircraft sometimes extend up to 2500 feet above the ground. Therefore, pilots of en route aircraft should be constantly on the alert for other aircraft in traffic patterns and avoid these areas whenever possible. Traffic pattern altitudes should be maintained unless otherwise required by the applicable distance from cloud criteria (FAR 91.105).

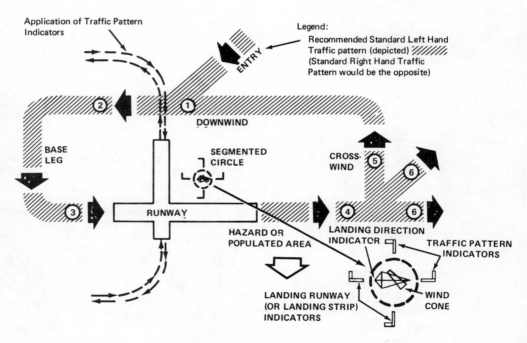

① Enter pattern in level flight, abeam the midpoint of the runway, at pattern altitude. (1000' AGL is recommended pattern altitude unless established otherwise.)

② Maintain pattern altitude until abeam approach end of the landing runway, on downwind leg.

③ Complete turn to final at least 1/4 mile from the runway.

④ Continue straight ahead until beyond departure end of runway.

⑤ If remaining in the traffic pattern, commence turn to crosswind leg beyond the departure end of the runway, within 300 feet of pattern altitude.

⑥ If departing the traffic pattern, continue straight out, or exit with a 45° left turn beyond the departure end of the runway, after reaching pattern altitude.

Figure 4–6—RECOMMENDED TRAFFIC PATTERNS AT NON-TOWER AIRPORTS

224. UNEXPECTED MANEUVERS IN THE AIRPORT TRAFFIC PATTERN

There have been several incidents in the vicinity of controlled airports that were caused primarily by aircraft executing unexpected maneuvers. Airport traffic control service is based upon observed or known traffic and airport conditions. Controllers establish the sequence of arriving and departing aircraft by requiring them to adjust flight as necessary to achieve proper spacing. These adjustments can only be based on observed traffic, accurate pilot reports, and anticipated aircraft maneuvers. Pilots are expected to cooperate so as to preclude disruption of traffic flow or creation of conflicting patterns. The pilot in command of an aircraft is directly responsible for and is the final authority as to the operation of that aircraft. On occasion it may be necessary for a pilot to maneuver his aircraft to maintain spacing with the traffic he has been sequenced to follow. The controller can anticipate minor maneuvering such as shallow "S" turns. The controller cannot however, anticipate a major maneuver such as a 360 degree turn. If a pilot makes a 360 degree turn after he has obtained a landing sequence the result is usually a gap in the landing interval and more importantly it causes a chain reaction which may result in a conflict with following traffic and interruption of the sequence established by the tower or approach controller. Should a pilot decide he needs to make maneuvering turns to maintain spacing behind a preceding aircraft, he should always advise the controller if at all possible. Except when requested by the controller or in emergency situations, a 360 degree turn should never be executed in the traffic pattern or when receiving radar service without first advising the controller.

225. WIND DIRECTION AND VELOCITY

Wind direction issued by air traffic facilities is magnetic and wind velocity is in knots.

226. USE OF RUNWAYS

a. Runways are numbered to correspond to their magnetic bearing. Runway 27, for example, has a bearing of 270 degrees. Wind direction issued by the tower is also magnetic.

(1) At airports where an informal or formal runway use program is not established, ATC clearances may specify: (1) the runway most nearly aligned with the wind when it is five knots or more, (2) the "calm wind" runway when wind is less than five knots, or (3) another runway if operationally advantageous. It is not necessary for a controller to specifically inquire if the pilot will use a specific runway or to offer him a choice of runways. If a pilot prefers to use a different runway than that specified or the one most nearly aligned with the wind, he is expected to inform ATC accordingly.

(2) At airports where an informal runway use program is established, for noise abatement purposes, ATC will assign runways deemed to have the least noise impact if the wind directions is within 90 degrees of the runway heading and wind velocity does not exceed 15 knots, and runways are clear and dry. If the pilot prefers to use a different runway than that specified, he is expected to inform ATC accordingly. Such re-

quests will be honored and, when appropriate, pilots will be advised the requested runway is noise sensitive.

(3) At airports where a formal runway use programs is established. ATC will assign runways as specified in a Letter of Agreement between the aircraft operators which regularly use the airport, the airport proprietor, and the control tower. In some cases, there will exist an established order of runway selection for landing and another for takeoff, or a different order of runway selection for turbojet aircraft than that established for conventional aircraft. Pilot requests for use of other runways for reasons of safety will be honored and the pilot advised that the assigned runway is specified in the formal runway use program.

(4) If a pilot prefers to use a different runway than that specified, he is expected to advise ATC accordingly. When use of a different runway is requested, pilot cooperation is solicited to preclude disruption of the traffic flow or creation of conflicting patterns.

227–229. RESERVED

230. INTERSECTION TAKEOFFS

a. In order to enhance airport capacities, reduce taxiing distances, minimize departure delays, and provide for more efficient movement of air traffic, controllers may initiate intersection takeoffs as well as approve them when the pilot requests. If for ANY reason a pilot prefers to use a different intersection or the full length of the runway or desires to obtain the distance between the intersection and the runway end, HE IS EXPECTED TO INFORM ATC ACCORDINGLY.

b. Controllers are required to separate small propeller driven aircraft (less than 12,500 pounds) taking off from an intersection on the same runway (same or opposite direction takeoff) following a large aircraft (12,500 pounds or more) by ensuring that at least a 3-minute interval exists between the time that the preceding large aircraft has taken off and the succeeding aircraft begins takeoff roll. To inform the pilot of the required 3-minute wait, the controller will state "Hold for Wake Turbulence." If after considering wake turbulence hazards the pilot feels that a lesser time interval is appropriate, he may request a waiver to the 3-minute interval. Pilots must initiate such a request by stating "REQUEST WAIVER TO 3 MINUTE INTERVAL," or by making a similar statement. Controllers may then issue a takeoff clearance if other traffic permits, since the pilot has accepted responsibility for his own wake turbulence separation. A pilot may not waive the 3 minute interval when departing behind a heavy jet.

231. SIMULTANEOUS OPERATIONS ON INTERSECTING RUNWAYS

a. Despite the many new and lengthened runways which have been added to the nation's airports in recent years, limited runway availability remains a major contributing factor to operational delays. Many high-density airports have gained operational experience with intersecting runways which clearly indicates that simultaneous operations are safe and feasible. Tower controllers may authorize simultaneous landings and, at designated locations, simultaneous landing and takeoffs on intersecting runways when the following conditions are met:

(1) The runways are dry and the controller has received no reports that braking action is less than good.

(2) Simultaneous landings are conducted in VFR conditions unless visual separation is applied. Simultaneous landings and takeoffs are conducted in VFR conditions only and only between sunrise and sunset.

(3) Instructions are issued to restrict one aircraft from entering the intersecting runway being used by another aircraft.

(4) Traffic information is issued to and acknowledged for by the pilots of both aircraft.

(5) The measured distance from runway threshold to intersection is issued if the pilot requests it.

(6) The conditions specified in 3, 4, and 5 are met at or before issuance of the landing clearance.

(7) The distance from landing threshold to the intersection is adequate for the category of aircraft being held short. Controllers are provided a general table of aircraft category/minimum runway length requirements as a guide. Operators of STOL aircraft should identify their aircraft as such on initial contact with the tower, unless a letter of agreement concerning this fact, is in effect. IT IS INCUMBENT ON THE PILOT TO DETERMINE HIS ABILITY TO HOLD SHORT OF AN INTERSECTION AFTER LANDING, WHEN SO INSTRUCTED.

b. THE SAFETY AND OPERATION OF AN AIRCRAFT REMAIN THE RESPONSIBILITY OF THE PILOT. IF FOR ANY REASON (e.g. DIFFICULTY IN DISCERNING LOCATION OF AN INTERSECTION AT NIGHT, INABILITY TO HOLD SHORT OF AN INTERSECTION, WIND FACTORS, ETC.) A PILOT ELECTS TO USE THE FULL LENGTH OF THE RUNWAY, A DIFFERENT RUNWAY OR DESIRES TO OBTAIN THE DISTANCE FROM THE LANDING THRESHOLD TO THE INTERSECTION, HE IS EXPECTED TO PROMPTLY INFORM ATC ACCORDINGLY.

232. LOW APPROACH

a. A low approach (sometimes referred to as a low pass) is the go-around maneuver following approach. Instead of landing or making a touch-and-go, a pilot may wish to go around (low approach) in order to expedite a particular operation—a series of practice instrument approaches is an example of such an operation. Unless otherwise authorized by ATC, the low approach should be made straight ahead, with no turns or climb made until the pilot has made a thorough visual check for other aircraft in the area.

b. When operating within an airport traffic area, a pilot intending to make a low approach should contact the tower for approval. This request should be made prior to starting the final approach.

c. When operating to an airport not within an airport traffic area; a pilot intending to make a low approach should, prior to leaving the final approach fix inbound, so advise the FSS, UNICOM, or make a broadcast, as

appropriate (see 155—AIRPORT ADVISORY PRACTICES AT NONTOWER AIRPORTS.)

233. TRAFFIC CONTROL LIGHT SIGNALS

a. The following procedures are used by airport traffic control towers in the control of aircraft not equipped with radio. These same procedures will be used to control aircraft equipped with radio if radio contact cannot be established. Airport traffic control personnel use a directive traffic control signal which emits an intense narrow beam of a selected color (either red, white, or green) when controlling traffic by light signals. Although the traffic signal light offers the advantage that some control may be exercised over non-radio equipped aircraft, pilots should be cognizant of the disadvantages which are:

(1) The pilot may not be looking at the control tower at the time a signal is directed toward him.

(2) The directions transmitted by a light signal are very limited since only approval or disapproval of a pilot's anticipated actions may be transmitted. No supplement or explanatory information may be transmitted except by the use of the "General Warning Signal" which advises the pilot to be on the alert.

b. Between sunset and sunrise, a pilot wishing to attract the attention of the control tower should turn on a landing light and taxi the aircraft into a position, clear of the active runway, so that light is visible to the tower. The landing light should remain on until appropriate signals are received from the tower.

c. Portable traffic control light signals:

Color and Type of Signal	On the Ground	In Flight
STEADY GREEN	Cleared for take-off	Cleared to land
FLASHING GREEN	Cleared to taxi	Return for landing (to be followed by steady green at proper time)
STEADY RED	Stop	Give way to other aircraft and continue circling
FLASHING RED	Taxi clear of landing area (runway) in use	Airport unsafe—do not land
FLASHING WHITE	Return to starting point on airport	
ALTERNATING RED & GREEN	General Warning Signal—Exercise Extreme Caution	

d. During daylight hours, acknowledge tower transmissions or light signals by moving the ailerons or rudder. At night, acknowledge by blinking the landing or navigation lights. If radio malfunction occurs after departing the parking area, watch the tower for light signals or monitor tower frequency.

234. AIRPORT ROTATING BEACON

During the hours of daylight the lighting of the rotating beacon will mean that ground visibility is less than three miles and/or that the ceiling is less than 1000 feet. The operation of the rotating beacon indicates that a clearance from air traffic control is necessary for landing, takeoff, or flight in the traffic pattern if the airport is within a control zone. (See paragraph 52–d)

235. COMMUNICATIONS

a. Pilots of departing aircraft should communicate with the control tower on the appropriate ground control/clearance delivery frequency prior to starting engines to receive engine start time, taxi and/or clearance information. Unless otherwise advised by the tower, remain on that frequency during taxiing and runup, then change to local control frequency when ready to request takeoff clearance. (See 161—AUTOMATIC TERMINAL INFORMATION SERVICE (ATIS) for continuous broadcast of terminal information.)

b. Ground control frequencies are provided in the 121.6–121.9 MHz band to eliminate frequency congestion on the tower (local control) channel. These ground control frequencies, whose use is limited to communications between the tower and aircraft on the ground and between the tower and utility vehicles on the airport, provide a clear VHF channel for arriving and departing aircraft. They are used for issuance of taxi information, clearances, and other necessary contacts between the tower and aircraft or other vehicles operated on the airport. A pilot who has just landed should not change from the tower frequency to the ground control frequency until he is directed to do so by the controller. Normally, only one ground control frequency is assigned at an airport; however, at locations where the amount of traffic so warrants, a second ground control frequency and/or another frequency designated as a clearance delivery frequency, may be assigned.

c. The controller may omit the frequency or the numbers preceding the decimal point in the frequency when directing the pilot to change to a VHF ground control frequency if, in the controller's opinion, this usage will be clearly understood by the pilot; e.g. 121.7–'Contact ground' or 'Contact ground point seven'.

236. GATE HOLDING DUE TO DEPARTURE DELAYS

Pilots should contact ground control/clearance delivery prior to starting engines as gate hold procedures will be in effect whenever departure delays exceed or are anticipated to exceed 5 minutes. The sequence for departure will be maintained in accordance with initial call up unless modified by flow control restrictions. Pilots should monitor the ground control/clearance delivery frequency for engine startup advisories or new proposed start time if the delay changes.

237–239. RESERVED

240. FUEL ADVISORY DEPARTURE PROCEDURES

a. The Air Traffic Service has undertaken several programs designed to conserve aviation fuel. Fuel Advisory Departure (FAD) Procedures is one such program.

b. FAD is designed to operate when conditions at an airport are such that arrival delays will exceed one hour, and that the hour or more delay will continue for an extended period. FAD is not designed to eliminate delays, but to absorb, with engine off, any excess of the anticipated one hour delay at the departure terminal. This means absorbing the excess of the hour arrival delay at the departure gate, being assigned a new departure time and then proceeding to destination and holding an hour or less at the destination.

c. Subject to the availability of holding space, FAD offers the pilot/operator options to absorb the delay in the air or on the ground. Of course, delay on the ground with engine off is the key to fuel savings. Options include: ground delay, airborne delay, split ground/airborne delay, intermediate landing (delay at the intermediate airport is credited) or flight substitution.

d. System users are appraised of the imposition of FAD through ATC Systems Command Center advisories transmitted to all Flight Service Stations, and Airline Dispatch Offices. When notified that FAD procedures are in effect, operators are requested to file flight plans to the impacted airport at least 4 hours in advance of departure. The flight plan should include the estimated time enroute.

e. FAD procedures were tested in a live enviromnent at the Chicago O'Hare airport. The tests and subsequent programs indicated that significant fuel savings can be realized when the ground delay option is exercised.

241. TAXIING

a. Approval must be obtained prior to moving an aircraft or vehicle onto the movement area during the hours an airport traffic control tower is in operation. Always state your position on the airport when calling the tower for taxi instructions. The movement area is normally described in local bulletins issued by the airport manager or control tower. These bulletins may be found in FSSs, fixed base operators offices, air carrier offices and operations offices. The control tower also issues bulletins describing areas where they cannot provide airport traffic control service due to nonvisibility or other reasons. In addition, a clearance must be obtained prior to taxiing on a runway, taking off or landing during the hours an airport traffic control tower is in operation. When ATC clears an aircraft to "taxi to" an assigned takeoff runway, the absence of holding instructions authorizes the aircraft to "cross" all runways which the taxi route intersects except the assigned takeoff runway. It does not include authorization to "taxi onto" or "cross" the assigned takeoff runway at any point. In the absence of holding instructions, a clearance to "taxi to" any point other than an assigned takeoff runway is a clearance to cross all runways that intersect the taxi route to that point.

b. ATC clearances or instructions pertaining to taxiing are predicated on known traffic and known physical airport conditions. Therefore, it is important that pilots clearly understand the clearance or instruction. Although an ATC clearance is issued for taxiing purposes, when operating in accordance with the FARs, it is the responsibility of the pilot to avoid collision with other aircraft. Since "the pilot in command of an aircraft is directly responsible for, and is the final authority as to, the operation of that aircraft" the pilot should obtain clarification of any clearance or instruction which is not understood.

c. At those airports where the United States Government operates the control tower and ATC has authorized non-compliance with the requirement for two-way radio communications while operating within the airport traffic area, or at those airports where the United States Government does not operate the control tower and radio communications cannot be established, pilots shall obtain a clearance by visual light signal prior to taxiing on a runway and prior to take-off and landing.

d. The following phraseologies and procedures are used in radio-telephone communications with aeronautical ground stations.

(1) Aircraft identification, location, type of operation planned (VFR or IFR) and the point of first intended landing.

Example:

Aircraft: "WASHINGTON GROUND BEECHCRAFT ONE THREE ONE FIVE NINER AT HANGAR EIGHT, READY TO TAXI, IFR TO CHICAGO OVER"

Tower: "BEECHCRAFT ONE THREE ONE FIVE NINER, RUNWAY THREE SIX, WIND ZERO THREE ZERO DEGREES AT TWO FIVE, ALTIMETER THREE ZERO ZERO FOUR, HOLD SHORT OF RUNWAY THREE."

(2) Air route traffic control clearances are relayed to pilots by airport traffic controllers in the following manner:

Example:

Tower: BEECHCRAFT ONE THREE ONE FIVE NINER CLEARED TO THE CHICAGO MIDWAY AIRPORT, VIA VICTOR EIGHT, MAINTAIN EIGHT THOUSAND, OVER.

Aircraft: "BEECHCRAFT ONE THREE ONE FIVE NINER CLEARED TO THE CHICAGO MIDWAY AIRPORT, VIA VICTOR EIGHT, MAINTAIN EIGHT THOUSAND, OVER."

NOTE.—Normally, an ATC IFR clearance is relayed to a pilot by the ground controller. At busy locations, however, pilots may be instructed by the ground controller to "CONTACT CLEARANCE DELIVERY" on a frequency designated for this purpose. No surveillance or control over the movement of traffic is exercised by this position of operation. See Clearance Readback in ATC Clearances/Separations.

(3) Aircraft identification, location and request for taxi instructions after landing.

Example:

Aircraft: "DULLES GROUND BEECHCRAFT ONE FOUR TWO SIX ONE CLEARING RUNWAY ONE RIGHT ON TAXIWAY E3, REQUEST CLEARANCE TO PAGE."

Tower: "BEECHCRAFT ONE FOUR TWO SIX ONE, TAXI TO PAGE VIA TAXIWAYS E3, E1 AND E9."

242. TAXI DURING LOW VISIBILITY

Pilots and aircraft operators should be constantly aware that during certain low visibility conditions the movement of aircraft and vehicles on airports may not be visible to the tower controller. This may prevent visual confirmation of an aircraft's adherence to taxi instructions. Pilots should, therefore, exercise extreme vigilance and proceed cautiously under such conditions.

Of vital importance is the need for pilots to notify the controller when difficulties are encountered or at the first indication of becoming disoriented. Pilots should proceed with extreme caution when taxiing toward the sun. When vision difficulties are encountered pilots should immediately inform the controller.

243. PRACTICE INSTRUMENT APPROACHES

a. Various air traffic incidents required adoption of measures to achieve more organized and controlled operations where practice instrument approaches are conducted. Practice instrument approaches are considered to be instrument approaches made by either a VFR aircraft not on an IFR flight plan or an aircraft on an IFR flight plan. To achieve this and thereby enhance air safety, it is Air Traffic Service policy to provide for separation of such operations at locations where approach control facilities are located and, as resources permit, at certain other locations served by Air Route Traffic Control Centers or approach control facilities. Pilot requests to practice instrument approaches may be approved by ATC subject to traffic and workload conditions. Pilots should anticipate that in some instances the controller may find it necessary to deny approval or withdraw previous approval when traffic conditions warrant. It must be clearly understood, however, that even though the controller may be providing separation, pilots on VFR flight plans are required to comply with basic visual flight rules (FAR 91.105). Application of ATC procedures or any action taken by the controller to avoid traffic conflictions does not relieve IFR and VFR pilots of their responsibility to see and avoid other traffic while operating in VFR conditions. (FAR 91.67) In addition to the normal IFR separation minima (which includes visual separation) during VFR conditions, 500 feet vertical separation may be applied between VFR aircraft and between a VFR aircraft and an IFR aircraft. Pilots not on IFR flight plans desiring practice instrument approaches should always state 'practice' when making requests to ATC. This will preclude the controller from thinking a pilot is requesting flight in accordance with instrument flight rules. Accordingly, it will preclude the controller from expecting a pilot to cancel the IFR flight plan when the approach is made to an airport where there is no functioning control tower.

b. Before practicing an instrument approach, pilots should inform the approach control facility or the tower of the type of practice approach they desire to make and how they intend to terminate it; i.e., full-stop landing, touch-and-go, or missed/low approach maneuver. This information may be furnished progressively when conducting a series of approaches. The controller will control flights practicing instrument approaches so as to ensure that they do not disrupt the flow of arriving and departing itinerant IFR or VFR aircraft. The priority afforded itinerant aircraft over practice instrument approaches is not intended to be so rigidly applied that it causes inefficient application of services. A minimum delay to itinerant traffic may be appropriate to allow an aircraft practicing an approach to complete that approach.

c. At airports without a tower, pilots wishing to make practice instrument approaches should notify the facility having control jurisdiction of the desired approach as indicated on the approach chart. All approach control facilities and Air Route Traffic Control Centers are required to publish a facility bulletin depicting those airports where they provide standard separation to both VFR and IFR aircraft conducting practice instrument approaches.

d. When authorization is granted to make practice approaches to airports where an approach control facility is located and to certain other airports served by approach control or an Air Route Traffic Control Center, the controller will approve the practice approach, instruct the aircraft maintain VFR conditions, if appropriate, and will provide approved standard separation between aircraft he has authorized to practice instrument approaches and between such aircraft and any IFR aircraft.

e. Visual flight rules aircraft practicing instrument approaches will not be provided separation during a missed approach unless the missed approach is requested by the pilot and approved by ATC.

f. Except in an emergency, aircraft cleared to practice instrument approaches must not deviate from the approved procedure until cleared to do so by the controller.

g. At radar approach control locations when a full approach procedure (procedure turn, etc.) cannot be approved, pilots should expect to be vectored to a final approach course for a practice instrument approach which is compatible with the general direction of traffic at that airport.

h. When granting approval for a practice instrument approach, the controller will usually ask the pilot to report to the tower prior to or over the final approach fix inbound.

i. When authorization is granted to conduct practice instrument approaches to an airport with a tower but where approved standard separation is not provided to aircraft conducting practice instrument approaches, the tower will approve the practice approach, instruct the aircraft to maintain VFR if appropriate, and issue traffic information, as required.

j. When air aircraft notifies a flight service station providing Airport Advisory Service of intent to conduct a practice instrument approach and if separation will be provided, you will be instructed to contact the appropriate facility on a specified frequency prior to initiating the approach. At airports where separation is not provided, the flight service station will acknowledge the message and issue known traffic information but will neither approve or disapprove the approach.

k. Pilots conducting practice instrument approaches should be particularly alert for other aircraft operating in the local traffic pattern or in proximity to the airport.

244. OPTION APPROACH

The "Cleared for the Option" procedure will permit an instructor pilot/flight examiner/pilot the option to make a touch-and-go, low approach, missed approach, stop-and-go, or full stop landing. This procedure can be very beneficial in a training situation in that neither the student pilot nor examinee would know what maneuver would be accomplished. The pilot should make his request for this procedure passing the final approach fix inbound on an instrument approach or entering downwind for a VFR traffic pattern. The advantages of this procedure as a training aid are that it enables

an instructor/examiner to obtain the reaction of a trainee/examinee under changing conditions, the pilot would not have to discontinue an approach in the middle of the procedure due to student error or pilot proficiency requirements, and finally it allows more flexibility and economy in training programs. This procedure will only be used at those locations with an operational control tower and will be subject to ATC approval/disapproval.

245. CLEARING THE RUNWAY AFTER LANDING

After landing, unless otherwise instructed by the control tower, aircraft should continue to taxi in the landing direction, proceed to the nearest turnoff and exit the runway without delay. Do not turn on to another runway or make a 180 degree turn to taxi back on an active runway or change to ground control frequency while on the active runway without authorization from the tower.

246. USE OF AIRCRAFT LIGHTS

a. Operation of Aircraft Rotating Beacon.

(1) There have been several incidents in which small aircraft have overturned or damaged by prop/jet blast forces from taxiing large aircraft. A small aircraft taxiing behind any large aircraft with its engines operating could meet with the same results. In the interest of preventing ground upsets and injuries to ground personnel due to prop/jet engine blast forces, the FAA has recommended to air carriers/commercial operators that they establish procedures for the operation of the aircraft rotating beacon any time the engines are in operation.

(2) General aviation pilots utilizing aircraft equipped with rotating beacons are also encouraged to participate in this program and operate the beacon any time the aircraft engines are in operation as an alert to other aircraft and ground personnel that prop/jet engine blast forces may be present. Caution must be exercised by all personnel not to rely solely on the rotating beacon as an indication that aircraft engines are in operation, since participation in this program is voluntary.

b. Operation of Aircraft Operation Lights.

(1) FAA has initiated a voluntary pilot safety program, "Operation Lights On" to enhance the "see-and-be-seen" concept of averting collisions both in the air and on the ground, and to reduce bird strikes. All pilots are encouraged to turn on their anti-collision lights any time the engine(s) are running day or night. All pilots are further encouraged to turn on their landing lights when operating within 10 miles of any airport (day and night), in conditions of reduced visibility and in areas where flocks of birds may be expected, i.e., coastal areas, lake areas, swamp areas, around refuse dumps, etc.

(2) Although turning on aircraft lights does enhance the "see-and-be-seen" concept, pilots should not become complacent about keeping a sharp outlook for other aircraft. Not all aircraft are equipped with lights and some pilots may not have their lights turned on. The aircraft manufacturers' recommendations for operation of landing lights and electrical systems should be observed.

c. Aircraft Strobe Lights.

(1) Pilots are reminded to extinguish aircraft strobe lights when on the ground, because of the flash intensity and irritating effect on ground personnel and other pilots.

247. HAND SIGNALS

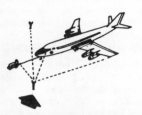

SIGNALMAN DIRECTS TOWING

SIGNALMAN'S POSITION

FLAGMAN DIRECTS PILOT TO SIGNALMAN IF TRAFFIC CONDITIONS REQUIRE

ALL CLEAR (O.K.)

POINT TO ENGINE TO BE STARTED

START ENGINE

PULL CHOCKS

COME AHEAD

LEFT TURN

RIGHT TURN

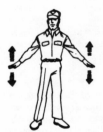

SLOW DOWN

STOP

INSERT CHOCKS

CUT ENGINES

NIGHT OPERATION
(Uses same hand movements as day operation)

EMERGENCY STOP

248–259. RESERVED

260. CLEARANCE

A clearance issued by ATC is predicated on known traffic and known physical airport conditions. An ATC clearance means an authorization by ATC, for the purpose of preventing collision between known aircraft, for an aircraft to proceed under specified conditions within controlled airspace. IT IS NOT AUTHORIZATION FOR A PILOT TO DEVIATE FROM ANY RULE, REGULATION OR MINIMUM ALTITUDE NOR TO CONDUCT UNSAFE OPERATION OF HIS AIRCRAFT. FAR 91.3 (a) states: "The pilot in command of an aircraft is directly responsible for, and is the final authority as to, the operation of that aircraft." If ATC issues a clearance that would cause a pilot to deviate from a rule or regulation, or in the pilot's opinion, would place the aircraft in jeopardy, IT IS THE PILOT'S RESPONSIBILITY TO REQUEST AN AMENDED CLEARANCE. Similarly, if a pilot prefers to follow a different course of action, such as make a 360 degree turn for spacing to follow traffic when established in a landing or approach sequence, land on a different runway, takeoff from a different intersection, takeoff from the threshold instead of an intersection or delay his operation, HE IS EXPECTED TO INFORM ATC ACCORDINGLY. When he requests a different course of action, however, the pilot is expected to cooperate so as to preclude disruption of traffic flow or creation of conflicting patterns. *When weather conditions permit, during the time an IFR flight is operating, it is the direct responsibility of the pilot to avoid other aircraft since VFR flights may be operating in the same area without the knowledge of ATC and traffic clearances provide standard separation only between IFR flights.*

261. CLEARANCE PREFIX

A clearance, information, or request for information originated by an ATC facility and relayed to the pilot through an air/ground communication station will be prefixed by "ATC CLEARS," "ATC ADVISES," or "ATC REQUESTS."

262. CLEARANCE ITEMS.

a. ATC clearances normally contain the following:

(1) **Clearance Limit.**—The traffic clearance issued prior to departure will normally authorize flight to the airport of intended landing. Under certain conditions, at some locations a short range clearance procedure is utilized whereby a clearance is issued to a fix within or just outside of the terminal area and the pilot is advised of the frequency on which he will receive the long range clearance direct from the center controller.

(2) **Departure Procedure.**—Headings to fly and altitude restrictions may be issued to separate a departure from other air traffic in the terminal area. (See **322**—ABBREVIATED IFR DEPARTURE CLEARANCE PROCEDURES and **325**—INSTRUMENT DEPARTURES.) Where the volume of traffic warrants, Standard Instrument Departures (SIDS) have been developed.

(3) **Route of Flight.**

(a) Clearances are normally issued for the altitude/flight level and route filed by the pilot. However, due to traffic conditions, it is frequently necessary for ATC to specify an altitude/flight level or route different from that requested by the pilot. In addition, flow patterns have been established in certain congested areas, or between congested areas, whereby traffic capacity is increased by routing all traffic on preferred routes. Information on these flow patterns is available in offices where pre-flight briefing is furnished or where flight plans are accepted.

(b) Air traffic clearances include data to assist pilots in identifying radio reporting points for where there is more than one type with the same name, for example: "Denver VOR." It is the responsibility of a pilot to notify air traffic control immediately if his radio equipment cannot receive the type of signals he must utilize to comply with his clearance.

(4) **Altitude Data.**

(a) The altitude/flight level instructions in an ATC clearance normally require that a pilot "MAINTAIN" the altitude/flight level at which the flight will operate when in controlled airspace. Altitude/flight level changes while en route should be requested prior to the time the change is desired.

(b) When possible, if the altitude assigned is different than that requested by the pilot, ATC will inform an aircraft when to expect climb or descent clearance or to request altitude change from another facility. If this has not been received prior to crossing the boundary of the ATC facility's area and assignment at a different flight level is still desired, the pilot should reinitiate his request with the next facility.

(c) The term "CRUISE" may be used instead of "MAINTAIN" to signify to the pilot that climb to or descent from assigned altitude may be commenced at his discretion without further clearance from ATC. "CRUISE" is normally used only for relatively short flights in uncongested areas and is authorized for the flight to proceed to, and make an approach at, destination.

NOTE.—See definition of CRUISE in the Pilot/Controller Glossary.

(5) **Holding Instructions.**

(a) Whenever an aircraft has been cleared to a point other than the destination airport, it is the responsibility of the ATC controller to furnish the pilot with an additional clearance prior to the time the flight arrives at the clearance limit. This clearance may authorize flight beyond the clearance limit or contain holding instructions for the flight.

(b) When an aircraft is 3 minutes or less from a clearance limit and a clearance beyond the fix has not been received, the pilot is expected to start a speed reduction so that he will cross the fix, initially, at or below the maximum holding airspeed.

(c) When the aircraft reaches the clearance limit and holding instructions or a clearance beyond the fix has not been received, the pilot should begin holding and immediately request further clearance. Holding shall be effected in accordance with the holding pattern depicted on the appropriate U.S. Government or commercially produced (meeting FAA requirements) low/high altitude en route, area or STAR chart for the clearance limit, maintaining the last assigned altitude/flight level.

If no holding pattern is charted, the pilot is expected to begin holding in a standard holding pattern on the course on which he approaches the fix. If no holding pattern is charted, the pilot is expected to begin holding in a standard holding pattern on the course on which he approaches the fix.

(d) The altitude/flight level of the aircraft at this clearance limit will be protected so that separation will exist in the event the aircraft holds awaiting further clearance. The pilot should report to ATC the time and altitude/flight level at which the aircraft reaches the holding fix or clearance limit and report leaving any assigned holding fix or point. (These reports are not required when in radar contact.)

NOTE.—The foregoing should not be construed as being related in any way to the procedures which apply when a two-way radio failure occurs—FAR 91.127.

263. AMENDED CLEARANCES

a. Amendments to the initial clearance will be issued at any time an air traffic controller deems such action necessary to avoid possible confliction between aircraft. Clearances will require that a flight "hold" or change altitude prior to reaching the point where standard separation from other IFR traffic would no longer exist. Some pilots have questioned this action and requested "traffic information" and were at a loss when the reply indicated "no traffic reported." In such cases the controller has taken action to prevent a traffic confliction which would have occurred at a distant point.

b. A pilot may wish an explanation of the handling of his flight at the time of occurrence; however, controllers are not able to take time from their immediate control duties nor can they afford to overload the ATC communications channels to furnish explanations. Pilots may obtain an explanation by directing a letter or telephone call to the chief controller of the facility involved.

c. The pilot has the privilege of requesting a different clearance from that which has been issued by ATC if he feels that he has information which would make another course of action more practicable or if aircraft equipment limitations or company procedures forbid compliance with the clearance issued.

d. Pilots should pay particular attention to the clearance and not assume that the route and altitude/flight level are the same as requested in the flight plan. It is suggested that pilots make a written report of clearances at the time they are received, and verify, by a repeat back, any portions that are complex or about which a doubt exists. It will be the responsibility of each pilot to accept or refuse the clearance issued.

264. SPECIAL VFR CLEARANCES (Special VFR Flight Clearance Procedures (F.A.R. Part 91.107)

a. An ATC clearance must be obtained *prior* to operating within a control zone when the weather is less than that required for VFR flight. A VFR pilot may request and be given a clearance to enter, leave or operate within most control zones in special VFR conditions, traffic permitting, and providing such flight will not delay IFR operations. The visibility requirements for Special VFR fixed-wing aircraft are: 1 mile flight visibility for operations within the control zone and mile ground visibility if taking off or landing. All special VFR flights must remain clear of clouds. When a control tower is located within the control zone, requests for clearances should be to the tower. If no tower is located within the control zone, a clearance may be obtained from the nearest tower, flight service station or center.

b. It is not necessary to file a complete flight plan with the request for clearance but the pilot should state his intentions in sufficient detail to permit air traffic control to fit his flight into the traffic flow. The clearance will not contain a specific altitude as the pilot must remain clear of clouds. The controller may require the pilot to fly at or below a certain altitude due to other traffic, but the altitude specified will permit flight at or above the minimum safe altitude. In addition, at radar locations, flights may be vectored if necessary for control purposes or on pilot request.

c. Special VFR clearances are effective within control zones only. ATC does not provide separation after an aircraft leaves the control zone on a special VFR clearance.

d. Special VFR operations by fixed-wing aircraft are prohibited in some control zones due to the volume of IFR traffic. A list of these control zones is contained in FAR 93.113, and also depicted on Sectional Aeronautical Charts.

e. ATC provides separation between special VFR flights and between them and other IFR flights.

f. Special VFR operations by fixed-wing aircraft are prohibited between sunset and sunrise unless the pilot is instrument rated and the aircraft is equipped for IFR flight.

265. PILOT RESPONSIBILITY UPON CLEARANCE ISSUANCE

a. RECORD ATC CLEARANCE—When conducting an IFR operation, make a written record of your clearance. The specified conditions which are a part of your air traffic clearance may be somewhat different from those included in your flight plan. Additionally, Air Traffic Control may find it necessary to ADD conditions, such as a particular departure route. The very fact that Air Traffic Control specifies different or additional conditions means that other aircraft are involved in the traffic situation.

b. ATC CLEARANCE/INSTRUCTION READBACK—Pilots of airborne aircraft should read back *those parts* of ATC clearances/instructions containing altitude assignments or vectors, as a means of mutual verification. The readback of the "numbers" serves as a double check between pilots and controllers, and such, it is an invaluable aid in reducing the kinds of communication errors that occur when a number is either "misheard" or is incorrect.

(1) Precede all readbacks/acknowledgements with the aircraft identification. This should assure that controllers can determine that the correct aircraft received the clearance/instruction. The requirement to include aircraft identification in all readbacks/acknowledgments becomes more important as frequency congestion increases and when aircraft with similar call signs are on the same frequency.

(2) Read back altitudes, altitude restritcions, and vectors in the same sequence as they are given in the clearance/instruction.

(3) Altitudes contained in charted procedures such as SIDs, instrument approaches, etc., should not be read back unless they are specifically stated by the controller.

266–269. RESERVED

270. ADHERENCE TO CLEARANCE

a. When air traffic clearance has been obtained under either the Visual or Instrument Flight Rules, the pilot in command of the aircraft shall not deviate from the provisions thereof unless an amended clearance is obtained. The addition of a VFR or other restriction, i.e., climb/descent point or time, crossing altitude, etc., does not authorize a pilot to deviate from the route of flight or any other provision of the air traffic control clearance.

b. In case emergency authority is used to deviate from provisions of an ATC clearance the pilot in command shall notify ATC as soon as possible and obtain an amended clearance. In an emergency situation which results in no deviation from the Rules prescribed in Part 91 but which requires air traffic control to give priority to an aircraft, the pilot of such aircraft shall when requested by ATC make a report within 48 hours of such emergency situation to the chief of that ATC facility.

c. When air traffic control issues an instruction, pilots are expected to comply with its provision upon receipt. ATC, in certain situations, will include the word "IMMEDIATELY" in an instruction to impress urgency of an imminent situation and expeditious compliance by the pilot is expected and necessary for safety.

d. When air traffic control issues a clearance, pilots are expected to execute its provisions upon acceptance. The term "at pilot's discretion" included in the altitude information of an air traffic control clearance means that ATC has offered the pilot the option to start climb/descent when he wishes. He is authorized to conduct the climb/descent at any rate he wishes, and to temporarily level off at any intermediate altitude he may desire. However, once he has vacated an altitude, he may not return to that altitude.

e. When ATC has not used the term 'AT PILOT'S DISCRETION' nor imposed any climb/descent restrictions, pilots should initiate climb or descent promptly on acknowledgement of the clearance. Descend or climb at an optimum rate consistent with the operating characteristics of the aircraft to 1,000 feet above or below the assigned altitude, and then attempt to descend or climb at a rate of 500 feet per minute until the assigned altitude is reached. If at anytime the pilot is unable to climb/descend at a rate of at least 500 feet a minute, advise ATC. If it is necessary to level off at an intermediate altitude during climb or descent, advise ATC, except for level off at 10,000 feet MSL on descent or 3,000 feet above airport elevation (prior to entering an airport traffic area), when required for speed reduction (FAR 91.70).

NOTE.—Leveling off at 10,000 feet MSL on descent, or 3,000 feet above airport elevation (prior to entering in an airport traffic area), to comply with FAR 91.70 airspeed restrictions, is commonplace. Controllers anticipate this action and plan accordingly. Leveling off at any other time, on climb or descent, may seriously affect air traffic handling by ATC. Consequently, it is imperative that pilots make every effort to fulfill the above expected actions to aid ATC in safely handling and expediting traffic.

f. If the altitude information of an air traffic control DESCENT clearance includes a provision to "CROSS (fix) AT/AT OR ABOVE/BELOW (altitude)," "the manner in which the descent is executed to comply with the crossing altitude is at the pilot's discretion." This authorization to descend at pilot's discretion is only applicable to that portion of the flight to which the crossing altitude restriction applies, and the pilot is expected to comply with the crossing altitude as a provision of the clearance. Any other clearance in which pilot execution is optional will so state: "AT PILOT'S DISCRETION."

(1) Examples:

(a) "UNITED FOUR SEVENTEEN, DESCEND AND MAINTAIN SIX THOUSAND."

The pilot is expected to commence descent upon receipt of the clearance, and to descend at the suggested rates specified in paragraph E, until reaching the assigned altitude of 6,000 feet.

(b) "UNITED FOUR SEVENTEEN, DESCEND AT PILOT'S DISCRETION, MAINTAIN SIX THOUSAND."

The pilot is authorized to conduct descent within the context of the term AT PILOT'S DISCRETION as described above.

(c) "UNITED FOUR SEVENTEEN, CROSS LAKEVIEW VOR AT OR ABOVE FLIGHT LEVEL TWO ZERO ZERO, DESCEND AND MAINTAIN SIX THOUSAND."

The pilot is authorized to conduct descent AT PILOT'S DISCRETION until reaching Lakeview VOR. He must comply with the clearance provision to cross the Lakeview VOR at or above FL 200. After passing Lakeview VOR he is expected to descend at the rates specified in paragraph E until reaching the assigned altitude of 6,000 feet.

(d) "UNITED FOUR SEVENTEEN, CROSS LAKEVIEW VOR AT SIX THOUSAND, MAINTAIN SIX THOUSAND."

The pilot is authorized to conduct descent AT PILOT'S DISCRETION, however, he must comply with the clearance provision to cross the Lakeview VOR at 6,000 feet.

(e) "UNITED FOUR SEVENTEEN, DESCEND NOW TO FLIGHT LEVEL TWO SEVEN ZERO, CROSS LAKEVIEW VOR AT OR BELOW ONE ZERO THOUSAND, DESCEND AND MAINTAIN SIX THOUSAND."

The pilot is expected to promptly execute and complete descent to FL 270 upon receipt of the clearance. After reaching FL 270 he is authorized to descend "at pilot's discretion" until reaching Lakeview VOR. He must comply with the clearance provision to cross Lakeview VOR at or below 10,000 feet. After Lakeview VOR he is expected to descend at the rates specified in paragraph 7 until reaching 6,000 feet.

g. The guiding principle is that the last ATC clearance has precedence over the previous ATC clearance. When the route or altitude in a previously issued clearance is amended, the controller will restate applicable altitude restrictions. If altitude to maintain is changed or restated whether prior to departure or while airborne, and previously issued altitude restritcions are omitted, altitude restritcions are canceled, including SID altitude restrictions.

(1) Examples:

(a) A departure flight receives a clearance to destination airport to maintain Flight Level 290. The clearance incorporates a SID which has certain altitude crossing restrictions. Shortly after takeoff, the flight receives a new clearance changing the maintaining Flight Level from 290 to 250. If the altitude restrictions are still applicable, the controller restates them.

(b) A departing aircraft is cleared to cross Mount Vernon intersection at or above 3,000, Gordonville VOR at or above 12,000, maintain FL 200. Shortly after departure, the altitude to be maintained is changed to FL 240. If the altitude restrictions are still applicable, the controller issues an amended clearance as follows:

"cross Mount Vernon intersection at or above three thousand, cross Gordonsville VOR at or above one two thousand, maintain flight level two four zero."

(c) An arriving aircraft is cleared to destination airport V45 Delta VOR direct, cross Delta at 10,000, maintain 6,000. Prior to Delta VOR, the controller issues amended clearance as follows:

"Turn right heading one eight zero for vector to Runway three six ILS approach, maintain 6,000."

NOTE.—Because the altitude restriction "cross Delta VOR at 10,000" was omitted from the amended clearance, it is no longer in effect.

h. Pilots of turbojet aircraft equipped with afterburner engines should advise ATC prior to takeoff if they intend to use afterburning during their climb to the en route altitude. Often, the controller may be able to plan his traffic to accommodate a high performance climb and allow the pilot to climb to his planned altitude without restriction.

271. IFR SEPARATION STANDARDS

a. Air traffic control effects separation of aircraft vertically by assigning different altitudes; longitudinally by providing an interval expressed in time or distance between aircraft on the same, converging, or crossing courses; and laterally by assigning different flight paths.

b. Standard separation will be provided between all aircraft operating on IFR flight plans except when "VFR Conditions-on-Top" has been requested by a pilot and authorized by ATC in lieu of a specific cruising or holding altitude or when clearances specifying that climb or descent or any portion of the flight shall be conducted in "VFR Conditions" are issued. A pilot may specifically request IFR separation while conducting a practice instrument approach.

c. When radar is employed in the separation of aircraft at the same altitude, a minimum of 3 miles separation is provided between aircraft operating within 40 miles of the radar antenna site, and 5 miles between aircraft operating beyond 40 miles from the antenna site. These minima may be increased or decreased in certain specific situations.

272. SPEED ADJUSTMENTS

a. To avoid excessive vectoring, ATC may request pilots of radar controlled aircraft to adjust speed.

b. Pilots complying with speed adjustments are expected to maintain a speed within ten knots of the specified speed. All speed adjustments shall be expressed in terms of knots based on indicated air speed (IAS).

c. Unless pilot concurrence is obtained, ATC requests for speed adjustments will be in accordance with the following minima:

(1) To aircraft operating between FL280 and 10,000 feet, a speed not less than 250 knots.

(2) To turbojet aircraft operating below 10,000 feet

(a) A speed not less than 210 knots, except;

(b) Within 20 miles of the airport of intended landing, a speed not less than 170 knots.

(3) Propeller aircraft within 20 miles of the airport of intended landing, a speed not less than 150 knots.

(4) Departures, a speed not less than 230 knots.

d. When ATC combines a speed adjustment with a descent clearance, the sequence of delivery, with the word "then" between, indicates the expected order of execution; i.e., "Descend and Maintain (altitude) then Reduce Speed to (speed)," or "Reduce Speed to (speed) then Descend and Maintain (altitude)." However, the maximum speeds below 10,000 feet as established in FAR 91.70 still apply. If there is any doubt concerning the manner in which such a clearance is to be executed request clarification from ATC.

e. If ATC determines (before an approach clearance is issued) that it is no longer necessary to apply speed adjustment procedures, they will inform the pilot to resume normal speed. Approach clearances supersede any prior speed adjustment assignments and pilots are expected to make their own speed adjustments, as necessary, to complete the approach. Under certain circumstances, however, it may be necessary for ATC to request further speed adjustments after approach clearance is issued to maintain separation between successive arrivals. Under such circumstances previously issued speed adjustments will be restated if that speed is to be maintained or additional speed adjustments requested. ATC must obtain pilot concurrence for speed adjustment after approach clearances are issued.

f. Controllers have been advised that utilization of the minimum speeds set forth above for propeller-driven aircraft will sometimes be impractical, since some aircraft in this category cruise at lower speeds and cannot attain the speeds specified.

g. Speed adjustment of propeller-driven aircraft which cannot attain the minimum speeds set forth above, shall be accomplished by requesting such flights to, if practicable:

(1) Maintain a specified speed equivalent to that of the preceding/succeeding aircraft; or

(2) Increase or decrease speed utilizing increments of 10 knots or multiples thereof.

h. The pilots retain the prerogative of rejecting the application of speed adjustment by ATC if the minimum safe airspeed for any particular operation is greater than the speed adjustment. IN SUCH CASES, PILOTS ARE EXPECTED TO ADVISE ATC OF THE SPEED THAT WILL BE USED.

i. Pilots are reminded that they are responsible for rejecting the application of speed adjustment by ATC if, in their opinion, it will cause them to exceed the maximum indicated airspeed prescribed by FAR 91.70 (a). IN SUCH CASES, THE PILOT IS EXPECTED TO SO INFORM ATC. Pilots operating at or above 10,000 feet MSL who are issued speed adjustments which exceed 250 knots IAS and are subsequently cleared below 10,000 feet MSL are expected to comply with FAR 91.70(a).

j. For operations in an airport traffic area, ATC is authorized to request or approve a speed greater than the maximum indicated airspeeds prescribed for operation within that airspace—FAR 91.70(b).

273. VISUAL SEPARATION

a. Visual separation is a means employed by ATC to separate aircraft only in terminal areas. There are two methods employed to effect this separation:

(1) The tower controller sees the aircraft involved and issues instructions, as necessary, to ensure that the aircraft avoid each other.

(2) A pilot sees the other aircraft involved and upon instructions from the controller provides his own separation by maneuvering his aircraft as necessary to avoid it. This may involve following in-trail behind another aircraft or keeping it in sight until it is no longer a factor.

b. A pilot's acceptance of traffic information and instructions to follow another aircraft or provide visual separation from it is considered by the controller as acknowledgment that the pilot sees the other aircraft and will maneuver his aircraft as necessary to avoid it. In operations conducted behind heavy jet aircraft the pilot's acceptance of traffic information and instructions to follow the heavy jet or provide visual separation from it is considered by the controller as acknowledgment that the pilot sees the heavy jet and accepts the responsibility of providing his own wake turbulence separation.

c. When pilots have been told to follow another aircraft or to provide visual separation from it, they should promptly notify the controller if they do not sight the other aircraft involved, if weather conditions are such that they cannot maintain visual contact with the other aircraft to avoid it, or if for any reason they cannot accept the responsibility to provide their own separation under these circumstances.

d. Pilots should remember, however, that they have a regulatory responsibility (FAR 91.67a) to see and avoid other aircraft when weather conditions permit.

274. IFR CLEARANCE WITH VFR RESTRICTIONS

a. ATC will not issue a clearance to an IFR flight specifying that climb, descent, or any portion of the flight be conducted in VFR conditions unless one of the following exists:

(1) The pilot requests the VFR restriction.

(2) For noise abatement benefits where part of the IFR departure route does not conform with an FAA approved noise abatement route or altitude.

b. If you are operating on an IFR flight plan and are given a VFR restriction, ATC will not apply IFR separation during the "VFR Restriction" portion of the flight.

c. If after receiving a VFR restriction you find that compliance with the clearance is not feasible, maintain VFR and request an amended clearance.

275. RUNWAY SEPARATION

Tower controllers establish the sequence of arriving and departing aircraft by requiring them to adjust flight or ground operation as necessary to achieve proper spacing. They may "HOLD" an aircraft short of the runway to achieve spacing between it and another arriving aircraft; the controller may instruct a pilot to "EXTEND DOWNWIND" in order to establish spacing from another arriving or departing aircraft. At times a clearance may include the word "IMMEDIATE." For example: "CLEARED FOR IMMEDIATE TAKEOFF." In such cases "IMMEDIATE" is used for purposes of *air traffic separation.* It is up to the pilot to refuse the clearance if, in his opinion, compliance would adversely affect his operation.

276–289. RESERVED

290. PREFLIGHT PREPARATION

a. Every pilot is urged to receive a preflight briefing and to file a flight plan. This briefing would consist of weather, airport, and enroute navaid information. Briefing service may be obtained from a Flight Service Station either by telephone/interphone, by radio when airborne, or by a personal visit to the Station.

b. You are urged to use the Pilot's Preflight Check List which is on the reverse of the flight plan form. The Check List is a reminder of items you should be aware of before beginning flight. Also provided beneath the Check List is a Flight Log for your use if desired.

c. Consult your local flight service station (FSS), combined station/tower (CS/T), or National Weather Service Office (NWSO) for preflight weather briefing. FSS and NWSO personnel are certificated pilot weather briefers; however, since CS/T personnel are not certificated pilot weather briefers, weather briefings they furnish are limited to factual data derived directly from weather sequence and forecast information.

d. FSSs are required to advise of pertinent NOTAMs, but if they are overlooked, don't hesitate to remind the specialist that you have not received NOTAM information. Additionally, NOTAMs which are known in sufficient time for publication and are of 7 days duration or longer are normally incorporated into the Notices to Airmen (Class II) publication and carried there until cancellation time. FDC NOTAMs, which apply to instrument flight procedures, are also included in the Notices to Airmen publication up to and including the number indicated in the FDC NOTAM legend. These NOTAMs are not provided during a briefing unless specifically requested by the pilot since the FSS specialist has no way of knowing whether the pilot has already checked the Notices to Airmen publication prior to calling. Remember to *ask* for NOTAMs in the Notices to Airmen publication—they are not normally furnished during your briefing.

e. Pilots are urged to use only the latest issue of aeronautical charts in planning and conducting flight operations. Aeronautical charts are revised and reissued on a periodic basis to ensure that depicted data are current and reliable. In the conterminous United States, sectional charts are updated each 6 months, IFR en route charts each 56 days, and amendments to civil IFR approach charts are accomplished on a 56-day cycle with a change notice volume issued on the 28 day mid-cycle. Charts that have been supersedede by those of a more recent date may contain obsolete or incomplete flight information.

f. When telephoning for information, use the following procedure:

(1) Identify yourself as a pilot. (Many persons calling WB stations want information for purposes other than flying.)

(2) State your intended route, destination, proposed departure time, estimated time en route and type of aircraft.

(3) Advise if you intend to fly only VFR.

(4) When talking to an FSS, you will be asked your aircraft identification for activity record purposes.

NOTE.—Telephone briefings by the specialist may be monitored and/or recorded by management personnel on an unscheduled basis for purposes of quality control training or evaluation of specialist performance.

g. In addition to the filing of a flight plan, if the flight will traverse or land in one or more foreign countries, it is particularly important that pilots leave a complete itinerary with someone directly concerned, keep that person advised of the flight's progress and inform him that, if serious doubt arises as to the safety of the flight, he should first contact the FSS.

h. Pilots operating under provisions of FAR Part 135, ATCO, certificate and not having an FAA assigned 3-letter designator, are urged to prefix the normal registration (N) number with the letter "T" on flight plan filing (e.g., TN1234B).

291. NOTICE TO AIRMEN (NOTAM) SYSTEM

a. Time-critical aeronautical information which is of a temporary nature or is not sufficiently known in advance to permit publication on aeronautical charts or in other operational publications, receives immediate dissemination via the National Notice to Airmen (NOTAM) Service A telecommunications system.

b. Information maintained as NOTAM is categorized into two types. They are the NOTAM-D and the NOTAM-L categories.

(1) NOTAM-D information is that information which could affect a pilot's decision to make a flight. It includes such information as primary runway or airport closure, interruptions in service of navigational aids, instrument landing systems, radar service availability, and other information essential to planned enroute, terminal or landing operations. NOTAM-D information is disseminated for all navigational facilities, all IFR airports with approved Instrument Approach Procedures and for those VFR airports annotated with the symbol § in the Airport/Facility Directory. NOTAM-D information is maintained in the Kansas City National Communications Center computer data base for the length of its validity or until its publication. NOTAM-D information is distributed automatically by the National Communications Center, according to predetermined address listings, to both local and distant air traffic facilities. All facilities, however, do have immediate access upon request to all NOTAM-D information on file in the National Communications Center computer data base via the Notice to Airmen telecommunications system.

(2) NOTAM-L information is that information which is of an advisory, or nice to know, nature. It includes such information as taxiway closings, men and equipment near, or crossing, runways, and information on airports not annotated with the symbol § in the Airport/Facility Directory. NOTAM-L information is maintained on file only at those local air traffic facilities concerned with the operations at these airports. NOTAM-L information, however, can be made available upon specific request to the local Flight Service Station having responsibility for the airport concerned.

c. On those occasions when it becomes necessary to disseminate information which is regulatory in nature, such as to amend current aeronautical charts, Instrument Approach Procedures, or to effect restrictions to flight, the National Flight Data Center in Washington, D.C., will issue the NOTAM containing the regulatory information as an FDC NOTAM. FDC NOTAMs are distributed through the National Communications Center in Kansas City, for transmission to all air traffic facilities having telecommunications access.

d. An integral part of the Notice to Airmen (NOTAM) system is the biweekly Notice to Airmen (Class II)* publication. This publication contains three basic subdivisions, or parts.

> * NOTE.—The term Class II refers to the fact that the NOTAMs, or notices, appear in printed form for mail distribution as opopsed to NOTAMs which are distributed via telecommunications. The latter are considered Class I.

(1) The first part consists of notices which meet the criteria for NOTAM (D) and are expected to remain in effect for an extended period. These NOTAMs are included to reduce congestion on the teletype circuits. NOTAM(L) and, occasionally, special notices are included when their inclusion will contribute to flight safety. All information contained in the publication will be carried until the information becomes expired, is cancelled or, in the case of permanent information, is published in other permanent publications, such as the Airport/Facility Directory. All new notices entered into this part will be included only if the information contained is expected to remain in effect for at least seven days after the effective date of the publication.

(2) The second part contains all FDC NOTAMS which were current at the time of publication. The number of the last FDC NOTAM included in the publication is noted to aid the user in updating the listing contained with any FDC NOTAMs which may have been issued after publication.

(3) The third part contains notices that, either because they are too long or because they concern a wide or unspecified geographic area, are not suitable for inclusion in the first part of this publication. The content of these notices vary widely and there are not specific criteria for their inclusion, other than their enhancement of flight safety.

292. FLIGHT PLAN—VFR FLIGHTS

a. Except for operations in or penetrating a Coastal or Domestic ADIZ or DEWIZ, a flight plan is not required for VFR flight; however, it is strongly recommended that one be filed.

b. To obtain maximum benefits of the flight plan program, flight plans should be filed directly with the nearest flight service station. For your convenience, FSSs provide one-call (telephone/interphone) or one-stop (personal) aeronautical and meteorological briefings while accepting flight plans. Radio may be used to file if no other means are available. Also, some states operate aeronautical communications facilities which will accept and forward flight plans to the FSS for further handling.

c. When a "stopover" flight is anticipated to cover an extended period of time, it is recommended that a separate flight plan be filed for each "leg" when the stop is expected to be more than one hour duration.

d. Pilots are encouraged to give their departure times directly to the flight service station with which the flight plan was filed. This will ensure more efficient flight plan service and permit the FSS to advise you of significant changes in aeronautical facilities or meteorological conditions. The following procedures are in effect: when a VFR flight plan is filed, it will be held until one hour after the proposed departure time and then canceled unless:

(1) The actual departure time is received.

(2) A revised proposed departure time is received.

(3) At a time of filing, the FSS is informed that the proposed departure time will be met, but actual time cannot be given because of inadequate communications.

e. On pilot's request, at a location having an active tower, the aircraft identification will be forwarded to the tower for reporting the actual departure time. This procedure should be avoided at busy airports.

f. Although position reports are not required for VFR flight plans, periodic reports to FAA Flight Service Stations along the route are good practice. Such contacts permit significant information to be passed to the transiting aircraft and also serve to check the progress of the flight should it be necessary for any reason to locate the aircraft.

Examples:

(1) Bonanza 314K, over Kingfisher at (time), VFR flight plan, Tulsa to Amarillo.

(2) Cherokee 5133J, over Oklahoma City at (time), Shreveport to Denver, no flight plan.

g. Pilots not operating on an IFR flight plan, and when in level cruising flight, are cautioned to conform with VFR cruising altitudes appropriate to direction of flight. During climb or descent, pilots are encouraged to fly to the right side of the center line of the radial forming the airway in order to avoid IFR and VFR cruising traffic operating along the center line of the airway.

h. Indicate aircraft equipment capabilities when filing VFR flight plans by appending the appropriate suffix to aircraft type in the same manner as that prescribed for IFR flight (see 295—FLIGHT PLAN-IFR FLIGHTS). Under some circumstances, ATC computer tapes can be useful in constructing the radar history of a downed or crashed aircraft. In each case, knowledge of the aircraft's transponder equipment is necessary in determining whether or not such computer tapes might prove effective.

293. FLIGHT PLAN—DEFENSE VFR (DVFR) FLIGHTS

VFR flights into a Coastal or Domestic ADIZ/DEWIZ are required to file a VFR flight plan for security purposes. Detailed ADIZ procedures are found in the National Security section of this chapter. (See FAR 99.)

294. COMPOSITE FLIGHT PLAN (VFR–IFR) FLIGHTS

a. Flight plans which specify VFR operation for one portion of a flight, and IFR for another portion, will be accepted by the FSS at the point of departure. If VFR flight is conducted for the first portion of the flight, the pilot should report his departure time to the FSS with which he filed his VFR/IFR flight plan; and, subsequently, close the VFR portion and request ATC clearance from the FSS nearest the point at which change from VFR to IFR is proposed. Regardless of the type facility you are communicating with (FSS, center, or tower), it is the pilot's responsibility to request that facility to "CLOSE VFR FLIGHT PLAN." The pilot must remain in VFR weather conditions until operating in accordance with the IFR clearance.

b. When a flight plan indicates IFR for the first portion of flight and VFR for the latter portion, the pilot will normally be cleared to the point at which the change is proposed. Once the pilot has reported over the clearance limit and does not desire further IFR clearance, he should advise Air Traffic Control to cancel the IFR portion of his flight plan. Further clearance will not be necessary for VFR flight beyond that point. If the pilot desires to continue his IFR flight plan beyond the clearance limit, he should contact Air Traffic Control at least five minutes prior to the clearance limit and request further IFR clearance. If the requested clearance is not received prior to reaching the clearance limit fix, the pilot will be expected to establish himself in a standard holding pattern on the radial/course to the fix unless a holding pattern for the clearance limit fix is depicted on a U.S. Government or commercially produced (meeting FAA requirements) low/high altitude en route, area or STAR chart. In this case the pilot will hold according to the depicted pattern.

295. FLIGHT PLAN—IFR FLIGHTS

a. GENERAL

(1) Prior to departure from within, or prior to entering controlled airspace, a pilot must submit a complete flight plan and receive an air traffic clearance, if weather conditions are below VFR minimums. Instrument flight plans may be submitted to the nearest Flight Service Stations or airport traffic control tower either in person or by telephone (or by radio if no other means are available). Pilots should file IFR flight plans at least 30 minutes prior to estimated time of departure to preclude possible delay in receiving a departure clearance from ATC. To minimize your delay in entering the control zone at destination when IFR weather conditions exist or are forecast at that airport, an IFR flight plan should be filed before departure. Otherwise, a 30-minute delay is not unusual in receiving an ATC clearance because of time spent in processing flight plan data. Traffic saturation frequently prevents control personnel from accepting flight plans by radio. In such cases, the pilot is advised to contact the nearest flight service station for the purpose of filing the flight plan.

NOTE.—There are several methods of obtaining IFR clearances at non-tower, non-flight service stations, and outlying airports. The procedure may vary due to geographical features, weather conditions, and the complexity of the ATC system. To determine the most effective means of receiving an IFR clearance, pilots should ask the nearest flight service station the most appropriate means of obtaining the IFR clearance.

(2) When filing an IFR flight Plan for a 'Heavy' aircraft, add the prefix H to the aircraft type.

Example:

H/DC10/U

(3) When filing an IFR flight plan for flight in an aircraft equipped with a radar beacon transponder, DME equipment, TACAN-only equipment or a combination of both, identify equipment capability by adding a suffix to the AIRCRAFT TYPE preceded by a slant, as follows:

/X   no transponder.

/T   transponder with no altitude encoding capability.

/U   transponder with altitude encoding capability.

/D   DME, no transponder.

/B   DME, transponder with no altitude encoding capability.

/A   DME, transponder with altitude encoding capability.

/M   TACAN-only, no transponder.

/N   TACAN-only, transponder with no altitude encoding capability.

/P   TACAN-only, transponder with altitude encoding capability.

/C   RNAV, transponder with no altitude encoding capability.

/F   RNAV, transponder with altitude encoding capability.

/W   RNAV, no transponder.

NOTE.—RNAV refers to airborne area navigation systems certificated for flying RNAV routes in accordance with FAA Advisory Circular 90-45A.

(4) It is recommended that pilots file the maximum transponder/navigation capability of their aircraft in the equipment suffix. This will provide air traffic control with the necessary information to utilize all facets of navigational equipment and transponder capabilities available. In the case of area navigation equipped aircraft which have been certificated in accordance with Advisory Circular 90–45A, pilots should file on the flight plan the /C, /F, or /W capability of the aircraft even though an area navigation route has not been requested. This will ensure ATC awareness in the event an area navigation route is available and may be utilized to expedite the flight.

NOTE.—The suffix is not to be added to the aircraft identification or be transmitted by radio as part of the aircraft identification.

b. AIRWAYS/JET ROUTES DEPICTION ON FLIGHT PLAN

(1) It is vitally important that the route of flight be accurately and completely described in the flight plan. To simplify definition of the proposed route, and to facilitate air traffic control, pilots are requested to file via airways or jet routes established for use at the altitude or flight level planned.

(a) If flight is to be conducted via designated airways or jet routes, describe the route by indicating the type and number of the airway(s) or jet route(s) requested. If more than one airway or jet route is to be used, clearly indicate points of transition. If the transition is made at an unnamed intersection, show the next succeeding navaid or named intersection on the intended route and the complete route from that point. Reporting points may be identified by using authorized Location Identifiers; however, if these are not known, the name of the reporting point should be used.

Example 1:

FL 250 ALB J37 ATL J14 BHM

Spelled Out: Requesting Flight Level 250 from Albany, New York, via Jet Route 37 to Atlanta, Georgia, and Jet Route 14 to Birmingham, Alabama.

Example 2:

FL 250 ALB J37 ENO J14 RIC J14 BHM

Spelled Out: Requesting Flight Level 250 from Albany, New York, via Jet Route 37 and Jet Route 14 to Richmond, Virginia, (transitioning to Jet Route 14 at Kenton VORTAC (ENO) thence via Jet Route 14 to Birmingham, Alabama.

(b) The route of flight may also be described by naming the reporting points over which the flight will pass, provided the points named are established for use at the altitude/flight level planned (see DIRECT FLIGHTS).

Example:

30 DCA RVD BAL

Spelled Out: Requesting 3000 feet from Washington National, via direct Riverdale direct Baltimore-Washington International.

(c) When the route of flight is defined by named reporting points, whether alone or in combination with airways or jet routes, and the navigational aids (VOR, VORTAC, TACAN, LF, RBN) to be used for the flight are a combination of different types of aids, enough information should be included to clearly indicate the route requested.

Example:

FL 310 LAX J5 LKV J3 GEG YXC FL 330 HL500 VLR HL515 YWG

Spelled Out: Requesting Flight Level 310 from Los Angeles International via Jet Route 5 Lakeview, Jet Route 3 Spokane, direct Kimberly, British Columbia Low Frequency Range, Flight Level 330 High Level Airway 500 to Langruth, Manitoba VOR, High Level Airway 515 to Winnepeg, Manitoba.

(d) When filing IFR, it is to the pilots' advantage to file a "preferred route."

(e) ATC may issue Standard Instrument Departure (SID) or a Standard Terminal Arrival Route (STAR) as appropriate. (See Instrument Departure in the DEPARTURES—IFR section and Standard Terminal Arrival Routes in the ENROUTE—IFR section.)

NOTE.—Pilots not desiring a SID/STAR should so indicate in the remark section of the flight plan as "NO SID" or "NO STAR."

c. DIRECT FLIGHTS

(1) All or any portions of the route which will not be flown on the radials/courses of established airways or routes, e.g., direct route flights, must be defined by indicating the radio fixes over which the flight will pass. Fixes selected to define the route shall be those over which the position of the aircraft can be accurately determined. Such fixes automatically become compulsory reporting points for the flight, unless advised otherwise by ATC. Only those navigational aids established for use in a particular structure, i.e., in the Low or High structures, may be used to define the en route phase of a direct flight within that structure.

(2) The azimuth feature of VOR aids and the azimuth and distance (DME) features of VORTAC/TACAN aids are assigned certain frequency protected areas of airspace which are intended for application to established airway and route use, and to provide guidance for planning flights outside of established airways or routes. These areas of airspace are expressed in terms of cylindrical service volumes of specified dimensions called "class limits" or "categories." An operational service volume has been established for each class in which adequate signal coverage and frequency protection can be assured. To facilitate use of VOR, VORTAC or TACAN aids, consistent with their operational service volume limits, pilot use of such aids for defining a direct route of flight in controlled airspace should not exceed the following:

(a) Operations above Flight Level 450-use aids not more than 200 nautical miles apart. These aids are depicted on the En Route High Altitude Chart-U.S.

(b) Operation off established routes from 18,000 feet MSL to Flight Level 450-use aids not more than 260 nautical miles apart. These aids are depicted on the En Route High Altitude Chart—U.S.

(c) Operation off established airways below 18,000 feet MSL—use aids not more than 80 nautical miles apart. These aids are depicted on the En Route, Low Altitude Chart—U.S.

(d) Operation off established airways between 14,500 feet MSL and 17,999 feet MSL in the conterminous United States—(H) facilities not more than 200 NM apart may be used.

(3) Increasing use of self-contained airborne navigational systems which do not rely on the VOR/VORTAC/TACAN system has resulted in pilot requests for direct routes which exceed NAVAID service volume limits. These direct route requests will be approved only in a radar environment, with approval based on pilot responsibility for navigation on the authorized direct route. "Radar flight following" will be provided by ATC for air traffic control purposes.

(4) At times, ATC will initiate a direct route in a radar environment which exceeds NAVAID service volume limits. In such cases ATC will provide "radar monitoring" and navigational assistance as necessary.

(5) Airway or jet route numbers, appropriate to the stratum in which operation will be conducted, may also be included to describe portions of the route to be flown.

Example:

140 MDW V262 BDF V10 BRL STJ SLN GCK

Spelled Out: Requesting 14,000 feet from Chicago Midway Airport via Victor 262 to Bradford, Victor 10 to Burlington, Iowa, direct St. Joseph, Missouri, direct Salina, Kansas, direct Garden City Kansas.

NOTE.—When route of flight is described by radio fixes, the pilot will be expected to fly a direct course between the points named.

(6) Pilots are reminded that they are responsible for adhering to obstruction clearance requirements on those segments of direct routes that are outside of controlled airspace. The MEA's and other altitudes shown on low altitude IFR enroute charts pertain to those route segments within controlled airspace, and those altitudes may not meet obstruction clearance criteria when oper-

ating off those routes. When planning a direct flight, check your Sectional or other VFR charts too!

d. AREA NAVIGATION (RNAV) ROUTES

(1) Some aircraft are equipped with approved area navigation systems that permit direct flight via a selected course to a predefined point without having to fly directly toward or away from a navigational aid. This capability is commonly termed RNAV and routes have been established or designated to accommodate such direct flights. Pilots of RNAV certificated aircraft have the option of filing and operating in accordance with established or designated route criteria or may file for random (impromptu) RNAV routes.

(2) The complexities involved in determining route width, with reference to facility usable distance, requires that random RNAV routes only be approved in a radar environment. ATC will radar monitor each flight, however, navigation on the random RNAV route is the responsibility of the pilot. Factors that will be considered by ATC in approving random RNAV routes, include the capability to provide radar monitoring and compatibility with traffic volume and flow. When operationally feasible, pilots are urged to file established or designated RNAV routes in lieu of random RNAV routes.

(3) Pilots requesting ATC clearance for random RNAV routes are expected to do the following:

(a) File airport to airport flight plans prior to departure.

(b) File the appropriate RNAV capability certification suffix in the flight plan.

(c) Plan the random route portion of the flight plan to begin and end over appropriate arrival/departure transition fixes or appropriate navigation aids for the altitude stratum within which the flight will be conducted.

(d) File route structure transitions to and from the random route portion in the flight plan. The use of normal preferred departure and arrival routes, such as SID/STAR where established, is recommended.

(e) Define random routes by waypoints. File route description waypoints by using degree-distance in reference to navigation aids for the appropriate altitude stratum.

(f) File a minimum of one route description waypoint for each ARTC Center's area over which the random portion of flight will be conducted. Such waypoints must be located within 200 NM of the boundary of the preceding centers flight advisory area.

(g) File an additional route description waypoint for each turnpoint in the route.

(h) Though not required in the flight plan, plan additional waypoints necessary to ensure accurate navigation via the file route of flight. Navigation is the pilot's responsibility unless ATC assistance is requested.

(i) Plan the route of flight so as to avoid Prohibited and Nonjoint use Restricted Airspace unless pilots have obtained permission to operate in that airspace and so informs the appropriate ATC facility. Avoid flight planning through other uncontrolled airspace unless specifically desiring flight through such airspace.

e. VFR OPERATIONS ON IFR FLIGHT PLAN

(1) A pilot on an IFR flight plan operating in VFR weather conditions above a cloud, haze, smoke, or other meteorological formation may request "VFR Conditions On Top" in lieu of an assigned altitude. This would permit the pilot to select an altitude/flight level of his choice. Upon receiving authorization from ATC to maintain "VFR Conditions On Top," the pilot is now concerned with adhering to both the IFR and the VFR Flight Rules as follows:

(a) If operating more than 3,000 feet above the surface, he is expected to fly at a VFR altitude/flight level appropriate for the direction of flight and to keep ATC advised of his altitude/flight level.

(b) Flight must be conducted in VFR weather conditions.

(c) ATC may issue traffic information of other pertinent IFR traffic, however, they do not provide separation between the "VFR-on-top" pilot and other aircraft. Remember, it is the pilot's responsibility to avoid other aircraft when operating in VFR weather conditions or on a "VFR Conditions On Top" clearance.

(d) The pilot is required to adhere to IFR Flight Rules that are applicable to any IFR flight: minimum IFR altitudes, position reporting, radio communications, change in flight plan notification, adherence to ATC clearance.

(e) ATC will not authorize "VFR Conditions On Top" operation in positive control areas. Requirements for operating in positive control areas defined in the Airspace Chapter of this manual.

(2) Departing instrument-rated pilots who wish an IFR clearance only to climb through a layer of overcast or reduced visibility, and then continue flight VFR may request ATC clearance "TO VFR CONDITIONS ON TOP". This request may be made through a Flight Service Station, by telephone to ATC, or by request to the Tower before taxiing out. The clearance, which authorizes IFR flight through the cloud layer, will contain a near-by clearance limit, routing, and a request to report reaching "VFR CONDITIONS ON TOP". When the pilot reaches "VFR CONDITIONS ON TOP" and desires to cancel the IFR portion of his flight, he should so state. This type of operation can be combined with a VFR Flight Plan to destination.

296–299. RESERVED

300. CHANGE IN FLIGHT PLAN

In addition to altitude/flight level, destination and/or route changes, increasing or decreasing the speed of an aircraft constitutes a change in a flight plan. Therefore, at any time the average true airspeed at cruising altitude between reporting points varies or is expected to vary from that given in the flight plan by *plus or minus 5 percent, or 10 knots, whichever is greater*, air traffic control should be advised.

301. CHANGE IN PROPOSED DEPARTURE TIME

a. To prevent computer saturation in the en route environment, time out parameters have been established to delete non-activated proposed departure flight plans. Most centers have this parameter set so as to delete these flight plans a minimum of 1 hour after the proposed departure time. To ensure flight plan remains active, pilots whose actual departure time will be delayed 1 hour or more beyond their filed departure time, are requested to notify ATC of their departure time.

b. Due to traffic saturation, control personnel frequently will be unable to accept these revisions via radio. It is recommended that you forward these revisions to the nearest flight service station.

302. CLOSING VFR/DVFR FLIGHT PLANS

A pilot is responsible for ensuring that his VFR or DVFR flight plan is cancelled (See FAR 91.83). You should close your flight plan with the nearest Flight Service Station, or if one is not available you may request any ATC facility to relay your cancellation to the FSS. *Control towers do not automatically close VFR or DVFR flight plans* as they may not be aware that a particular VFR aircraft is on a flight plan. If you fail to report or cancel your flight plan within ½ hour after your ETA, Search and Rescue procedures are started.

303. CANCELLING IFR FLIGHT PLAN

a. FAR 91.83 includes the statement "When a flight plan has been filed, the pilot in command, upon cancelling or completing the flight under the flight plan, shall notify the nearest Flight Service Station or ATC facility."

b. An IFR flight plan may be cancelled at any time the flight is operating in VFR conditions outside positive controlled airspace by the pilot stating "CANCEL MY IFR FLIGHT PLAN" to the controller or air/ground station with which he is communicating. Immediately after cancelling an IFR flight plan, a pilot should take necessary action to change to appropriate: air/ground frequency; VFR radar beacon code; VFR altitude/flight level. ATC separation and information services will be discontinued, including radar services (where applicable). Consequently, if the cancelling flight desires VFR radar advisory service the pilot must specifically request it. In addition, pilots must be aware that other procedures may be applicable to a flight that cancels an IFR flight plan within an area where a special program has been established, e.g., a designated Terminal Radar Service Area or Terminal Control Area.

c. If a DVFR flight plan requirement exists the pilot is responsible for filing this flight plan to replace the cancelled IFR flight plan. If a subsequent IFR operation becomes necessary, a new IFR flight plan must be filed and an ATC clearance obtained before operating in IFR conditions.

d. If operating on an IFR flight plan to an airport with a functioning control tower, the flight plan is automatically closed upon landing.

e. If operating on an IFR flight plan to an airport where there is no functioning control tower, the pilot must initiate cancellation of the IFR flight plan. This can be done after landing if .there is a functioning Flight Service Station or other means of direct communications with ATC. In the event there is no Flight Service Station and air/ground communications with ATC is not possible below a certain altitude, the pilot should, weather conditions permitting, cancel his IFR flight plan while still airborne and able to communicate with ATC by radio. This will not only save the time and expense of cancelling the flight plan by telephone but will quickly release the airspace for use by other aircraft.

304. GENERAL INSTRUCTIONS FOR THE FAA FLIGHT PLAN FORM

a. Explanation of Flight Plan Items.

Block 1. Check the type flight plan. Check both the VFR and IFR blocks if composite VFR/IFR.

*†Block 2. Enter your complete aircraft identification including the prefix "N" if applicable.

*†Block 3. Enter the designator for the aircraft or, if unknown, the aircraft manufacturer's name (e.g., Cessna); followed by a slant (/) and the transponder/DME equipment code letter (e.g., C–182/U).

*Block 4. Enter your computer true airspeed. (If IFR and the average TAS changes plus or minus 5 percent or 10 knots, whichever is greater, advise ATC).

*Block 5. Enter the departure point/airport identifier code (or the name if identifier is unknown) (Note: Use of identifier codes will expedite the processing of your flight plan.)

*Block 6. Enter the proposed departure time in Greenwich Mean Time (GMT) (Z). If airborne, specify the actual or proposed departure time as appropriate.

*Block 7. VFR: enter the appropriate VFR altitude (to assist the briefer in providing weather/wind information).

IFR: Enter the requested enroute altitude or flight level. When more than one altitude/flight level is desired along the route of flight, it is best to make a subsequent reqest direct to the controller.

*Block 8. Define the route of flight by using navaid/identifier codes (or names if the code is unknown), airways, jet routes, and waypoints (for RNAV). Use navaids or waypoints to define direct routes and radials/bearings to define other unpublished routes.

*†Block 9. Enter the destination airport identifier code (or name if identifier is unknokn). Include the city name (or even the state name) if needed for clarity.

*†Block 10. Enter your estimated time enroute based on latest forecast winds.

*Block 11. Enter only those remarks pertinent to ATC or to the clarification of other flight plan information. Items of a personnel nature are not accepted. Do not assume that remarks will be automatically transmitted to every controller. Specific requests should be made to the appropriate controller.

Block 12. Specify the fuel on board computed from the departure point.

Block 13. Specify an alternate airport if desired or required. (Do NOT include routing.)

Block 14. Enter your complete name, address, and telephone number. Enter sufficient information to identify home base, airport, or operator. This information would be essential in the event of search and rescue operation.

Block 15. Enter the total number of persons on board including crew.

Block 16. Enter the predominant color(s).

Last Block. For VFR flight plans, record the FSS name for closing the flight plan. If the flight plan is closed with a different FSS or facility, state the recorded FSS name that would normally have closed your flight plan. (Close IFR flight plans with tower, approach control, or ARTCC's, or if unable, with FSS. When landing at an airport with a functioning control tower, IFR flight plans are automatically cancelled.)

†Indicates information transmitted to destination FSS for VFR Flight Plans. (ETE is converted to an ETA for VFR Flight Plans.)

*Indicates information transmitted to the ARTCC for IFR Flight Plans—(Note: The destination FSS does NOT receive information on civil IFR Flight Plans. If you "cancel IFR" with ATC, your flight plan is closed, and you must file a VFR flight plan with FSS if you desire to remain on a flight plan.)

b. A description of the International Flight Plan Form is contained in the International Flight Information Manual.

c. Flight Plan Form.

Form Approved: OMB No. 04-R0072

| DEPARTMENT OF TRANSPORTATION FEDERAL AVIATION ADMINISTRATION **FLIGHT PLAN** | CIVIL AIRCRAFT PILOTS. FAR Part 91 requires you file an IFR flight plan to operate under instrument flight rules in controlled airspace. Failure to file could result in a civil penalty not to exceed $1,000 for each violation (Section 901 of the Federal Aviation Act of 1958, as amended). Filing of a VFR flight plan is recommended as a good operating practice. See also Part 99 for requirements concerning DVFR flight plans. |

1. TYPE	2. AIRCRAFT IDENTIFICATION	3. AIRCRAFT TYPE/ SPECIAL EQUIPMENT	4. TRUE AIRSPEED	5. DEPARTURE POINT	6. DEPARTURE TIME		7. CRUISING ALTITUDE
VFR IFR DVFR			KTS		PROPOSED (Z)	ACTUAL (Z)	

8. ROUTE OF FLIGHT

9. DESTINATION (Name of airport and city)	10. EST. TIME ENROUTE		11. REMARKS
	HOURS	MINUTES	

12. FUEL ON BOARD		13. ALTERNATE AIRPORT(S)	14. PILOT'S NAME, ADDRESS & TELEPHONE NUMBER & AIRCRAFT HOME BASE	15. NUMBER ABOARD
HOURS	MINUTES			

16. COLOR OF AIRCRAFT	**CLOSE VFR FLIGHT PLAN WITH**_____**FSS ON ARRIVAL**

FAA Form 7233-1 (5-77)

305–319. RESERVED

320. PRE-TAXI CLEARANCE PROCEDURES

a. Certain airports have established programs whereby pilots of departing IFR aircraft may elect to receive their IFR clearances before they start taxiing for takeoff. The following provisions are included in such procedures:

(1) Pilot participation is not mandatory.

(2) Participating pilots call clearance delivery/ground control not more than 10 minutes before proposed taxi time.

(3) IFR clearance (or delay information, if clearance cannot be obtained) is issued at the time of this initial call-up.

(4) When the IFR clearance is received on clearance delivery frequency, pilots call ground control when ready to taxi.

(5) Normally, pilots need not inform ground control that they have received IFR clearance on clearance delivery frequency. Certain locations may, however, require that the pilot inform ground control of a portion of his routing or that he has received his IFR clearance.

(6) If a pilot cannot establish contact on clearance delivery frequency or has not received his IFR clearance before he is ready to taxi, he contacts ground control and informs the controller accordingly.

b. Location where these procedures are in effect are indicated in the Airport/Facility Directory.

321. TAXI CLEARANCE

Pilots on IFR flight plans should communicate with the control tower on the appropriate ground control/clearance delivery frequency prior to starting engines to receive engine start time, taxi and/or clearance information.

322. ABBREVIATED IFR DEPARTURE CLEARANCE (CLEARED . . . AS FILED) PROCEDURES

a. ATC facilities will issue an abbreviated IFR departure clearance based on the ROUTE of flight filed in the IFR flight plan, provided the filed route can be approved with little or no revision. These abbreviated clearance procedures are based on the following conditions:

(1) The aircraft is on the ground or it has departed VFR and the pilot is requesting IFR clearance while airborne.

(2) That a pilot will not accept an abbreviated clearance if the route or destination of a flight plan filed with ATC has been changed by him or the company or the operations officer before departure.

(3) That it is the responsibility of the company or operations office to inform the pilot when they make a change to the filed flight plan.

(4) That is the responsibility of the pilot to inform ATC in his initial call-up (for clearance) when the filed flight plan has been (1) amended or (2) cancelled and replaced with a new filed flight plan.

NOTE: The facility issuing a clearance may not have received the revised route or the revised flight plan by the time a pilot requests clearance.

b. The controller will issue a detailed clearance when he knows that the original filed flight plan has been changed or when the pilot requests a full route clearance.

c. The clearance as issued will include the destination airport filed in the flight plan.

d. ATC procedures now require the controller to state the SID name, the current number and the SID Transition name in addition to the phrase "Cleared (to destination) airport as filed" for ALL departure clearances when the SID or SID Transition is to be flown. The procedure applies whether or not the SID is filed in the flight plan.

e. STARs, when filed in a flight plan, are considered a part of the filed route of flight and will not normally be stated in an initial departure clearance. If the ARTCC's jurisdictional airspace includes both the departure airport and the fix where a STAR or STAR Transition begins, the STAR name, the current number and the STAR Transition name MAY be stated in the initial clearance.

f. "Cleared to (destination) airport as filed" does NOT include the enroute altitude filed in a flight plan. An enroute altitude will be stated in the clearance or the pilot will be advised to expect an assigned/filed altitude within a given time frame or at a certain point after departure. This may be done verbally in the departure instructions or stated in the SID.

g. In a radar and a non-radar environment, the controlelr will state "Cleared to (destination) airport as filed" and:

(1) If a SID or SID Transition is to be flown, specify the SID name, the current SID number, the SID Transition name, the assigned altitude/flight level, and any additional instructions (departure control frequency, beacon code assignment etc.) necessary to clear a departing aircraft via the SID/SID Transition and the route filed.

Example:

National Seven Twenty Cleared to Miami Airport As Filed, Intercontinental One Departure, Lake Charles Transition, Maintain Flight Level Two Seven Zero.

(2) When there is no SID or when the pilot cannot accept a SID, specify the assigned altitude/flight level, and any additional instructons necessary to clear a departing aircraft via an appropriate departure routing and the route filed.

NOTE: A detailed departure route description or a radar vector may be used to achieve the desired departure routing.

(3) If necessary to make a minor revision to the filed route, specify the assigned SID/SID Transition (or departure routing), the revision to the filed route, the assigned altitude/flight level and any additional instructions necessary to clear a departing aircraft.

Example:

Jet Star One Four Two Four Cleared to Atlanta As Filed Except Change Route to Read South Boston Victor 20 Greensboro, South Boston Two Departure, Maintain Flight Level Two Three Zero.

(4) Additionally, in a non-radar environment, specify one or more fixes as necessary to identify the initial route of flight.

Example:

Cessna Three One Six Zero Foxtrot Cleared to Charlotte Airport As Filed Via Brooke, Maintain Seven Thousand.

h. To ensure success of the program, pilots should.

(1) Avoid making changes to a filed flight plan just prior to departure.

(2) State the following information in the initial call-up to the facility when no change has been made to the filed flight plan: Aircraft call sign, location, type operation (IFR) and the name of the airport (or fix) to which you expect clearance.

Example:

"WASHINGTON CLEARANCE DELIVERY (OR GROUND CONTROL IF APPROPRIATE) THIS IS AMERICAN SEVENTY SIX AT GATE ONE, IFR LOS ANGELES."

(3) If the flight plan has been changed, state the change and request a full route clearance.

Example:

"WASHINGTON CLEARANCE DELIVERY, THIS IS AMERICAN SEVENTY SIX AT GATE ONE IFR SAN FRANCISCO MY FLIGHT PLAN ROUTE HAS BEEN AMENDED (OR DESTINATION CHANGED) REQUEST FULL ROUTE CLEARANCE."

(4) Request verification or clarification from ATC if ANY portion of the clearance is not clearly understood.

(5) When requesting clearance for the IFR portion of a VFR-IFR flight, request such clearance prior to the fix where IFR operation is proposed to commence in sufficient time to avoid delay. Use the following phraseology:

Example:

"LOS ANGELES CENTER, THIS IS APACHE SIX ONE PAPA, VFR ESTIMATING PASO ROBLES VOR AT THREE TWO, ONE THOUSAND FIVE HUNDRED, REQUEST IFR TO BAKERSFIELD."

323. CLEARANCE VOID TIMES

a. If operating from an airport not served by a control tower, the pilot may receive a clearance containing a provision that if the flight has not departed by a specific time, the clearance is void. In this situation, the pilot who does not depart prior to the void time must advise ATC as soon as possible, but no later than 30 minutes, of his intentions.

b. Failure to take this action can result in costly delays and reroutes of other IFR traffic because ATC will take action on the assumption that the pilot departed as cleared. Additionally, extensive search and rescue operations may be initiated if nothing is heard from the pilot after he accepts the ATC clearance.

c. Example:

CLEARANCE VOID IF NOT OFF BY (time). IF NOT OFF BY (clearance void time) ADVISE (facility) NOT LATER THAN (time) OF INTENTIONS.

324. DEPARTURE CONTROL

a. Departure Control is an approach control function responsible for ensuring separation between departures. So as to expedite the handling of departures, Departure Control may sugest a take-off direction other than that which may normally have been used under VFR handling. Many times it is preferred to offer the pilot a runway that will require the fewest turns after take-off to place the pilot on his filed course or selected departure route as quickly as possible. At many locations particular attention is paid to the use of preferential runways for local noise abatement programs, and route departures away from congested areas.

b. Departure Control utilizing radar will normally clear aircraft out of the terminal area using standard instrument departures (SID) via radio navigation aids. When a departure is to be vectored immediately following takeoff, the pilot will be advised prior to take-off of the initial heading to be flown but may not be advised of the purpose of the heading. Pilots operating in a radar environment are expected to associate departure headings with vectors to their planned route or flight. When given a vector taking his aircraft off a previously assigned nonradar route, the pilot will be advised briefly what the vector is to achieve. There after, radar service will be provided until the aircraft has been re-established "on-course" using an appropriate navigation aid and the pilot has been advised of his position; or, a handoff is made to another radar controller with further surveillance capabilities.

c. Controllers will inform pilots of the departure control frequencies and, if appropriate, the transponder code before take-off. Pilots should not operate their transponder until ready to start the take-off roll or change to the departure control frequency until requested.

325. INSTRUMENT DEPARTURES

a. STANDARD INSTRUMENT DEPARTURES (SIDS)

(1) A Standard Instrument Departure (SID) is an air traffic control coded departure procedure which has been established at certain airports to simplify clearance delivery procedures.

(2) Pilots of civil aircraft operating from locations where SID procedures are effective may expect ATC clearances containing a SID. Use of a SID requires pilot possession of at least the textual description of the approved effective SID. If the pilot does not possess a preprinted SID description or for any other reason does not wish to use a SID, he is expected to advise ATC. Notification may be accomplished by filing "NO SID" in the remarks section of the filed flight plan or by the less desirable method of verbally advising ATC.

(3) All effective SIDs are published in textual and graphic form by the National Ocean Survey in East and West SID booklets.

b. OBSTRUCTION CLEARANCE DURING DEPARTURE

(1) IFR departure procedures have been established to assist the pilots conducting IFR flight in avoiding obstructions during climbout to minimum enroute altitude. These procedures are established only at locations where instrument approach procedures are published and when required due to obstructions.

DEPARTURES—IFR

(2) These procedures may be a weather ceiling and visibility requirement due to obstructions close in to the airport, or detailed flight maneuvers particularly at locations in mountainous terrain. In many cases obstruction avoidance procedures are incorporated into established SIDs and the SID is referenced as the obstruction avoidance procedure. In this case when a pilot desires to utilize the SID, it should be filed in the flight plan as the first item of the requested routing.

(3) Crossing restrictions used in a SID may be established for traffic separation or to assist the pilot in obstacle avoidance. When a crossing restriction is established for either reason, pilots are expected to cross the fix as charted and continue to make good a minimum climb of 152 feet per mile after crossing the fix until reaching the MEA or assigned altitude. A SID without a crossing restriction or an accelerated climb requirement will have no penetrations of the 40:1 departure surface (152'/mile) overlying the departure area.

(4) Instrument take-off minimums and departure procedures are published with U.S. Government instrument approach procedure charts. These are described in airport listings on separate pages included with each area approach chart book. Only those airports having non-standard take-off minimums or prescribed departure procedures are listed. The approach charts for such airports will display the symbol ▼ in the space beneath the minimums section to indicate that the separate listing should be consulted. (Following is an example of this listing.)

(a) Example:

Instrument Approach Procedures (Charts)
Northeast United States

▼ IFR TAKE-OFF MINIMUMS AND DEPARTURE PROCEDURES

FAR 91.116(c) prescribes take-off rules and establishes standard take-off minimums as follows:

(1) Aircraft having two engines or less—one statute mile.

(2) Aircraft having more than two engines—one-half statute mile.

Aerodromes within this geographical area with IFR take-off minimums other than standard are listed below alphabetically by aerodrome name. Departure procedures and/or ceiling visibility minimums are established to assist pilots conducting IFR flight in avoiding obstructions during climb to the minimum enroute altitude.

Take-off minimums and departure procedures apply to all runways unless otherwise specified.

AERODROME NAME	TAKE-OFF MINIMUMS
AUGUSTA STATE	Rwy 17, 200–1*
Augusta, Maine	Rwy 26, 300–1**

*or standard with a minimum climb of 320' per NM to 800.
**or standard with a minimum climb of 200' per NM to 800.
Rwy 17 climb on 150° heading to 1000 before turning W bound.

BALTIMORE-WASHINGTON INTL	Rwy 10, RVR/18*
Baltimore, Maryland	Rwy 15R, ½ mile*
*(FAR 135)	Rwy 28, RVR/40*

BAR HARBOR	Rwys 4, 29, 35, 300–1
Bar Harbor Maine	Rwys 11–29, 17–35, Night NA

Climb on 218° heading to 1200, climbing right turn to 2700 direct NDB*. Climb in the holding pattern to MEA for direction of flight.
*BH NDB, LOC Rwy 22; LME NDB, NDB-B

BARNES MUNI

Westfield, Massachusetts

Rwy 20 requires 225' per NM rate of climb to 1200'. Rwy 15 800–1 day, 800–2 night; right turn to 210° as soon as practicable. Rwys 2, 33 700–1 day, 800–2 night.

BEAVER COUNTY	Rwy 10, 200–1
Beaver Falls, Pennsylvania	

(5) Each pilot, prior to departing an airport on an IFR flight should consider the type of terrain and other obstructions on or in the vicinity of the departure airport and take the following action.

(a) Determine whether a departure procedure and/or Standard Instrument Departure (SID) is available for obstruction avoidance.

(b) Determine if obstruction avoidance can be maintained visually or that the departure procedure should be followed.

(c) At airports where instrument approach procedures have not been published, hence no published departure procedure, determine what action will be necessary and take such action that will assure a safe departure.

326–339. RESERVED

340. ARTCC COMMUNICATIONS

a. DIRECT COMMUNICATIONS—CONTROLLERS/PILOTS

(1) Air Route Traffic Control Centers are capable of direct communications with IFR air traffic on certain frequencies. Maximum communications coverage is possible through the use of Remote Center Air/Ground (RCAG) sites comprised of VHF and UHF transmitters and receivers. These sites are located throughout the United States. Although they may be several hundred miles away from the ARTCC, they are remoted to the various centers by land lines or microwave links. As IFR operations are expedited through the use of direct communications, pilots are requested to use these frequencies strictly for communications pertinent to the control of IFR aircraft. Flight plan filing, en route weather, weather forecasts and similar data should be requested through Flight Service Stations, company radio, or appropriate military facilities capable of performing these services.

(2) An ARTCC is divided into sectors. Each sector is handled by one or a team of controllers and has its own sector discrete frequency. As a flight progresses from one sector to another, the pilot is requested to change to the appropriate sector discrete frequency.

(3) ATC Frequency Change Procedures:

(a) The following phraseology will be used by controllers to effect a frequency change: "(Aircraft Identification) CONTACT (facility name or location name and terminal function) (frequency) AT (time, fix or altitude) OVER. Pilots are expected to maintain a listening watch on the transferring controller's frequency until the time, fix or altitude specified. ATC will omit frequency change restrictions whenever pilot compliance is expected upon receipt."

(b) The following phraseology should be utilized by pilots for establishing contact with the designated facility:

1. When a position report will be made:

"(Name) CENTER, (aircraft identification), (position), OVER."

2. When no position report will be made:

"(Name) CENTER, (aircraft identification), ESTIMATING (reporting point) (time) AT (altitude/flight level) CLIMBING/DESCENDING TO MAINTAIN (altitude/flight level) OVER."

3. When operating in a radar environment and no position report is required.

(Name) CENTER, (aircraft identification) AT (exact altitude/flight level); or, if appropriate, LEAVING (exact altitude/flight level) CLIMBING/DESCENDING TO MAINTAIN (altitude/flight level) OVER.

NOTE—Exact altitude/flight level means to the nearest 100 foot increment. Exact altitude/flight level reports on initial contact provide air traffic control with information required prior to using MODE C altitude information for separation purposes.

(c) At times controllers will ask pilots to vertify the fact that they are at a particular altitude. The phraseology used will be: 'VERIFY AT (altitude).' In climbing/descending situations, controllers may ask pilots to "VERIFY ASSIGNED ALTITUDE AS (altitude)." Pilots should confirm that they are at the altitude stated by the controller or that the assigned altitude is correct as stated. If this is not the case, they should inform the controller of the actual altitude being maintained or the different assigned altitude. *Pilots should not take action to change their actual altitude or different assigned altitude to that stated in the controllers verification request unless the controller specifically authorizes a change.*

(4) ARTCC Radio Frequency Outage:

(a) ARTCCs normally have at least one back-up radio receiver and transmitter system for each frequency which can usually be pressed into service quickly with little or no disruption of ATC service. Occasionally, technical problems may cause a delay but switchover seldom takes more than 60 seconds. When it appears that the outage will not be quickly remedied, the ARTCC will usually request a nearby aircraft, if there is one, to switch to the affected frequency to broadcast communications instructions. It is important, therefore, that the pilot wait at least 1 minute before deciding that the ARTCC has actually experienced a bona fide radio frequency failure. When such an outage does occur, the pilot should, if workload and equipment capability permit, maintain a listening watch on the affected frequency while attempting to comply with the recommended communications procedures which follow.

(b) If two-way communications cannot be established with the ARTCC after changing frequencies, a pilot should attempt to recontact the transferring controller for the assignment of an alternative frequency or other instructions.

(c) When an ARTCC radio frequency failure occurs after two-way communications have been established, the pilot should attempt to re-establish contact with the center on any other known ARTCC frequency, preferably that of the next responsible sector when practicable, and ask for instructions. However, when the next normal frequency change along the route is known to involve another ATC facility, the pilot should contact that facility, if feasible, for instructions. If communications cannot be re-established by either method, the pilot is expected to request communications instructions from the FSS appropriate to the route of flight.

(d) The exchange of information between an aircraft and an ARTCC through an FSS is quicker than relay via company radio because the FSS has direct interphone lines to the responsible ARTCC sector. Accordingly, when circumstances dictate a choice between the two, during an ARTCC frequency outage, relay via FSS radio is recommended.

341. POSITION REPORTING

The safety and effectiveness of traffic control depends to a large extent on accurate position reporting. In order to provide the proper separation and expedite aircraft movements, air traffic control must be able to make accurate estimates of the progress of every aircraft operating on an IFR flight plan.

a. POSITION IDENTIFICATION

(1) When a position report is to be made passing a VOR radio facility, the time reported should be the time at which the first complete reversal of the "to-from" indicator is accomplished.

(2) When a position report is made passing a facility by means of an airborne ADF, the time reported should be the time at which the indicator makes a complete reversal.

(3) When an aural or light-panel indication is used to determine the time passing a reporting point, such as a fan marker, Z marker, cone of silence or intersection of range courses, the time should be noted when the signal is first received and again when it ceases. The mean of these two times should then be taken as the actual time over the fix.

(4) If a position is given with respect to distance and direction from a reporting point, the distance and direction should be computed as accurately as possible.

(5) Except for terminal area transition purposes, position reports or navigation with reference to aids not established for use in the structure in which flight is being conducted will not normally be required by ATC.

b. POSITION REPORTING POINTS

Federal Aviation Regulations require pilots to maintain a listening watch on the appropriate frequency and, unless operating under the provisions of (c), to furnish position reports passing certain reporting points. Reporting points are indicated by symbols on en route charts. The designated compulsory reporting point symbol is the solid triangle (▲) ; the "on request" reporting point symbol is the open triangle (△). Reports passing an "on request" reporting point are only necessary when requested by ATC.

c. POSITION REPORTING REQUIREMENT

(1) **Flights along airways/routes**—A position report is required by all flights regardless of altitude, including those operating in accordance with an ATC clearance specifying "VFR conditions on top," over each designated compulsory reporting point along the route being flown.

(2) **Flight Along a Direct Route**—Regardless of the altitude or flight level being flown, including flights operating in accordance with an ATC clearance specifying "VFR conditions-on-top," pilots shall report over each reporting point used in the flight plan to define the route of flight.

(3) **Flights in a Radar Environment**—ATC will inform a pilot that he is in "RADAR CONTACT" (a) when his aircraft is initially identified in the ATC system ; and (b) when radar identification is re-established after radar service has been terminated or radar contact lost. Subsequent to being advised that the controller has established radar contact, this fact will not be repeated to the pilot when handed off to another controller. At times, the aircraft identity will be *confirmed* by the receiving controller ; however, this should not be construed to mean that radar contact has been lost. The identity of transponder equipped aircraft will be confirmed by asking the pilot to "IDENT," "SQUAWK STANDBY," or to change codes. Aircraft without transponders will be advised of their position to confirm identity. In this case, *the pilot is expected to advise the controller if he disagrees with the position given.* If the pilot cannot confirm the accuracy of the position given because he is not tuned to the NAVAID referenced by the controller, the pilot should ask for another radar position relative to the NAVAID to which he is tuned.

(a) When informed by ATC that their aircraft are in "RADAR CONTACT," PILOTS SHOULD DISCONTINUE POSITION REPORTS OVER DESIGNATED REPORTING POINTS. They should resume normal position reporting when ATC advises "RADAR CONTACT LOST" or "RADAR SERVICE TERMINATED."

d. POSITION REPORT ITEMS

Position reports should include the following items:

(1) Identification,

(2) Position,

(3) Time,

(4) Altitude or flight level (include actual altitude or flight level when operating on a clearance specifying "VFR conditions-on-top"),

(5) Type of flight plan (not required in IFR position reports made directly to ARTC Centers or approach control),

(6) ETA and name of next reporting point,

(7) The name only of the next succeeding reporting point along the route of flight, and

(8) Pertinent remarks.

342. ADDITIONAL REPORTS

a. The following reports should be made to ATC or FSS facilities without request :

(1) At all times :

(a) When vacating any previously assigned altitude/flight level for a newly assigned altitude/flight level.

(b) That an altitude change will be made if operating on a clearance specifying "VFR conditions-on-top."

(c) When approach has been missed. (Request clearance for specific action ; i.e., to alternative airport, another approach, etc.)

(2) When not in "radar contact" :

(a) The time and altitude/flight level reaching a holding fix or point to which cleared.

(b) When leaving any assigned holding fix or point.

(c) When leaving final approach fix inbound on final approach.

(d) A corrected estimate at anytime it becomes apparent that an estimate as previously submitted is in error in excess of 3 minutes.

b. Pilots encountering weather conditions which have not been forecast, or hazardous conditions which have been forecast, are expected to forward a report of such weather to air traffic control. (See **520**—PILOT WEATHER REPORTS (PIREPS) and FAR 91.125(b) and (c).)

343. AIRWAYS/ROUTE SYSTEMS

a. Three route systems have been established for air navigation purposes. They are the VOR and L/MF system, the jet route system, and the area navigation (RNAV) route system.

(1) The VOR and L/MF Airway System consists of airways designated from 1200 feet above the surface (or in some instances higher) to but not including 18,000 feet MSL and is designed to serve aircraft which operate at these altitudes. These airways are depicted on En Route Low Altitude Charts—U.S. Series L–1 through L–28.

(a) THE VOR AIRWAYS are predicated solely on VOR/VORTAC navigation aids, except in Alaska, and are depicted on aeronautical charts by a "V" ("Victor") followed by the airway number, e.g., V 12. Segments of VOR airways and jet routes in Alaska are based on L/MF navigation aids and charted in brown color instead of blue on enroute charts. These airways are numbered similarly to U.S. highways. As in the highway numbering system, a segment of an airway which is common to two or more routes carries the numbers of all the airways which coincide for that segment. When such is the case, a pilot in filing a flight plan needs to indicate only that airway number of the route which he is using. *Alternate Airways* are identified by their location with respect to the associated main airway. "Victor 9 West" indicates an alternate airway associated with, and lying to the west of Victor 9.

(b) A pilot who intends to make an airway flight, using VOR facilities, will simply specify the appropriate "Victor" airway(s) in his flight plan. For example, if a flight is to be made from Chicago to New Orleans at 8000 feet, using omniranges only, the route may be indicated as "Departing from Chicago-Midway, cruising 8000 feet via Victor 9 to Moisant International." If flight is to be conducted in part by means of L/MF navigation aids and in part on omniranges, specifications of the appropriate airways in the flight plan will indicate which types of facilities will be used along the described routes, and, for IFR flight, permit ATC to issue a traffic clearance accordingly. A route may also be described by specifying the station over which the flight will pass, but in this case since many VOR's and L/MF aids have the same name, the pilot must be careful to indicate which aid will be used at a particular location. This will be indicated in the route of flight portion of the flight plan by specifying the type of facility to be used after the location name in the following manner: Newark L/MF, Allentown VOR.

(c) With respect to position reporting, reporting points are designated for VOR Airway Systems. Flights using Victor Airways will report over these points unless advised otherwise by ATC.

(d) THE L/MF AIRWAYS are predicated solely on L/MF navigation aids and are depicted on aeronautical charts by color and number; e.g., Amber One. Green and Red airways are plotted east and west. Amber and Blue airways are plotted north and south. The colored airway system exists only in the State of Alaska. All such airways formerly designated within the conterminous United States have been rescinded.

(2) THE JET ROUTE SYSTEM consists of jet routes established from 18,000 feet MSL to FL 450 inclusive designed to serve aircraft which customarily operate at these altitudes.

(3) The RNAV route system presently consist of a skeletal structure of approximately 165 high altitude routes (18,000 feet MSL to flight level 450) embracing the 48 states. Properly equipped and certificated aircraft may use these routes (see Advisory Circular AC 90–45A, Approval of Area Navigation Systems For Use in the U.S. National Airspace System). A distinct feature of RNAV is the provision for flight along a predetermined track without the need to overfly ground-based navigation facilities. Low altitude (below 18,000 feet MSL) RNAV routes are planned for the future.

(4) RNAV equipment may be used to navigate Jet Routes, Victor Airways, DME Holding and those Terminal Arrival/Departure routes which are based on VOR/DME facility defining the route. RNAV equipment should *not* be used as the primary navigational reference for instrument approaches other than RNAV procedures unless specifically approved for such use in the operating manual for that equipment.

(5) OPERATION ABOVE FL 450 may be conducted on a point-to-point basis. Navigational guidance is provided on an area basis utilizing those facilities depicted on the En Route High Altitude Charts—U.S. Series H–1 through H–4.

b. To the extent possible, the VOR airway and jet route systems have been aligned in an overlying manner to facilitate transition between each. To simplify definition of route and to facilitate air traffic control, pilot are requested to file via the airways/jet routes published for the altitude/flight level planned.

c. Radar Vectors. Controllers may vector aircraft within controlled airspace for separation purposes, noise abatement considerations, when an operational advantage will be realized by the pilot or the controller, or when requested by the pilot. Vectors outside of controlled airspace will be provided only on pilot request. Pilots will be advised as to what the vector is to achieve when the vector is controller initiated and will take the aircraft off a previously assigned nonradar route. To the extent possible, aircraft operating on RNAV routes will be allowed to remain on their own navigation.

d. Pilots are cautioned when flying in Canadian airspace, to review Canadian Air Regulations.

(1) Special attention should be given to the parts which differ from U.S. Federal Aviation Regulations. The Canadian airways "Block Airspace" restriction is an example:

"Block airspace" means the airspace within designated low level airways—

   (a) extending upwards from 9,500 feet above mean sea level, east of longitude 114° West and

   (b) extending upwards from 12,500 feet above mean sea level, west of longitude 114° West except on Amber Airway 2, Victor Airway 301 and Victor Airway 301W between Edmonton and Calgary, Alberta where "block airspace" includes the airspace between 9,500 feet and 12,500 feet above mean sea level. ("Low level airway" means an airspace designated and defined as such in the *Designated Airspace Handbook.*)

(2) Regardless of the weather conditions or the height of the terrain, no person shall operate an aircraft under VFR conditions within block airspace except in accordance with a clearance for VFR flight issued by ATC.

(3) Unless otherwise authorized by the Director General, Civil Aeronautics of the Department of Transport, no person holding a commercial or private pilot license without an instrument rating shall operate an aircraft in VFR flight within block airspace unless he has successfully completed a written examination demonstrating his knowledge of radio navigation and of air traffic control procedures applicable to IFR flight in

cluding clearances and position reports, and his pilot license is endorsed to that effect.

(4) Segments of VOR airways and high level routes in Canada are based on L/MF navigation aids and are charted in brown color instead of blue on enroute charts.

344. AIRWAY/ROUTE COURSE CHANGES

a. Pilots of aircraft are required to adhere to airways/ routes being flown. Special attention must be given to this requirement during course changes. Each course change consists of variables that make the technique applicable in each case a matter only the pilot can resolve. Some variables which must be considered are turn radii, wind effect, airspeed, degree of turn, and cockpit instrumentation. An early turn, as illustrated below, is one method of adhering to airways/routes. The use of any available cockpit instrumentation, such as distance measuring equipment, may be used by the pilot to lead his turn when making course changes. This *is consistent* with the intent of FAR 91.123 which requires pilots to operate along the centerline of an airway and along the direct course between navigational aids or fixes.

b. Turns which begin at or after fix passage may exceed airway/route boundaries. The following illustration contains an example flight track depicting this, together with an example of an early turn.

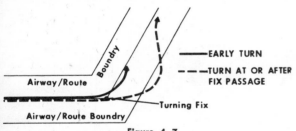

Figure 4—7

c. Without such actions, as leading a turn, aircraft operating in excess of 290 knots true airspeed (TAS) can exceed the normal airway/route boundaries depending on the amount of course change required, wind direction and velocity, the character of the turn fix (DME, overhead navigation aid, or intersection), and the pilot's technique in making a course change. For example, a flight operating at 17,000 feet MSL with a TAS of 400 knots, a 25 degree bank, and a course change of more than 40 degrees would exceed the width of the airway/route; i.e., 4 nautical miles each side of centerline. However, in the airspace below 18,000 feet MSL, operations in excess of 290 knots TAS are not prevalent and the provision of additional IFR separation in all course change situations for the occasional aircraft making a turn in excess of 290 knots TAS creates an unacceptable waste of airspace and imposes a penalty upon the preponderance of traffic which operate at low speeds. Consequently, the FAA expects pilots to lead turns and take other actions they consider necessary during course changes to adhere as closely as possible to the airways/route being flown.

d. Due to the high airspeeds used at 18,000 feet MSL and above, FAA provides additional IFR separation protection for course changes made at such altitude levels.

345. CHANGEOVER POINT (COP's)

COP's are prescribed for Federal airways, jet routes, area navigation routes, or other direct routes for which an MEA is designated under Part 95, FAR. The COP is a point along the route or airway segment between two adjacent navigation facilities or way points where changeover in navigation guidance should occur. At this point, the pilot should change navigation receiver frequency from the station behind the aircraft to the Station ahead. A symbol ⬛ is used on aeronautical charts to indicate the COP when offset from the midway point along straight route segments. Without the symbol, the COP is midway between the navigation facilities for straight route segments, or at the intersection of radials or courses forming a dogleg in the case of dogleg route segments. COP's are established for the purpose of preventing loss of navigation guidance, to prevent frequency interference from other facilities, and to prevent use of different facilities by different aircraft in the same airspace. Pilots are urged to observe COP's to the fullest extent.

346. OPERATION IN RESTRICTED AIRSPACE

a. ATC facilities apply the following procedures when aircraft are operating on an IFR clearance (including those cleared by ATC to maintain VFR conditions on top) via a route which lies within joint-use restricted airspace.

(1) The ATC facility controlling an aircraft immediately before it would enter the restricted airspace will coordinate as necessary with the ATC facility designated as the controlling facility or with the using agency to obtain permission for the aircraft to operate in the restricted airspace.

(2) If permission is obtained, the ATC facility will allow the aircraft to operate in the restricted airspace without issuing specific clearance for it to do so.

(3) If permission cannot be obtained, the ATC facility will issue an amended clearance so the aircraft will avoid the restricted airspace.

b. Note that the above apply only to joint-use restricted airspace and not to prohibited and nonjoint-use airspace. For the latter categories, the ATC facility will issue a clearance so the aircraft will avoid the restricted airspace unless it is on an approved altitude reservation mission or has obtained its own permission to operate in the airspace and so informs the controlling facility.

c. Restricted airspace is depicted on the En Route Chart appropriate for use at the altitude or flight level being flown. For joint-use restricted areas, the name of the controlling agency is shown on these charts. For all prohibited areas and non-joint use restricted areas unless otherwise requested by the using agency, the phrase "NO A/G" is shown.

347. HOLDING

NOTE.—See CLEARANCE ITEMS—when further clearance has not been received.

a. When holding at a VOR station pilots should begin the turn to the outbound leg at the time of the first complete reversal of the "to-from" indicator. See Two-Way Communications Failure for holding at the approach fix when radio failure occurs.

b. Patterns at the most generally used holding fixes are depicted on U.S. Government or commercially produced (meeting FAA requirements) low/high altitude en route, area and STAR charts. Pilots are expected to hold in the pattern depicted unless specifically advised otherwise by ATC.

c. ATC clearance requiring that an aircraft be held at a holding point where the pattern is not depicted will include the following information:

(1) General Holding Instructions.

(a) The direction to hold from holding point; (The direction to hold with relation to the holding fix will be specified as one of eight general points of the compass; i.e., north, northeast, east, etc.).

(b) Holding fix;

(c) On (specified) radial, course, magnetic bearing, airway number or jet route;

(d) Outbound leg length in nautical miles if DME is to be used;

(e) Left turns, if nonstandard patterns is to be used;

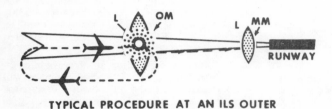

TYPICAL PROCEDURE AT AN ILS OUTER MARKER SITE

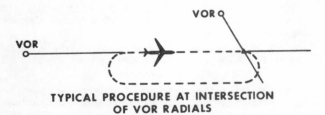

TYPICAL PROCEDURE AT INTERSECTION OF VOR RADIALS

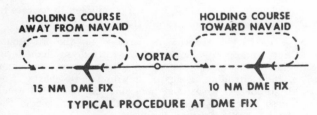

TYPICAL PROCEDURE AT DME FIX

Figure 4–8—HOLDING PATTERN EXAMPLES

(f) Time to expect further clearance, or time to expect approach clearance.

(2) Detailed holding instructions: Same as (1)—(a), (b) and (c) above with following additions:

(a), or minute/s if DME is not to be used.

(b), or right turns if standard patterns is to be used.

d. Holding pattern airspace protection is based on the following procedures. They are the only procedures for entry and holding recommended by FAA.

(1) Descriptive Terms

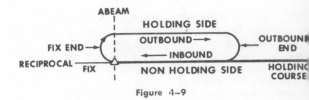

Figure 4–9

| Standard Pattern | : | Right turns (illustrated) |
| Nonstandard Pattern | : | Left turns |

(2) Airspeeds (maximum)

(a) Propeller-driven _____ 175K IAS

(b) Civil turbojet

1. MHA through 6,000 feet _____ 200K IAS
2. Above 6,000 feet through 14,000 feet _____ 210K IAS
3. Above 14,000 feet _____ 230K IAS

(c) Military turbojet

1. All–except aircraft listed below in 2,3,4 and 5 _____ 230K IAS
2. F–84F, F–100[1], F–102, F–104[1] F–106, T–38, F–4, F–8, F–11, F–14, F–15, F–16, A–5, A–7 (USAF only), AV–8 _____ 265K IAS
3. F–4 (USAF only) _____ 280K IAS
4. F–100[1], F/RF–101, F–104[1], F–105, F–111, SR–71 _____ 310K IAS
5. T–37 _____ 175K IAS

Holding speed depends upon weight and drag configuration.

(3) Entry

(a) Parallel Procedure—Parallel holding course, turn left, and return to holding fix or intercept holding course.

(b) Teardrop Procedure—Proceed on outbound track of 30° (or less) to holding course, turn right to intercept holding course.

(c) Direct Entry Procedure—Turn right and fly the pattern.

STANDARD PATTERN

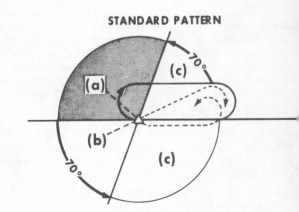

Figure 4–10—ENTRY PROCEDURES

(4) Timing

(a)	At or below 14,000 ft. MSL	Above 14,000 ft. MSL
INBOUND leg*	1 min.	1½ min.

*NOTE.—The *initial* outbound leg should be flown for 1 min. or 1½ min. (appropriate to altitude). Timing for subsequent outbound legs should be adjusted as necessary to achieve proper inbound leg time.

(b) Outbound timing begins *over* or *abeam* the fix, whichever occurs later. If the *abeam* position cannot be determined, start timing when turn to outbound is completed.

(5) Distance Measuring Equipment (DME)

DME holding is subject to the same entry and holding procedures except that distances (nautical miles) are used in lieu of time values. The *outbound course* of a DME holding pattern is called the outbound leg of the pattern. The length of the outbound leg will be specified by the controller. The end of the outbound leg is determined by the odometer reading.

(a) Example:

When the inbound course is *toward* the navaid and the fix distance is 10 NM, and the leg length is 5NM, then the end of the outbound leg will be reached when the odometer reads 15 NM.

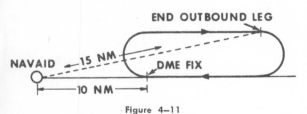

Figure 4—11

(b) Example:

When the inbound course is *away* from the navaid and the fix distance is 28 NM and the leg length is 8 NM, then the end of the outbound leg will be reached when the odometer reads 20 NM.

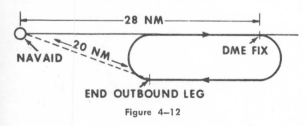

Figure 4—12

(6) Pilot Action

(a) Start speed reduction when 3 minutes or less from the holding fix. Cross the holding fix, initially, at or below the maximum holding airspeed.

(b) Make all turns during entry and while holding at: (1) 3° per second, or (2) 30° bank angle, or (3) 25° bank angle provided a flight director system is used: whichever requires the least bank angle.

(c) Compensate for known effect of wind, except when turning.

(d) Determine entry turn from aircraft heading upon arrival at the holding fix. Plus or minus 5° in heading is considered to be within allowable good operating limits for determining entry.

(e) Advise ATC immediately if any increased airspeed is necessary due to turbulence, icing, etc., or if unable to accomplish any part of the holding procedures. After such higher speeds are no longer necessary, operate according to the appropriate published holding speed and notify ATC.

NOTE.—Airspace protection for turbulent air holding is based on a maximum of 280K IAS or Mach 0.8, whichever is lower. Considerable impact on traffic flow will result when turbulent air holding patterns are used; thus, pilot discretion will ensure their use is limited to bona fide conditions/requirements.

(7) Nonstandard Holding Pattern—Fix end and outbound end turns are made to the left. Entry procedures to a nonstandard pattern are oriented in relation to the 70° line on the holding side just as in the standard pattern.

e. When holding at a fix and instructions are received specifying the time of departure from the fix, the pilot should adjust his flight path within the limits of the established holding pattern in order to leave the fix at the exact time specified. After departing the holding fix, normal speed is to be resumed with respect to other governing speed requirements such as terminal area speed limits, specific ATC requests, etc. Where the fix is associated with an instrument approach, and timed approaches are in effect, a procedure turn shall not be executed unless the pilot advises ATC, since aircraft holding are expected to proceed inbound on final approach directly from the holding pattern when approach clearance is received.

f. RADAR SURVEILLANCE OF OUTER FIX HOLDING PATTERN AIRSPACE AREAS.

(1) Whenever aircraft are holding at an outer fix, ATC will usually provide radar surveillance of the outer fix holding pattern airspace area, or any portion of it, if it is shown on the controller's radar scope.

(2) The controller will attempt to detect any holding aircraft that stray outside the holding pattern airspace area and will assist any detected aircraft to return to the assigned airspace area.

(3) Many factors could prevent ATC from providing this additional service, such as workload, number of targets, precipitation, ground clutter, and radar system capability. These circumstances may make it unfeasible to maintain radar identification of aircraft or to detect aircraft straying from the holding pattern. The provision of this service depends entirely upon whether the controller believes he is in a position to provide it and does not relieve a pilot of his responsibility to adhere to an accepted ATC clearance.

g. If an aircraft is established in a published holding pattern at an assigned altitude above the published minimum holding altitude and subsequently cleared for the approach, the pilot may descend to the published minimum holding altitude. The holding pattern would only be a segment of the instrument approach procedure *if* it is published on the instrument procedure chart and is used in lieu of a procedure turn.

h. For those holding patterns where there are no published minimum holding altitudes, the pilot, upon receiving an approach clearance, must maintain his last assigned altitude until leaving the holding pattern and established on the inbound course. Thereafter, the published minimum altitude of the route segment being flown will apply. It is expected that the pilot will be assigned a holding altitude that will permit a normal descent on the inbound course.

348—359. RESERVED

360. STANDARD TERMINAL ARRIVAL ROUTES (STARS)

a. A standard terminal arrival route (STAR) is an air traffic control coded instrument flight rules (IFR) arrival route established for application to arriving IFR aircraft destined for certain airports. Its purpose is to simplify clearance delivery procedures.

b. Pilots of IFR civil aircraft destined to locations for which STARs have been published may be issued a clearance containing a STAR whenever ATC deems it appropriate. Until military STAR publications and distribution is accomplished, STARs will be issued to military pilots only when requested in the flight plan or verbally by the pilot.

c. Use of STARs requires pilot possession of at least the approved textual description. As with any ATC clearance or portion thereof, it is the responsibility of each pilot to accept or refuse an issued STAR. A pilot should notify ATC if he does not wish to use a STAR by placing "NO STAR" in the remark section of the flight plan or by the less desirable method of verbally stating the same to ATC.

d. A bound booklet containing all STAR charts is available on subscription from the National Ocean Survey. STAR's implemented on an urgent/emergency basis will be published in textual form in the Notices to Airmen (Class II) publication until charted.

361. LOCAL FLOW TRAFFIC MANAGEMENT— PROFILE DESCENT

a. This program is a continuing effort by the FAA to enhance safety by reducing low-altitude flying time of high performance aircraft. For the purpose of this program, high performance aircraft are all turbojet aircraft and any turboprop weighing more than 12,500 pounds. In addition to enhanced safety through reduced low-altitude flying time of high performance aircraft, other objectives of this program are: fuel conservation, reduction of aircraft noise for airport neighbors, standardized arrival procedure for high performance aircraft, and equitable distribution of arrival delays.

b. A profile descent is basically an uninterrupted descent (except where level flight is required for speed adjustment) from cruising altitude to interception of a minimum altitude specified for the initial or intermediate segment of an instrument approach.

c. Profile descent procedures are based on an altitude loss of approximately 300 feet per flying mile from cruise altitude. Actual altitude loss will vary depending on aircraft characteristics and the most economical descent for that flight.

d. When crossing altitudes and speed restrictions are depicted on profile descent charts or issued verbally, ATC will expect the pilot to descend first to the crossing altitude and then reduce speed.

e. Acceptance by the pilot of a RUNWAY PROFILE DESCENT clearance requires the pilot to adhere to the altitudes, speeds, and headings depicted on the chart, unless otherwise instructed by ATC. At locations without published RUNWAY PROFILE DESCENT charts, pilots will be issued clearance which will usually permit an uninterrupted descent in accord with the profile procedure.

f. ALL PILOTS RECEIVING A CLEARANCE FOR A RUNWAY PROFILE DESCENT ARE EXPECTED TO ADVISE ATC IF THEY DO NOT HAVE RUNWAY PROFILE DESCENT CHARTS OR ARE UNABLE TO COMPLY WITH THE CLEARANCE.

362. APPROACH CONTROL

a. Approach control is responsible for controlling all instrument flight operating within its area of responsibility. Approach control may serve one or more airfields, and control is exercised primarily by direct pilot/controller communications. Prior to arriving at the destination radio facility, instructions will be received from ARTCC to contact approach control on a specified frequency.

b. Radar Approach Control

(1) Where radar is approved for approach control service, it is used not only for radar approaches (ASR and PAR) but is also used to provide vectors in conjunction with published nonradar approaches based on radio navaids(ILS, VOR, NDB, TACAN). Radar vectors can provide course guidance and expedite traffic to the final approach course of any established instrument approach procedure or to the traffic pattern for a visual approach. Approach control facilities that provide this radar service will operate in the following manner.

(2) Arriving aircraft are either cleared to an outer fix most appropriate to the route being flown with vertical separation and, if required, given holding information or, when radar handoffs are effected between the ARTCC and approach control, or between two approach control facilities, aircraft are cleared to the airport or to a fix so located that the handoff will be completed prior to the time the aircraft reaches the fix. When radar handoffs are utilized, successive arriving flights may be handed off to approach control with radar separation in lieu of vertical separation. After release to approach control, aircraft are vectored to the appropriate final approach course (ILS, VOR, ADF, etc.). Radar vectors and altitude/flight levels will be issued as required for spacing and separating aircraft. *Therefore, pilots must not deviate from the headings issued by approach control.* Aircraft will normally be informed when it is necessary to vector across the final approach course for spacing or other reasons. If approach course crossing is imminent and the pilot has not been informed that he will be vectored across the final approach course, he should query the controller. The pilot is not expected to turn inbound on the final approach course unless an approach clearance has been issued. This clearance will normally be issued with the final vector for interception of the final approach course, and the vector will be such as to enable the pilot to establish his aircraft on the final approach course prior to reaching the final approach fix. In the case of aircraft already inbound on the final approach course, approach clearance will be issued prior to the aircraft reaching the final approach fix. When established inbound on the final approach course, radar separation will be maintained and the pilot will be expected to complete the approach utilizing the approach aid designated in the clearance (ILS, VOR, radio beacons, etc.) as the primary means of navigation. Therefore, once established on the final approach course,

pilots must not deviate from it unless a clearance to do so is received from air traffic control. After passing the final approach fix on final approach, aircraft are expected to continue inbound on the final approach course and complete the approach or effect the missed approach procedure published for that airport.

(3) Whether aircraft are vectored to the appropriate final approach course or provide their own navigation on published routes to it, radar service is automatically terminated when the landing is completed or the tower controller has the aircraft in sight, whichever occurs first.

363. ADVANCE INFORMATION ON INSTRUMENT APPROACH

a. When landing at airports with approach control services and where two or more instrument approach procedures are published, pilots will be provided in advance of their arrival with the type of approach to expect or that they may be vectored for a visual approach. This information will be broadcast either by a controller or on ATIS. It will not be furnished when the visibility is three miles or better and the ceiling is at or above the highest initial approach altitude established for any low altitude instrument approach procedure for the airport. The purpose of this information is to aid the pilot in planning arrival actions; however, it is not an ATC clearance or commitment and is subject to change. Pilots should bear in mind that fluctuating weather, shifting winds, blocked runway, etc., are conditions which may result in changes to approach information previously received. It is important that the pilot advise ATC immediately if he is unable to execute the approach ATC advised will be used, or if he prefers another type of approach.

364. INSTRUMENT APPROACH PROCEDURE CHARTS

a. FAR 91.116a (Instrument Approaches to Civil Airports) requires the use of standard instrument approach procedures unless otherwise authorized by the Administrator (including ATC.) FAR 91.116d (Military Airports) requires civil pilots flying into or out of military airports to comply with the instrument approach procedures and takeoff and landing minimums prescribed by the authority having jurisdiction at those airports. All instrument approach procedures (standard and special, civil and military) are based on joint civil/military criteria contained in the U.S. Standard for Terminal Instrument Procedures (TERPs). The design of instrument approach procedures (IAPs) based on criteria contained in TERPs, takes into account the interrelationship between airports, facilities, and the surrounding environment, terrain, obstacles, noise sensitivity, etc. Appropriate altitudes, courses, headings, distances, and other limitations are specified and, once approved, the procedures are published and distributed by government and commercial cartographers as instrument approach charts. All IAPs are not published in chart form. Radar instrument approach procedures are established where requirements and facilities exist but they are printed in tabular form in appropriate U.S. Government Flight Information Publications. A pilot adhering to the altitudes, flight paths, and weather minimums depicted on the IAP chart or vectors and altitudes issued

by the radar controller, is assured of terrain and obstruction clearance and runway/airport alignment during approach for landing. IAPs are designed to provide an IFR descent from the enroute environment to a point where a safe landing can be made. They are prescribed and approved by appropriate civil or military authority to ensure a safe descent during instrument flight conditions at a specific airport. It is important that pilots understand these procedures and their use prior to attempting to fly instrument approaches. TERPs criteria are provided for the following types of instrument approach procedures:

(1) Precision approaches where an electronic glide slope is provided (PAR and ILS) and,

(2) Nonprecision approaches where glide slope information is not provided (all approaches except PAR and ILS).

b. The method used to depict prescribed altitudes on instrument approach charts differs according to techniques employed by different chart publishers. Prescribed altitudes may be depicted in three different configurations: Minimum, maximum, and mandatory. Altitudes depicted on one commercial publishers charts are minimum altitudes unless specifically identified as "maximum" or "mandatory." The U.S. Government distributes charts produced by Defense Mapping Agency (DMA) and National Ocean Survey (NOS). Altitudes are depicted on these charts in the profile view with underline, overline, or both to identify them as minimum, maximum, or mandatory as in the following examples:

(1) $\underline{2500}$—Minimum Altitude. Aircraft is required to maintain altitude at or above the depicted value.

(2) $\overline{3500}$—Maximum Altitude. Aircraft is required to maintain atitude at or below the depicted value.

(3) $\overline{\underline{4500}}$—Mandatory Altitude. Aircraft is required to maintain altitude at the depicted value.

The underline/overline to identify mandatory altitudes and the overline to identify maximum altitudes are used almost exclusively by DMA for military charts. With very few exceptions, civil approach charts produced by NOS utilize only the underline to identify minimum altitudes. Pilots are cautioned to adhere to altitudes as prescribed because, in certain instances, they may be used as the basis for vertical separation of aircraft by ATC. When a depicted altitude is specified in the ATC clearance, that altitude becomes mandatory as defined in b.(3) above.

c. Minimum Safe Altitudes (MSAs) are published for emergency use on approach procedure charts utilizing NDB or VOR type facilities. The altitude shown provides at least 1,000 feet of clearance above the highest obstacle in the defined sector to a distance of 25 NM from the facility. As many as four sectors may be depicted with different altitudes for each sector displayed in rectangular boxes in the plan view of the chart. A single altitude for the entire area may be shown in the lower right portion of the plan view. Navigational course guidance is not assured at the MSA within these sectors.

d. Minimum Vectoring Altitudes (MVAs) are established for use by ATC when radar air traffic control is exercised. MVA charts are prepared by air traffic facilities at locations where there are numerous different minimum IFR altitudes. Each MVA chart has sectors large enough to accommodate vectoring of aircraft within the sector at the MVA. Each sector boundary is at least 3 miles from the obstruction determining the MVA. To avoid a large sector with an execessively high MVA due to an isolated prominent obstruction, the obstruction may be enclosed in a buffer area whose boundaries are at least 3 miles from the obstruction. This is done to facilitate vectoring around the obstruction.

e. The minimum vectoring altitude in each sector provides 1000 feet above the highest obstacle in nonmountainous areas and 2000 feet above the highest obstacle in designated mountainous areas. Where lower MVAs are required in designated mountainous areas to achieve compatibility with terminal routes or to permit vectoring to an instrument approach procedure, 1000 feet of obstacle clearance may be authorized with the use of Airport Surveillance Radar (ASR). The minimum vectoring altitude will provide at least 300 feet above the floor of controlled airspace.

f. Because of differences in the areas considered for MVA, and those applied to other minimum altitudes, and the ability to isolate specific obstacles, some MVAs may be lower than the non-radar MEAs/MOCAs or other minimum altitudes depicted on charts for a given location. While being radar vectored, IFR altitude asssignments by ATC will be at or above MVA.

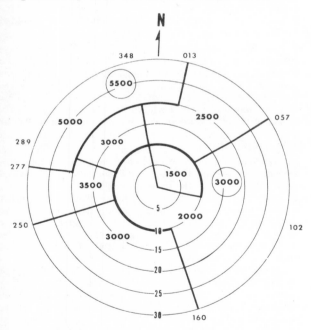

Figure 4–13—TYPICAL MVA CHART

g. Visual Descent Point (VDP). VDP is being incorporated in selected nonprecision approach procedures. The VDP is a defined point on the final approach course of a nonprecision straight-in approach procedure from which normal descent from the MDA to the runway touchdown point may be commenced, provided visual reference required by FAR 91.117(b) is established.

The VDP will normally be identified by DME on VOR and LOC procedures. VDPs are not a mandatory part of the procedure, but are intended to provide additional guidance where they are implemented. VASI will normally be available where VDPs are established. No special technique is required to fly a procedure with a VDP. The pilot should not descend below the MDA prior to reaching the VDP and acquiring the necessary visual reference in accordance with FAR 91.117(b). Pilots not equipped to receive the VDP should fly the approach procedure as though no VDP had been provided. The VDP is identified on the profile view of the approach chart by the symbol: V.

365. APPROACH CLEARANCE

a. An aircraft which has been cleared to a holding fix and subsequently "cleared . . . approach" has not received new routing. Even though the "cleared . . . approach" may have been issued or received prior to the aircraft reaching the holding fix, ATC would expect the pilot to proceed via the holding fix (his last assigned route), a transition if one exists, and then to the initial approach fix to commence his approach. If a transition fix is located along the route of flight en route to the holding fix and clearance for an approach is received, he should commence his approach from the transition fix if not already passed it. If a route of flight directly to the initial approach fix is desired, it should be so stated by the controller with phraseology to include the words "direct . . .," "proceed direct" or similar phrase which the pilot can interpret without question. If the pilot is uncertain of his clearance, he should immediately query ATC as to what route of flight is desired.

366–369. RESERVED

370. INSTRUMENT APPROACH PROCEDURES

a. Minimums are specified for various aircraft approach categories based on speed/weight combinations. Speeds are based upon a value 1.3 times the stalling speed of the aircraft in the landing configuration at maximum certificated gross landing weight. Thus they are COMPUTED values. See FAR 97.3(b). An aircraft can fit into only one category, that being the highest category in which it meets either specification. For example, a 30,000 pound aircraft landing weight combined with a computed approach speed of 130 knots would place the aircraft in Category C. If it is necessary, however, while circling to land, to maneuver at speeds more than 5 knots in excess of the upper limit of the speed range for each category, due to the possibility of extending the circling maneuver beyond the area for which obstruction clearance is provided, the circling minimum for the next higher approach category should be used. For example, an aircraft which falls in Category C, but is circling to land at a speed in excess of 145 knots, should use the approach category 'D' minimum when circling to land. This clarification is issued pending revision of AC No. 90–1A.

b. Pilots are reminded that when operating on an unpublished route or while being radar vectored, the pilot, when an approach clearance is received, shall, in addition to complying with the minimum altitudes for IFR operations (FAR 91.119), maintain his last assigned altitude unless a different altitude is assigned by ATC, or until the aircraft is established on a segment of a published route or instrument approach procedure. After the aircraft is so established, published altitudes apply to descent within each succeeding route or approach segment unless a different altitude is assigned by ATC. Notwithstanding this pilot responsibility, for aircraft operating on unpublished routes or while being radar vectored, ATC will, except when conducting a radar approach, issue an IFR approach clearance only after the aircraft is established on a segment of a published route or instrument approach procedure, or is assigned an altitude to maintain until the aircraft is established on a segment of a published route or instrument approach procedure. Example—'Cross Redding VOR at or above five thousand, cleared for VOR Runway three four approach,' '5 miles from outer marker, turn right heading three three zero, maintain two thousand until established on the localizer, cleared for ILS Runway three six approach.' The altitude assigned will assure IFR obstruction clearance from the point at which the approach clearance is issued until established on a segment of a published route or instrument approach procedure. If a pilot is uncertain of the meaning of his clearance, he shall immediately request clarification from ATC.

c. Several instrument approach procedures, using various navigation/approach aids may be authorized for an airport. ATC may advise that a particular approach procedure is being used, primarily to expedite traffic. If a pilot is issued a clearance that specifies a particular approach procedure, he is expected to notify ATC immediately if he desires a different one. In this event it may be necessary for ATC to withhold clearance for the different approach until such time as traffic conditions permit. However, if the pilot is involved in an emergency situation he will be given priority. If the pilot is not familiar with the specific approach procedure, ATC should be advised and they will provide detailed information on the execution of the procedure.

d. At times ATC may not specify a particular approach procedure in the clearance, but will state "CLEARED FOR APPROACH." Such clearance indicates that the pilot may execute any one of the authorized instrument approach procedures for that airport. This clearance does not constitute approval for the pilot to execute a contact approach or a visual approach.

e. When cleared for a specifically prescribed instrument approach procedure, i.e., "cleared for ILS runway one niner approach" or when "cleared for approach" i.e., execution of any procedure prescribed for the airport, pilots shall execute the entire procedure as described on the Instrument Approach Procedure Chart unless an appropriate new or revised ATC clearance is received, or the IFR flight plan is cancelled.

f. Pilots planning flights to locations served by special instrument approach procedures should obtain advance approval from the owner of the procedure. Approval by the owner is necessary because special procedures are for the exclusive use of a single interest unless otherwise authorized by the owner. Additionally, some special approach procedures require certain crew qualifications, training, or other special considerations in order to execute the approach. Also, some of these approach procedures are based on privately owned navigational aids. Owners of aids that are not for public use may elect to turn off the aid for whatever reason they may have; i.e., maintainance, conservation, etc. Air traffic controllers are not required to question pilots to determine if they have permission to use the procedure. Controllers presume a pilot has obtained approval and is aware of any details of the procedure if he files an IFR flight plan to that airport.

g. When executing an instrument approach and in radio contact with an FAA facility, unless in "radar contact," report passing the final approach fix inbound.

h. If a missed approach is required, advise ATC and include the reason (unless initiated by ATC). Comply with the missed approach instructions for the instrument approach procedure being executed, unless otherwise directed by ATC. (See **382** and **404**—MISSED APPROACH.)

371. PROCEDURE TURN

a. A procedure turn is specified when it is necessary to reverse direction to establish the aircraft inbound on an intermediate or final approach course. The instrument approach procedure specifies the outbound and inbound courses, the distance within which the procedure turn shall be completed, and the side of the inbound course (by the magnetic compass direction) on which the turn should be made. Unless otherwise restricted (Limitations on Procedure Turns, below) the type and rate of the turn and the point at which the turn is begun is left to the discretion of the pilot. However, the maneuver must be completed within the prescribed procedure turn distance and not below the minimum altitude specified for its completion.

(1) When the approach procedure involves a procedure turn, a maximum speed of not greater than 250 knots (IAS) should be observed and the turn should be executed within the distance specified in the profile view. The normal procedure turn distance is 10 miles. This may be reduced to a minimum of 5 miles where only Category A or helicopter aircraft are to be operated or increased to as much as 15 miles to accommodate high performance aircraft.

(2) Where a holding pattern is specified in lieu of a procedure turn, the holding maneuver must be executed within the one minute time limitation or published leg length. The maneuver is completed when the aircraft is established on the inbound course after executing the appropriate holding pattern entry. Criteria for entry into the holding pattern and applicable airspeed to be flown is as prescribed in the EN ROUTE-IFR, Holding Section. If cleared for the approach prior to returning to the holding fix, and the aircraft is at the prescribed altitude, additional circuits of the holding pattern are not necessary nor expected by air traffic control. If the pilot elects to make additional circuits to lose excessive altitude or to become better established on course, it is his responsibility to so advise air traffic control when he receives his approach clearance.

(3) In order to provide proper separation from departing aircraft, ATC may specify the point at which the turn should be executed, which will be consistent with the limitations of the specific approach procedure for the airport.

(4) A teardrop procedure/penetration turn may be specified in some procedures for a required course rever-

sal. The teardrop procedure consists of departure from an initial approach fix on a outbound course followed by a turn toward and intercepting the inbound course at or prior to the intermediate fix or point. Its purpose is to permit an aircraft to reverse direction and lose considerable altitude within reasonably limited airspace. Where no fix is available to mark the beginning of the intermediate segment, it shall be assumed to commence at a point 10 miles prior to the final approach fix. When the facility is located on the airport, an aircraft is considered to be on final approach upon completion of the penetration turn. However, the final approach segment begins on the final approach course 10 miles from the facility.

(5) A procedure turn may not be established when an approach can be made from a properly aligned holding pattern. In such cases, the holding pattern is established over an intermediate fix or a final approach fix and, as in the procedure turn, the descent from the minimum holding pattern altitude to the final approach fix altitude may not commence until the aircraft is established on the inbound course.

(6) A procedure turn is not required when an approach can be made directly from a specified intermediate fix to the final approach fix. In such cases, the term "NoPT" is used with the appropriate course and altitude to denote that the procedure turn is not required. If a procedure turn is desired, and when cleared to do so by ATC, descent below the procedure turn altitude should not be made until the aircraft is established on the inbound course, since some NoPT altitudes may be lower than the procedure turn altitudes.

b. Limitations on Procedure Turns.

(1) In the case of a radar initial approach to a final approach fix or position, or a timed approach from a holding fix, or where the procedure specifies "NoPT", no pilot may make a procedure turn unless, when he receives his final approach clearance, he so advises ATC and a clearance is received.

(2) When a teardrop procedure turn is depicted and a course reversal is required, this type turn must be executed.

(3) When a one minute holding pattern replaces the procedure turn, the standard entry and the holding pattern shall be followed except when RADAR VECTORING is provided.

(4) As otherwise restricted by notes and symbols on the procedure charts.

372. TIMED APPROACHES FROM A HOLDING FIX

a. TIMED APPROACHES may be conducted when the following conditions are met:

(1) A control tower is in operation at the airport where the approaches are conducted.

(2) Direct communications is maintained between the pilot and the center/approach controller until the pilot is instructed to contact the tower.

(3) If more than one missed approach procedure is available, none require a course reversal.

(4) If only one missed approach procedure is available, the following conditions are met:

(a) Course reversal is not required; and,

(b) Reported ceiling and visibility are equal to or greater than the highest prescribed circling minimums for the instrument approach procedure.

(5) When cleared for the approach, pilots shall not execute a procedure turn. (Ref: FAR 91.116(h))

b. Although the controller will not specifically state that "timed approaches are in progress", his assigning a time to depart the final approach fix inbound is indicative that timed approach procedures are being utilized, or in lieu of holding, he may use radar vectors to the final approach course to establish a mileage interval between aircraft that will insure the appropriate time sequence between the final approach fix and the airport

c. Each pilot in an approach sequence will be given advance notice as to the time he should leave the holding point on approach to the airport. When a time to leave the holding point has been received, the pilot should adjust his flight path to leave the fix as closely as possible to the designated time.

d. Time Approach Example.

Figure 3–16 depicts a final approach procedure from a holding pattern at a final approach fix (FAF).

At 12:03 local time, in the example shown, a pilot holding, receives instructions to leave the fix inbound at 12:07. These instructions are received just as the pilot has completed turn at the outbound end of the holding pattern and is proceeding inbound towards the fix. Arriving back over the fix, the pilot notes that the time is 12:04 and that he has three minutes to lose in order to

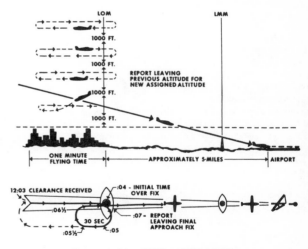

Figure 4–14—TIMED APPROACHES

leave the fix at the assigned time. Since the time remaining is more than two minutes, the pilot plans to fly a race track pattern rather than a 360° turn, which would use up two minutes. The turns at the ends of the race track pattern will consume approximately two minutes. Three minutes to go, minus two minutes required for turns, leaves one minute for level flight. Since two portions of level flight will be required to get back to the fix inbound, the pilot halves the one minute remaining and plans to fly level for 30 seconds outbound before starting his turn back toward the fix on final approach. If the winds were negligible at flight altitude, this procedure would bring the pilot inbound across the fix precisely at the specified time of 12:07. However, if the pilot expected a headwind on final approach, he should shorten his 30 seconds outbound course somewhat, knowing that the wind will carry him away from the fix faster while outbound and decrease his ground speed while returning to the fix. On the other hand, if the pilot knew he would have a tailwind on final approach, he should lengthen his calculated 30-second outbound heading somewhat, knowing that the wind would tend to hold him closer to the fix while outbound and increase his ground speed while returning to the fix.

373. RADAR APPROACHES

a. The only airborne radio equipment required for radar approaches is a functioning radio transmitter and receiver. The radar controller vectors the aircraft to align it with the runway centerline. The controller continues the vectors to keep the aircraft on course until the pilot can complete the approach and landing by visual reference to the surface There are two types of radar approaches "Precision" (PAR) and "Surveillance" (ASR).

b. A radar approach may be given to any aircraft upon request and may be offered to pilots of aircraft in distress or to expedite traffic, however, a surveillance approach might not be approved unless there is an ATC operational requirement, or in an unusual or emergency situation. Acceptance of a precision or surveillance approach by a pilot does not waive the prescribed weather minimums for the airport or for the particular aircraft operator concerned. The decision to make a radar approach when the reported weather is below the established minimums rests with the pilot.

c. Precision and surveillance approach minimums are published on separate pages in the National Ocean Survey Instrument Approach Procedure Charts.

(1) A PRECISION APPROACH (PAR) is one in which a controller provides highly accurate navigational guidance in azimuth and elevation to a pilot. Pilots are given headings to fly, to direct them to, and keep their aircraft aligned with the extended centerline of the landing runway. They are told to anticipate glide path interception approximately 10 to 30 seconds before it occurs and when to start descent. The published decision height will be given only if the pilot requests it. If the aircraft is observed to deviate above or below the glide path, the pilot is given the relative amount of deviation by use of terms "slightly" or "well" and is expected to adjust his rate of descent to return to the glide path. Range from touchdown is given at least once each mile. If an aircraft is observed by the controller to proceed outside of specified safety zone limits in azimuth and/or elevation and continue to operate outside these prescribed limits, the pilot will be directed to execute a missed approach or to fly a specified course unless he has the runway environment (runway, approach lights, etc.) in sight. Navigational guidance in azimuth and elevation is provided the pilot until the aircraft reaches the published Decision Height (DH). Advisory course and glidepath information is furnished by the controller until the aircraft passes over the landing threshold, at which point the pilot is advised of any deviation from the runway centerline. Radar service is automatically terminated upon completion of the approach.

(2) A SURVEILLANCE APPROACH is one in which a controller provides navigational guidance in azimuth only. The pilot is furnished headings to fly to align his aircraft with the extended centerline of the landing runway. Since the radar information used for a surveillance approach is considerably less precise than that used for a precision approach, the accuracy of the approach will not be as great and higher minimums will apply. Guidance in elevation is not possible but the pilot will be advised when to commence descent to the minimum descent altitude (MDA) or, if appropriate, to an intermediate 'step down fix' minimum crossing altitude and subsequently to the prescribed MDA. In addition, the pilot will be advised of the location of the missed approach point (MAP) prescribed for the procedure and his position each mile on final from the runway, airport/heliport or MAP, as appropriate. If requested by the pilot, recommended altitudes will be issued at each mile, based on the descent gradient established for the procedure, down to the last mile that is at or above the MDA. Normally, navigational guidance will be provided until the aircraft reaches the MAP. Controllers will terminate guidance and instruct the pilot to execute a missed approach unless at the MAP the pilot has the runway, airport/heliport in sight or, for a helicopter point-in-space approach, the prescribed visual reference with the surface is established. Also, if, at any time during the approach the controller considers that safe guidance for the remainder of the approach can not be provided, he will terminate guidance and instruct the pilot to execute a missed approach. Similarly, guidance termination and missed approach will be effected upon pilot request and, for civil aircraft only, controllers may terminate guidance when the pilot reports the runway, airport/heliport or visual surface route (point-in-space approach) in sight or otherwise indicates that continued guidance is not required. Radar service is automatically terminated at the completion of a radar approach.

NOTE.—The published minimum descent altitude (MDA) for straight-in approaches will be given to the pilot before he begins his descent; however, if the circling MDA is required it will be given only on request and the pilot must furnish his aircraft category at the time of the request.

(3) A NO-GYRO APPROACH is available to a pilot under radar control who experiences circumstances wherein his directional gyro or other stabilized compass is inoperative or inaccurate. When this occurs, he should so advise air traffic control and request a No-Gyro vector or approach. Pilots of aircraft not equipped with a directional gyro or other stabilized compass who desire radar handling may also request a No-Gyro vector or approach. The pilot should make all turns at standard rate and should execute the turn immediately upon receipt of instructions. For example, "TURN RIGHT," "STOP TURN." When a surveillance or precision approach is made, the pilot will be advised after his aircraft has been turned onto final approach to make turns at half standard rate.

374. RADAR MONITORING OF INSTRUMENT APPROACHES

a. Precision Approach Radar (PAR) facilities operated by the FAA and the military services at some joint-use (civil/military) and military installations monitor aircraft on instrument approaches and issue radar advisories to the pilot when weather is below VFR minima (1,000 and 3), at night, or when requested by a pilot. This service is provided only when the PAR final approach course coincides with the final approach of the navigational aid and only during the operational hours of the PAR. The radar advisories serve only as a secondary aid since the pilot has selected the navigational aid as the primary aid for the approach.

b. Prior to starting final approach, the pilot will be advised of the frequency on which the advisories will be transmitted. If, for any reason, radar advisories cannot be furnished, the pilot will be so advised.

c. Advisory information, derived from radar observations, includes information on:

(1) Passing the final approach fix. (At this point, the pilot may be requested to report sighting the approach lights or the runway.)

(2) Trend advisories with respect to elevation and/or azimuth radar position and movement will be provided. Whenever the aircraft nears the PAR safety limit the pilot will be advised that he is well above or below the glidepath or well left or right of course *(glidepath information given only to those aircraft executing a precision approach; e.g., ILS).*

> NOTE.—Altitude information is not transmitted to aircraft executing other than precision approaches because the descent portions of these approaches generally do not coincide with the depicted PAR glide path.

(3) If, after repeated advisories, the aircraft proceeds outside the PAR safety limit or if a radical deviation is observed, the pilot will be advised to execute a missed approach if not visual.

d. Radar service is automatically terminated upon completion of the approach.

375. SIMULTANEOUS ILS APPROACHES

a. System: An approach system permitting simultaneous ILS approaches to airports having parallel runways separated by at least 4,300 feet between centerlines. Integral parts of a total system are ILS, radar, communications, ATC procedures, and appropriate airborne equipment. The Approach Procedure Chart permitting simultaneous approaches will contain the note "simultaneous approach authorized rwys 14L and 14R" identifying the appropriate runways as the case may be. When advised that simultaneous ILS approaches are in progress, pilots shall advise approach control immediately of malfunctioning or inoperative receivers or if simultaneous approach is not desired.

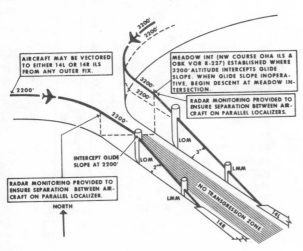

Figure 4-15—SIMULTANEOUS ILS APPROACHES

b. Radar Monitor Service: This service is provided for each ILS to insure prescribed lateral separation during approaches. Pilots will be assigned frequencies to receive advisories and instructions. Aircraft deviating from either localizer to the point where the no transgression zone (an area at least 2,000 feet wide) may be penetrated will be instructed to take corrective action. If an aircraft fails to respond to such instruction, the aircraft on the adjacent localizer may be instructed to alter course.

c. Radar Advisories: Whenever simultaneous ILS approaches are in progress radar advisories will be provided on the tower frequency.

(1) The monitor controller will have the capability of overriding the tower controller on the tower frequency.

(2) The pilot will be advised to monitor the tower frequency.

(3) The monitor will automatically be terminated at 1 mile, or if procedurally required at a specific location, at the ILS middle marker.

(4) The monitor controller will *not* advise when the monitor is terminated.

376. PARALLEL APPROACHES

a. Parallel approaches are an air traffic control procedure permitting parallel ILS approaches to airports having parallel runways separated by at least 3,000 feet between centerlines. Integral parts of a total system are ILS, radar, communications, ATC procedures, and appropriate airborne equipment.

b. A parallel approach differs from a simultaneous approach in that the minimum distance between parallel runway centerlines is reduced; there is no requirement for radar monitoring or advisories; and, a staggered sepaartion of aircraft on the adjacent localizer course is required.

c. Aircraft are afforded a minimum of 2 miles radar separation between successive aircraft on the adjacent localizer course and a minimum of 3 miles radar separation from aircraft on the same localizer course. In addition, a minimum of 1000 feet vertical or a minimum of 3 miles radar separation is provided between aircraft during turn-on.

d. Whenever parallel approaches are in progress, aircraft are informed that approaches to both runways are in use. In addition, the radar controller will have the capability of overriding the tower controllers frequency where the responsibility for radar separation is not performed by the tower controller.

377-379. RESERVED

380. SIDE-STEP MANEUVER

Air Traffic Control may authorize an approach procedure which serves either one of parallel runways that are separated by 1,200 feet or less followed by a straight-in landing on the adjacent runway. Aircraft that will execute a side-step maneuver will be cleared for a specified approach and landing on the adjacent parallel runway. Example, "cleared for ILS runway 07 left approach, side-step to runway 07 right." Pilots are expected to commence the side-step maneuver as soon as possible after the runway or runway environment is in sight. Landing minima to the adjacent runway will be higher than the minima to the primary runway, but will normally be lower than the published circling minima. ATC will not clear aircraft for landing on an adjacent runway unless weather conditions will permit successful completion of the side-step maneuver.

381. WEATHER MINIMUMS

a. **LANDING MINIMUMS.** The rules applicable to landing minimums are contained in FAR 91.116 and FAR 91.117. Detailed information regarding civil use of the U.S. Government instrument approach charts is found in Advisory Circular AC–90–1A. This circular can be obtained from Distribution Operations TAD–482.41, Department of Transportation, Washington, D.C. 20590.

(1) *Straight-in-minimums* are shown on instrument approach procedure charts when the final approach course of the instrument approach procedure is within 30° of the runway alignment and a normal descent can be made from the IFR altitude shown on the instrument approach procedures to the runway surface. When either the normal rate of descent or the runway alignment factor of 30° is exceeded, a straight-in minimum is not published and a circling minimum applies. The fact that a straight-in minimum is not published does not preclude the pilot from landing straight-in if he has the active runway in sight in sufficient time to make a normal approach for landing. Under such conditions and when Air Traffic Control has cleared him for landing on that runway, he is not expected to circle even though only circling minimums are published. If he desires to circle, he should advise ATC.

(2) *Side-Step Maneuver Minimums*—Landing minima for a side-step maneuver to the adjacent runway will be higher than the minima to the primary runway but will normally be lower than the published circling minima.

(3) *Circling Minimum*—The circling minimums published on the instrument approach chart provide adequate obstruction clearance and the pilot should not descend below the circling altitude until the aircraft is in a position to make final descent for landing. Sound judgement and knowledge of his and the aircraft capabilities are the criteria for a pilot to determine the exact maneuver in each instance since airport design and the aircraft position, altitude and airspeed must all be conisdered. The following basic rules apply.

(a) Maneuver the shortest path to the base or downwind leg as appropriate under minimum weather conditions. There is no restriction from passing over the airport or other runways.

(b) It should be recognized that many circling maneuvers may be made while VFR or other flying is in progress at the airport. Standard left turns or specific instruction from the controller for maneuvering must be considered when circling to land.

(c) At airports without a control tower, it may be desirable to fly over the airport to determine wind and turn indicators, and to observe other traffic which may be on the runway or flying in the vicinity of the airport.

(4) *Instrument Approach At A Military Field.* When instrument approaches are conducted by civil aircraft at military airports, they shall be conducted in accordance with the procedures and minimums approved by the military agency having jurisdiction over the airport.

382. MISSED APPROACH

a. When a landing cannot be accomplished, advise ATC and, upon reaching the missed approach point defined on the approach procedure chart, the pilot must comply with the missed approach instructions for the procedure being used or with an alternate missed approach procedure specified by Air Traffic Control.

b. Protected obstacle clearance areas for missed approach are predicated on the assumption that the abort is initiated at the missed approach point not lower than the MDA or DH. Reasonable buffers are provided for normal maneuvers. However, no consideration is given to an abnormally early turn. Therefore when an early missed approach is executed, pilots should—unless otherwise cleared by ATC—fly the instrument approach procedure as specified on the approach plate to the missed approach point at or above the MDA or DH before executing a turning maneuver.

c. If visual reference is lost while circling to land from an instrument approach, the missed approach specified for that particular procedure must be followed (unless an alternate missed approach procedure is specified by Air Traffic Control). To become established on the prescribed missed approach course, the pilot should make an initial climbing turn toward the landing runway and continue the turn until he is established on the missed approach course. Inasmuch as the circling maneuver may be accomplished in more than one direction, different patterns will be required to become established on the prescribed missed approach course depending on the aircraft position at the time visual reference is lost. Adherence to the procedure will assure that an aircraft will remain within the circling and missed approach obstruction clearance areas.

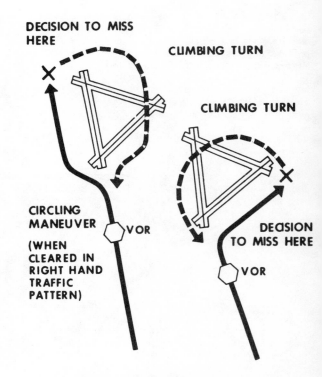

Figure 4–16—MISSED APPROACH EXAMPLE

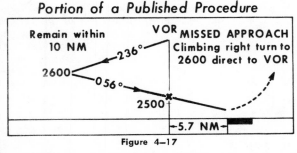

Portion of a Published Procedure

Figure 4—17

d. At locations where ATC Radar Service is provided the pilot should conform to radar vectors when provided by ATC in lieu of the published missed approach procedure.

e. When approach has been missed, request clearance for specific action; i.e., to alternative airport, another approach, etc.

383. VISUAL APPROACH

a. ATC may authorize an aircraft to conduct a "visual approach" to an airport or to follow another aircraft when flight to and landing at the airport can be accomplished in VFR weather. The aircraft must have the airport or the identified preceding aircraft in sight before the clearance is issued. If the aircraft has the airport in sight but cannot see the aircraft he is following, ATC may still clear the aircraft for a visual approach; however, ATC retains both separation and wake vortex separation responsibility. When visually following a preceding aircraft, acceptance of a visual approach clearance, constitutes acceptance of pilot responsibility for maintaining a safe approach interval and adequate wake turbulence separation.

NOTE.—At some locations, visual approach flight procedures for turbine-powered aircraft are charted.

b. When operating to an airport with an operating control tower, aircraft may be authorized to conduct a "visual approach" to one runway while other aircraft are conducting IFR or VFR approaches to another runway. When operating to airports with parallel runways separated by less than 2,500 feet, the succeeding aircraft must report sighting the preceding aircraft before ATC may authorize it to conduct a "visual approach." When the parallel runways are separated by 2,500 feet or more, or converging runways are in use, ATC may authorize a "visual approach" after advising all aircraft involved

that other aircraft are conducting approaches to the other runway.

c. When operating to an airport without an operating control tower and no weather reporting facility is available, ATC may authorize a "visual approach" only if the aircraft reports that descent and flight to the destination airport can be made in VFR.

d. Authorization to conduct a "visual approach" is an IFR authorization and does not alter IFR flight plan cancellation responsibility. (See **303**—CANCELING IFR FLIGHT PLAN.)

384. CONTACT APPROACH

a. Pilots operating in accordance with an IFR flight plan, provided they are clear of clouds and have at least 1 mile flight visibility and can reasonably expect to continue to the destination airport in those conditions, may request ATC authorization for a "contact approach,"

b. Controllers may authorize a "contact approach" provided:

(1) The Contact Approach is specifically requested by the pilot. ATC cannot initiate this approach.

Example:

REQUEST CONTACT APPROACH.

(2) The reported ground visibility at the destination airport is at least 1 statute mile.

(3) The contact approach will be made to an airport having a standard or special instrument approach procedure.

(4) Approved separation is applied between aircraft so cleared and between these aircraft and other IFR or special VFR aircraft.

Example:

CLEARED FOR CONTACT APPROACH, and if required AT OR BELOW (altitude) (Routing) IF NOT POSSIBLE (alternative procedures) AND ADVISE.

c. A Contact Approach is an approach procedure that may be used by a pilot (with prior authorization from ATC) in lieu of conducting a standard or special instrument approach procedure to an airport. It is not intended for use by a pilot on an IFR flight clearance to operate to an airport not having an authorized instrument approach procedure. Nor is it intended for an aircraft to conduct an instrument approach to one airport and then, when "in the clear", to discontinue that approach and proceed to another airport. In the execution of a contact approach, the pilot assumes the responsibility for obstruction clearance. If radar service is being received, it will automatically terminate when the pilot is told to contact the tower.

385. LANDING PRIORITY

A clearance for a specific type of approach (ILS, ADF, VOR or Straight-in Approach) to an aircraft operating on an IFR flight plan does not mean that landing priority will be given over other traffic. Traffic control towers handle all aircraft, regardless of the type of flight plan, on a "first-come, first-served" basis. Therefore, because of local traffic or runway in use, it may be necessary for the controller. in the interest of safety, to provide a different landing sequence. In any case, a landing sequence will be issued each aircraft as soon as possible to enable the pilot to properly adjust his flight path.

386—399. RESERVED

Section 9. PILOT/CONTROLLER ROLES AND RESPONSIBILITIES

400. GENERAL

a. The roles and responsibilities of the pilot and controller for effective participation in the ATC system are contained in several documents. Pilot responsibilities are in the Federal Aviation Regulations (FARs) and the air traffic controller's are in the Air Traffic Control Handbook (7110.65) and supplemental FAA directives. Additional and supplemental information for pilots can be found in the current Airman's Information Manual (AIM), Notices to Airmen, Advisory Circulars and aeronautical charts. Since there are many other excellent publications produced by non-government organizations, as well as other government organizations, with various updating cycles, questions concerning the latest or most current material can be resolved by cross-checking with the above mentioned documents.

b. The pilot in command of an aircraft is directly responsible for, and is the final authority as to the safe operation of that aircraft. In an emergency requiring immediate action, the pilot in command may deviate from any rule in the General Subpart A and Flight Rules Subpart B in accordance with FAR 91.3.

c. The air traffic controller is responsible to give first priority to the separation of aircraft and to the issuance of radar safety advisories, second priority to other services that are required, but do not involve separation of aircraft and third priority to additional services to the extent possible.

d. In order to maintain a safe and efficient air traffic system, it is necessary that each party fulfill his responsibilities to the fullest.

e. The responsibilities of the pilot and the controller intentionally overlap in many areas providing a degree of redundancy. Should one or the other fail in any manner, this overlapping responsibility is expected to compensate, in many cases, for failures that may affect safety.

f. The following, while not intended to be all inclusive, is a brief listing of pilot and controller responsibilities for some commonly used procedures or phases of flight. More detailed explanations are contained in other portions of this publication, the appropriate Federal Aviation Regulations, Advisory Circulars and similar publications. The information provided is an overview of the principles involved and is not meant as an interpretation of the rules nor is it intended to extend or diminish responsibilities.

401. AIR TRAFFIC CLEARANCE

A. Pilot

– Acknowledge receipt and understanding of an ATC clearance.

– Request clarification or amendment, as appropriate, any time a clearance is not fully understood, or considered unacceptable from a safety standpoint.

– Comply with an air traffic clearance upon receipt except as necessary to cope with an emergency. If deviation is necessary, advise ATC as soon as possible and obtain an amended clearance.

B. Controller

– Issues appropriate clearances for the operation being or to be conducted in accordance with established criteria.

– Assigns altitudes in IFR clearances that are at or above the minimum IFR altitudes in controlled airspace.

402. CONTACT APPROACH

A. Pilot

– This approach must be requested by the pilot, and is made in lieu of a standard or special instrument approach.

– By requesting the contact approach, the pilot indicates that the flight is operating clear of clouds, has at least 1 mile flight visibility, and can reasonably expect to continue to the destination airport in those conditions.

– Be aware that while conducting a contact approach, the pilot assumes responsibility for obstruction clearance.

– Advise ATC immediately if you are unable to continue the contact approach or if you encounter less than 1 mile flight visibility.

B. Controller

– Issues clearance for contact approach only when requested by the pilot. Does not solicit the use of this procedure.

– Before issuing clearance, ascertains that reported ground visibility at destination airport is at least 1 mile.

– Provides approved separation between aircraft cleared for contact approach and other IFR or special VFR aricraft. When using vertical separation, does not assign a fixed altitude but clears the aircraft at or below an altitude which is at least 1,000 feet below any IFR traffic but not below minimum safe altitudes prescribed in FAR 91.79.

– Issues alternative instructions if, in his judgment, weather conditions may make completion of the approach impracticable.

403. INSTRUMENT APPROACH

A. Pilot

– Be aware that the controller issues clearance for approach based only on known traffic.

– Follow the procedure as shown on the instrument approach chart, including all restrictive notations, such as—

   (a) Procedure not authorized at night;

   (b) Approach not authorized when local area altimeter not available;

   (c) Procedure not authorized when control tower not in operation;

   (d) Procedure not authorized when glide slope not used; or

   (e) Straight-in minima not authorized at night; etc.

-- Upon receipt of an approach clearance while on an unpublished route or being radar vectored:

    (a) Comply with the minimum altitude for IFR and;

    (b) Maintain last assigned altitude until established on a segment of a published route or IAP, at which time published altitudes apply.

B. Controller

-- Issues an approach clearance based on known traffic.

-- Issues an IFR approach clearance only after the aircraft is established on a segment of published route or IAP, or assigns an appropriate altitude for the aircraft to maintain until so established.

404. MISSED APPROACH

A. Pilot

-- Execute a missed approach when one of the following conditions exist:

    (a) Arrival at the missed approach point (MAP) or the decision height (DH) and visual reference to the runway environment is insufficient to complete the landing.

    (b) Determined that a safe landing is not possible.

    (c) Instructed to do so by ATC.

-- Advise ATC that a missed approach will be made. Include the reason for the missed approach unless initiated by ATC.

-- Comply with the missed approach instructions for the instrument approach procedure being executed unless other *missed approach* instructions are specified by ATC.

-- If executing a missed approach prior to reaching the MAP or DH, fly the instrument procedure to the MAP at an altitude at or above the MDA or DH before executing a turning maneuver.

-- Radar vectors issued by ATC when informed that a missed approach is being executed supersedes the previous missed approach procedure.

-- If making a missed approach from a radar approach, execute the missed approach procedure previously given or climb to the altitude and fly the heading specified by the controller.

-- Following missed approach, request clearance for specific action; i.e., to alternative airport, another approach, etc.

-- Advise ATC of your intentions; i.e., whether you wish to hold, proceed to another airport, or execute another approach, etc.

B. Controller

-- Issues an approved alternate missed approach procedure if it is desired that the pilot execute a procedure other than as depicted on the instrument approach chart.

-- May vector a radar identified aircraft executing a missed approach when operationally advantageous to the pilot or the controller.

-- In response to the pilots' stated intentions, issues a clearance to an alternate airport, to a holding fix, or for reentry into the approach sequence, as traffic conditions permit.

405. RADAR VECTORS

A. Pilot

-- Comply with headings and altitudes assigned to you by the controller.

-- Question any assigned heading or altitude believed to be incorrect.

-- If operating VFR and compliance with any radar vector or altitude would cause a violation of any FAR, advise ATC and obtain a revised clearance or instruction.

B. Controller

-- Vectors aircraft in controlled airspace:

    (a) For separation.

    (b) For noise abatement.

    (c) To obtain an operational advantage for the pilot or controller.

-- Vectors aircraft in controlled and uncontrolled airspace when requested by the pilot.

-- Vectors IFR aircraft at or above minimum vectoring altitudes.

-- Is permitted to vector VFR aircraft below minimum vectoring altitudes.

406. SAFETY ADVISORY

A. Pilot

-- Initiate appropriate action if a safety advisory is received from ATC.

-- Be aware that this service is not always available and that many factors affect the ability of the controller to be aware of a situation in which unsafe proximity to terrain, obstructions or another aircraft may be developing.

-- This service is not a substitute for pilot adherence to safe operating practices.

B. Controller

-- Issues a safety advisory if he is aware an aircraft under his control is at an altitude which, in the controller's judgment, places the aircraft in unsafe proximity to terrain, obstructions or another aircraft. Types of safety advisories are:

    (a) Terrain/Obstruction Advisory—Immediately issue to an aircraft under his control if he is aware the aircraft is at an altitude believed to place the aircraft in unsafe proximity to terrain/obstructions.

    (b) Aircraft Conflict Advisory—Immediately issued to an aircraft under his control if he is aware of an aircraft not under his control at an altitude believed to place the aircraft in unsafe proximity to each other. With the alert, he offers the pilot an alternative, if feasible.

-- Discontinues further advisories if informed by the pilot that he is taking action to correct the situation or that he has the other aircraft in sight.

407. SEE AND AVOID

A. Pilot

-- When meteorological conditions permit, regardless of type of flight plan, whether or not under control of a radar facility, the pilot is responsible to see and avoid other traffic, terrain or obstacles.

B. Controller

- Provides radar traffic information to radar identified aircraft operating outside positive control airspace on a workload permitting basis.
- Issues a safety advisory to an aircraft under his control if he is aware the aircraft is at an altitude believed to place the aircraft in unsafe proximity to terrain, obstructions or other aircraft.

408. SPEED ADJUSTMENTS

A. Pilot

- Advise ATC any time cruising airspeed varies plus or minus 5 percent, or 10 knots, whichever is greater, from that given in the flight plan.
- Comply with speed adjustments from ATC unless:
  - (a) The minimum or maximum safe airspeed for any particular operation is greater or less than the requested airspeed. In such cases, advise ATC.
  - (b) Operating at or above 10,000 feet MSL on an ATC assigned SPEED ADJUSTMENT of more than 250 knots IAS and subsequent clearance is received for descent below 10,000 feet MSL. In such cases, pilots are expected to comply with FAR 91.70(a).
- When complying with speed adjustment assignment, maintain an indicated airspeed within plus or minus 10 knots of the requested airspeed.

B. Controller

- Assigns aircraft to speed adjustments when necessary but not as a substitute for good vectoring technique.
- Adheres to the restrictions of 7110.65 as to when speed adjustment procedures may be applied.
- Avoids speed adjustments requiring alternate decreases and increases.
- Assigns speed adjustments to a specified IAS or to increase or decrease speed utilizing increments of 10 knots or multiples thereof.
- Advises pilots to resume normal speed when speed adjustments are no longer required.
- Gives due consideration to aircraft capabilities to reduce speed while descending.

409. TRAFFIC ADVISORIES (Traffic Information)

A. Pilot

- Acknowledge receipt of traffic advisories.
- Inform controller if traffic in sight.
- Advise ATC if a vector to avoid traffic is desired.
- Do not expect to receive radar traffic advisories on all traffic. Some aircraft may not appear on the radar display. Be aware that the controller may be occupied with higher priority duties and unable to issue traffic information for a variety of reasons.
- Advise controller if service not desired.

B. Controller

- Issues radar traffic to the maximum extent consistent with higher priority duties except in positive controlled airspace.
- Provides vectors to assist aircraft to avoid observed traffic when requested by the pilot.
- Issues traffic information to aircraft in the airport traffic area for sequencing purposes.

410. VISUAL APPROACH

A. Pilot

- If a visual approach is not desired, advise ATC.
- Comply with controller's instructions for vectors toward the airport of intended landing or to a visual position behind a preceding aircraft.
- After being cleared for a visual approach, proceed to the airport in a normal manner or follow designated traffic and/or charted flight procedures, as appropriate remaining in VFR at all times.
- Acceptance of a visual approach clearance to visually follow a preceding aircraft is pilot acknowledgement that he will establish a safe landing interval behind the preceding aircraft and that he accepts responsibility for his own wake turbulence separation.
- Advise ATC immediately if you are unable to continue following a designated aircraft or encounter less than basic VFR weather conditions.
- Be aware that radar service is automatically terminated without advising the pilot when the aircraft is instructed to contact the tower.
- Be aware that there may be other traffic in the traffic pattern and the landing sequence may differ from the traffic sequence assigned by the approach control or air route traffic control center.

B. Controller

- Does not clear an aircraft for visual approach unless it is at the minimum vectoring altitude (MVA) or reports indicate that descent to MVA can be made in VFR conditions.
- Provides radar separation until the pilot accepts a visual approach clearance.
- Continues flight following and traffic information until the aircraft is instructed to contact the tower.
- Issues visual approach clearance when the pilot reports sighting the airport or a preceding aircraft which is to be followed.
- Informs the pilot conducting the visual approach of the aircraft class when pertinent traffic is known to be a heavy aircraft.

411. VISUAL SEPARATION

A. Pilot

- If instructed by ATC to follow another aircraft for the purpose of maintaining visual separation, notify the controller if you do not see it, are unable to maintain visual contact with it, or for any other reason you cannot accept the responsibility for your separation under these conditions.
- Acceptance of both traffic information and instructions to follow another aircraft is pilot acknowledgement that he sees the other aircraft and will maneuver his aircraft as necessary to avoid it or maintain in-trail separation.
- The pilot also accepts responsibility for wake turbulence separation under these conditions.

B. Controller

- Applies visual separation only within a terminal area when a controller has both aircraft in sight or by instructing a pilot who sees the other aircraft to maintain visual separation from it.

412. INSTRUMENT DEPARTURES
A. Pilot
- Prior to Departure: Consider the type of terrain and other obstructions on or in the vicinity of the departure airport.
- Determine if obstruction avoidance can be maintained visually or that the departure procedure should be followed.
- Determine whether a departure procedure and/or Standard Instrument Departure (SID) is available for obstruction avoidance.
- At airports where instrument approach procedures have not been published, hence no published departure procedure, determine what action will be necessary and take such action that will assure a safe departure.

B. Controller
- At locations with airport traffic control service, when necessary, specifies direction of takeoff/turn or initial heading to be flown after takeoff.
- At locations without airport traffic control service, but within a control zone when necessary to specify direction of takeoff/turn or initial heading to be flown, obtains pilot's concurrence that the procedure will allow him to comply with local traffic patterns, terrain, and obstruction avoidance.
- Includes established departure procedures as part of the air traffic control clearance when pilot compliance is necessary to ensure separation.

413–429. RESERVED

Section 10. NATIONAL SECURITY AND INTERCEPTION PROCEDURES

430. NATIONAL SECURITY

a. National security in the control of air traffic is governed by Federal Air Regulation (FAR) Part 99.

b. All aircraft entering domestic U.S. airspace from points outside, must provide for identification prior to entry. To facilitate early aircraft identification of all aircraft in the vicinity of U.S.-International airspace boundaries, Air Defense Identification Zones (ADIZ) have been established.

c. ADIZ boundaries for the U.S. is graphically represented in paragraph 433.

d. Operational requirements for aircraft entering an ADIZ are as follows:

(1) Flight Plan—A flight plan must be on file in all ADIZ/DEWIZ areas, for flights in the Panama Canal Zone ADIZ and in the U.S. Domestic ADIZ, the flight plan must be approved through ATC. In the Alaskan DEWIZ (Distant Early Warning Identification Zone), the flight plan must be filed before departure, except as otherwise permitted in FAR 99.13.

(2) Two-way Radio—All operative, two-way radio must be avaialble in all ADIZ/DEWIZ areas. Exceptions are only as provided for in FAR 99.1(c), and as applicable to the U.S. domestic and coastal ADIZ areas.

(3) Position Reporting—Normal IFR position reports are required in all ADIZ/DEWIZ areas. In the domestic and coastal ADIZ areas, flights under Defense VFR (DVFR) flight plans must give the estimated time of ADIZ penetration at least 15 minutes prior to penetration. In the coastal ADIZ, inbound foreign aircraft must report at least one hour prior to ADIZ penetration. In the Alaskan DEWIZ, DVFR flights must report prior to penetration (correlation of ground filed flight plan data may be required).

(4) Aircraft Position Tolerances—In all ADIZ/DEWIZ areas, recommended tolerances are no more than within 5 minutes of position estimate and no more than 10 miles from course centerline.

e. Aircraft operating within an ADIZ may be exempted from the National Security requirements of FAR Part 99 (except as may be applicable under FAR section 99.7) if the aircraft is operating:

(1) Within the 48 contiguous states and the District of Columbia, or within the state of Alaska, and remains within 10 miles of departure point.

(2) In Coastal or Domestic ADIZ north of 25° N or west of 85° W at a true air speed (TAS) of less than 180 knots.

(3) In Alaskan DEWIZ at TAS of less than 180 knots while pilot maintains listening watch on appropriate frequency.

(4) Over or within three miles of any island in Hawaiian Coastal ADIZ.

f. Exemptions (except for FAR section 99.7) may also be granted by and Air Route Traffic Control Center (ARTCC), on a local basis, for some operations within an ADIZ.

g. An Airfiled VFR Flight Plan makes an aircraft subject to interception for positive identification when entering an ADIZ. Pilots are therefore urged to fil the required DVFR flight plan either in person or b telephone prior to departure.

h. Special Security Instructions

(1) During defense emergency or air defense emer gency conditions, additional special security instruction may be issued in accordance with the Security Contro of Air Traffic and Air Navigation Aids (SCATANA Plan.

(2) Under the provisions of the SCATANA Plan, th military will direct the action to be taken—in regar to landing, grounding, diversion, or dispersal of aircra and the control of air navigation aids—in the defens of the United States during emergency conditions.

(3) At the time a portion or all of SCATANA implemented, ATC facilities will broadcast appropriat instructions received from the military over availab ATC frequencies. Depending on instructions receive from the military. VFR flights may be directed to lan at the nearest available airport, and IFR flights wi be expected to proceed as directed by ATC.

(4) Pilots on the ground may be required to file flight plan and obtain an approval (through FAA) prio to conducting flight operation.

(5) In view of the above, all pilots should guard a ATC or FSS frequency at all times while conductin flight operations.

431. INTERCEPTION PROCEDURES

a. General

During peacetime, intercepted aircraft will be ap proached from the stern. Generally two intercepto states of readiness. Unless otherwise directed by th control agency, intercepted aircraft will be identified b type only. When specific information is required (i. markings, serial numbers, etc.) the interceptor aircre will respond only if the request can be conducted in safe manner. During hours of darkness or Instrumen Meteorological Conditions (IMC), identification of u known aircraft will be by type only. The interceptio pattern described below is the typical peacetime metho used by air interceptor aircrews. In all situations, th interceptor aircrew will use caution to avoid startlin the intercepted aircrew and/or passengers.

b. Intercept phases

(1) Phase One—Approach Phase

During peacetime, intercepted aircraft will be ap proached from the stern. Generally two intercepto aircraft will be employed to accomplish the identifica tion. The flight leader and his wingman will coordinat their individual positions in conjunction with the groun controlling agency. Their relationship will resemble line abreast formation. At night or in IMC, a con fortable radar trail tactic will be used. Safe vertica separation between interceptor aircraft and unknow aircraft will be maintained at all times.

(2) Phase Two—Identification Phase

The intercepted aircraft should expect to visually ac quire the lead interceptor and possibly the wingma during this phase in visual meteorological condition

(VMC). The wingman will assume a surveillance position while the flight leader approaches the unknown aircraft. Intercepted aircraft personnel may observe the use of different drag devices to allow for speed and position stabilization during this phase. The flight leader will then initiate a gentle closure toward the intercepted aircraft, stopping at a distance no closer than absolutely necessary to obtain the information needed. The interceptor aircraft will use every possible precaution to avoid startling intercepted aircrew or passengers. Additionally, the interceptor aircrews will constantly keep in mind that maneuvers considered normal to a fighter aircraft may be considered hazardous to passengers and crews of non-fighter aircraft. When interceptor aircrews know or believe that an unsafe condition exists, the identification phase will be terminated. As previously stated, during darkness or IMC identification of unknown aircraft will be by type only. Positive vertical separation will be maintained by interceptor aircraft throughout this phase.

(3) Phase Three—Post Intercept Phase

Upon identification phase completion, the flight leader will turn away from the intercepted aircraft. The wingman will remain well clear and accomplish a rejoin with his leader.

c. Communication interface between interceptor aircrews and the ground controlling agency is essential to ensure successful intercept completion. Flight Safety is paramount. An aircraft which is intercepted by another aircraft shall immediately:

(1) follow the instructions given by the intercepting aircraft, interpreting and responding to the visual signals;

(2) notify, if possible, the appropriate air traffic services unit;

(3) attempt to establish radio communication with the intercepting aircraft or with the appropriate intercept control unit, by making a general call on the emergency frequency 243.0 MHz and repeating this call on the emergency frequency 121.5 MHz, if practicable, giving the identity and position of the aircraft and the nature of the flight;

(4) if equipped with SSR transponder, select mode 3/A Code 7700, unless otherwise instructed by the appropiate air traffic services unit. If any instructions received by radio from any sources conflict with those given by the intercepting aircraft by visual or radio signals, the intercepted aircraft shall request immediate clarification while continuing to comply with the instructions given by the intercepting aircraft.

INTERCEPTION PATTERNS FOR IDENTIFICATION OF INTERCEPTED AIRCRAFT (TYPICAL)

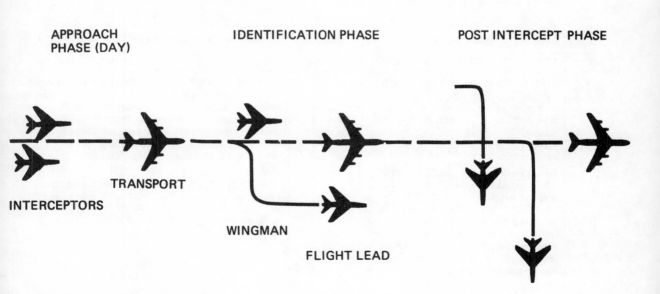

Figure 4—18

432. INTERCEPTION SIGNALS

Signals initiated by intercepting aircraft and responses by intercepted aircraft

Series	INTERCEPTING Aircraft Signals	Meaning	INTERCEPTED Aircraft Responds	Meaning
1	DAY—Rocking wings from a position in front and, normally, to the left of intercepted aircraft and, after acknowledgement, a slow level turn, normally to the left, on to the desired course. NIGHT—Same and, in addition, flashing navigational and, if available, landing lights at irregular intervals. *Note.—Meteorological conditions or terrain may require the intercepting aircraft to take up a position in front and to the right of the intercepted aircraft and to make the subsequent turn to the right.*	You have been intercepted. Follow me.	DAY—Rocking wings and following. NIGHT—Same and, in addition, flashing navigational and, if available, landing lights at irregular intervals.	Understood, will comply.
2	DAY OR NIGHT—An abrupt break-away maneuver from the intercepted aircraft consisting of a climbing turn of 90 degrees or more without crossing the line of flight of the intercepted aircraft.	You may proceed.	DAY OR NIGHT—Rocking wings.	Understood, will comply.
3	DAY—Circling aerodrome, lowering landing gear and overflying runway in direction of landing. NIGHT—Same and, in addition, showing steady landing lights.	Land at this aerodrome.	DAY—Lowering landing gear, following the intercepting aircraft and, if after overflying the runway landing is considered safe, proceeding to land. NIGHT—Same and, in addition, showing steady landing lights (if carried).	Understood, will comply.

Signals initiated by intercepted aircraft and responses by intercepting aircraft

Series	INTERCEPTED Aircraft Signals	Meaning	INTERCEPTING Aircraft Responds	Meaning
4	DAY—Raising landing gear while passing over landing runway at a height exceeding 300 m (1,000 ft) but not exceeding 600 m (2,000 ft) above the aerodrome level, and continuing to circle the aerodrome. NIGHT—Flashing landing lights while passing over landing runway at a height exceeding 300 m (1,000 ft) but not exceeding 600 m (2,000 ft) above the aerodrome level, and continuing to circle the aerodrome. If unable to flash landing lights, flash any other lights available.	Aerodrome you have designated is inadequate.	DAY OR NIGHT—If it is desired that the intercepted aircraft follow the intercepting aircraft to an alternate aerodrome, the intercepting aircraft raises its landing gear and uses the Series 1 signals prescribed for intercepting aircraft. If it is decided to release the intercepted aircraft, the intercepting aircraft uses the Series 2 signals prescribed for intercepting aircraft.	Understood, follow me. Understood, you may proceed.

433. ADIZ DEFENSE AND DESIGNATED MOUNTAINOUS AREAS

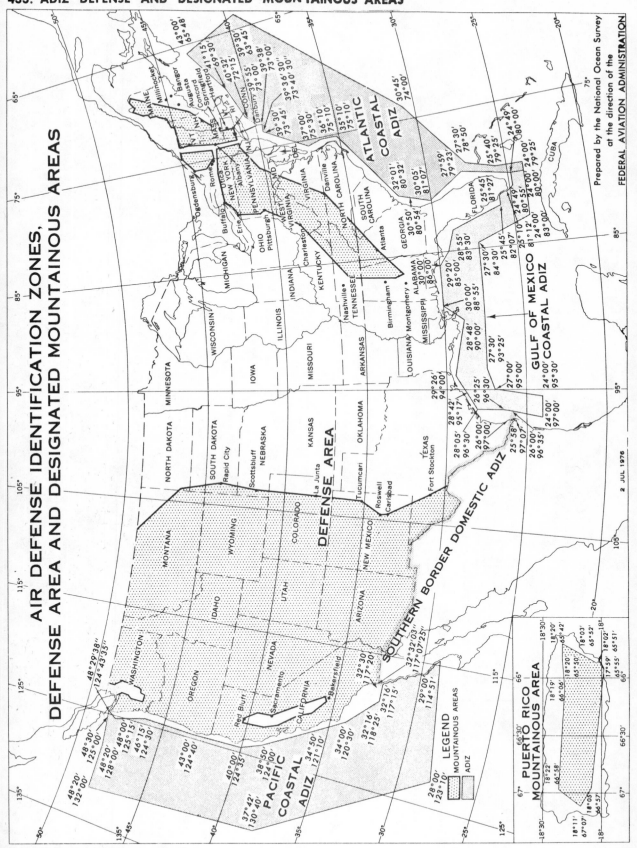

AIR DEFENSE IDENTIFICATION ZONES, DEFENSE AREA AND DESIGNATED MOUNTAINOUS AREAS

ATLANTIC COASTAL ADIZ

GULF OF MEXICO COASTAL ADIZ

SOUTHERN BORDER DOMESTIC ADIZ

DEFENSE AREA

PACIFIC COASTAL ADIZ

PUERTO RICO MOUNTAINOUS AREA

LEGEND
MOUNTAINOUS AREAS
ADIZ

Prepared by the National Ocean Survey
at the direction of the
FEDERAL AVIATION ADMINISTRATION

2 JUL 1976

Chapter 5. EMERGENCY PROCEDURES

Section 1. GENERAL

440. ACCIDENT CAUSE FACTORS

a. The ten most frequent cause factors for General Aviation Accidents in 1978 that involve the pilot in command are:
—Inadequate preflight preparation and/or planning
—Failure to obtain/maintain flying speed
—Failure to maintain direction control
—Improper level off
—Failure to see and avoid objects or obstructions
—Mismanagement of fuel
—Improper in-flight decisions or planning
—Misjudgment of distance and speed
—Selection of unsuitable terrain
—Improper operation of flight controls.

b. The above factors have continued to plague General Aviation pilots over the years. This list remains relatively stable and points out the need for continued refresher training to establish a higher level of flight proficiency for all pilots. A part of the FAA's continuing effort to promote increased aviation safety is the General Aviation Accident Prevention Program. For information on Accident Prevention activities contact your nearest General Aviation or Flight Standards District Office.

c. ALERTNESS—Be alert at all times, especially when the weather is good. Most pilots pay attention to business when they are operating in full IFR weather conditions, but strangely, air collisions almost invariably have occurred under ideal weather conditions. Unlimited visibility appears to encourage a sense of security which is not at all justified. Considerable information of value may be obtained by lisenting to advisories being issued in the terminal area, even though controller workload may prevent a pilot from obtaining individual service.

d. GIVING WAY—If you think another aircraft is too close to you, give way instead of waiting for the other pilot to respect the right-of-way to which you may be entitled. It is a lot safer to pursue the right-of-way angle after you have completed your flight.

441. VFR IN CONGESTED AREAS

"A high percentage of near midair collisions occur below 8,000 feet AGL and within 30 miles of an airport —————." When operating VFR in these highly congested areas, whether you intend to land at an airport within the area or are just flying through, it is recommended that extra vigilance be maintained and that you monitor an appropriate control frequency. Normally the appropriate frequency is an approach control frequency. By such monitoring action you can "get the picture" of the traffic in your area. When the approach controller has radar, traffic advisories may be given to VFR pilots who requests them, subject to the provisions included in paragraph **162**—RADAR TRAFFIC INFORMATION SERVICE.

442. ASK FOR ASSISTANCE

"I'm not lost, I just don't know for sure where I am, but a familiar landmark will show up soon." "I *think* I have enough fuel to get there." "I think it will be smoother if I go above these clouds, there are bound to be some holes I can get down through when I get near home." "I'd look pretty silly if I asked for help and then found out I didn't really need it." The first time one of these thoughts pop into your mind, *it is time* to ask for assistance. Do not wait until the situation has deteriorated into an emergency before letting ATC know of your predicament. A little embarrassment is better than a big accident!

443. AVOID FLIGHT BENEATH UNMANNED BALLOONS

a. The majority of unmanned free balloons currently being operated have, extending below them, either a suspension device to which the payload or instrument package is attached, or a trailing wire antenna, or both. In many instances these balloon subsystems may be invisible to the pilot until his aircraft is close to the balloon, thereby creating a potentially dangerous situation. Therefore, good judgment on the part of the pilot dictates that aircraft should remain well clear of all unmanned free balloons and flight below them should be avoided at all times.

b. Pilots are urged to report any unmanned free balloons sighted to the nearest FAA ground facility with which communication is established. Such information will assist FAA ATC facilities to identify and flight follow unmanned free balloons operating in the airspace.

444. EMERGENCY LOCATOR TRANSMITTERS

a. GENERAL

Emergency Locator Transmitters (ELT) are required for most general aviation airplanes (reference: FAR 91.52). ELTs of various types have been developed as a means of locating downed aircraft and their occupants. These electronic, battery operated transmitters emit a distinctive downward swept audio tone on 121.5 MHz and/or 243.0 MHz. The equipment is capable of providing continuous operations for at least 48 hours at a wide range of ambient temperatures. Aircraft owners and operators should be aware of the battery expiration date on their ELTs. Careful planning should be made to insure timely replacement of batteries. It can expedite search and rescue operations and save lives.

b. ELT TESTING

(1) Caution should be exercised to prevent the inadvertent actuation of locator transmitters in the air or while they are being handled on the ground. Operational testing of transmitters should be carried out only in shielded areas under controlled conditions. False signals on the distress frequencies can interfere with actual distress transmissions as well as decrease the degree of urgency that should be attached to such signals.

(2) "Aircraft operational testing is authorized on 121.5 MHz as follows:

(a) Tests should be no longer than three audio sweeps.

(b) If the antenna is removable, a dummy load should be substituted during test procedures.

(c) Tests shall be conducted only within the time period made up of the first five minutes after every hour. Emergency tests outside of this time have to be coordinated with the nearest FSS or Control Tower. Airborne ELT tests are not authorized."

c. ELT REPORTING PROCEDURES

(1) Pilots are encouraged to periodically monitor the emergency frequencies of 121.5 MHz and/or 243.0 MHz to assist in identifying possible emergency ELT tranmissions. On receiving a signal from an Emergency Locator Transmitter report the following information to the nearest FAA facility:

(a) Aircraft position and time the signal was first heard.

(b) Aircraft position and time the signal was last heard.

(c) Aircraft position at maximum signal strength.

(d) Flight altitude and frequency of the emergency signal. (121.5/243.0)

NOTE.—If the aircraft is equipped with homing equipment provide the bearing to the emergency signal with each aircraft position report.

445. MOUNTAIN FLYING

a. Your first experience of flying over mountainous terrain (particularly if most of your flight time has been over the flatlands of the midwest) could be a never-to-be-forgotten nightmare if proper planning is not done and if you are not aware of the potential hazards awaiting. Those familiar section lines are not present in the mountains; those flat, level fields for forced landings are practically non-existent; abrupt changes in wind direction and velocity occur; severe updrafts and downdrafts are common, particularly near or above abrupt changes of terrain such as cliffs or rugged areas; even the clouds look different and can build up with startling rapidity. Mountain flying need not be hazardous if you follow the recommendations below:

b. File a flight plan. Plan your route to avoid topography which would prevent a safe forced landing.

The route should be over populated areas and well known mountain passes. Sufficient altitude should be maintained to permit gliding to a safe landing in the event of engine failure.

c. Don't fly a light aircraft when the winds aloft, at your proposed altitude, exceed 35 miles per hour. Expect the winds to be of much greater velocity over mountain passes than reported a few miles from them. Approach mountain passes with as much altitude as possible. Downdrafts of from 1500 to 2000 feet per minute are not uncommon on the leeward side.

d. Don't fly near or above abrupt changes in terrain. Severe turbulence can be expected, especially in high wind conditions.

e. Some canyons run into a dead-end. Don't fly so far up a canyon that you get trapped. ALWAYS BE ABLE TO MAKE A 180 DEGREE TURN!

f. Plan your trip for the early morning hours. As a rule, the air starts to get bad at about 10 a.m., and grows steadily worse until around 4 p.m., then gradually improves until dark Mountain flying at night in a single engine light aircraft is asking for trouble.

g. When landing at a high altitude field, the same indicated airspeed should be used as at low elevation fields. *Remember:* that due to the less dense air at altitude, this same indicated airspeed actually results in a higher true airspeed, a faster landing speed, and more important, a longer landing distance. During gusty wind conditions which often prevail at high altitude fields, a power approach and power landing is recommended. Additionally, due to the faster groundspeed, your takeoff distance will increase considerably over that required at low altitudes.

h. *Effects of Density Altitude.* Performance figures in the aircraft owner's handbook for length of takeoff run, horsepower, rate of climb, etc., are generally based on standard atmosphere conditions (59° F, pressure 29.92 inches of mercury) at sea level. However, inexperienced pilots as well as experienced pilots may run into trouble when they encounter an altogether different set of conditions. This is particularly true in hot weather and at higher elevations. Aircraft operations at altitudes above sea level and at higher than standard temperatures are commonplace in mountainous areas. Such operations quite often result in a drastic reduction of aircraft performance capabilities because of the changing air density. Density altitude is a measure of air density. It is not to be confused with pressure altitude—true altitude or absolute altitude. It is not to be used as a height reference, but as a determining criteria in the performance capability of an aircraft. Air density decreases with altitude. As air density decreases, density altitude increases. The further effects of high temperature and high humidity are cumulative, resulting in an increasing high density altitude condition. High density altitude reduces all aircraft performance parameters. To the pilot, this means that— the normal horsepower output is reduced, propeller efficiency is reduced and a higher true airspeed is required to sustain the aircraft throughout its operating parameters. It means an increase in runway length requirements for takeoff and landings, and a decreased rate of climb. An average small airplane, for example, requiring 1,000 feet for takeoff at sea level under standard atmospheric conditions will require a takeoff run of approximately 2,000 at an operational altitude of 5,000 feet.

NOTE.—A turbo-charged aircraft engine provides some slight advantage in that it provides sea level horsepower up to a specified altitude above sea level.

(1) *Density Altitude Advisories*—at airports with elevations of 2,000 feet and higher, control towers and flight service stations will broadcast the advisory "Check Density Altitude" when the temperature reaches a predetermined level. These advisories will be broadcast on appropriate tower frequencies or, where available, ATIS. Flight service stations will broadcast these advisories as a part of Airport Advisory Service, and on TWEB.

(2) These advisories are provided by air traffic facilities, as a reminder to pilots that high temperatures and high field elevations will cause significant changes in aircraft characteristics. The pilot retains the responsibility to compute density altitude, when appropriate, as a part of preflight duties.

NOTE.—All flight service stations will compute the current density altitude upon request.

i. *Mountain Wave.* Many pilots go all their lives without understanding what a mountain wave is. Quite a few have lost their lives because of this lack of understanding. One need not be a licensed meteorologist to understand the mountain wave phenomenon.

(1) Mountain waves occur when air is being blown over a mountain range or even the ridge of a sharp bluff area. As the air hits the upwind side of the range, it starts to climb, thus creating what is generally a smooth updraft which turns into a turbulent downdraft as the air passes the crest of the ridge. From this point, for many miles downwind, there will be a series of downdrafts and updrafts. Satellite photos of the Rockies have shown mountain waves extending as far as 700 miles downwind of the range. Along the east coast area, such photos of the Appalachian chain have picked up the mountain wave phenomenon over a hundred miles eastward. All it takes to form a mountain wave is wind blowing across the range at 15 knots or better at an intersection angle of not less than 30 degrees.

(2) Pilots from flatland areas should understand a few things about mountain waves in order to stay out of trouble. Approaching a mountain range from the upwind side (generally the west), there will usually be a smooth updraft; therefore, it is not quite as dangerous an area as the lee of the range. From the leeward side, it is always a good idea to add an extra thousand feet or so of altitude because downdrafts can exceed the climb capability of the aircraft. Never expect an updraft when approaching a mountain chain from the leeward. Always be prepared to cope with a downdraft and turbulence.

(3) When approaching a mountain ridge from the downwind side, it is recommended that the ridge be approached at approximately a 45° angle to the horizontal direction of the ridge. This permits a safer retreat from the ridge with less stress on the aircraft should severe turbulence and downdraft be experienced. If severe turbulence is encountered, simultaneously reduce power and adjust pitch until aircraft approaches maneuvering speed, then adjust power and trim to maintain maneuvering speed and fly away from the turbulent area.

446–449. RESERVED

Section 2. SEARCH AND RESCUE COORDINATION CENTERS

450. NATIONAL SEARCH AND RESCUE PLAN

a. Under the National Search and Rescue Plan, the U.S. Coast Guard is responsible for coordination of search and rescue for the Maritime Region, and the U.S. Air Force is responsible for coordination of search and rescue for the Inland Region. In order to carry out this responsibility the Air Force and the Coast Guard have established Rescue Coordination Centers to direct search and rescue activities within their regions. This service is available to all persons and property in distress, both civilian and military. Normally, for aircraft incidents, information will be passed to the Rescue Coordination Centers through the appropriate Air Route Traffic Control Center or Flight Service Station.

451. SEARCH AND RESCUE FACILITIES INCLUDE

(1) Rescue Coordination Centers;

(2) Search and Rescue aircraft;

(3) Rescue vessels;

(4) Pararescue and ground rescue teams;

(5) Emergency radio fixing.

452. COAST GUARD RESCUE COORDINATION CENTERS

a. Locations:

Boston, Mass.
617–223–3645

New York, N.Y.
212–688–7055

Portsmouth, Va.
804–398–6231

Miami, Florida
305–350–5611

Long Beach, Calif.
213–590–2225

San Francisco, Calif.
415–556–5500

Seattle, Wash.
206–442–5886

Juneau, Alaska
907–568–7340

New Orleans, La.
504–589–6225

Cleveland, Ohio
216–522–3984

St. Louis, Mo.
314–425– 4614

Honolulu, Hawaii
808–546–7109

Kodiak, Alaska
907–487–5888

San Juan, Puerto Rico
809–722–2943

b. Coast Guard Rescue Coordination Centers are served by major radio stations which guard 500 kHz (CW) and 2182 kHz (voice). In addition, San Francisco and Honolulu guard 8364 kHz and 247 Coast Guard units along the sea coasts of the United States and shores of the Great Lakes guard 2182 kHz (voice). All of these facilities are available for reporting distress or potential distress. THE CALL "NCU" (CW) or "COAST GUARD" (VOICE) ALERTS ALL COAST GUARD RADIO STATIONS WITHIN RANGE.

453. AIR FORCE RESCUE COORDINATION CENTER

a. Continental U.S.:

Scott Air Force Base, IL_____All contiguous U.S.	
Commercial	618–256–4815
WATS	800–851–3051
AUTOVON	638–4815
FTS	255–4815 or 4810

b. Air Force Rescue Coordination Center—Alaska:
Alaskan Air Command/RCC
Elmendork AFB, AK
907–227–2131

c. Air Force Rescue Coordination Center—Pacific:
Commander
USAF Pacific Region
Search and Rescue Coordinator
Hickman AFB,
Hawaii

454–459. RESERVED

Section 3. PROCEDURES AND SIGNALS FOR AIRCRAFT IN EMERGENCY

460. GENERAL

a. Search and Rescue (SAR) is a life-saving service provided through the combined efforts of the FAA, Air Force, Coast Guard, State Aeronautic Commissions or other similar state agencies who are assisted by other organizations such as the Civil Air Patrol, Sheriffs Air Patrol, State Police, etc. It provides search, survival aid, and rescue of personnel of missing or crashed aircraft.

b. Prior to departure on every flight, local or otherwise, someone at the departure point should be advised of your destination and the route of flight if other than direct. Search efforts are often wasted and rescue is often delayed because of pilots who thoughtlessly take off without telling anyone where they are going.

c. All you need to remember to obtain this valuable protection is:

(1) File a Flight Plan with an FAA Flight Service Station in person or by telephone or radio.

(2) Close your flight plan with the appropriate authority immediately upon landing.

(3) If you land at a location other than the intended destination, report the landing to the nearest FAA Flight Service Station.

(4) If you land en route and are delayed more than 30 minutes, report this information to the nearest FSS.

(5) Remember that if you fail to report within one-half hour after your ETA, a search will be started to locate you.

d. To assist survival and rescue in the event of a crash landing the following advice is given:

(1) For flight over uninhabited land areas, it is wise to take suitable survival equipment depending on type of climate and terrain.

(2) If forced landing occurs at sea, chances for survival are governed by degree of crew proficiency in emergency procedures and by effectiveness of water survival equipment.

e. Remember the Four C's

(1) **Confess** your predicament to any ground radio station. Do not wait too long. Give SAR a chance!

(2) **Communicate** with your ground link and pass as much of the distress message on first transmission as possible. We need information for best SAR action!

(3) **Climb** if possible for better radar and DF detection. If flying at low altitude, the chance of establishing radio contact is improved by climbing.

NOTE.—Unauthorized climb of descent under IFR conditions within controlled airspace is not permitted except in emergency. Any variation in altitude will be unknown to Air Traffic Control except at radar locations having height finding capabilities. Air Traffic Control will operate on the assumption that the provisions of FAR 91.127 are being followed by the pilot.

(4) **Comply**—especially *Comply*—with advice and instructions received, if you really want help. Assist the ground "communications control" station to control communications on the distress frequency on which you are working (as that is the distress frequency for your case). Tell interfering stations to maintain silence until you call. Cooperate!

f. Observance of a Downed Aircraft

(1) Determine if crash is marked with yellow cross: if so, the crash has already been reported and identified.

(2) Determine, if possible, type and number of aircraft and whether there is evidence of survivors.

(3) Fix, as accurately as possible, exact location of crash.

(4) If circumstances permit, orbit scene to guide in other assisting units or until relieved by another aircraft.

(5) Transmit information to nearest FAA or other appropriate radio facility.

(6) Immediately after landing, make a complete report to nearest FAA, Air Force, or Coast Guard installation. Report may be made by long distance collect telephone.

461. OBTAINING EMERGENCY ASSISTANCE

When a pilot is in doubt of his position, or feels apprehensive for his safety, he should not hesitate to request assistance. Search and Rescue facilities, including Radar, Radio, and DF stations, are ready and willing to help. There is no penalty for using them. Delay has caused accidents and cost lives. *Safety is not a luxury.* Take Action!

a. A pilot in any emergency phase (uncertainty, alert, or distress) should do three things to obtain assistance:

(1) *If equipped with a radar beacon transponder and if unable to establish voice communications with an air traffic control facility, switch to Mode 3/A and Code 7700. Military transponder should also be placed in the Emergency position. If crash is imminent and equipped with a Locator Beacon, actuate the emergency signal.*

(2) *Contact controlling agency and give nature of distress and pilot's intentions.* If unable to contact controlling agencies, attempt to contact any agency on assigned frequency or any of the following frequencies (transmit and receive):

Frequency	Emission	Effective Range in Nautical Miles	Guarded By
121.5 MHz	Voice	Generally limited to radio line-of-sight	All military towers, most civil towers, VHF direction finding stns, radar facilities. Flight Service Stations.
243.0 MHz	Voice	Generally limited to radio-line-of-sight	All military towers, most civil towers, UHF direction finding stns, radar facilities. Flight Service Stations.
2182 kHz	Voice	Generally less than 300 miles for average aircraft installations	Some ships and boats, Coast Guard stations, most commercial coast stations.

Frequency	Emission	Effective Range in Nautical Miles	Guarded By
500 kHz	CW	Generally less than 100 miles for average aircraft installations	Most large ships, most Coast Guard radio stations, most commercial coast stations.
8364 kHz	CW	Up to several thousand miles, depending upon propagation conditions. Subject to "skip."	U.S.N. Direction Finding Stations, most Coast Guard radio stations and some FAA International Flight Service Stations (IFSS).

(3) Content of an emergency transmission—transmit as much of the following as possible:

(a) MAYDAY, MAYDAY, MAYDAY (if distress), or PAN, PAN, PAN (if uncertainty or alert). If CW transmission, use SOS (distress) or XXX (uncertainty or alert).

(b) Aircraft identification repeated three times.

(c) Type of aircraft.

(d) Position or estimated position (stating which).

(e) Heading (true or magnetic) (stating which).

(f) True airspeed or estimated true airspeed (stating which).

(g) Altitude.

(h) Fuel remaining in hours and minutes.

(i) Nature of distress.

(j) Pilot's intentions (bailout, ditch, crash landing, etc.).

(k) Assistance desired (fix, steer, bearing, escort, etc.).

(l) Two 10-second dashes with mike button (voice) or key (CW) followed by aircraft identification (once) and OVER (voice) or K (CW).

NOTE.—ARTCC emergency frequency capability normally does not extend to radar coverage limits. If the ARTCC does not respond to transmission on emergency frequency 121.5 MHz or 243.0 MHz pilots should initiate a call to the nearest Flight Service Station or Airport Traffic Control Tower.

(4) Comply with information and clearance received. Accept the communications control offered to you by the ground radio station, silence interfering radio stations, and do not shift frequency or shift to another ground station unless absolutely necessary.

b. Pilots of IFR flights experiencing two-way radio failure are expected to adhere to the procedures prescribed under "RADIO COMMUNICATIONS FAILURE" (FAR Part 91.127).

(1) The pilot should remember that he has two means of declaring an emergency:

(a) Emergency SQUAWK (Code 7700) from transponders

(b) Sending emergency message

(2) Some ground stations have *three* electronic means of assisting:

(a) Receipt of emergency message

(b) DF bearings; and

(c) Detection of transponder emergency SQUAWK (Code 7700).

462. DIRECTION FINDING INSTRUMENT APPROACH PROCEDURE

a. Direction finding (DF) equipment has long been used to locate lost aircraft, to guide aircraft to areas of good weather or to airports; and now at most DF equipped airports, DF instrument approaches may be given to aircraft in emergency.

b. Experience has shown that a majority of actual emergencies requiring DF assistance involve pilots with a minimum of flight experience, particularly IFR experience. With this in mind, a DF approach procedure provides for maximum flight stability in the approach by utilizing small degrees of turn, and descents when the aircraft is in a wings level attitude. The DF specialist will give the pilot headings to fly and tell the pilot when to begin descent.

c. DF instrument approach procedures are for emergency use, this type of approach will not be given in IFR weather conditions unless the pilot has declared an emergency.

d. To become familiar with the procedures and other benefits of DF, pilots are urged to request practice guidance and approaches in VFR weather conditions. DF specialists welcome the practice and, workload permitting, will honor such requests.

463. DOWNED AIRCRAFT

a. The rapidity of rescue on land or water will depend on how accurately your position may be determined. If a flight plan has been followed and your position is on course, rescue will be expedited.

b. For bailout, set radio for continuous emission. For ditching or crash landing, radio should, if it is considered that there is no additional risk of fire and if circumstances permit be set for continuous transmission.

c. If it becomes necessary to ditch, distressed aircraft should make every effort to ditch near a surface vessel. If time permits, the position of the nearest vessel can be obtained from a Coast Guard Rescue Coordination Center through the FAA facility.

d. Unless you have good reason to believe that you will not be located by search aircraft, it is better to remain near your aircraft and prepare means for signalling whenever aircraft approach your position.

464. DITCHING PROCEDURES

a. In order to select a proper ditching course for an aircraft, a basic knowledge of sea evaluation and other factors involved is required. Selection of the ditching heading may well determine the difference between survival and disaster.

b. Definition of oceanographic terminology:

(1) Sea. The condition of the surface that is the result of both waves and swells.

(2) Wave. (or Chop). The condtiion of the surface caused by the local winds.

(3) Swell. The condition of the surface which has been caused by a distant disturbance.

(4) Swell Face. The side of the swell toward the observer. The backside is the side away from the observer. These definitions apply regardless of the direction of swell movement.

(5) Primary Swell. The swell system having the greatest height from trough to crest.

(6) Secondary Swells. Those swell systems of less height than the primary swell.

(7) Fetch. The distance the waves have been driven by a wind blowing in a constant direction, without obstruction.

(8) Swell Period. The time interval between the passage of two successive crests at the same spot in the water, measured in seconds.

(9) Swell Velocity. The velocity with which the swell advances with relation to a fixed reference point, measured in knots. There is little movement of water in the horizontal direction. Swells move primarily in a vertical motion, similar to the motion observed when shaking out a carpet.

(10) Swell Direction. The direction *from* which a swell is moving. This direction is not necessarily the result of the wind present at the scene. The swell encountered may be moving into or across the local wind. Swells, once set in motion, tend to maintain their original direction for as long as they continue in deep water, regardless of changes in wind direction.

(11) Swell Height. The height between crest and trough, measured in feet. The vast majority of ocean swells are lower than 12 to 15 feet, and swells over 25 feet are not common at any spot on the oceans. Successive swells may differ considerably in height.

c. It is extremely dangerous to land into the wind without regard to sea conditions. The swell system, or systems, must be taken into consideration.

(1) In ditching parallel to the swell, it makes little difference whether touchdown is on top of the crest or in the trough. It is preferable, if possible to land on the top or back side of the swell.

(2) If only one swell system exists, the problem is relatively simple—even with a high, fast system. Unfortunately, most cases involve two or more systems running in different directions. With many systems present, the sea presents a confused appearance. One of the most difficult situations occurs when two swell systems are at right angles. For example, if one system is 8 feet high, and the other 3 feet, a landing parallel to the primary system, and down swell on the secondary system is indicated. If both systems are of equal height, a compromise may be advisable—selecting an intermediate heading at 45 degrees down swell to both systems. When landing down a secondary swell, attempt to touch down on the back side, not on the face of the swell. Remember one axiom—AVOID THE FACE OF A SWELL.

(3) *If the swell system is formidable, it is considered advisable, in landplanes, to accept more crosswind in order to avoid landing directly into the swell.*

(4) The secondary swell system is often from the same direction as the wind. Here, the landing may be made parallel to the primary system, with the wind and secondary system at an angle. There is a choice of two headings paralleling the primary system. One heading is downwind and down the secondary swell; and the other is into the wind and into the secondary swell. The choice of heading will depend on the velocity of the wind versus the velocity and height of the secondary swell.

d. The simplest method of estimating the wind direction and velocity is to examine the wind streaks on the water. These appear as long streaks up and down wind. Some persons may have difficulty determining wind direction after seeing the streaks on the water. Whitecaps fall forward with the wind but are overrun by the waves thus producing the illusion that the foam is sliding backward. Knowing this, and by observing the direction of the streaks, the wind direction is easily determined. Wind velocity can be accurately estimated by noting the appearance of the whitecaps, foam and wind streaks.

e. A successful aircraft ditching is dependent on three primary factors. In order of importance they are:

> Sea conditions and wind.
> Type of aircraft.
> Skill and technique of pilot.

(1) The behavior of the aircraft on making contact with the water will vary within wide limits according to the state of the sea. If landed parallel to a single swell system, the behavior of the aircraft may approximate that to be expected on a smooth sea. If landed into a heavy swell or into a confused sea, the deceleration forces may be extremely great—resulting in breaking up of the aircraft. Within certain limits, the pilot is able to minimize these forces by proper sea evaluation and selection of ditching heading.

(2) When on final approach the pilot should look ahead and observe the surface of the sea. They may be shadows and whitecaps—signs of large seas. Shadows and whitecaps close together indicate that the seas are short and rough. Touchdown in these areas is to be avoided. Select and touchdown in any area (only about 500 feet is needed) where the shadows and whitecaps are not so numerous.

(3) Touchdown should be at the *lowest* speed and rate of descent which permit safe handling and optimum nose up attitude on impact. Once first impact has been made, there is often little the pilot can do to control a landplane.

f. Once pre-ditching preparations are completed, the pilot should turn to the ditching heading and commence let-down. The aircraft should be dragged low over the water, and slowed down until ten knots or so above stall. At this point, additional power should be used to overcome the increased drag caused by the noseup attitude. When a smooth stretch of water appears ahead, cut power, and touchdown at the best recommended speed as fully stalled as possible. By cutting power when approaching a relatively smooth area, the pilot will prevent over shooting and will touchdown with less chance of planing off into a second uncontrolled landing. Most experienced seaplane pilots prefer to make contact with the water in a semi-stalled attitude, cutting power as the tail makes contact. This technique eliminates the chance of misjudging altitude with a resultant heavy drop in a fully stalled condition. Care must be taken not to drop the aircraft from too high altitude, or to balloon due to excessive speed. The altitude above water depends on the aircraft. Over glassy smooth water, or at night without sufficient light, it is very easy for even the most experienced pilots to misjudge altitude by 50 feet or more. Under such conditions, carry enough power to maintain nine to twelve degrees noseup attitude, and 10 to 20% over stalling speed until contact is made with the water. The proper use of power on the approach is of great importance. If power is available on one side only, a little power should be used to flatten the approach; however, the engine should not be used to such an extent that the aircraft cannot be turned against the good engines right down to the stall with a margin of rudder movement available. When near the stall, sudden application of excessive unbalanced power may result in loss of directional control. If power is available on one side only, a slightly higher than normal glide approach speed should be used. This will insure good control and some margin of speed after leveling off without excessive use of power. The use of power in ditching is so important that when it is certain that the coast cannot be reached, the pilot should, if possible, ditch before fuel is exhausted. The use of power in a night or instrument ditching is far more essential than under daylight contact conditions.

(1) If no power is available, a greater than normal approach speed should be used down to the flare-out. This speed margin will allow the glide to be broken early and more gradually, thereby giving the pilot time and distance to feel for the surface—decreasing the possibility of stalling high or flying into the water. When landing parallel to a swell system, little difference is noted between landing on top of a crest or in the trough. If the wings of the aircraft are trimmed to the surface of the sea rather than the horizon, there is little need to worry about a wing hitting a swell crest. The actual slope of a swell is very gradual. If force to land into a swell, touchdown should be made just after passage of the crest. If contact is made on the face of the swell, the aircraft may be swamped or thrown violently into the air, dropping heavily into the next swell. If control surfaces remain intact, the pilot should attempt to maintain the proper nose attitude by rapid and positive use of the controls.

g. After Touchdown: In most cases drift caused by crosswind can be ignored; the forces acting on the aircraft after tourcdown are of such magnitude that drift will be only a secondary consideration. If the aircraft is under good control, the "crab" may be kicked out with rudder just prior to touchdown. This is more important with high wing aircraft, for they are laterally unstable on the water in a crosswind, and may roll to the side in ditching.

> NOTE: This information has been extracted from the publication "Aircraft Emergency Procedures Over Water".

465. FUEL DUMPING

a. Should it become necessary to dump fuel, the pilot should immediately advise Air Traffic Control. Upon receipt of advice that an aircraft will dump fuel, Air Traffic Control will broadcast or cause to be broadcast immediately and every 3 minutes thereafter on appropriate Air Traffic Control, Flight Service Station and airline company radio frequencies the following:

ADVISORY TO AIRCRAFT NOT ON ATC CLEARANCE—FUEL DUMPING IN PROGRESS—(aircraft type) (present position) course/s) (altitude)—AVOID FLIGHT WITHIN 5 NAUTICAL MILES IF AT THIS ALTITUDE. IF WITHIN FIVE NAUTICAL MILES, REMAIN AT LEAST

ONE THOUSAND FEET ABOVE OR AT LEAST TWO THOUSAND FEET BELOW THE AIRCRAFT.

b. Upon receipt of such a broadcast, pilots of aircraft affected, which are not on IFR flight plans or special VFR clearances, should clear the area specified in the advisory. Aircraft on IFR flight plans or special VFR clearances will be provided specific separation by Air Traffic Control. At the termination of the fuel dumping operation, pilots should advise Air Traffic Control. Upon receipt of such information, Air Traffic Control will issue, on appropriate frequencies, the following:

ADVISORY TO ALL CONCERNED—(aircraft type) FUEL DUMP TERMINATED.

466. SPECIAL EMERGENCY (AIR PIRACY)

a. A special emergency is a condition of air piracy, or other hostile act by a person(s) aboard an aircraft, which threatens the safety of the aircraft or its passengers.

b. The pilot of an aircraft reporting a special emergency condition should:

(1) If circumstances permit, distress or urgency radio-telephony should be applied. Include the details of the condition.

(2) If circumstances do not permit the use of prescribed distress or urgency procedures, the message sent by the aircraft should:

(a) Be sent on the air-ground frequency in use at the time.

(b) Consist of as many as possible of the following elements spoken distinctly and in the following order:

1. Name of the station addressed (time and circumstances permitting).

2. The identification of the aircraft and present position.

3. The nature of the special emergency condition and pilot intentions (circumstances permitting).

4. If unable to provide this information, use code words and/or transponder setting for indicated meanings as follows:

Spoken Words
TRANSPONDER SEVEN FIVE ZERO ZERO

Meaning
Am being hijacked/forced to a new destination

Transponder Setting
Mode 3/A, Code 7500

c. RECOMMENDED PROCEDURES FOR U.S. PASSENGER AIRCRAFT HIJACKED TO THE SOVIET UNION, PEOPLE'S REPUBLIC OF CHINA, VIETNAM AND NORTH KOREA.—If it is possible to do so without jeopardizing the safety of the flight, the pilot of a hijacked U.S. passenger aircraft after departing from the cleared routing over which the aircraft was operating will attempt to do one or more of the following things, insofar as circumstances may permit: (A) maintain a true airspeed of no more than 400 knots, and preferably an altitude of between 10,000 and 25,000 feet, (B) fly a course toward the destination which the hijacker has announced, and (C) transmit the international distress signal, MAYDAY, on any of the international distress frequencies available to him (243.0 MHz,

121.5 MHz, 2182 kHz). If these procedures result in either radio contact or air intercept, the pilot will attempt to comply with any instructions received which may direct him to an appropriate landing field. Additionally, if the aircraft is equipped with an operational transponder, the pilot may use transponder Mode A (Military Mode 3) Code 7500 to indicate his aircraft has been hijacked or Code 7700 to indicate his aircraft is in distress.

d. Code 7500 will never be assigned by air traffic control without prior notification from the pilot that his aircraft is being subjected to unlawful interference. The pilot should refuse the assignment of code 7500 in any other situation and inform the controller accordingly. Code 7500 will trigger the special emergency indicator in all radar ATC facilities.

e. Air traffic controllers will acknowledge and confirm receipt of transponder code 7500 by asking the pilot to verify it. If the aircraft is not being subjected to unlawful interference, the pilot should respond to the query by broadcasting in the clear that he is not being subjected to unlawful interference. Upon receipt of this information, the controller will request the pilot to verify the code selection depicted in the code selector windows in the transponder control panel and change the code to the appropriate setting. If the pilot replies in the affirmative or does not reply, the controller will not ask further questions but will flight follow, respond to pilot requests and notify appropriate authorities.

467. FAA SPONSORED EXPLOSIVES DETECTION (DOG/HANDLER TEAM) LOCATIONS

a. At many of our major airports a program has been established by the FAA and Law Enforcement Assistance Administration to make available explosives detection dog/handler teams. The dogs are trained by the Air Force and the overall program is run by FAA's Civil Aviation Security Service. Local police departments are the caretakers of the dogs and are allowed to use the dogs in their normal police patrol functions. The local airport, however, has first call on the teams' services. The explosives detection teams were established so that no aircraft in flight is more than one hour from an airport at which it can be searched if a bomb threat is received. The following list contains those locations that presently have a team in existence. This list will be updated as more teams are established. If you desire this service, notify your company or an FAA facility.

b. Team Locations:

Airport Symbol	Location
ABQ	Albuquerque, New Mexico
ATL	Atlanta, Georgia
BAL	Baltimore, Maryland
BIS	Bismarck, North Dakota
BOS	Boston, Massachusetts
BUF	Buffalo, New York
CLE	Cleveland, Ohio
DFW	Dallas, Texas
DEN	Denver, Colorado
GEG	Spokane, Washington
IAH	Houston, Texas
JAX	Jacksonville, Florida
MCI	Kansas City, Missouri
LAX	Los Angeles, California
MEM	Memphis, Tennessee
MIA	Miami, Florida
MSP	Minneapolis, Minnesota
BNA	Nashville, Tennessee
MSY	New Orleans, Louisiana
OKC	Oklahoma City, Oklahoma
PHX	Phoenix, Arizona
PIT	Pittsburgh, Pennsylvania
SJU	San Juan, Puerto Rico
SLC	Salt Lake City, Utah
SAN	San Diego, California
SFO	San Francisco, California
SEA	Seattle, Washington
STL	St. Louis, Missouri
TUS	Tucson, Arizona

468—479. RESERVED

PROCEDURES AND SIGNALS FOR AIRCRAFT IN EMERGENCY
WIND-SWELL-DITCH HEADING SITUATIONS

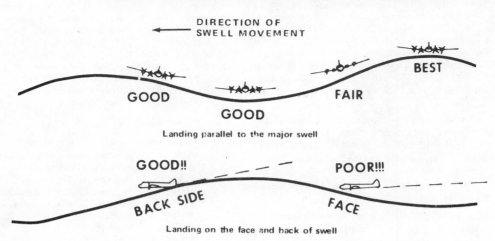

DIRECTION OF SWELL MOVEMENT

BEST

GOOD   FAIR
      GOOD

Landing parallel to the major swell

GOOD!!   POOR!!!

BACK SIDE   FACE

Landing on the face and back of swell

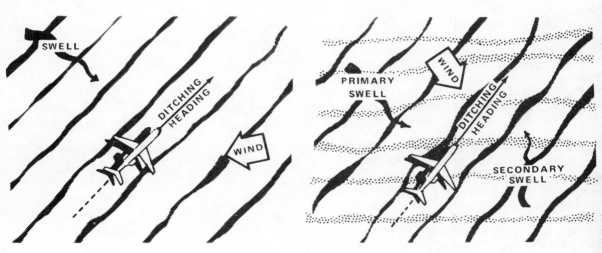

Single Swell System - Wind 15 knots

Double Swell System - Wind 15 knots

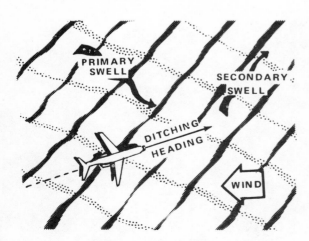

Double Swell System - Wind 30 knots

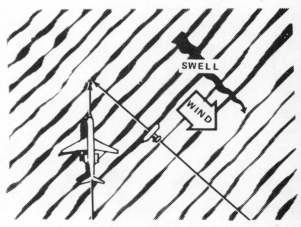

Wind - 50 knots

Aircraft with low landing speeds - land into the wind.

Aircraft with high landing speeds - choose compromise heading between wind and swell.

Both - Land on back side of swell.

Figure 5—1

PROCEDURES AND SIGNALS FOR AIRCRAFT IN EMERGENCY
GROUND-AIR VISUAL CODE FOR USE BY SURVIVORS

Message	Symbol	Message	Symbol	Message	Symbol
REQUIRE DOCTOR SERIOUS INJURIES	I	REQUIRE SIGNAL LAMP WITH BATTERY, AND RADIO	I	REQUIRE FUEL AND OIL	L
REQUIRE MEDICAL SUPPLIES	II	INDICATE DIRECTION TO PROCEED	K	ALL WELL	LL
UNABLE TO PROCEED	X	AM PROCEEDING IN THIS DIRECTION	↑	NO	N
REQUIRE FOOD AND WATER	F	WILL ATTEMPT TAKE-OFF	 ▷	YES	Y
REQUIRE FIREARMS AND AMMUNITION	 V	AIRCRAFT SERIOUSLY DAMAGED	 L7	NOT UNDERSTOOD	JL
REQUIRE MAP AND COMPASS	□	PROBABLY SAFE TO LAND HERE	△	REQUIRE MECHANIC	W

IF IN DOUBT, USE INTERNATIONAL SYMBOL   SOS

INSTRUCTIONS

1. Lay out symbols by using strips of fabric or parachutes, pieces of wood, stones, or any available material.
2. Provide as much color contrast as possible between material used for symbols and background against which symbols are exposed.
3. Symbols should be at least 10 feet high or larger. Care should be taken to lay out symbols exactly as shown.
4. In addition to using symbols, every effort is to be made to attract attention by means of radio, flares, smoke, or other available means.
5. On snow covered ground, signals can be made by dragging, shoveling or tramping. Depressed areas forming symbols will appear black from the air.
6. Pilot should acknowledge message by rocking wings from side to side.

GROUND-AIR VISUAL CODE FOR USE BY GROUND SEARCH PARTIES

NO.	MESSAGE	CODE SYMBOL
1	Operation completed.	LLL
2	We have found all personnel.	 LL
3	We have found only some personnel.	 ╫
4	We are not able to continue. Returning to base.	X X
5	Have divided into two groups. Each proceeding in direction indicated.	 ⚡
6	Information received that aircraft is in this direction.	➡
7	Nothing found. Will continue search.	NN

"Note: These visual signals have been accepted for international use and appear in Annex 12 to the Convention on International Civil Aviation."

Figure 5–2

VISUAL EMERGENCY SIGNALS

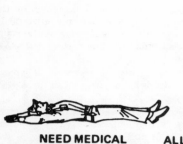

NEED MEDICAL ASSISTANCE—URGENT
Used only when life is at stake

ALL OK—DO NOT WAIT
Wave one arm overhead

CAN PROCEED SHORTLY— WAIT IF PRACTICABLE
One arm horizontal

NEED MECHANICAL HELP OR PARTS—LONG DELAY
Both arms horizontal

USE DROP MESSAGE
Make throwing motion

OUR RECEIVER IS OPERATING
Cup hands over ears

DO NOT ATTEMPT TO LAND HERE
Both arms waved across face

LAND HERE
Both arms forward horizontally, squatting and point in direction of landing—Repeat

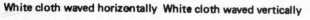

NEGATIVE (NO)
White cloth waved horizontally

AFFIRMATIVE (YES)
White cloth waved vertically

PICK US UP— PLANE ABANDONED
Both arms vertical

AFFIRMATIVE (YES)
Dip nose of plane several times

NEGATIVE (NO)

Fishtail plane

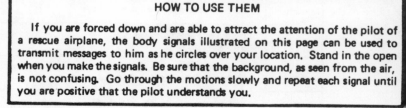

HOW TO USE THEM

If you are forced down and are able to attract the attention of the pilot of a rescue airplane, the body signals illustrated on this page can be used to transmit messages to him as he circles over your location. Stand in the open when you make the signals. Be sure that the background, as seen from the air, is not confusing. Go through the motions slowly and repeat each signal until you are positive that the pilot understands you.

Figure 5—3

116

Section 4. TWO-WAY RADIO COMMUNICATIONS FAILURE

480. TWO-WAY RADIO COMMUNICATIONS FAILURE

a. It is virtually impossible to provide regulations and procedures applicable to all possible situations associated with two-way radio communications failure. During two-way radio communications failure when confronted by a situation not covered in the regulation, pilots are expected to exercise good judgment in whatever action they elect to take. Should the situation so dictate they should not be reluctant to use the emergency action contained in FAR 91.3(b).

b. Whether two-way communications failure constitutes an emergency depends on the circumstances, and, in any event, it is a determination made by the pilot. FAR 91.3 authorizes a pilot to deviate from any rule to the extent required to meet an emergency.

c. In the event of two-way radio communications failure, ATC service will be provided on the basis that the pilot is operating in accordance with FAR 91.127. A pilot experiencing two-way communications failure should (unless emergency authority is exercised) comply with AR 91.127 as indicated below.

(1) General. Unless otherwise authorized by ATC, each pilot who has two-way radio communications failure when operating under IFR shall comply with the following:

(2) VFR conditions. If the failure occurs in VFR conditions, or if VFR conditions are encountered after the failure, each pilot shall continue the flight under VFR and land as soon as practicable. This procedure also applies when two-way radio failure occurs while operating in Positive Control Airspace (PCA). The primary objective of this provision in FAR 91.127 is to preclude extended IFR operation in the air traffic control system in VFR weather conditions. Pilots should recognize that operation under these conditions may unnecessarily as well as adversely affect other users of the airspace, since ATC may be required to reroute or delay other users in order to protect the failure aircraft. However, it is not intended that the requirement to "land as soon as practicable" be construed to mean "as soon as possible." The pilot retains his prerogative of exercising his best judgment and is not required to land at an unauthorized airport, at an airport unsuitable for the type of aircraft flown, or to land only minutes short of his destination.

(3) IFR conditions. If the failure occurs in IFR conditions, or if paragraph (2) of this section cannot be complied with, each pilot shall continue the flight according to the following:

(a) Route.

1. By the route assigned in the last ATC clearance received;

2. If being radar vectored, by the direct route from the point of radio failure to the fix, route, or airway specified in the vector clearance;

3. In the absence of an assigned route, by the route that ATC has advised may be expected in a further clearance; or

4. In the absence of an assigned route or a route that ATC has advised may be expected in a further clearance, by the route filed in the flight plan.

(b) Altitude. At the HIGHEST of the following altitudes or flight levels FOR THE ROUTE SEGMENT BEING FLOWN:

1. The altitude or flight level assigned in the last ATC clearance received except that the altitude in "2" below shall apply for only the segment/s of the route where the minimum altitude is higher than the ATC assigned altitude.

2. The minimum altitude (converted, if appropriate, to minimum flight level as prescribed in § 91.81 (c)) for IFR operations; or

3. The altitude or flight level ATC has advised may be expected in a further clearance except that the altitude in "2" above shall apply for only the segment/s of the route where the minimum altitude is higher than the expected altitude. ATC is required to assign either the altitude filed by the aircraft or an altitude within the highest route stratum filed and as near as possible to the altitude filed by the aircraft before the aircraft reaches the fix or prior to the time specified in the EXPECT (altitude) AT (time) or (fix) clearance. When the aircraft has proceeded past the specified fix or the time has expired, the altitude to be expected is no longer applicable.

4. The intent of the rule is that a pilot who has experienced two-way radio failure should, during any segment of his route, fly at the appropriate altitude specified in the rule for that *particular segment*. The appropriate altitude is whichever of the three is *highest* in each given phase of flight: (1) the altitude or flight level last assigned; (2) the MEA; or (3) the altitude or flight level the pilot has been advised to expect in a further clearance.

(c) Examples:

1. A pilot with two-way radio failure had an assigned altitude of 7,000 feet, and while enroute comes to a route segment for which the MEA was 9,000 feet. He would climb to 9,000 feet at the time or place where it became necessary to comply with the 9,000 feet MEA. (See FAR 91.119(b)) If later, while still proceeding to his destination, the MEA dropped from 9,000 feet to 5,000 feet, he would descent to *7,000 feet* (the last assigned altitude), because that altitude is *higher* than the MEA.

2. The Mea between **A** and **B**—5,000 feet.
The MEA between **B** and **C**—5,000 feet.
The MEA between **C** and **D**—11,000 feet.
The Mea between **D** and **E**—7,000 feet.

A pilot had been cleared via **A**, **B**, **C**, **D**, to **E**. His assigned altitude was 6,000 feet and he was told to except a clearance to 8,000 feet at **B**. Prior to receiving the higher altitude assignment, he experienced two-way failure. The pilot would maintain 6,000 to **B**, then climb to 8,000 feet (the altitude he was advised to expect.) He would maintain 8,000 feet, then climb to 11,000 at **C**, or prior to **C** if necessary to comply with an MCA at **C**. (FAR 91.119(b)). Upon reaching **D**, the pilot would descend to *8,000 feet* (even though the MEA was 7,000 feet), as 8,000 was the highest of the altitude situations stated in the rule, FAR 91.127.

(d) Leaving holding fix.

1. If holding instructions have been received, leave the holding fix at the expect-further-clearance time received, or, if an expected approach clearance time has been received, leave the holding fix in order to arrive over the fix from which the approach begins as close as possible to the expected approach clearance time.

2. If holding instructions have not been received and the aircraft is ahead of its ETA, the pilot is expected to hold at the fix from which the approach begins. If more than one approach fix is available, it is pilot choice and ATC protects airspace at all of them. Descent for approach begins at the ETA shown in the flight plan, as amended with ATC.

(e) Descent for approach. Begin descent from the en route altitude or flight level upon reaching the fix from which the approach begins, but not before—

1. The expect-approach-clearance time has been ceived) ; or

2. If no expect-approach-clearance time has been received, at the estimated time of arrival, shown on the flight plan, as amended with ATC.

3. If holding is necessary at the radio fix to be used for the approach at the destination airport, holding and descent to the initial approach altitude shall be accomplished in a holding pattern in accordance with the pattern depicted on the approach chart. If no holding pattern is depicted, holding and descent will be accomplished in a holding pattern on the side of the final approach course on which the procedure turn is prescribed.

481. TRANSPONDER OPERATION DURING TWO-WAY COMMUNICATIONS FAILURE

a. Should the pilot of an aircraft equipped with a coded radar beacon transponder experience a loss of two-way radio capability he should:

(1) adjust his transponder to reply on Mode A/3, Code 7700 for a period of 1 minute,

(2) then change to Code 7600 and remain on 7600 for a period of 15 minutes or the remainder of the flight, whichever occurs first.

(3) repeat steps a and b, as practicable.

b. The pilot should understand that he may not be in an area of radar coverage. Many radar facilities are also not presently equipped to automatically display Code 7600 and will interrogate 7600 only when the aircraft is under direct radar control at the time of radio failure. However, replying on Code 7700 first increases the probability of early detection of a radio failure condition.

482. RE-ESTABLISHING RADIO CONTACT

a. In addition to monitoring the NAVAID voice feature, the pilot should attempt to reestablish communications by attempting contact:

(1) on the previously assigned frequency, or

(2) with an FSS or ARINC.

b. If communications are established with an FSS or ARINC, the pilot should advise of the aircraft's position, altitude, last assigned frequency and then request further clearance from the controlling facility. The preceding does not preclude the use of 121.5 MHz. There is no priority on which action should be attempted first. If the capability exists, do all at the same time.

NOTE.—ARINC is a commercial communications corporation which designs, constructs, operates, leases or otherwise engages in radio activities serving the aviation community. ARINC has the capability of relaying information to/from ATC facilities throughout the country.

483–489. RESERVED

Section 5. SAFETY, ACCIDENT AND HAZARD REPORTS

490. AVIATION SAFETY REPORTING PROGRAM

a. The Federal Aviation Administration (FAA) has established a voluntary program designed to stimulate the free and unrestricted flow of information concerning deficiencies and discrepancies in the aviation system. This is a positive program intended to ensure the safest possible system by identifying and correcting unsafe conditions before they lead to accidents. The primary objective of the program is to obtain information to evaluate and enhance the safety and efficiency of the present system.

b. This program, however, will initially apply to that part of the System involving the safety of aircraft operations, including departure, en route, approach and landing operations and procedures, air traffic control procedures, pilot/controller communications, the aircraft movement area of the airport, and near mid-air collisions. Pilots, air traffic controllers, and all other members of the aviation community and the general public are asked to file written reports of any discrepancy or deficiency noted in these areas.

c. To ensure receipt of this information, the program provides for the waiver of certain disciplinary actions against persons, including pilots and air traffic controllers, who file timely written reports concerning potentially unsafe incidents. To be considered timely, reports must be delivered or postmarked within five days of the incident unless that period is extended for good cause. Reporting forms are available at FAA facilities.

d. The FAA has modified the present Aviation Safety Reporting Program by utilizing the National Aeronautics and Space Administration (NASA) to act as an independent third party to receive and analyze reports submitted under the Program. This modification to the Program is described in Advisory Circular 00–46A. The Aviation Safety Reporting Program is also described in AC 00–46A.

e. NASA ARC Form 277 is available in FAA offices for persons who wish to report deficiencies and discrepancies in the National Airspace System.

f. The report should give the date, time, location, persons and aircraft involved (if applicable), nature of the event, and all pertinent details.

491. RULES PERTAINING TO AIRCRAFT ACCIDENTS INCIDENTS, OVERDUE AIRCRAFT, AND SAFETY INVESTIGATIONS (NATIONAL TRANSPORTATION SAFETY BOARD, PROCEDURAL REGULATION, 49 CFR 830 (IN PART))

a. INCIDENTS REQUIRING NOTIFICATION

The operator of an aircraft shall immediately, and by the most expeditious means available, notify the nearest National Transportation Safety Board, Bureau of Aviation Safety Field Office when:

(1) An aircraft accident or any of the following listed incidents occur:

(a) Flight control system malfunction or failure;

(b) Inability of any required flight crewmember to perform his normal flight duties as a result of injury or illness;

(c) Turbine engine rotor failures excluding compressor blades and turbine buckets;

(d) In-flight fire;

(e) Aircraft collide in flight.

(2) An aircraft is overdue and is believed to have been involved in an accident.

b. MANNER OF NOTIFICATION

(1) The most expeditious method of notification to the National Transportation Safety Board by the operator will be determined by the circumstances existing at that time. The National Transportation Safety Board has advised that any of the following would be considered examples of the type of notification that would be acceptable:

(a) Direct telephone notification.

(b) Telegraphic notification.

(c) Notification to the Federal Aviation Administration who would in turn notify the NTSB by direct communication; i.e., dispatch or telephone.

c. ITEMS TO BE NOTIFIED

The notification required above shall contain the following information, if available:

(1) Type, nationality, and registration marks of the aircraft;

(2) Name of the pilot-in-command;

(3) Date and time of the accident;

(4) Last point of departure and point of intended landing of the aircraft;

(5) Position of the aircraft with reference to some easily defined geographical point;

(6) Number of persons aboard, number killed, and number seriously injured;

(7) Nature of the accident, the weather, and the extent of damage to the aircraft, so far as is known; and

(8) A description of any explosives, radioactive materials, or other dangerous articles carried.

d. FOLLOW UP REPORTS

(1) The operator shall file a report on NTSB Form 6120.1 or 6120.2, available from the National Transportation Safety Board Field Offices, or the National Transportation Safety Board, Washington, D.C.:

(a) Within ten (10) days after an occurrence for which notification is required;

(b) When, after seven (7) days, an overdue aircraft is still missing;

(c) Upon request of an authorized representative of the National Transportation Safety Board;

(2) Each crew member, if physically able at the time the report is submitted, shall attach thereto a statement setting forth the facts, conditions and circumstances relating to the accident or occurrence as they appear to him to the best of his knowledge and belief. If the crew member is incapacitated, he shall submit the statement as soon as he is physically able.

e. WHERE TO FILE THE REPORTS

(1) The operator of an aircraft shall file with the Field Office of the National Transportation Safety Board

nearest the accident or incident any report required by this section.

(2) The National Transportation Safety Board field offices are listed under U.S. Government in the telephone directories in the following cities: Anchorage, Alaska; Chicago, Ill.; Denver, Colo.; Fort Worth, Texas; Kansas City, Mo.; Los Angeles, Calif.; Miami, Fla.; New York, N.Y.; Oakland, Calif.; Seattle, Wash.; Washington, D.C.

492. NEAR MIDAIR COLLISION REPORTING

a. The FAA is continuing to encourage the transmission of near midair collision reports; however, enforcement of applicable FAA regulations that might be identified during the investigation of such incidents will be pursued.

b. The agency is vitally interested in all near midair collision incidents. Each reported incident is thoroughly investigated by the agency as soon as received in accordance with the established procedures. In order to ensure expeditious handling, all airmen are urged to report each incident immediately to:

(1) Nearest FAA Air Traffic Control facility or Flight Service Station by radio.

(2) Telephone report at next point of landing to nearest FAA Air Traffic Control facility or Flight Service Station.

(3) Written, in lieu of (1) and (2) above, to the nearest Air Carrier District Office or General Aviation District Office.

c. The following information should be reported if available:

(1) Date and time (GMT) of incident.

(2) Location of incident and altitude.

(3) Identification and type of reporting aircraft; aircrew destination; name and home base of pilot.

(4) Identification and type of other aircraft; aircrew destination; name and home base of pilot.

(5) Type of flight plans; station altimeter setting used.

(6) Detailed weather conditions at flight altitude/level.

(7) Approximate courses of both aircraft: indicate if one or both aircraft were climbing/descending.

(8) Reported separation in distance at first sighting; proximity at closest point horizontally and vertically; length of time in sight prior to evasive action.

(9) Degree of evasive action taken, if any (from both aircraft, if possible); injuries, if any.

493–499. RESERVED

Chapter 6. SAFETY OF FLIGHT

Section 1. WEATHER

500. GENERAL

a. The National Weather Service (NWS) maintains a comprehensive surface and upper air weather observing program and a nation-wide aviation weather forecasting and pilot briefing service. Weather observations are made each hour or more often at over 600 locations in the United States. These observations may be used to determine the present weather conditions for flight planning purposes.

b. Aviation forecasts are prepared by 51 Weather Service Forecast Offices (WSFO's). These WSFO's prepare and distribute a total of 452 terminal forecasts 3 times daily for specific airports in the 50 states and the Caribbean. They are valid to 24 hours with the last 6 hours as categorical outlooks of LIFR (low), IFR, MVFR (marginal) VFR, and the cause of these conditions. They also prepare a total of 306 route forecasts and 39 synopsis 3 times daily for the conterminous U.S. used for PATWAS, TWEB, and briefing purposes. Forecasts issued morning and mid-day are valid for 12 hours, the forecast issued in the evening is valid for 18 hours. Twelve WSFO's also prepare area forecasts (FA) twice per day, each valid for 18 hours with an additional 12 hour categorical outlook. Winds aloft forecasts are also provided for 120 locations in the United States and Alaska for flight operational purposes. All of the above flying weather forecasts are given wide distribution via teletypewriter circuits and request reply procedures from the Weather Message Switching Center in Kansas City.

(1) Categorical outlook terms, describing general ceiling and visibility conditions for advanced planning purposes, are defined as follows:

(a) LIFR (Low IFR) —Ceiling less than 500 feet and/or visibility less than 1 mile.

(b) IFR —Ceiling 500 to less than 1,000 feet and/or visibility 1 to less than 3 miles.

(c) MVFR (Marginal VFR)—Ceiling 1,000 to 3,000 feet and/or visibility 3 to 5 miles inclusive.

(d) VFR —Ceiling greater than 3,000 feet and visibility greater than 5 miles; includes sky clear.

(2) The cause of LIFR, IFR, or MVFR is also given by either ceiling or visibility restrictions or both. The contraction "CIG" and/or weather and obstruction to vision symbols are used. If winds or gusts of 25 knots or greater are forecast for the outlook period, the word "WIND" is also included for all categories including VFR.

Examples:

LIFR CIG	—Low IFR due to low ceiling.
IFR F	—IFR due to visibility restricted by fog.
MVFR CIG H K	—Marginal VFR due both to ceiling and to visibility restricted by haze and smoke.
IFR CIG R WIND	—IFR due both to low ceiling and to visibility restricted by rain; wind expected to be 25 knots or greater.

501. INFLIGHT WEATHER ADVISORIES

a. The NWS issues in-flight weather advisories designated as either SIGMETs (nonconvective–WS; convective–WST) or AIRMETs–WA. These advisories are issued individually and their information may be included in relevant portions of Aviation Area Forecasts (FAs). Normally, WSs, WSTs and WAs which are issued separately will automatically amend the relevant portion of the FA for the period of the advisory, but separate FA amendments can also be issued whenever a significant change occurs. The purpose of this service is to notify en route pilots of the possibility of encountering hazardous flying conditions which may not have been provided in preflight briefings. Whether or not the condition described is potentially hazardous to a particular flight is for the pilot to evaluate on the basis of his own experience and the operational limits of his aircraft.

b. Convective SIGMETs (WST) will be issued for the following phenomena:

(1) Tornadoes.

(2) Lines of thunderstorms.

(3) Embedded thunderstorms.

(4) Thunderstorm areas greater than or equal to thunderstorm intensity level 4 with an areal coverage of 4/10 (40%) or more.

(See RADAR WEATHER ECHO INTENSITY LEVELS in Pilot/Controller Glossary.)

(5) Hail greater than or equal to ¾ inch diameter.

NOTE.—Since thunderstorms are the reason for issuing the convective SIGMET, severe or greater turbulence, severe icing, and low-level wind shear (gust fronts, etc.) are implied and will not be specified in the advisory.

(a) Three Convective SIGMET bulletins specifying the Eastern (E), Central (C), and Western (W) U.S. will be issued, when required, on a scheduled basis hourly at 55 minutes past the hour (H+55) and as specials on an unscheduled basis. The boundaries that separate the Eastern and Central, and the Central and Western U.S. are 87 and 107 degrees West, respectively. (See figure 6–1 for a chart of VORs and major locations used as reference points for the In-Flight Weather Advisory messages.)

(b) Each of the Convective SIGMET bulletins will be:

1. Made up of one or more individually numbered Convective SIGMETs,

2. Valid for one hour, and

3. Removed from system automatically at 40 minutes past the hour (H+40).

(c) The following are complete examples of Convective SIGMET bulletins for the Central U.S. as transmitted on teletype.

Example 1

ZCZC
MKCC WST 221655
CONVECTIVE SIGMET 17C
KS OK TX
(WRN KS OK AND TX PNHDL) or (VCNTY GLD-CDS LN)
NO SIG TSTMS RPRTD
FCST TO 1855Z
LN TSTMS DVLPG BY 1755Z WL MOV EWD 30–35 KTS
HAIL TO 1½ IN PSBL
ADP
NNNN

Example 2

ZCZC
MKCC WST 221855
CONVECTIVE SIGMET 19C
KS OK
FROM 30E GCK TO 20E GAG
LN TSTMS 25 MI WIDE MOVG FROM 2315. MAX TOPS TO 450.
HAIL TO 1 IN . . . WIND GUSTS TO 55
FCST TO 2055Z
DSIPTG LN WL CONT MOVG NEWD 25–30 KTS THRU 2055Z
CONVECTIVE SIGMET 20C
ND SD
FROM 90 W MOT TO GFK TO ABR TO RAP
AREA TSTMS MOVG FROM 2530, MAX TOPS TO 450
TORNADO RPRTD 1820Z 20NE RAP . . . HAIL TO 1 IN . . . WIND GUSTS TO 55
FCST TO 2055Z
INTSFYG AREA WL MOV NWD 15 KTS THRU 2055Z
HAIL TO ¾ IN PSBL
ADP
NNNN

Notes:

1. Each WST will be numbered consecutively (01–99) each day, beginning with the 0055Z issuance.

2. Width of line and tops of thunderstorms will be included if available from radar, satellite pictures, or PIREP's.

c. Nonconvective SIGMETs (WS) within the conterminous U.S. will be issued by the FA Centers for their area of responsibility for the following weather phenomena:

(1) Severe and extreme turbulence.

(2) Severe icing.

(3) Widespread duststorms/sandstorms lowering visibilities to below three miles.

d. AIRMETs (WA) will only be issued to amend the FA regarding weather phenomena that may be potentially hazardous to aircraft concerning the following:

(1) Moderate icing.

(2) Moderate turbulence.

(3) Sustained winds of 30 knots or more at the surface.

(4) Widespread areas of ceilings less than 1000 feet and/or visibility less than three miles.

(5) Extensive mountain obscurement.

NOTE.—If the above phenomena are adequately forecast in the FA, an AIRMET will not be issued.

e. Advisories are identified with a letter and number beginning 0000 GMT by the issuing office. Nonconvective SIGMET alphanumeric series are "ALPHA-NOVEMBER;" AIRMETs series are "OSCAR-ZULU."

The first SIGMET is identified as "ALFA 1"; each succeeding related advisory retains the same letter designator until cancelled, but is given the next number; i.e., "ALFA 2", etc. A SIGMET or AIRMET automatically cancels a preceding advisory of the same category and lettering. For example, SIGMET BRAVO 2 supersedes SIGMET BRAVO 1 and AIRMET PAPA 2 cancels AIRMET PAPA 1.

f. FAA flight service stations (FSSs) broadcast SIGMETs and AIRMETs during their valid period when they pertain to the area within 150 NM of the FSS as follows:

(1) SIGMETs—At 15 minute intervals (H+00, H+15*, H+30 and H+45); and AIRMETs—at 30 minute intervals (H+15* and H+45) during the first hour after issuance.

(2) Thereafter, a summarized alert notice will be broadcast at H+15* and H+45 during the valid period of the advisories.

Example:

"A SIGMET is current for a squall line running north and south through Central Nebraska."

* Included in the scheduled weather broadcast.

g. Pilots, upon hearing the alert notice, if they have not received the advisory or are in doubt, should contact the nearest FSS and ascertain whether the advisory is pertinent to their flights.

h. Air Route Traffic Control Centers and Terminal Control facilities broadcast a SIGMET alert message once on all nonemergency frequencies within a 150 mile radius of the SIGMET geographical area. These broadcasts contain a brief description of the weather activity and the general area affected.

Example 1:

"Attention all aircraft, SIGMET delta three. From Myton to Tuba City to Milford. Severe turbulence

FIGURE 6–1. IN-FLIGHT WEATHER ADVISORY PROGRAM

and severe clear icing below one zero thousand feet. Reported by several aircraft. Expected to continue beyond zero three zero zero Greenwich."

Example 2:

"Attention all aircraft, convective SIGMET two seven eastern. From the vicinity of Elmira to Phillipsburg. Scattered embedded thunderstorms moving east at one zero knots. A few intense level five cells, maximum tops flight level four five zero."

502. PRE-FLIGHT BRIEFING SERVICES

a. Available aviation weather reports and forecasts are displayed at each Weather Service Office and FAA Flight Service Station. Pilots should feel free to help themselves to this information or to ask the assistance of the duty employee.

b. When telephoning for information, use the following procedures:

(1) Identify yourself as a pilot and give aircraft identification if known. (Many persons calling Weather Service Offices want information for purposes other than flying.)

(2) State your intended route, destination, proposed departure time, estimated time en route and type of aircraft.

(3) Advise if prepared to fly IFR.

c. Combined station/tower (CS/T) personnel are not certificated pilot weather briefers; however, they can assist you by providing factual data from weather reports and forecasts.

503. PILOTS AUTOMATIC TELEPHONE WEATHER ANSWERING SERVICE (PATWAS)

a. At some locations the numbers of pilots requiring flight weather briefings are too numerous for person-to-person briefings. To assist in this important service, recorded weather briefings are available at several locations. This service is called Pilots Automatic Telephone Weather Answering Service (PATWAS).

b. The PATWAS locations are found in the Airport/Facility Directory under the FSS-CS/T Weather Service Telephone Numbers section.

NOTE.—As of July 1, 1979, FAA facilities providing PATWAS will have implemented new operational procedures which will greatly enhance the dissemination of meteorological and aeronautical data. Recent tests of these procedures indicated user acceptance provided certain conditions are inherent. These are: currency, accuracy, availability, and user awareness. As long as these parameters are maintained, user acceptance has been excellent. New procedures place a higher operational priority on the PATWAS, this will insure the information is current and accurate. Information is tailored to provide data for a local flight, or is route-oriented. Data available between 2200 LST and 0500 LST may be a genral outlook for the PATWAS area. You are invited to forward your suggestions and comments on these new procedures to:

DOT/FAA
ATTN: AAT–360
800 Independence Ave., S.W.
Washington, D.C. 20591

504. FLIGHT SERVICE STATION PRE-FLIGHT BRIEFING

a. Flight Service Specialists are qualified and certificated by the NOAA/NWS as Pilot Weather Briefers. They are not authorized to make original forecasts but are authorized to translate and interpret available forecasts and reports directly into terms of the weather conditions which you can expect along your flight route and at destination. They also will assist you in selecting an alternate course of action in the event adverse weather is encountered. It is not necessary to be thoroughly familiar with the standard phraseologies and procedures for air/ground communications. A brief call stating your message in your own words will receive immediate attention. If a complete weather briefing is desired, advise the FSS accordingly. The FSS only provides that weather information which is specifically requested.

505. EN ROUTE FLIGHT ADVISORY SERVICE (EFAS)

a. EFAS is a service specifically designed to provide en route aircraft with timely and meaningful weather advisories pertinent to the type of flight intended, route of flight and altitude. It is normally available throughout the counterminous U.S. from 6 a.m. to 10 p.m. at a service criterion of 5,000 feet above ground level. EFAS will be provided by specially trained specialists from selected FSSs controlling one or more remote communications outlets covering a large geographical area. All communications will be conducted on the designated frequency, 122.0 MHz using the radio call (name of FSS) FLIGHT WATCH.

b. To contact a flight watch facility on 122.0 MHz use the name of the controlling FSS and the words FLIGHT WATCH or, if the controlling FSS is unknown, simply call "FLIGHT WATCH" and give the aircraft position.

Example:

OAKLAND FLIGHT WATCH, LEAR TWO THREE FOUR FIVE KILO, etc. FLIGHT WATCH, COMMANDER FIVE SIX SEVEN LIMA FOXTROT OVER VIENNA VOR, OVER

c. En Route Flight Advisory Service has been implemented at the following FSSs:

Boston, MA	New Orleans, LA
Montpelier, VT	Fort Worth, TX
Buffalo, NY	El Paso, TX
Charleston, WV	Lubbock, TX
Pittsburgh, PA	Omaha, NE
Teterboro, NJ	Des Moines, IA
Washington, DC	Albuquerque, NM
Atlanta, GA	Phoenix, AZ
Birmingham, AL	Las Vegas, NV
Charleston, SC	Denver, CO
Jackson, MS	Grand Forks, ND
Memphis, TN	Huron, SD
Miami, FL	Casper, WY
Raleigh, NC	Great Falls, MT
Chicago, IL	Boise, ID
Detroit, MI	Salt Lake City, UT
Indianapolis, IN	Oklahoma City, OK
Minneapolis, MN	Oakland, CA
Kansas City, MO	Los Angeles, CA
St. Louis, MO	Portland, OR
Houston, TX	Seattle, WA
San Antonio, TX	Walla Walla, WA

d. EFAS is not intended to be used for filing or closing flight plans, position reporting, to get a complete pre-flight briefing, or to obtain random weather reports and forecasts. In such instances, the flight watch specialist will provide the name and radio frequency of the FSS to contact for such services. Weather reports along the proposed route of flight, destination, or alternate airport, and terminal forecasts for the destination or alternate airport will be given when requested. Pilot participation is essential to the success of EFAS through a continuous exchange of information on winds, turbulence, visibility, icing, etc., between pilots inflight and flight watch specialists on the ground. Pilots are encouraged to report good as well as bad and expected as well as unexpected inflight conditions to flight watch facilities.

506. TRANSCRIBED WEATHER BROADCASTS (TWEB)

a. Equipment is provided at selected FAA FSSs by which meteorological and Notice to Airmen data are recorded on tapes and broadcast continuously over the low-frequency (200–415 kHz) navigational aid (L/MF range or H facility) and VOR. Broadcasts are made from a series of individual tape recordings. The first three tapes identify the station, give general weather forecast conditions in the area, pilot reports (PIREP), radar reports when available, and winds aloft data. The remaining tapes contain weather at selected locations within a 400-mile radius of the central point. Changes, as they occur are transcribed onto the tapes.

507. SCHEDULED WEATHER BROADCASTS (SWB)

a. All flight service stations having voice facilities on radio ranges (VORs) or radio beacons (NDBs) broadcast weather reports and Notice to Airmen information at 15 minutes past each hour from reporting points within approximately 150 miles from the broadcast station.

b. UNSCHEDULED BROADCASTS

These broadcasts will be made at random times and will begin with the announcement "Aviation broadcast" followed by identification of the data. (See para 501 for information on broadcast of inflight advisories.)

Example:

Aviation Broadcast, Special Weather Report, (Notice to Airmen, Pilot Report, etc.) (location name twice) three seven (past the hour) observation . . . etc.

508–509. RESERVED

510. WEATHER RADAR SERVICES

a. The National Weather Service operates a 90-station network of weather radars. These stations are generally spaced in such a manner as to enable them to detect and identify the type and characteristics of most of the precipitation east of the Continental Divide. In addition, 32 radars of the Department of Defense and 18 FAA radars augment the network in the conterminous U.S.

In Alaska data from 15 DOD radars are collected and summarized by the Anchorage Forecast Center.

b. When precipitation is being detected, a scheduled radar observation is taken at 40 minutes past each hour, and more often under certain conditions. These observations are transmitted to many Weather Service Stations and FAA stations and are available for use in pre-flight and in-flight planning. In addition, an hourly plain language radar summary and sixteen radar summary facsimile charts per day are prepared by the Radar Analysis and Development Unit in Kansas City, Missouri. The hourly radar summary is transmitted on Service A teletypewriter to all NWS and Flight Service Stations, and the radar chart is available to all subscribers to the facsimile circuit.

c. Some Flight Service Stations located near radar equipped Weather Service Stations have weather radar repeaterscopes. The FSS specialist at these locations are certified to make interpretations of the weather displayed on the radar scope. They can brief a pilot on the displayed weather pattern as to the area covered and the weather movement. However technical analysis of the intensity of precipitation and cells is made by the NWS, who in turn forwards this information to the FSS pilot briefer. The weather radar presents a very dependable display of the weather within 100 miles, and storms of considerable heights and intensities can be seen at ranges of more than 100 miles. Through the combined efforts of the NWS and the FSS, a pilot can receive a comprehensive picture of the weather to assist him in planning a safe flight.

511. ATC IN-FLIGHT WEATHER AVOIDANCE ASSISTANCE

a. ATC Radar Weather Display.

(1) Areas of weather clutter are radar echoes from rain or moisture. *Radars cannot detect turbulence.* The determination of the intensity of the weather displayed is based on its precipitation density. Generally the turbulence associated with a very heavy rate of rainfall will normally be significantly more severe than any associated with a very light rainfall rate.

(2) ARTCCs are phasing in computer-generated digitized radar displays to replace the heretofore standard broadband radar display. The new system known as Narrowband Radar provides the controller with two distinct levels of weather intensity by assigning radar display symbols for specific precipitation densities measured by the narrowband system.

b. Weather Avoidance Assistance.

(1) To the extent possible, controllers will issue pertinent information on weather or chaff areas and assist pilots in avoiding such areas when requested. Pilots should respond to a weather advisory by either acknowledging the advisory or by acknowledging the advisory and requesting an alternative course of action as follows:

(a) Request to deviate off course by stating the number of miles and the direction of the requested deviation. In this case, when the requested deviation is approved the pilot is expected to provide his own navigation, maintain the altitude assigned by ATC and to remain within the specific mileage of his original course.

(b) Request a new route to avoid the affected area.

(c) Request a change of altitude.

(d) Request radar vectors around the affected areas.

(2) For obvious reasons of safety, an IFR pilot must not deviate from the course or altitude/flight-level without a proper ATC clearance. When weather conditions encountered are so severe that an immediate deviation is determined to be necessary and time will not permit approval by ATC, the pilot's emergency authority may be exercised.

(3) When the pilot requests clearance for a route deviation or for an ATC radar vector, the controller must evaluate the air traffic picture in the affected area, and coordinate with other controllers (if ATC jurisdictional boundaries may be crossed) before replying to the request.

(4) It should be remembered that the controller's primary function is to provide safe separation between aircraft. Any additional service, such as weather avoidance assistance, can only be provided to the extent that it does not derogate the primary function. It's also worth noting that the separation workload is generally greater than normal when weather disrupts the usual flow of traffic. ATC radar limitations (see RADAR SERVICES AND PROCEDURES) and frequency congestion may also be a factor in limiting the controller's capability to provide additional service.

(5) It is very important therefore, that the request for deviation or radar vector be forwarded to ATC as far in advance as possible. Delay in submitting it may delay or even preclude ATC approval or require that additional restrictions be placed on the clearance. Insofar as possible the following information should be furnished to ATC when requesting clearance to detour around weather activity:

(a) Proposed point where detour will commence.

(b) Proposed route and extent of detour (direction and distance).

(c) Point where original route will be resumed.

(d) Flight conditions (IFR or VFR).

(e) Any further deviation that may become necessary as the flight progresses.

(f) Advise if the aircraft is equipped with functioning airborne radar.

(6) To a large degree, the assistance that might be rendered by ATC will depend upon the weather information available to controllers. Due to the extremely transitory nature of severe weather situations, the controller's weather information may be of only limited value if based on weather observed on radar only. Frequent updates by pilots giving specific information as to the area affected, altitudes intensity and nature of the severe weather can be of considerable value. Such reports are relayed by radio or phone to other pilots and controllers and also receive widespread teletypewriter dissemination.

(7) Obtaining IFR clearance or an ATC radar vector to circumnavigate severe weather can often be accommodated more readily in the enroute areas away from terminals because there is usually less congestion and, therefore, greater freedom of action. In terminal areas, the problem is more acute because of traffic density, ATC coordination requirements, complex departure and arrival routes, adjacent airports, etc. As a consequence, controllers are less likely to be able to

WEATHER

accommodate all requests for weather detours in a terminal area or be in a position to volunteer such route to the pilot. Nevertheless, pilots should not hesitate to advise controllers of any observed severe weather and should specifically advise controllers if they desire circumnavigation of observed weather.

512. RUNWAY VISUAL RANGE (RVR)

a. Runway visual range visibility values are measured by transmissometers mounted on towers along the runway. A full RVR system consists of:

(1) Transmissometer projector and related items.

(2) Transmissometer receiver (detector) and related items.

(3) Analogue recorder.

(4) Signal data converter and related items.

(5) Remote digital or remote display programmer.

b. The transmissometer projector and receiver are mounted on towers either 250 or 500 feet apart. A known intensity of light is emitted from the projector and is measured by the receiver. Any obscuring matter such as rain, snow, dust, fog, haze or smoke reduces the light intensity arriving at the receiver. The resultant intensity measurement is then converted to an RVR value by the signal data converter. These values are displayed by readout equipment in the associated air traffic facility and updated approximately once every minute for controller issuance to pilots.

c. The signal data converter receives information on the high intensity runway edge light setting in use (step 3, 4, or 5); transmission values from the transmissometer; and the sensing of day or night conditions. From the three data sources, the system will compute appropriate RVR values. Due to variable conditions, the reported RVR values may deviate somewhat from the true observed visual range due to the slant range consideration, brief time delays between the observed RVR conditions and the time they are transmitted to the pilot, and rapidly changing visibility conditions.

d. An RVR transmissometer established on a 500-foot baseline provides digital readouts to a minimum of 1000 feet. A system established on a 250-foot baseline provides digital readouts to a minimum of 600 feet, which are displayed in 200-foot increments to 3000 feet and in 500-foot increments from 3000 feet to a maximum value of 6000 feet.

e. RVR values for Category IIIa operations extend down to 700 feet RVR; however, only 600 and 800 feet are reportable RVR increments. The 800 RVR reportable value covers a range of 701 feet to 900 feet and is therefore a valid minimum indication of Category IIIa operations.

f. Approach categories with the corresponding minimum RVR values are as follows:

Category	Visibility (RVR)
Nonprecision	2400 feet
Category I	1800 feet
Category II	1200 feet
Category IIIa	700 feet
Category IIIb	150 feet
Category IIIc	0

g. Ten-minute maximum and minimum RVR values for the designated RVR runway are reported in the remarks section of the aviation weather report when the prevailing visibility is less than 1 mile and/or the RVR is 6000 feet or less. Air traffic control towers report RVR when the prevailing visibility is 1½ miles or less and/or the RVR is 6000 feet or less.

h. Details on the requirements for the operational use of RVR are contained in FAA Advisory Circular 97–1, "Runway Visual Range." Pilots are responsible for compliance with minimums prescribed for their class of operations in appropriate Federal Aviation Regulations and/or operations specifications.

513. REPORTING OF CLOUD HEIGHTS

a. Ceiling, by definition in Part I Federal Aviation Regulations, and as used in Aviation Weather Reports and Forecasts, is the height *above ground (or water) level* of the lowest layer of clouds or obscuring phenomenon that is reported as "broken", "overcast", or "obscuration" and not classified as "thin" or "partial". For example, a forecast which reads "CIGS WILL BE GENLY 1 TO 2 THSD FEET" refers to heights *above ground level* (AGL). On the other hand, a forecast which reads "BRKN TO OVC LYRS AT 8 TO 12 THSD MSL" states that the height is *above mean sea level* (MSL).

b. Pilots usually report height values above mean sea level, since they determine heights by the altimeter. This is taken in account when disseminating and otherwise applying information received from pilots. ("Ceilings" heights are always above ground level.) In reports disseminated as PIREP's, height references are given the same as received from pilots, that is above mean sea level (MSL or ASL). In the following example, however, a pilot report of the heights of the bases and tops of an overcast layer in the terminal area is used in two ways in a surface aviation weather report:

E12 OVC 2FK 132/49/47/0000/002/ OVC 23

In this example the weather station has converted the pilot's report of the height of base of the overcast from the height (MSL) indicated on the pilot's altimeter to height above ground. The height of cloud tops shown in remarks (OVC 23) is *above mean sea level* (ASL or MSL) as initially reported by the pilot.

c. In aviation forecasts (Terminal, Area, or In-flight Advisories), ceiling are denoted by the prefix "C" when used with sky cover symbols as in "LWRG TO C5 OVC-1TRW", or by the contraction "CIG" before, or the contraction "AGL" after, the forecast cloud height value. When the cloud base is given in height above mean sea level, it is so indicated by the contraction "MSL" or "ASL" following the height value. The heights of clouds tops, freezing level, icing and turbulence are always given in heights above mean sea level (ASL or MSL).

514. ESTIMATING INTENSITY OF PRECIPITATION (OTHER THAN DRIZZLE) ON RATE-OF-FALL BASIS

a. LIGHT   Scattered drops or flakes that do not completely wet or cover an exposed surface, regardless of duration, to 0.10 inch per hour; maximum 0.01 inch in 6 minutes.

126

b. MODERATE 0.11 inch to 0.30 inch per hour; more than 0.01 inch to 0.03 inch in 6 minutes.

c. HEAVY More than 0.30 inch per hour; more than 0.03 inch in 6 minutes.

515. ESTIMATING INTENSITY OF DRIZZLE ON RATE-OF-FALL BASIS

a. LIGHT Scattered drops that do not completely wet an exposed surface, regardless of duration, to 0.01 inch per hour.

b. MODERATE More than 0.01 inch to 0.02 inch per hour.

c. HEAVY More than 0.02 inch per hour.

516. INTENSITY OF DRIZZLE OR SNOW WITH VISIBILITY AT USUAL POINT OF OBSERVATION AS CRITERIA

a. LIGHT Visibility ⅝ statute mile or more.

b. MODERATE Visibility less than ⅝ statute mile but not less than ⁵⁄₁₆ statute mile.

c. HEAVY Visibility less than ⁵⁄₁₆ statute mile.

517. AUTOMATIC WEATHER OBSERVATION SYSTEMS (AUTOB)

a. The National weather service is installing seven automatic weather reporting systems (AUTOB). There will be two locations in Alaska and five locations in the conterminous U.S. AUTOB is a completely automatic system that reports sky condition, visibility, precipitation occurrence, temperature,, dewpoint, wind speed, wind direction, altimeter setting, peak wind speed and precipitation accumulation. A typical report would appear as follows: ENV AUTOB −X ES BKN 45 OVC BV130P 54/49/2913/028 PK WND 18 001 HIR CLDS DETECTED

This report would be decoded as follows:

ENV —Wendover, Utah.

AUTOB —Completely automatic observation.

−X —Obscuring phenomena present may be obscuring part of the sky. (A report of WX would indicate obscuring phenomena present may be obscuring *all* the sky.)

E8 BKN —Ceiling estimated 800 feet broken.

45 OVC —Cloud layer 4,500 feet overcast.

BV130 —Visibility is now less than 1½ mile but more than ¾ mile, the maximum in the past 10 minutes was between 2½ and 3½ miles, and the minimum in the past 10 minutes was less than ¾ mile.

P* —Precipitation has occurred in the 10 minutes prior to the observation— precipitation is probably occurring now.

54/49/ —Temperature 54°F, dewpoint 49°F.

2913/ —Wind from 290° True at 13 knots.

028 —Altimeter setting 30.28 inches of mercury.

PK WND 18 —Highest wind speed measured since last hourly observation is 18 knots.

001 —Precipitation accumulated since the most recent 0000, 0600, 1200, or 1800 GMT observation is 0.01 inch.

HIR CLDS DETECTED* —Indication that a layer of clouds was detected above the overcast (but still within the 6,000 foot range of the ceilometer).

The element with asterisks (*) will not appear in the AUTOB observations until late 1979. Until then you will also see the visibility group (BVxxx) reported near the end of the report and a group SKY XXXX XXXX at the very end of the report. In this SKY group the first set of four digits indicate the percent of time in the past 30 minutes clouds were detected in the layers 0–500 feet, 500–1,000 feet, 1,000–2,000 feet and 2,000–6,000 feet. The second four digit group gives the same information except covers the period from 30 to 60 minutes before the observation. The percents are reported as follows: 0=0–10%, 1=10–20%, 2=20–30%, 3=30–40%, 4=40–50%, 5=50–60%, 6=60–70%, 7=70–80%, 8=80–90%, and 9=90–100%.

b. While the AUTOB report on Service A looks like an ordinary aviation observation, there are some significant differences—particularly in the way sky condition and visibility are handled.

(1) Most significant of these differences is the way an obscuration (X) is determined and reported. AUTOB will always report an obscuration, either partial (−X) or total (WX) if the visibility is less than 1½ miles. This is done for safety reasons since it's possible an obscuration will prevent the ceilometer from detecting some or all the clouds present. If the visibility is less than 1½ miles and some clouds are detected, AUTOB will report a −X followed by the cloud formation. If the visibility is less than 1½ miles and no clouds are detected, AUTOB assumes it can't see the clouds because of an obscuration and reports WX. No height is reported with the WX because the system can't measure vertical visibility.

(2) Another significant difference in the AUTOB report is that AUTOB only reports clouds up to 6,000 feet. If clouds are detected they're reported in the familiar SCT, BKN, and OVC format. However, if no clouds are detected, and the visibility is greater than 1½ miles, AUTOB reports CLR BLO 60. (Until late 1979 AUTOB will report 60 CLR.)

(3) Still another difference is the period during which AUTOB evaluates the sky condition. A human observer bases his sky condition on what he sees when he scans the sky for a relatively brief period of time just prior to making his report. AUTOB doesn't do this. It uses a ceilometer that can't scan. It can only see straight up. To compensate for this narrow field of view, AUTOB reports what the ceilometer has "seen" overhead in the past 30 minutes. The data gathered in the most recent 10 minutes is given double weight to make the report more current. Even so, it is possible that if sky condition changes drastically just prior to the transmission of the report, the report won't reflect the complete change. (This is of course true of human observations too if a change occurs just prior to transmission time.) Experience has shown this rarely happens—BUT YOU SHOULD BE AWARE OF THE POSSIBILITY WHEN USING AUTOB REPORTS.

(a) It's also possible for clouds to be present in the area but not reported by AUTOB. This happens if the clouds are localized and/or slow moving. AUTOB only reports clouds that pass over the ceilometer. AUTOB has absolutely no peripheral vision. If clouds don't pass over the ceilometer, they'll go undetected and unreported. Again, experience has shown the AUTOB rarely misses a cloud layer (within it's vertical range), BUT YOU SHOULD BE AWARE OF THE POSSIBILITY WHEN USING THE AUTOB REPORT.

(b) On rare occasions AUTOB may report clouds that aren't there. Great care has been taken to teach AUTOB to recognize clouds. However, nature being what it is, strong sunshine or other "noise" sometimes creates a signal in the system that to the AUTOB logic looks exactly like a cloud. When this happens, AUTOB is fooled and registers a cloud "hit" in the computer. If this happens enough times in the 30 minutes before the observation, a layer will be reported. This happens very rarely and never results in anything but a scattered layer, and even more rarely happens on two successive observations.

c. Visibility is reported by the group BVxxx. The BV indicates it is only an index of visibility conditions and is not Prevailing Visibility. The first digit after the BV is the present visibility. The second digit is the maximum visibility in the past 10 minutes and the last digit is the minimum visibility in the past 10 minutes. The visibility is reported in whole statute miles as follows: $0=0-\frac{3}{4}$, $1=\frac{3}{4}-1\frac{1}{2}$, $2=1\frac{1}{2}-2\frac{1}{2}$, $3=2\frac{1}{2}-3\frac{1}{2}$, $4=3\frac{1}{2}-4\frac{1}{2}$, $5=4\frac{1}{2}-5\frac{1}{2}$, $6=5\frac{1}{2}-6\frac{1}{2}$, $7=6\frac{1}{2}-7\frac{1}{2}$, $8=$ more than $7\frac{1}{2}$ miles.

(1) The AUTOB visibility is determined by a new instrument which measures the amount of projected light reflected back into a detector by particles in the air. These measurements are based on sampling a small volume of air at one location, the sensor site. If visibility is different at some other location on the airport, that fact won't be reflected in the AUTOB report. Differences in visibility at various locations on an airport occur more frequently than differences in cloud conditions over a small area—SO YOU SHOULD ALWAYS KEEP THIS IN MIND WHEN USING AN AUTOB REPORT.

d. AUTOB reports a P. if precipitation has been detected in the 10 minutes prior to the observation. The way this works is every time 0.01 inch of precipitation accumulates in the precipitation gage a pulse is sent to the AUTOB processor. If a pulse is received in the 10 minutes prior to the observation the P is reported immediately after the visibility group. If a pulse is not received in the 10 minutes prior to the observation the P is omitted from the report. If you see a P in the report you can be pretty certain precipitation was occurring at the time of the report. However, if you don't see the P it just may be enough precipitation didn't accumulate to cause the pulse to be sent to the processor—precipitation may be occurring. Look at the sky condition, visibility, temperature and dewpoint, and precipitation accumulation, compare the new report with the previous report and then make your decision as to whether or not it is raining.

e. What's in the future for AUTOB? Of course, you'll see more automatic systems. Now there are two systems. One at Wendover, Utah, the other at Summit, Alaska. By the end of the summer of 1979 there will be five more. They'll be at Winslow, Arizona; Sandberg, California; Del Rio, Texas; Fort Yukon, Alaska; and Unalakleet, Alaska. After that, you probably won't see any more AUTOB systems although you will certainly see more automatic stations. The new stations, those installed after 1979, will be improved. The range of the ceilometer will be greater, probably to 10,000 feet or more (possibly to 20,000). The system will be able to report the type of precipitation; e.g., whether its rain, snow, drizzle, or fog restricting visibility. The method of handling obscurations will also be improved so the system will report the equivalent of vertical visibility. As the new sensors and improvements come along the existing AUTOB sites will be modified or replaced to "keep up with the times."

518–519. RESERVED

520. PILOT WEATHER REPORTS (PIREP'S)

a. Whenever ceilings are at or below 5,000 feet, visibilities at or below five miles, or thunderstorms are reported or forecast, facilities are required to solicit and collect PIREP's which describe conditions aloft. Pilots are urged to cooperate and volunteer reports of cloud tops, upper cloud layers, thunderstorms, ice, turbulence, strong winds, and other significant flight condition information. Such conditions observed between weather reporting stations are vitally needed. The PIREP's should be given to the FAA ground facility with which communication is established, i.e., FSS, Air Route Traffic Control Center or terminal ATC facility. In addition to complete PIREP's. pilots can materially help round out the in-flight weather picture by adding to routine position reports, both VFR and IFR, the type of aircraft and the following phrases as appropriate:

ON TOP
BELOW OVERCAST
WEATHER CLEAR
MODERATE (or HEAVY) ICING
LIGHT, MODERATE, SEVERE, EXTREME
    TURBULENCE
FREEZING RAIN (or DRIZZLE)
THUNDERSTORM (location)
BETWEEN LAYERS
ON INSTRUMENTS
ON AND OFF INSTRUMENTS

b. If pilots are not able to make PIREP's by radio, reporting upon landing of the in-flight conditions encountered to the nearest Flight Service Station or Weather Service Office will be helpful. Some of the uses made of the reports are:

(1) The airport traffic control tower uses the reports to expedite the flow of air traffic in the vicinity of the field and also forwards reports to other interested offices.

(2) The Flight Service Station uses the reports to brief other pilots.

(3) The Flight Service Station Office uses the reports in briefing other pilots and in forecasting.

(4) The Air Route Traffic Control Center uses the reports to expedite the flow of en route traffic and determine most favorable altitudes.

(5) The Weather Service Forecast Office finds pilot reports very helpful in issuing advisories of hazardous weather conditions. This office also uses the reports to brief other pilots, and in forecasting.

521. PIREPS RELATING TO AIRFRAME ICING

a. The effects of ice accretion on aircraft are cumulative—Thrust is reduced, Drag increases, Lift lessens, Weight increases. The results are an increase in stall speed and a deterioration of aircraft performance. In extreme cases, 2 to 3 inches of ice can form on the leading edge of the airfoil in less than 5 minutes. It takes but ½ inch of ice to reduce the lifting power of some aircraft by 50% and increases the frictional drag by an equal percentage.

b. A pilot can expect icing when flying in visible precipitation such as rain or cloud droplets, and the temperature is 0 degrees Celsius or colder. When icing is detected, a pilot should do one of two things (particularly if the aircraft is not equipped with deicing equipment) he should get out of the area of precipitation or go to an altitude where the temperature is above freezing. This "warmer" altitude may not always be a lower altitude. Proper pre-flight action includes obtaining information on the freezing level and the above-freezing levels in precipitation areas. Report icing to ATC/FSS, and if operating IFR, request new routing or altitude if icing will be a hazard. Be sure to give type of aircraft to ATC when reporting icing. Following is a table that describes how to report icing conditions.

INTENSITY	ICE ACCUMULATION
Trace	Ice becomes perceptible. Rate of accumulation slightly greater than rate of sublimation. It is not hazardous even though deicing/anti-icing equipment is not utilized, unless encountered for an extended period of time (over 1 hour).
Light	The rate of accumulation may create a problem if flight is prolonged in this environment (over 1 hour). Occasional use of deicing/anti-icing equipment removes/prevents accumulation. It does not present a problem if the deicing/anti-icing equipment is used.
Moderate	The rate of accumulation is such that even short encounters become potentially hazardous and use of deicing/anti-icing equipment or diversion is necessary.
Severe	The rate of accumulation is such that deicing/anti-icing equipment fails to reduce or control the hazard. Immediate diversion is necessary.

Pilot Report: Aircraft Identification, Location, Time (GMT), Intensity of Type,* Altitude/FL, Aircraft Type, IAS.

* Rime Ice: Rough, milky, opaque ice formed by the instantaneous freezing of small supercooled water droplets.

Clear Ice: A glossy, clear, or translucent ice formed by the relatively slow freezing of large supercooled water droplets.

522. WIND SHEAR PIREPS

a. Because unexpected changes in wind speed and direction can be hazardous to aircraft operations at low altitudes on approach to and departing from airports, pilots are urged to volunteer reports to controllers of wind shear conditions they encounter. An advance warning of this information will assist other pilots in avoiding or coping with a wind shear on approach or departure.

b. When describing conditions, use of the terms "negative" or "positive" wind shear should be avoided. PIREPs of *negative* wind shear on final," intended to describe loss of airspeed and lift, have been interpreted to mean that *no* wind shear was encountered. The recommended method for wind shear reporting is to state the loss/gain of airspeed and the altitude/s at which it was encountered. Examples are: "Denver Tower, Cessna 1234 encountered wind shear, loss of 20 knots at 400 feet," Tulsa Tower, American 721 encountered wind shear on final, gained 25 knots between 600 and 400 feet followed by loss of 40 knots between 400 feet and surface." Pilots who are not able to report wind shear in these specific terms are encouraged to make reports in terms of the effect upon their aircraft. For example: "Miami Tower, Gulfstream 403 Charlie encountered an abrupt wind shear at 800 feet on final, max thrust required."

c. Pilots using Inertial Navigation Systems should report the wind and altitude both above and below the shear layer.

523. CLEAR AIR TURBULENCE (CAT) PIREPS

Clear air turbulence (CAT) has become a very serious operational factor to flight operations at all levels and especially to jet traffic flying in **excess of** 15,000 feet. The best available information on this phenomena must come from pilots via the PIREP's procedures. All pilots encountering CAT conditions are urgently requested to report *time, location* and *intensity* (light, moderate, severe or extreme) of the element to the FAA facility with which they are maintaining radio contact. If time and conditions permit, elements should be reported according to the standards for other PIREP'S and position reports. (See **527**—TURBULENCE REPORTING CRITERIA TABLE.)

524. THUNDERSTOMS

a. Turbulence, hail, rain, snow, lightning, sustained updrafts and downdrafts, icing conditions—all are present in thunderstorms. While there is some evidence that maximum turbulence exists at the middle level of a thunderstorm, recent studies show little variation of turbulence intensity with altitude.

b. There is no useful correlation between the external visual appearance of thunderstorms and the severity or amount of turbulence or hail within them. Too, the visible thunderstorm cloud is only a portion of a turbulent system whose updrafts and downdrafts often extend far beyond the visible storm cloud. Severe turbulence can be expected up to 20 miles from severe thunderstorms. This distance decreases to about 10 miles in less severe storms. These turbulent areas may appear as a well defined echo on weather radar.

c. Weather radar, airborne or ground based, will normally reflect the areas of moderate to heavy precipitation (radar does not detect turbulence). The frequency and severity of turbulence generally increases with the radar reflectivity which is closely associated with the areas of highest liquid water content of the storm. NO FLIGHT PATH THROUGH AN AREA OF STRONG OR VERY STRONG RADAR ECHOS SEPARATED BY 20–30 MILES OR LESS MAY BE CONSIDERED FREE OF SEVERE TURBULENCE.

d. Turbulence beneath a thunderstorm should not be minimized. This is especially true when the relative humidity is low in any layer between the surface and 15,000 feet. Then the lower altitudes may be characterized by strong out-flowing winds and severe turbulence.

e. The probability of lightning strikes occurring to aircraft is greatest when operating at altitudes where temperatures are between −5°C and +5°C. Lightning can strike aircraft flying in the clear in the vicinity of a thunderstorm.

f. The National Weather Service recognizes only 2 classes of intensities of Thunderstorms as applied to aviation surface weather observations:

Thunderstorm T; Severe T+

g. National Weather Service radar systems are able to objectively determine radar weather echo intensity levels by use of Video Integrator Processor (VIP) equipment. These thunderstorm intensity levels are on a scale of one to six. (See RADAR WEATHER ECHO INTENSITY LEVELS in the Pilot/Controller Glossary.)

(1) Example of alert provided by an ATC facility to an aircraft:

(AIRCRAFT IDENTIFICATION) LEVEL FIVE INTENSE WEATHER ECHO BETWEEN TEN O'CLOCK AND TWO O'CLOCK, ONE ZERO MILES MOVING EAST AT TWO ZERO KTS, TOP FL THREE NINE ZERO.

(2) Example of alert provided by a Flight Service Station:

(AIRCRAFT IDENTIFICATION) LEVEL FIVE INTENSE WEATHER ECHO TWO ZERO MILES WEST OF ATLANTA VOR TWO FIVE MILES WIDE, MOVING EAST AT TWO ZERO KTS, TOPS FL THREE NINE ZERO.

525. DO'S AND DONT'S OF THUNDERSTORM FLYING

a. Above all, remember this: never regard any thunderstorm as "light" even when radar observers report the echoes are of light intensity. Avoiding thunderstorms is the best policy. Following are some Do's and Don'ts of thunderstorm avoidance:

(1) Don't land or take off in the face of an approaching thunderstorm. A sudden wind shift or low level turbulence could cause loss of control.

(2) Don't attempt to fly under a thunderstorm even if you can see through to the other side. Turbulence under the storm could be disastrous.

(3) Don't try to circumnavigate thunderstorms covering 6/10 of an area or more either visually or by airborne radar.

(4) Don't fly without airborne radar into a cloud mass containing scattered embedded thunderstorms. Scattered thunderstorms not embedded usually can be visually circumnavigated.

(5) Do avoid by at least 20 miles any thunderstorm identified as severe or given an intense radar echo. This is especially true under the anvil of a large cumulonimbus.

(6) Do clear the top of a known or suspected severe thunderstorm by at least 1,000 feet altitude for each 10 knots of wind speed at the cloud top. This would exceed the altitude capability of most aircraft.

(7) Do remember that vivid and frequent lightning indicates a severe thunderstorm.

(8) Do regard as severe any thunderstorm with tops 35,000 feet or higher whether the top is visually sighted or determined by radar.

b. If you cannot avoid penetrating a thunderstorm, following are some Do's *before* entering the storm:

(1) Tighten your safety belt, put on your shoulder harness if you have one and secure all loose objects.

(2) Plan your course to take you through the storm in a minimum time and hold it.

(3) To avoid the most critical icing, establish a penetration altitude below the freezing level or above the level of −15°C.

(4) Turn on pitot heat and carburetor or jet inlet heat. Icing can be rapid at any altitude and cause almost instantaneous power failure or loss of airspeed indication.

(5) Establish power settings for reduced turbulence penetration airspeed recommended in your aircraft manual. Reduced airspeed lessens the structural stresses on the aircraft.

(6) Turn up cockpit lights to highest intensity to lessen danger of temporary blindness from lightning.

(7) If using automatic pilot, disengage altitude hold mode and speed hold mode. The automatic altitude and speed controls will increase maneuvers of the aircraft thus increasing structural stresses.

(8) If using airborne radar, tilt your antenna up and down occasionally. Tilting it up may detect a hail shaft that will reach a point on your course by the time you do. Tilting it down may detect a growing thunderstorm cell that may reach your altitude.

c. Following are some Do's and Don'ts *during* thunderstorm penetration:

(1) Do keep your eyes on your instruments. Looking outside the cockpit can increase danger of temporary blindness from lightning.

(2) Don't change power settings; maintain settings for reduced airspeed.

(3) Do maintain a constant attitude; let the aircraft "ride the waves." Maneuvers in trying to maintain constant altitude increases stresses on the aircraft.

NOTE.—When the pilot anticipates that he will be required to 'ride the waves' as described above, it is important that he notify ATC as soon as possible to insure that appropriate action is taken to insure separation from other aircraft. When this situation occurs suddenly, and the pilot executes his emergency authority to maintain a constant attitude, regardless of altitude, he should advise ATC as soon as possible.

(4) Don't turn back once you are in the thunderstorm. A straight course through the storm most likely will get you out of the hazards most quickly. In addition, turning maneuvers increase stresses on the aircraft.

526. KEY TO AVIATION WEATHER REPORTS AND FORECASTS

KEY TO AVIATION WEATHER REPORTS . . . .

NOAA/PA 73029

LOCATION IDENTIFIER AND TYPE OF REPORT*	SKY AND CEILING	VISIBILITY WEATHER AND OBSTRUCTION TO VISION	SEA-LEVEL PRESSURE	TEMPERATURE AND DEW POINT	WIND	ALTIMETER SETTING	RUNWAY VISUAL RANGE	CODED PIREPS
MKC	15 SCT M25 OVC	1R-K	132	/58/56	/ 18Ø7	/993/	RØ4LVR2ØV4Ø	/UA OVC 55

SKY AND CEILING

Sky cover contractions are in ascending order. Figures preceding contractions are heights in hundreds of feet above station. Sky cover contractions are:

CLR   Clear: Less than Ø.1 sky cover.
SCT   Scattered: Ø.1 to Ø.5 sky cover.
BKN   Broken: Ø.6 to Ø.9 sky cover.
OVC   Overcast: More than Ø.9 sky cover.

— Thin (When prefixed to the above symbols.)
—X Partial obscuration: Ø.1 to less than 1.Ø sky hidden by precipitation or obstruction to vision (bases at surface).
X Obscuration: 1 Ø sky hidden by precipitation or obstruction to vision (bases at surface).

Letter preceding height of layer identifies ceiling layer and indicates how ceiling height was obtained. Thus:

E	Estimated height	V	Immediately following numerical value, indicates a variable ceiling.
M	Measured		
W	Indefinite		

VISIBILITY

Reported in statute miles and fractions. (V=Variable)

WEATHER AND OBSTRUCTION TO VISION SYMBOLS

A	Hail	IC	Ice crystals	S	Snow
BD	Blowing dust	IF	Ice fog	SG	Snow grains
BN	Blowing sand	IP	Ice pellets	SP	Snow pellets
BS	Blowing snow	IPW	Ice pellet showers	SW	Snow showers
D	Dust	K	Smoke	T	Thunderstorms
F	Fog	L	Drizzle	T-	Severe thunderstorm
GF	Ground fog	R	Rain	ZL	Freezing drizzle
H	Haze	RW	Rain showers	ZR	Freezing rain

Precipitation intensities are indicated thus: —Light; (no sign) Moderate; + Heavy

WIND

Direction in tens of degrees from true north, speed in knots. ØØØØ indicates calm. G indicates gusty. Peak speed of gusts follows G or Q when gusts or squall are reported. The contraction WSHFT followed by GMT time group in remarks indicates windshift and its time of occurrence. (Knots X 1.15= statute mi/hr.)

EXAMPLES: 3627=360 Degrees, 27 knots; 3627G40 =360 Degrees, 27 knots, peak speed in gusts 40 knots.

ALTIMETER SETTING

The first figure of the actual altimeter setting is always omitted from the report.

RUNWAY VISUAL RANGE (RVR)

RVR is reported from some stations. Extreme values during 10 minutes prior to observation are given in hundreds of feet. Runway identification precedes RVR report.

CODED PIREPS

Pilot reports of clouds not visible from ground are coded with ASL height data preceding and/or following sky cover contraction to indicate cloud bases and/or tops, respectively. UA precedes all PIREPS.

DECODED REPORT

Kansas City: Record observation, 15ØØ feet scattered clouds, measured ceiling 25ØØ feet overcast, visibility 1 mile, light rain, smoke, sea-level pressure 1013.2 millibars, temperature 58°F, dewpoint 56°F, wind 18Ø°, 7 knots, altimeter setting 29.93 inches. Runway Ø4 left, visual range 2ØØØ feet variable to 4ØØØ feet. Pilot reports top of overcast 55ØØ feet.

*TYPE OF REPORT

The omission of type-of-report data identifies a scheduled record observation for the hour specified in the sequence heading. An out-of-sequence, special observation is identified by the letters "SP" following station identification and a 24-hour clock time group, e.g., "PIT SP Ø715 –X M1 OVC." A special report indicates a significant change in one or more elements.

KEY TO AVIATION WEATHER FORECASTS . . . .

TERMINAL FORECASTS contain information for specific airports on expected ceiling, cloud heights, cloud amounts, visibility, weather and obstructions to vision and surface wind. They are issued 3 times/day and are valid for 24 hours. The last six hours of each forecast are covered by a categorical statement indicating whether VFR, MVFR, IFR or LIFR conditions are expected. Terminal forecasts will be written in the following form:

CEILING: Identified by the letter "C"
CLOUD HEIGHTS: In hundreds of feet above the station (ground)
CLOUD LAYERS: Stated in ascending order of height
VISIBILITY: In statute miles but omitted if over 6 miles
WEATHER AND OBSTRUCTION TO VISION: Standard weather and obstruction to vision symbols are used
SURFACE WIND: In tens of degrees and knots; omitted when less than 10

EXAMPLE OF TERMINAL FORECAST

DCA 221Ø1Ø: DCA Forecast 22nd day of month—valid time 1ØZ–1ØZ.
1Ø SCT C18 BKN 5SW–3415G25 OCNL C8 X ½ SW: Scattered clouds at 1ØØØ feet, ceiling 18ØØ feet broken, visibility 5 miles, light snow showers, surface wind 34Ø degrees 15 knots Gusts to 25 knots, occasional ceiling 8 hundred feet sky obscured, visibility ½ mile in moderate snow showers.
12Z C5Ø BKN 3312G22: At 12Z becoming ceiling 5ØØØ feet broken, surface wind 33Ø degrees 12 knots Gusts to 22.
Ø4Z MVFR CIG: Last 6 hours of FT after Ø4Z marginal VFR due to ceiling.

AREA FORECASTS are 18-hour aviation forecasts plus a 12-hour categorical outlook prepared 2 times/day giving general descriptions of cloud cover, weather and frontal conditions for an area the size of several states. Heights of cloud tops, and icing are referenced ABOVE SEA LEVEL (ASL); ceiling heights, ABOVE GROUND LEVEL (AGL); bases of cloud layers are ASL unless indicated. Each SIGMET or AIRMET affecting an FA area will also serve to amend the Area Forecast.

SIGMET or AIRMET messages warn airmen in flight of potentially hazardous weather such as squall lines, thunderstorms, fog, icing, and turbulence. SIGMET concerns severe and extreme conditions of importance to all aircraft. AIRMET concerns less severe conditions which may be hazardous to some aircraft or to relatively inexperienced pilots. Both are broadcast by FAA on NAVAID voice channels.

WINDS AND TEMPERATURES ALOFT (FD) FORECASTS are 12-hour forecasts of wind direction (nearest 10° true N) and speed (knots) for selected flight levels. Temperatures aloft (°C) are included for all but the 3ØØØ-foot level.

EXAMPLES OF WINDS AND TEMPERATURES ALOFT (FD) FORECASTS:
FD WBC 121745
BASED ON 12120ØZ DATA
VALID 13000ØZ FOR USE 1800-0300Z. TEMPS NEG ABV 24000

FT	3000	6000	9000	12000	18000	24000	30000	34000	39000
BOS		3127	3425-07	3420-11	3421-16	3516-27	3512-38	311649	292451	283451
JFK		3026	3327-08	3324-12	3322-16	3120-27	2923-38	284248	285150	285749

At 6000 feet ASL over JFK wind from 330° at 27 knots and temperature minus 8°C

TWEB (CONTINUOUS TRANSCRIBED WEATHER BROADCAST)— Individual route forecasts covering a 25 nautical mile zone either side of the route. By requesting a specific route number, detailed en route weather for a 12 or 18-hour period (depending on forecast issuance) plus a synopsis can be obtained.

PILOTS . . . report in-flight weather to nearest FSS. The latest surface weather reports are available by phone at the nearest pilot weather briefing office by calling at H+10.

U.S. DEPARTMENT OF COMMERCE— NATIONAL OCEANIC AND ATMOSPHERIC ADMINISTRATION – NATIONAL WEATHER SERVICE –REVISED MARCH 1, 1976

527. TURBULENCE REPORTING CRITERIA TABLE

Intensity	Aircraft Reaction	Reaction Inside Aircraft	Reporting Term Definitio
LIGHT	Turbulence that momentarily causes slight, erratic changes in altitude and/or attitude (pitch, roll, yaw). Report as *Light Turbulence*;* or Turbulence that causes slight, rapid and somewhat rhythmic bumpiness without appreciable changes in altitude or attitude. Report as *Light Chop*.	Occupants may feel a slight strain against seat belts or shoulder straps. Unsecured objects may be displaced slightly. Food service may be conducted and little or no difficulty is encountered in walking.	Occasional—Less than 1/3 o the time. Intermittent—1/3 to 2/3. Continuous—More than 2/: NOTE—Pilots should repor location(s), time (GMT) intensity, whether in o near clouds, altitude, typ of aircraft and, when ap plicable, duration of tur bulence.
MODERATE	Turbulence that is similar to Light Turbulence but of greater intensity. Changes in altitude and/or attitude occur but the aircraft remains in positive control at all times. It usually causes variations in indicated airspeed. Report as *Moderate Turbulence*;* or Turbulence that is similar to Light Chop but of greater intensity. It causes rapid bumps or jolts without appreciable changes in aircraft altitude or attitude. Report as *Moderate Chop*.	Occupants feel definite strains against seat belts or shoulder straps. Unsecured objects are dislodged. Food service and walking are difficult.	Duration may be based o time between two location or over a single location All locations should b readily identifiable. Example: a. Over Omaha, 1232Z, Mod erate Turbulence, in clou Flight Level 310, B707. b. From 50 miles south o Albuquerque to 30 mile north of Phoennx, 1210 to 1250Z, occasional Mod erate Chop, Flight Leve 330, DC8.
SEVERE	Turbulence that causes large, abrupt changes in altitude and/or attitude. It usualy causes large variations in indicated airspeed. Aircraft may be momentarily out of control. Report as *Severe Turbulence*.*	Occupants are forced violently against seat belts or shoulder straps. Unsecured objects are tossed about. Food service and walking are impossible.	
EXTREME	Turbulence in which the aircraft is violently tossed about and is practically impossible to control. It may cause structural damage. Report as *Extreme Turbulence*.*		

* High level turbulence (normally above 15,000 feet ASL) not associated with cumuliform cloudiness, including thunderstorm should be reported as CAT (clear air turbulence) preceded by the appropriate intensity, or light or moderate chop.

528–529. RESERVED

Section 2.   ALTIMETER SETTING PROCEDURES

530. GENERAL

a. The accuracy of aircraft altimeters is subject to the following factors: (1) nonstandard temperatures of the atmosphere, (2) aircraft static pressure systems (position error); and (3) instrument error. Pilots should disregard the effect of nonstandard atmospheric temperatures except that low temperatures need to be considered for terrain clearance purposes.

> NOTE.—Standard temperature at sea level is 15°C (59° F). The temperature gradient from sea level is 2°C (3.5°F) per 1000 feet. Pilots should apply corrections for static pressure systems and/or instruments, if appreciable errors exist.

b. Experience gained through volume of operations has led to the adoption of a standard altimeter setting for flights operating in the higher altitudes. A standard setting eliminates altitude conflicts caused by altimeter settings derived from different geographical sources. In addition, it eliminates station barometer errors and some of the altimeter instrument errors.

531. PROCEDURES (See FAR 91.81)

a. The cruising altitude or flight level of aircraft shall be maintained by reference to an altimeter which shall be set, when operating:

(1) Below 18,000 feet MSL—to the current reported altimeter setting of a station along the route and within 100 nautical miles of the aircraft; or, there is no station within this area to the current reported altimeter setting of an appropriate available station. When an aircraft is enroute on an instrument flight plan, the ATC controller will furnish this information to the pilot at least once while the aircraft is in his area of jurisdiction. In the case of an aircraft not equipped with a radio, set to the elevation of the departure airport or use an appropriate altimeter setting available prior to departure.

(2) At or above 18,000 feet MSL—to 29.92″ Hg (standard setting). The lowest usable flight level is determined by the atmospheric pressure in the area of operation, as shown in the following table:

Altimeter Setting (Current Reported)	Lowest usable flight level
29.91 or higher	180
29.91 to 29.42	185
29.41 to 28.92	190
28.91 to 28.42	195
28.41 to 27.92	200

(3) Where the minimum altitude, as prescribed in FAR Parts 91.19 and 91.119, is above 18,000 feet MSL the lowest usable flight level shall be the flight level equivalent of the minimum altitude plus the number of feet specified in the following table:

Altimter Setting	Correction Factor
29.92 or higher	None
29.91 to 29.42	500 feet
29.41 to 28.92	1000 feet
28.91 to 28.42	1500 feet
28.41 to 27.92	2000 feet
27.91 to 27.42	2500 feet

> NOTE.—For example, the minimum safe altitude of a route is 19,000 feet MSL and the altimeter setting is reported between 29.92 and 29.42 Hg, the lowest usable flight level will be 195, which is the flight level equivalent of 19,500 feet MSL (minimum altitude plus 500 feet).

532. ALTIMETER ERRORS

a. The importance of frequently obtaining current altimeter settings cannot be overemphasized. If you do not reset your altimeter when flying *from* an area of high pressure or high temperatures *into* an area of low temperatures or low pressure, *your aircraft will be closer to the surface than the altimeter indicates.* An inch error on the altimeter equals 1,000 feet of altitude. To quote an old saying: "GOING FROM A HIGH TO A LOW, LOOK OUT BELOW."

b. A reverse situation—without resetting the altimeter when going from a low temperature or low pressure area into a high temperature or high pressure area, the aircraft will be higher than the altimeter indicates.

c. The possible result of the situation in **a.** above, is obvious, particularly if operating at the minimum altitude. In the situation in **b.** above, the result may not be as spectacular, but consider an instrument approach: If your altimeter is in error you may still be on instruments when reaching the minimum altitude (as indicated on the altimeter), whereas you might have been in the clear and able to complete the approach if the altimeter setting was correct.

533–539. RESERVED

Section 3. WAKE TURBULENCE

540. GENERAL

a. Every airplane generates a wake while in flight. Initially, when pilots encountered this wake in flight, the disturbance was attributed to "prop wash." It is known, however, that this disturbance is caused by a pair of counter rotating vortices trailing from the wing tips. The vortices from large aircraft pose problems to encountering aircraft. For instance, the wake of these aircraft can impose rolling moments exceeding the roll control capability of some aircraft. Further, turbulence generated within the vortices can damage aircraft components and equipment if encountered at close range. The pilot must learn to envision the location of the vortex wake generated by large aircraft and adjust his flight path accordingly.

b. During ground operations, jet engine blast (thrust stream turbulence) can cause damage and upsets if encountered at close range. Exhaust velocity versus distance studies at various thrust levels have shown a need for light aircraft to maintain an adequate separation during ground operations. Below are examples of the distance requirements to avoid exhaust velocities of greater than 25 mph:

25 MPH VELOCITY	B-727	DC-8	DC-10
Takeoff Thrust	550 Ft.	700 Ft.	2100 Ft.
Breakaway Thrust	200 Ft.	400 Ft.	850 Ft.
Idle Thrust	150 Ft.	35 Ft.	350 Ft.

c. Engine exhaust velocities generated by large jet aircraft during initial takeoff roll and the drifting of the turbulence in relation to the crosswind component dictate the desireability of lighter aircraft awaiting takeoff to hold well back of the runway edge of taxiway hold line; also, the desirability of aligning the aircraft to face the possible jet engine blast movement. Additionally, in the course of running up engines and taxiing on the ground, pilots of large aircraft in particular should consider the effects of their jet blasts on other aircraft.

d. The FAA has established new standards for the location of taxiway hold lines at airports served by air carriers as follows:

e. Taxiway holding lines will be established at 100 feet from the edge of the runway, except at locations where "heavy jets" will be operating, the taxiway holding line markings will be established at 150 feet. (The "heavy" category can include some B-707 and DC-8 type aircraft.)

541. VORTEX GENERATION

Lift is generated by the creation of a pressure differential over the wing surface. The lowest pressure occurs over the upper wing surface and the highest pressure under the wing. This pressure differential triggers the roll up of the airflow aft of the wing resulting in swirling air masses trailing downstream of the wing tips. After the roll up is completed, the wake consists of two counter rotating cylindrical vortices.

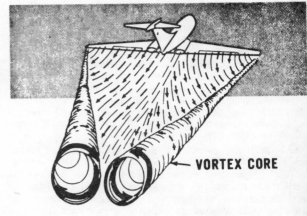

Figure 6-2

542. VORTEX STRENGTH

a. The strength of the vortex is governed by the weight, speed, and shape of the wing of the generating aircraft. The vortex characteristics of any given aircraft can also be changed by extension of flaps or other wing configuring devices as well as by change in speed. However, as the basic factor is weight, the vortex strength increases proportionately. During a recent test, peak vortex tangential velocities were recorded at 224 feet per second, or about 133 knots. The greatest vortex strength occurs when the generating aircraft is HEAVY—CLEAN—SLOW.

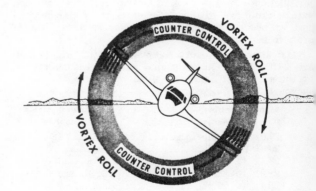

Figure 6-3

b. INDUCED ROLL

(1) In rare instances a wake encounter could cause in flight structural damage of catastrophic proportions. However, the usual hazard is associated with induced rolling moments which can exceed the rolling capability of the encountering aircraft. In flight experiments, aircraft have been intentionally flown directly up trailing vortex cores of large aircraft. It was shown that the capability of an aircraft to counteract the roll imposed by the wake vortex primarily depends on the wing span and counter control responsiveness of the encountering aircraft.

(2) Counter control is usually effective and induced roll minimal in cases where the wing span and ailerons of the encountering aircraft extend beyond the rotational flow field of the vortex. It is more difficult for aircraft with short wing span (relative to the generating aircraft) to counter the imposed roll induced by vortex flow. Pilots of short span aircraft, even of the high performance type, must be especially alert to vortex encounters.

(3) The wake of large aircraft requires the respect of all pilots.

543. VORTEX BEHAVIOR

a. Trailing vortices have certain behavioral characteristics which can help a pilot visualize the wake location and thereby take avoidance precautions.

(1) Vortices are generated from the moment aircraft leave the ground, since trailing vortices are a by-product of wing lift. Prior to takeoff or touchdown pilots should note the rotation or touchdown point of the preceding aircraft.

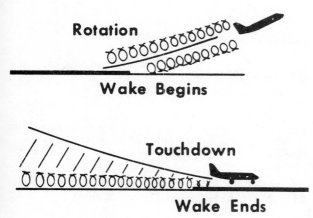

Figure 6—4

(2) The vortex circulation is outward, upward and around the wing tips when viewed from either ahead or behind the aircraft. Tests with large aircraft have shown that the vortex flow field, in a plane cutting thru the wake at any point downstream, covers an area about 2 wing spans in width and one wing span in depth. The vortices remain so spaced (about a wing span apart) even drifting with the wind, at altitudes greater than a wing span from the ground. In view of this, if persistent vortex turbulence is encountered, a slight change of altitude and lateral position (preferably upwind) will provide a flight path clear of the turbulence.

(3) Flight tests have shown that the vortices from large aircraft sink at a rate of about 400 to 500 feet per minute. They tend to level off at a distance about 900 feet below the flight path of the generating aircraft. Vortex strength diminishes with time and distance behind the generating aircraft. Atmospheric turbulence hastens breakup. Pilots should fly at or above the large aircraft's flight path, altering course as necessary to avoid the area behind and below the generating aircraft.

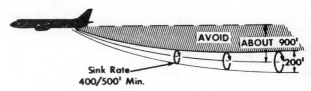

Figure 6—5

(4) When the vortices of large aircraft sink close to the ground (within about 200 feet), they tend to move laterally over the ground at a speed of about 5 knots.

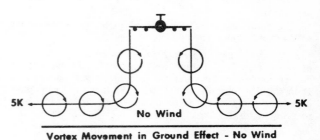

Vortex Movement in Ground Effect - No Wind

Figure 6—6

(5) A crosswind will decrease the lateral movement of the upwind vortex and increase the movement of the downwind vortex. Thus a light wind of 3 to 7 knots could result in the upwind vortex remaining in the touchdown zone for a period of time and hasten the drift of the downwind vortex toward another runway. Similarly, a tailwind condition can move the vortices of the preceding aircraft forward into the touchdown zone. THE LIGHT QUARTERING TAILWIND REQUIRES MAXIMUM CAUTION. Pilots should be alert to large aircraft upwind from their approach and takeoff flight paths.

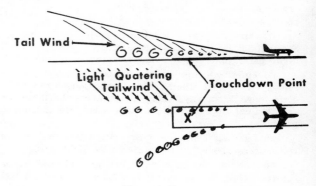

Figure 6—7

544. OPERATIONS PROBLEM AREAS

a. A wake encounter is not necessarily hazardous. It can be one or more jolts with varying severity depending upon the direction of the encounter, distance from the generating aircraft, and point of vortex encounter. The probability of induced roll increases when the encountering aircraft's heading is generally aligned with the vortex trail or flight path of the generating aircraft.

b. AVOID THE AREA BELOW AND BEHIND THE GENERATING AIRCRAFT, ESPECIALLY AT LOW ALTITUDE WHERE EVEN A MOMENTARY WAKE ENCOUNTER COULD BE HAZARDOUS.

c. Pilots should be particularly alert in calm wind conditions and situations where the vortices could:

(1) Remain in the touchdown area.

(2) Drift from aircraft operating on a nearby runway.

(3) Sink into takeoff or landing path from a crossing runway.

(4) Sink into the traffic patterns from other airport operations.

(5) Sink into the flight path of VFR flights operating at the hemispheric altitude 500 feet below.

d. Pilots of all aircraft should visualize the location of the vortex trail behind large aircraft and use proper vortex avoidance procedures to achieve safe operation. It is equally important that pilots of large aircraft plan or adjust their flight paths to minimize vortex exposure to other aircraft.

545. VORTEX AVOIDANCE PROCEDURES

a. *GENERAL.* Under certain conditions, airport traffic controllers apply procedures for separating aircraft from heavy jet aircraft. The controllers will also provide VFR aircraft, with whom they are in communication and which in the tower's opinion may be adversely affected by wake turbulence from a large aircraft, the position, altitude and direction of flight of the large aircraft followed by the phrase "CAUTION— WAKE TURBULENCE." WHETHER OR NOT A WARNING HAS BEEN GIVEN, HOWEVER, THE PILOT IS EXPECTED TO ADJUST HIS OPERATIONS AND FLIGHT PATH AS NECESSARY TO PRECLUDE SERIOUS WAKE ENCOUNTERS.

b. The following vortex avoidance procedures are recommended for the various situations:

(1) Landing behind a large aircraft—same runway: Stay at or above the large aircraft's final approach flight path—note his touchdown point—land beyond it.

(2) Landing behind a large aircraft—when parallel runway is closer than 2,500 feet: Consider possible drift to your runway. Stay at or above the large aircraft's final approach flight path—note his touchdown point.

(3) Landing behind a large aircraft—crossing runway: Cross above the large aircraft's flight path.

(4) Landing behind a departing large aircraft—same runway: Note large aircraft's rotation point—land well prior to rotation point.

(5) Landing behind a departing large aircraft—crossing runway: Note large aircraft's rotation point—if past the intersection—continue the approach—land prior to the intersection. If large aircraft rotates prior to the intersection, avoid flight below the large aircraft's flight path. Abandon the approach unless a landing is assured well before reaching the intersection.

(6) Departing behind a large aircraft: Note large aircraft's rotation point—rotate prior to large aircraft's rotation point—continue climb above and stay upwind of the large aircraft's climb path until turning clear of

his wake. Avoid subsequent headings which will cross below and behind a large aircraft. Be alert for any critical takeoff situation which could lead to a vortex encounter.

(7) Intersection takeoffs—same runway: Be alert to adjacent large aircraft operations particularly upwind of your runway. If intersection takeoff clearance is received, avoid subsequent heading which will cross below a large aircraft's path.

(8) Departing or landing after a large aircraft executing a low approach, missed approach or touch-and-go landing: Because vortices settle and move laterally near the ground, the vortex hazard may exist along the runway and in your flight path after a large aircraft has executed a low approach, missed approach or a touch-and-go landing, particularly in light quartering wind conditions. You should assure that an interval of at least 2 minutes has elapsed before your takeoff or landing.

(9) Enroute VFR—(thousand-foot altitude plus 500 feet). Avoid flight below and behind a large aircraft's path. If a large aircraft is observed above on the same track (meeting or overtaking) adjust your position laterally, preferably upwind.

546–549. RESERVED

550. HELICOPTERS

A hovering helicopter generates a downwash from its main rotor(s) similar to the prop blast of a conventional aircraft. However, in forward flight, this energy is transformed into a pair of trailing vortices similar to wing-tip vortices of fixed wing aircraft. Pilots of small aircraft should avoid the vortices as well as the downwash.

551. PILOT RESPONSIBILITY

a. Government and industry groups are making concerted efforts to minimize or eliminate the hazards of trailing vortices. However, the flight disciplines necessary to assure vortex avoidance during VFR operations must be exercised by the pilot. Vortex visualization and avoidance procedures should be exercised by the pilot using the same degree of concern as in collision avoidance.

b. Wake turbulence may be encountered by aircraft in flight as well as when operating on the airport movement area. (See WAKE TURBULENCE in the Pilot/Controller Glossary.)

c. Pilots are reminded that in operations conducted behind all aircraft, acceptance from ATC of:

(1) Traffic information, or

(2) Instructions to follow an aircraft, or

(3) The acceptance of a visual approach clearance, is an acknowledgment that the pilot will ensure safe takeoff and landing intervals and accepts the responsibility of providing his own wake turbulence separation.

d. For operations conducted behind heavy aircraft, ATC will specify the word 'heavy' when this information is known. Pilots of heavy aircraft should always use the word "heavy" in radio communications.

552. AIR TRAFFIC WAKE TURBULENCE SEPARATIONS

a. Air traffic controllers are required to apply specific separation intervals for aircraft operating behind a heavy jet because of the possible effects of wake turbulence.

b. The following separation is applied to aircraft operating directly behind a heavy jet at the same altitude or directly behind and less than 1,000 feet below:

    (1) Heavy jet behind another heavy jet—4 miles.

    (2) Small/Large aircraft behind a heavy jet—5 miles.

In addition, controllers provide a 6-mile separation for small aircraft landing behind a heavy jet and a 4-mile separation for small aircraft landing behind a large aircraft. This extra mile of separation is required at the time the preceding aircraft is over the landing threshold. (See AIRCRAFT CLASSES in the Pilot/Controller Glossary.)

c. Aircraft departing behind heavy jets are provided two minutes or the appropriate 4 or 5 mile radar separation. Controllers may disregard the separation if the pilot of a departing aircraft initiates a request to deviate from the separation requirement and indicates acceptance of responsibility for maneuvering his aircraft so as to avoid the possible wake turbulence hazard. However, occasions will arise when the controller must still hold the aircraft in order to provide separation required for other than wake turbulence purposes.

553–559. RESERVED

Section 4. BIRD HAZARDS AND MIGRATORY PATTERNS

560. BIRD HAZARDS

All pilots are requested to contact the nearest FAA Air Route Traffic Control Center, Flight Service Station, or tower (including non-federal towers) when they observe large flocks of birds and report the: (1)) Geographic location, (2) Bird Species (if known), (3) Approximate number, (4) Altitude, (5) Direction of bird flight path.

561. MIGRATORY PATTERNS

a. The birds considered of greatest potential hazard to aircraft because of large size, abundance, or habit of flying in dense flocks are the whistling swans, Canadian geese, blue geese, snow geese, white-fronted geese, mallards, pintails, gulls, vultures, starlings, and blackbirds. Birds of these species are considered particularly hazardous during spring and fall migrations and when they are concentrated in wintering areas. Swans make nonstop flights of several hundred miles (Chesapeake Bay to Lake Erie) at altitudes up to 6,000 feet. At some airports, there are large flocks of sandpipers, horned larks, blackbirds, tree swallows, longspurs, while pelicans, sandhill cranes, or other species which could be a hazardous problem during certain seasons. Notices of airports which have been reported to the FAA as having high density bird populations are published as Class two Notices to airmen until they can be transferred to the remarks section of the Airport acility Directory.

b. Since migrating waterfowl tend to dive when closely approach by aircraft, pilots are warned not to fly directly under migrating flocks of swans, geese or ducks.

c. Unfortunately, we do not have complete data for the United States concerning the migration paths of all of these species, or the exact times of migration, or the altitudes at which these birds fly, or the effects of weather on migration patterns. The migratory patterns of some species are described in Advisory Circular, AC/150/5200-3A.

562. REPORTING BIRD STRIKES OR INCIDENTS

a. Advisory Circular AC 150/5200-3A defines the actions requested of pilots involved in a bird strike or incident. This circular urges pilots to make a report using a special form developed for this purpose—FAA Form 3830, Bird Strike/Incident Report form. This form is available at any FAA Area Office, General Aviation District Office, Flight Service Station and Air Carrier District Office.

b. The data and information derived from these reports will be used to develop standards to cope with this expensive hazard to aircraft and for habitat control methods adjacent to airports.

563. WILDLIFE REFUGE AREAS

a. The Fish and Wildlife Service has the following regulation in effect governing the flight of aircraft on and over wildlife areas:

"This unauthorized operation of aircraft at low altitudes over, or the unauthorized landing of aircraft on a wildlife refuge area is prohibited, except in the event of emergency."

b. The Fish and Wildlife Service requests that pilots maintain a minimum altitude of 2,000 feet above the terrain of a wildlife refuge area.

564. NOISE-SENSITIVE AREAS

Pilots making VFR flights in fixed and rotary-wing aircraft over National Parks or other areas as identified below should make every effort to fly at not less than 2,000 feet above the surface, weather permitting, even though flight at a lower level may be consistent with the provisions of AR 91.79, Minimum Safe Altitudes:

National Parks
Primitive Areas
Recreational Areas
National Monuments
National Wildlife Refuge and Range Areas
National Forests
Wilderness Areas
National Seashores
National Lakeshores

565–569. RESERVED

Chapter 7. GOOD OPERATING PRACTICES

It should be remembered that adherence to air traffic rules does not eliminate the need for good judgment on the part of the pilot. Compliance with the following Good Operating Practices will greatly enhance the safety of every flight.

570. JUDGMENT IN VFR FLIGHT

a. General. Use reasonable restraint in exercising the prerogative of VFR flight, especially in terminal areas. The weather minimums and distances from clouds are minimums. Giving yourself a greater margin in specific instances is just good judgment.

b. Approach Area. Conducting a VFR operation in a Control Zone when the official visibility is 3 or 4 miles is not prohibited, but good judgment would dictate that you keep out of the approach area.

c. Reduced Visibility. It has always been recognized that precipitation reduces forward visibility. Consequently, although again it may be perfectly legal to cancel your IFR flight plan at any time you can proceed VFR, it is good practice, when precipitation is occurring, to continue IFR operation into a terminal area until you are reasonably close to your destination.

d. Simulated Instrument Flights. In conducting simulated instrument flights, be sure that the weather is good enough to compensate for the restricted visibility of the safety pilot and your greater concentration on your flight instruments. Give yourself a little greater margin when your flight plan lies in or near a busy airway or close to an airport.

e. Obstructions to VFR Flight. Extreme caution should be exercised when flying less than 2,100 feet above ground level (AGL) because there are more than 300 skeletal structures (radio and television antenna towers) exceeding 1,000 feet AGL with some extending higher than 2,000 feet AGL. In addition, more than 50 towers which exceed 1,000 feet AGL are either under construction or planned. Similar proposals are planned on a continuing basis. Most skeletal structures are supported by guy wires. The wires are difficult to see in good weather and can be totally obscured during periods of dusk and reduced visibility. These wires can extend about 1,500 feet horizontally from a structure; therefore, all skeletal structures should be avoided by at least 2,000 feet.

f. Overhead Wires. Overhead transmission and utility lines often span approaches to runway and scenic flyways such as lakes, rivers and canyons. The supporting structures of these lines may not always be readily visible and the wires may be virtually invisible under certain conditions. Most of these installations do not meet criteria to be determined to be obstructions to air navigation and therefore do not require marking and/or lighting. The supporting structures of some overhead transmission lines are equipped with flashing strobe lights. These lights indicate wires exist between the strobed structures.

571. USE OF VISUAL CLEARING PROCEDURES

a. Before Takeoff. Prior to taxiing onto a runway or landing area in preparation for takeoff, pilots should scan the approach areas for possible landing traffic, executing appropriate clearing maneuvers to provide him a clear view of the approach areas.

b. Climbs and Descents. During climbs and descents in flight conditions which permit visual detection of other traffic, pilots should execute gentle banks, left and right at a frequency which permits continuous visual scanning of the airspace about them.

c. Straight and level. Sustained periods of straight and level flight in conditions which permit visual detection of other traffic should be broken at intervals with approprate clearing procedures to provide effective visual scanning.

d. Traffic pattern. Entries into traffic patterns while descending create specific collision hazards and should be avoided.

e. Traffic at VOR sites. All operators should emphasize the need for sustained vigilance in the vicinity of VORs and airway intersections due to the convergence of traffic.

f. Training operations. Operators of pilot training programs are urged to adopt the following practices:

(1) Pilots undergoing flight instruction at all levels should be requested to verbalize clearing procedures (call out, "clear" left, right, above or below) to instill and sustain the habit of vigilance during maneuvering.

(2) High-wing airplane, momentarily raise the wing in the direction of the intended turn and look.

(3) Low-wing airplane, momentarily lower the wing in the direction of the intended turn and look.

(4) Appropriate clearing procedures should precede the execution of all turns including chandelles, lazy eights, stalls, slow flight, climbs, straight and level, spins and other combination maneuvers.

572. FOLLOW IFR PROCEDURES EVEN WHEN OPERATING VFR

a. To maintain IFR proficiency, pilots are urged to practice IFR procedures whenever possible, even when operating VFR. Some suggested practices include:

(1) Obtain a complete preflight and weather briefing. Check the NOTAMS.

(2) File a flight plan. This is an excellent low cost insurance policy. The cost is the time it takes to fill it out. The insurance includes the knowledge that someone will be looking for you if you become overdue at destination.

(3) Use current charts.

(4) Use the navigation aids. Practice maintaining a good course—keep the needle centered.

(5) Maintain a constant altitude (appropriate for the direction of flight).

(6) Estimate enroute position times.

(7) Make accurate and frequent position reports to the FSS's along your route of flight.

b. Simulated IFR flight is recommended (under the hood); however, pilots are cautioned to review and adhere to the requirements specified in FAR 91.21 before and during such flight.

573. VFR AT NIGHT

When flying VFR at night, in addition to the altitude appropriate for the direction of flight, pilots should maintain an altitude which is at or above the minimum enroute altitude as shown on charts. This is especially true in mountainous terrain, where there is usually very little ground reference. Don't depend on your being able to see those built-up rocks or TV towers in time to miss them.

574–579. RESERVED

580. FLIGHTS OUTSIDE THE UNITED STATES AND U.S. TERRITORIES

a. When conducting flights, particularly extended flights, outside the U.S. and its territories, full account should be taken of the amount and quality of air navigation services available in the airspace to be traversed. Every effort should be made to secure information on the location and range of navigational aids, availability of communications and meteorological services, the provision of air traffic services, including alerting service, and the existence of search and rescue services.

b. The filing of a flight plan—always good practice—takes on added significance for extended flights outside U.S. airspace and is, in fact, usually required by the laws of the countries being visited or overflown. It is also particularly important in the case of such flights that pilots leave a complete itinerary and schedule of the flight with someone directly concerned, keep that person advised of the flight's progress and inform him that if serious doubt arises as to the safety of the flight he should first contact the appropriate Flight Service Station.

c. All pilots should review the foreign airspace and entry restrictions published in the International Flight Information Manual during the flight planning process. Foreign airspace penetration without official authorization can involve both danger to the aircraft and the imposition of severe penalties and inconvenience to both passengers and crew. A flight plan on file with ATC authorities does not necessarily constitute the prior permission required by certain other authorities. The possibility of fatal consequences cannot be ignored in some areas of the world.

d. Current NOTAMs for foreign locations must also be reviewed. The publication International Notices to Airmen, published biweekly, contains considerable information pertinent to foreign flight. Current foreign NOTAMs are also available from the U.S. International NOTAM Office in Washington, D.C., through any local Flight Service Station.

581. PARACHUTE JUMP AIRCRAFT OPERATIONS

a. Procedures relating to parachute jump areas are contained in FAR Part 105. A tabulation of parachute jump areas in the U.S. is contained in the publication Graphic Notices and Supplemental Data.

b. Pilots of aircraft engaged in parachute jump operations are reminded that all reported altitudes must be with reference to mean sea level, or flight level as appropriate, to enable ATC to provide meaningful traffic information.

582–589. RESERVED

590. TO CONTACT AN FSS

Flight Service Stations are allocated frequencies for different functions, for Airport Advisory Service the pilot should contact the FSS on 123.6 MHz, for example. Other FSS frequencies are listed with the FSS in the Airport/Facility Directory. If you are in doubt as to what frequency to use to contact an FSS, transmit on 122.1 MHz and advise them of the frequency you are receiving on. (See Microphone Technique)

591. AIRCRAFT CHECKLISTS

Most Owners' Manuals contain recommended checklists for the particular type of aircraft. As checklists vary with different types of aircraft and equipments, it is not practical to recommend a complete set of checklists to cover all aircraft. Additions to the procedures in your Owners' Manual may better fill your personal preference or requirements. However, it is most important that checklists be designed to include all of the items in the Owners' Manual. By using these lists for every flight, the possibility of overlooking important items will be lessened.

592. IFR APPROACH TO A NONTOWER/NON FSS AIRPORT

a. AIRPORT ADVISORIES AT NONTOWER AIRPORTS in Chapter 4 outlines the practices, frequencies to use, and when to report your position and intentions when operating on or in the vicinity of airports not served by a tower or FSS. All pilots should monitor the appropriate frequency and make these reports, *including the pilot making an IFR approach to the airport.*

b. When making an IFR approach to an airport not served by a tower or FSS, after the ATC controller advises "CHANGE TO ADVISORY FREQUENCY APPROVED" you should broadcast your intentions, including the type of approach being executed, your position, and when over the final approach fix inbound. Continue to monitor the appropriate frequency (UNICOM, etc.) for reports from other pilots.

593–599. RESERVED

Chapter 8. MEDICAL FACTS FOR PILOTS

600. FITNESS FOR FLIGHT

a. Medical Certification

(1) All pilots except those flying gliders and free air balloons must possess valid medical certificates in order to exercise the privileges of their airman certificates. The periodic medical examinations required for medical certification are conducted by designated Aviation Medical Examiners, who are physicians with a special interest in aviation safety and training in aviation medicine.

(2) The standards for medical certification are contained in Part 67 of the Federal Aviation Regulations. Pilots who have a history of certain medical conditions described in these standards are mandatorily disqualified from flying. These medical conditions include a personality disorder manifested by overt acts, a psychosis, alcoholism, drug dependence, epilepsy, an unexplained disturbance of consciousness, myocardial infarction, angina pectoris and diabetes requiring medication for its control. Other medical conditions may be temporarily disqualifying, such as acute infections, anemia, and peptic ulcer. Pilots who do not meet medical standards may still be qualified under special issuance provisions or the exemption process. This may require that either additional medical information be provided or practical flight tests be conducted.

(3) Student pilots should visit an Aviation Medical Examiner as soon as possible in their flight training in order to avoid unnecessary training expenses should they not meet the medical standards. For the same reason, the student pilot who plans to enter commercial aviation should apply for the highest class of medical certificate that might be necessary in the pilot's career.

Caution: The Federal Aviation Regulations prohibit a pilot who possesses a current medical certificate from performing crewmember duties while the pilot has a known medical condition or increase of a known medical condition that would make the pilot unable to meet the standards for the medical certificate.

b. Illness

(1) Even a minor illness suffered in day-to-day living can seriously degrade performance of many piloting tasks vital to safe flight. Illness can produce fever and distracting symptoms that can impair judgment, memory, alertness, and the ability to make calculations. Although symptoms from an illness may be under adequate control with a medication, the medication itself may decrease pilot performance.

(2) The safest rule is not to fly while suffering from any illness. If this rule is considered too stringent for a particular illness, the pilot should contact an Aviation Medical Examiner for advice.

c. Medication

(1) Pilot performance can be seriously degraded by both prescribed and over-the-counter medications, as well as by the medical conditions for which they are taken. Many medications, such as tranquilizers, sedatives, strong pain relievers, and cough-suppressant preparations, have primary effects that may impair judgment, memory, alertness, coordination, vision, and the ability to make calculations. Others, such as antihistamines, blood pressure drugs, muscle relaxants, and agents to control diarrhea and motion sickness, have side effects that may impair the same critical functions. Any medication that depresses the nervous system, such as a sedative, tranquilizer or antihistamine, can make a pilot much more susceptible to hypoxia (see below).

(2) The Federal Aviation Regulations prohibit pilots from performing crewmember duties while using any medication that affects the faculties in any way contrary to safety. The safest rule is not to fly as a crewmember while taking any medication, unless approved to do so by the FAA.

d. Alcohol

(1) Extensive research has provided a number of facts about the hazards of alcohol consumption and flying. As little as one ounce of liquor, one bottle of beer, or four ounces of wine can impair flying skills, with the alcohol consumed in these drinks being detectable in the breath and blood for at least three hours. Even after the body completely destroys a moderate amount of alcohol, a pilot can still be severly impaired for many hours by hangover. There is simply no way of increasing the destruction of alcohol or alleviating a hangover. Alcohol also renders a pilot much more susceptible to disorientation and hypoxia (see below).

(2) A consistently high alcohol-related fatal aircraft accident rate serves to emphasize that alcohol and flying are a potentially lethal combination. The Federal Aviation Regulations prohibit pilots from performing crewmember duties within eight hours after drinking any alcoholic beverage or while under the influence of alcohol. However, due to the slow destruction of alcohol, a pilot may still be under influence eight hours after drinking a moderate amount of alcohol. Therefore, an excellent rule is to allow at least 12 to 24 hours between "bottle and throttle," depending on the amount of alcoholic beverage consumed.

e. Fatigue

(1) Fatigue continues to be one of the most treacherous hazards to flight, safety, as it may not be apparent to a pilot until serious errors are made. Fatigue is best described as either acute (short-term) or chronic (long-term).

(2) A normal occurrence of everyday living, acute fatigue is the tiredness felt after long periods of physical

and mental strain, including strenuous muscular effort, immobility, heavy mental workload, strong emotional pressure, monotony and lack of sleep. Consequently, coordination and alertness, so vital to safe pilot performance, can be reduced. Acute fatigue is prevented by adequate rest and sleep, as well as regular exercise and proper nutrition.

(3) Chronic fatigue occurs when there is not enough time for full recovery between episodes of acute fatigue. Performance continues to fall off, and judgment becomes impaired so that unwarranted risks may be taken. Recovery from chonic fatigue requires a prolonged period of rest.

f. Stress

(1) Stress from the pressures of everyday living can impair pilot performance, often in very subtle ways. Difficulties, particularly at work, can occupy thought processes enough to markedly decrease alertness. Distraction can so interfere with judgment that unwarranted risks are taken, such as flying into deteriorating weather conditions to keep on schedule. Stress and fatigue (see above) can be an extremely hazardous cominbation.

(2) Most pilots do not leave stress "on the ground." Therefore when more than usual difficulties are being experienced, a pilot should consider delaying flight until these difficulties are satisfactorily resolved.

g. Emotion

(1) Certain emotionally upsetting events, including a serious argument, death of a family member, separation or divorce, loss of job and financial catastrophe, can render a pilot unable to fly an aircraft safely. The emotions of anger, depression, and anxiety from such events not only decrease alertness but also may lead to taking risks that border on self-destruction. Any pilot who experiences an emotionally upsetting even should not fly until satisfactorily recovered from it.

h. Personal Checklist

(1) Aircraft accident statistics show that pilots should be conducting preflight checklists on themselves as well as their aircraft, for pilot impairment contributes to many more accidents than failures of aircraft systems. A personal checklist that can be easily committed to memory, which includes all of the categories of pilot impairment of discussed in this section, is being distributed by the FAA in the form of a wallet-sized card.

PERSONAL CHECKLIST

I'M physically and mentally
SAFE to fly—not being
impaired by

ILLNESS

MEDICATION.

STRESS

ALCOHOL

FATIGUE

EMOTION

601. EFFECTS OF ALTITUDE

a. Hypoxia

(1) Hypoxia is a state of oxygen deficiency in the body sufficient to impair functions of the brain and other organs. Hypoxia from exposure to altitude is due only to the reduced barometric pressures encountered at altitude, for the concentration of oxygen in the atmosphere remains about 21 percent from the ground out to space.

(2) Although a deterioration in night vision occurs at a cabin pressure altitude as low as 5,000 feet, other significant effects of altitude hypoxia usually do not occur in the normal healthy pilot below 12,000 feet. From 12,000 to 15,000 feet of altitude, judgment, memory, alertness, coordination and ability to make calculations are impaired, and headache, drowsiness, dizziness and either a sense of well-being (euphoria) or belligerence occur. The effects appear following increasingly shorter periods of exposure to increasing altitude. In fact, pilot performance can seriously deteriorate within 15 minutes at 15,000 feet.

(3) At cabin pressure altitudes above 15,000 feet, the periphery of the visual field grays out to a point where only central vision remains (tunnel vision). A blue coloration (cyanosis) of the fingernails and lips develops. The ability to take corrective and protective action is lost in 20 to 30 minutes at 18,000 feet and 5 to 12 minutes at 20,000 feet, followed soon thereafter by unconsciousness.

(4) The altitude at which significant effects of hypoxia occur can be lowered by a number of factors. Carbon monoxide inhaled in smoking or from exhaust fumes (see below), lowered hemoglobin (anemia), and certain medications can reduce the oxygen-carrying capacity of the blood to the degree that the amount of oxygen provided to body tissues will already be equivalent to the oxygen provided to the tissues when exposed to a cabin pressure altitude of several thousand feet. Small amounts of alcohol and low doses of certain drugs, such as antihistamines, tranquilizers, sedatives and analgesics can, through their depressant sections, render the brain much more susceptible to hypoxia. Extreme heat and cold, fever, and anxiety increase the body's demand for oxygen, and hence its susceptibility to hypoxia.

(5) The effects of hypoxia are usually quite difficult to recognize, especially when they occur gradually. Since symptoms of hypoxia do not vary in an individual, the ability to recognize hypoxia can be greatly improved by experiencing and witnessing the effects of hypoxia during an altitude chamber "flight." The FAA provides this opportunity through aviation physiology training, which is conducted at the FAA Civil Aeromedical Institute and at many military facilities across the United States. Pilots can apply for this training by contacting the Physiological Operations and Training Section, AAC–143, FAA Civil Aeromedical Institute, P.O. Box 25082, Oklahoma City, Oklahoma 73125.

(6) Hypoxia is prevented by heeding factors that reduce tolerance to altitude, by enriching the inspired air with oxygen from an appropriate oxygen system and by maintaining a comfortable, safe cabin pressure altitude. For optimum protection, pilots are encouraged

to use supplemental oxygen above 10,000 feet during the day, and above 5,000 feet at night. The Federal Aviation Regulations require that the minimum flight crew be provided with and use supplemental oxygen after 30 minutes of exposure to cabin pressure altitudes between 12,500 and 14,000 feet, and immediately on exposure to cabin pressure altitudes above 14,000 feet. Every occupant of the aircraft must be provided with supplemental oxygen at cabin pressure altitudes above 15,000 feet.

b. Ear Block

(1) As the aircraft cabin pressure decreases during ascent, the expanding air in the middle ear pushes the eustachian tube open and, by escaping down it to the nasal passages, equalizes in pressure with the cabin pressure. But during descent, the pilot must periodically open the eustachian tube to equalize pressure. This can be accomplished by swallowing, yawning, tensing muscles in the throat or, if these do not work, by the combination of closing the mouth, pinching the nose closed and attempting to blow through the nostrils (Valsalva maneuver).

(2) Either an upper respiratory infection, such as a cold or sore throat, or a nasal allergic condition can produce enough congestion around the eustachian tube to make equalization difficult. Consequently, the difference in pressure between the middle ear and aircraft cabin can build up to a level that will hold the eustachian tube closed, making equalization difficult if not impossible. The problem is commonly referred to as an "ear block."

(3) An ear block produces severe ear pain and loss of hearing that can last from several hours to several days. Rupture of the ear drum can occur in flight or after landing. Fluid can accumulate in the middle ear and become infected.

(4) An ear block is prevented by not flying with an upper respiratory infection or nasal allergic condition. Adequate protection is usually not provided by decongestant sprays or drops to reduce congestion around the eustachian tubes. Oral decongestants have side effects that can significantly impair pilot performance.

(5) If an ear block does not clear shortly after landing, a physician should be consulted.

c. Sinus Block

(1) During ascent and descent, air pressure in the sinuses equalizes with the aircraft cabin pressure through small openings that connect the sinuses to the nasal passages. Either an upper respiratory infection, such as a cold or sinusitis, or a nasal allergic condition can produce enough congestion around an opening to slow equalization and, as the difference in pressure between the sinus and cabin mounts, eventually plug the opening. This "sinus block" occurs most frequently during descent.

(2) A sinus block can occur in the frontal sinuses, located above each eyebrow, or in the maxillary sinuses, located in each upper cheek. It will usually produce excruciating pain over the sinus area. A maxillary sinus block can also make the upper teeth ache. Bloody mucus may discharge from the nasal passages.

(3) A sinus bolck is prevented by not flying with an respiratory infection or nasal allergic condition. Adequate protection is usually not provided by decongestant sprays or drops to reduce congestion around the sinus openings. Oral decongestants have side effects that can impair pilot performance.

(4) If a sinus block does not clear shortly after landing, a physician should be consulted.

d. Decompression Sickness After Scuba Diving

(1) A pilot or passenger who intends to fly after Scuba diving should allow the body sufficient time to rid itself of excess nitrogen absorbed during diving. If not, decompression sickness due to evolved gas can occur during exposure to low altitude and create a serious inflight emergency.

(2) The recommended waiting time before flight to cabin pressure altitudes of 8,000 feet or less is at least 2 hours after diving which has not required controlled ascent (non-decompression diving), and at least 24 hours after diving which has required controlled ascent (decompression diving). The waiting time before flight to cabin pressure altitudes above 8,000 feet should be at least 24 hours after any Scuba diving.

602. HYPERVENTILATION IN FLIGHT

a. Hyperventilation, or an abnormal increase in the volume of air breathed in and out of the lungs, can occur subconsciously when a stressful situation is encountered in flight. As hyperventilation "blows off" excessive carbon dioxide from the body, a pilot can experience symptoms of lightheadness, suffocation, drowsiness, tingling in the extremities, and coolness—and react to them with even greater hyperventilation. Incapacitation can eventually result from incoordination, disorientation, and painful muscle spasms. Finally, unconsciousness can occur.

b. The syptoms of hyperventilation subside within a few minutes after the rate and depth of breathing are consciously brought back under control. The buildup of carbon dioxide in the body can be hastened by controlled breathing in and out of a paper bad held over the nose and mouth.

c. Early symptoms of hyperventilation and hypoxia are similar. Moreover, hyperventilation and hypoxia can occur at the same time. Therefore, if a pilot is using an oxygen system when symptoms are experienced, the oxygen regulator should immediately be set to deliver 100 percent oxygen, and then the system checked to assure that it has been functioning effectively before giving attention to rate and depth of breathing.

603. CARBON MONOXIDE POISONING IN FLIGHT

a. Carbon monoxide is a colorless, odorless and tasteless gas contained in exhaust fumes. When breathed even in minute quantities over a period of time, it can significantly reduce the ability of the blood to carry oxygen. Consequently, effects of hypoxia occur (see above).

b. Most heaters in light aircraft work by air flowing over the manifold. Use of these heaters while exhaust fumes are escaping through manifold cracks and seals is responsible every year for several non-fatal and fatal aircraft accidents from carbon monoxide poisoning.

c. A pilot who detects the odor of exhaust or experiences symptoms of headache, drowsiness, or dizziness while using the heater should suspect carbon monoxide poisoning, and immediately shut off the heater and open air vents. If symptoms are severe, or continue after landing, medical treatment should be sought.

604. ILLUSIONS IN FLIGHT

a. Introduction

(1) Many different illusions can be experienced in flight. Some can lead to spatial disorientation. Others can lead to landing errors. Illusions rank among the most common factors cited as contributing to aircraft accidents.

b. Illusions Leading to Spatial Disorientation

(1) Various complex motions and forces and certain visual scenes encountered in flight can create illusions of motion and position. Spatial disorientation from these illusions can be prevented only by visual reference to reliabile, fixed points on the ground or to flight instruments.

(a) *The leans*—An abrupt correction of a banked attitude, which has been entered too slowly to stimulate the balance organs in the inner ear, can create the illusion of banking in the opposite direction. The disoriented pilot will roll the aircraft back into its original dangerous attitude or, if level flight is maintained, will feel compelled to lean in the preceived vertical plane until this illusion subsides.

(b) *Coriolis illusion*—An abrupt head movement in a constant-rate turn that has ceased stimulating the balance organs can create the illusion of rotation or movement in an entirely different plane. The disoriented pilot will maneuver the aircraft into a dangerous attitude in an attempt to stop rotation. This most overwhelmining of all illusions in flight may be prevented by not making sudden, extreme head movements, particularly while making prolonged constant-rate turns under IFR conditions.

(c) *Graveyard spin*—A proper recovery from a spin that has ceased stimulating the balance organs can create the illusion of spinning in the opposite direction. The disoriented pilot will return the aircraft to its original spin.

(d) *Graveyard spiral*—An observed loss of altitude during a coordinated constant-rate turn that has ceased stimulating the balance organs can create the illusion of being in a descent with the wings level. The disoriented pilot will pull back on the controls, tightening the spiral and increasing the loss of altitude.

(e) *Somatogravic illusion*—A rapid acceleration during takeoff can create the illusion of being in a nose-up attitude. The disoriented pilot will push the aircraft into a nose-low, or dive attitude. A rapid deceleration by rapid reduction of the throttles can have the opposite effect, with the disoriented pilot pulling the aircraft into a nose-up, or stall attitude.

(f) *Inversion illusion*—An abrupt transition from climb to straight and level flight can create the illusion of tumbling backwards. The disoriented pilot will push the aircraft abruptly into a nose-low attitude, possibly intensifying this illusion.

(g) *Elevator illusion*—An abrupt upward vertical acceleration, usually by an updraft, can create the illusion of being in a climb. The disoriented pilot will push the aircraft into a nose-low attitude. An abrupt downward vertical acceleration, usually by a downdraft, has the opposite effect, with the disoriented pilot pulling the aircraft into a nose-up attitude.

(h) *False horizon*—Sloping cloud formations, an obscured horizon, a dark scene spread with ground lights and stars, and certain geometric patterns of ground light can create illusions of not being aligned correctly with the actual horizon. The disoriented pilot will place the aircraft in a dangerous attitude.

(i) *Autokinesis*—In the dark, a static light will appear to move about when stared at for many seconds. The disoriented pilot will lose control of the aircraft in attempting to align it with the light.

c. Illusions Leading to Landing Errors

(1) Various surface features and atmospheric conditions encountered in landing can create illusions of incorrect height above and distance from the runway threshold. Landing errors from these illusions can be prevented by anticipating them during approaches, aerial visual inspection of unfamiliar airports before landing, using electronic glideslope or VASI systems when available, and maintaining optimum proficiency in landing procedures.

(a) *Runway width illusion*—A narrower-than-usual runway can create the illusion of the aircraft being at a greater height. The pilot who does not recognize this illusion will fly a lower approach, with the risk of striking objects along the approach path or landing short. A wider-than-usual runway can have the opposite effect, with the risk of leveling out high and landing hard or overshooting the runway.

(b) *Runway and terrain slopes illusion*—An upsloping runway, upsloping terrain, or both, can create the illusion of greater height. The pilot who does not recognize this illusion will fly a lower approach. A downsloping runway, downsloping approach terrain, or both, can have the opposite effect.

(c) *Featureless terrain illusion*—An absence of ground features, as when landing over water, darkened areas and terrain made featureless by snow, can create the illusion of greater height. The pilot who does not recognize this illusion will fly a lower approach.

(d) *Atmospheric illusions*—Rain on the windscreen can create the illusion of greater height, and atmospheric haze the illusion of greater distance. The pilot who does not recognize these illusions will fly a lower approach. Penetration of fog can create the illusion of pitching up. The pilot who does not recognize this illusion will steepen the approach, often quite abruptly.

(e) *Ground lighting illusios*—Lights along a straight path, such as a road, and even lights on moving trains can be mistaken for runway and approach lights. Bright runway and approach lighting systems, especially where few lights illuminate the surrounding terrain, may create the illusion of lesser distance. The pilot who does not recognize this illusion will fly a high approach.

605. VISION IN FLIGHT

a. Introduction

(1) Of the body senses, vision is the most important for safe flight. Major factors that determine how effectively vision can be used are the level of illumination and the technique of scanning the sky for other aircraft.

b. Vision Uder Dim and Bright Illumination

(1) Under conditions of dim illumination, small print and colors on aeronautical charts and aircraft instruments become unreadable unless adequate cockpit lighting is available. Moreover, another aircraft must be much closer to be seen unless its navigation lights are on.

(2) In darkness, vision becomes more sensitive to light, a process called dark adaptation. Although exposure to total darkness for at least 30 minutes is required for complete dark adaptation, the pilot can achieve a moderate degree of dark adaptation within 20 minutes under dim red cockpit lighting. Since red light severely distorts colors, especially on aeronautical charts, and can cause serious difficulty in focusing the eyes on objects inside the aircraft, its use is advisable only where optimum outside night vision capability is necessary. Even so, white cockpit lighting must be available when needed for map and instrument reading, especially under IFR conditions. Dark adaptation is impaired by exposure to cabin pressure altitudes above 5,000 feet, carbon monoxide inhaled in smoking and from exhaust fumes, deficiency of Vitamin A in the diet, and by prolonged exposure to bright sunlight. Since any degree of dark adaptation is lost within a few seconds of viewing a bright light, the pilot should close one eye when using a light to preserve some degree of night vision.

(3) Excessive illumination, especially from light reflected off the canopy, surfaces inside the aircraft, clouds, water, snow, and desert terrain, can produce glare, with uncomfortable squinting, watering of the eyes, and even temporary blindness. Sunglasses for protection from glare should absorb at least 85 percent of visible light (15 percent transmittance) and all colors equally (neutral transmittance), with negligible image distortion from refractive and prismatic errors.

c. Scanning for Other Aircraft

(1) Scanning the sky for other aircraft is a key factor in collision avoidance. It should be used continuously by the pilot and copilot (or right seat passenger) to cover all areas of the sky visible from the cockpit.

(2) Effective scanning is accomplished with a series of short, regularly spaced eye movements that bring successive areas of the sky into the central visual field. Each movement should not exceed 10 degrees, and each area should be observed for at least one second to enable detection. Although horizontal back-and-forth eye movements seem preferred by most pilots, each pilot should develop a scanning pattern that is most comfortable and then adhere to it to assure optimum scanning.

606–619. RESERVED

Chapter 9. AERONAUTICAL CHARTS AND RELATED PUBLICATIONS

620. GENERAL

Aeronautical charts for the United States and it's territories and possessions are produced by the National Ocean Survey, a part of the Department of Commerce, from information furnished by the Federal Aviation Administration.

621. OBTAINING AERONAUTICAL CHARTS

Enroute Aeronautical Charts, Enroute Supplements, Approach Procedure Charts, Regional Airport/Facility Directories and other publications described in this Chapter are available upon subscription from the:

National Ocean Survey
Distribution Division (C44)
650 Lafayette Ave.
Riverdale, Maryland 20840

622. TYPES OF CHARTS AVAILABLE

Sectional and VFR Terminal Area Charts
World Aeronautical Charts (U.S.)
Enroute Low Altitude Charts
Enroute High Altitude Charts
Area Navigation (RNAV) High Altitude Charts
Alaska Enroute Charts (Low and High)
Aircraft Position Charts
Planning Charts
Instrument Approach Procedure Charts
Standard Instrument Departure (SID) Charts
Standard Terminal Arrival Route (STAR) Charts
Alaska Terminal Publication

623. GENERAL DESCRIPTION OF EACH SERIES

a. Sectional and VFR Terminal Area Chrts

These charts are designed for visual navigation of slow and medium speed aircraft. They are produced to the following scales:

Sectional Charts—1:500,000 (1 in=6.86 NM)

VFR Terminal Area Charts—1:250,000 (1 in=3.43 NM)

Topographic information features the portrayal of relief and a judicious selection of visual check points for VFR flight (Terminal Area Charts include populated places, drainage, roads, railroads, and other distinctive landmarks). Aeronautical information includes visual and radio aids to navigation, aerodromes, controlled airspace, restricted areas, obstructions, and related data. The VFR Terminal Area Charts are also depict the airspace designated as "terminal control area" which provides for the control or segregation of all aircraft within the terminal control area. The Puerto Rico-Virgin Islands Terminal Area Chart contains basically the same information as that shown on the Sectional and Terminal Area Chart. It includes the Gulf of Mexico and Caribbean Planning Chart on the reverse side (See

PLANNING CHARTS). Charts are revised semi-annually except for several Alaskan Sectionals and the Puerto Rico-Virgin Islands Terminal Area which are revised annually.

b. World Aeronautical Charts

These charts are designed to provide a standard series of aeronautical charts, covering land areas of the world, at a size and scale convenient for navigation by moderate speed aircraft. They are produced at a scale of 1:1,000,000 (1 in=13.7 NM). Topographic information includes cities and towns, principal roads, railroads, distinctive landmarks, drainage and relief. The latter is shown by spot elevations, contours, and gradient tints. Aeronautical information includes visual and radio aids to navigation, aerodromes, airways, restricted areas, obstructions and other pertinent data. These charts are revised annually except for several Alaskan charts and the Mexican/Caribbean charts, which are revised every two years.

c. Enroute Low Altitude Charts

These charts are designed to provide aeronautical information for enroute navigation under Instrument Flight Rules (IFR) in the low altitude stratum. The series also includes enroute Area Charts which furnish terminal data at a large scale in congested areas, and is included with the subscription to the series. Information includes the portrayal of L/MF and VHF airways; limits of controlled airspace; position, identification and frequencies of radio aids; selected aerodromes; minimum enroute and obstruction clearance altitudes; airway distances; reporting points; special use airspace areas and related information. Charts are printed back to back. Charts are revised every 56 days effective with the date of airspace changes. An Enroute Change Notice may be issued as required on the mid-point 28-day cycle.

d. Enroute High Altitude Charts

These charts are designed to provide aeronautical information for enroute navigation under Instrument Flight Rules (IFR) in the high altitude stratum. Information includes the portrayal of jet routes; position, identification and frequencies of radio aids; selected aerodromes; distances; time zones; special use airspace areas and related information. Charts are revised every 56 days effective with the date of airspace changes. An Enroute Change Notice may be issued as required on the mid-point 28-day cycle.

e. Area Navigation (RNAV) High Altitude Charts

These charts are designed to provide aeronautical information for air routes established for aircraft equipped with area navigation. Information includes portrayal of RNAV routes, waypoints, track angles, changeover points, distances, selected navigational aids and aerodromes, special use airspace areas, oceanic routes, and other transitional information. Charts are revised every 56 days effective with the date of airspace changes. An Enroute Change Notice may be issued as required on the mid-point 28-day cycle.

f. Alaska Enroute Charts (Low and High)

These charts are produced in a low altitude and high altitude series with purpose and makeup identical to Low and High altitude charts described above. Charts are revised every 56 days effective with the date of airspace changes. An Enroute Change Notice may be issued as required on the mid-point 28-day cycle.

g. Aircraft Position Charts

These charts are designed to provide charts suitable for plotting lines of position from celestial observations and electronic aids. They are designed for long-range flights usually over extensive water or desert areas. They are produced at a scale of 1:5,000,000 to 1:6,750,000. Topographic information includes spot elevations, important drainage features, large cities and international boundaries. All enroute aeronautical data necessary for over-water flight is provided. This information varies with the area requirements and includes oceanic control areas, flight information regions, weather zones, normal positions of air-sea rescue vessels, and, if required, loran and consolan data. Charts are revised and issued as required.

h. Planning Charts

(1) VFR/IFR Planning Chart

These charts are designed to fulfill the requirements of pre-flight planning for flights under Visual or Instrument Flight Rules (VFR/IFR). They are produced at a scale of 1:2,333,232 (1 in=32 NM). The chart is printed in two parts in such a manner that, when assembled, it form a composite VFR Planning Chart on one side and IFR Planning Chart on the other. Information on the IFR chart includes low altitude airways and mileages, navigational facilities, special use airspace areas, time zones, airports, isogonic lines, and related data. Information on the VFR chart includes selected populated places, large bodies of water, major drainage, shaded relief, navigational facilities, airports, special use airspace areas, and related data.

(2) Flight Case Planning Chart

The chart is designed for pre-flight and enroute flight planning for VFR flights. It is produced at a scale of 1:4,374,803 (1 in=60 NM). This chart contains basically the same information as the VFR/IFR Planning Chart with the addition of selected FSS and Weather Service Offices located at airport sites, parachute jumping areas, a tabulation of special use airspace areas, a mileage table listing distances between 174 major airports and a city/areodrome location index.

(3) Gulf of Mexico and Caribbean Plannig Chart

This chart is designated for pre-flight planning for VFR flights. It is produced at a scale of 1:6,270,551 (1 in=86 NM). This chart is on the reverse of the Puerto Rico-Virgin Islands Terminal Area Chart. Information includes mileage between Airports of Entry, a selection of special use airspace areas and a Directory of Aerodromes with their available facilities and servicing.

i. Istrument Approach Procedure (IAP) Charts

Instrument approach procedure charts portray the aeronautical data which is required to execute instrument approaches to airports. These charts are published in 15 bound volumes covering the conterminous U.S. and the Puerto Rico-Virgin Islands. Each new volume is superseded by a new volume each 56 days. Changes to procedures occurring between the 56 day publication cycle is reflected in a change notice volume issued on the 28 day mid-cycle. These changes are in the form of a new chart. The publication of a new 56 day volume incorporates all the changes and replaces the preceding volume and the change notice. The bound volumes are 5¼ x 8½ inches and bound on the top edge. Each chart contained depicts the Instrument Approach Procedure, all related navigation data, communications information and an airport diagram. Each procedure is designated for use with a specific electronic navigational aid, such as ILS, VOR, NDB, RNAV, etc. Airport Taxi Charts, where published, are included.

j. Standard Instrument Departure (SID) Charts

These Charts are designed to expedite clearance delivery and to facilitate transition between take-off and enroute operations. They are published in a bound book 5½" x 8½", and furnish pilots departure routing clearance information in graphic and textual form. These are two bound volumes which are issued every 56 days.

k. Standard Terminal Arrival Route (STAR) Charts

These charts are designed to expedite air traffic control arrival route procedures and to facilitate transition between enroute and instrument approach operations. These charts, published in a bound book, 5¼" x 8¼", present to the pilot preplanned instrument flight rules (IFR) air traffic control arrival route procedure in graphic and textual form. Each STAR procedure is presented as a separate chart and may serve a single airport or more than one airport in a given geographic location. One bound volume of STAR charts for the United States, excluding Alaska, is issued every 56 days.

l. Alaska Terminal Publication

This publication contains charts depicting all terminal flight procedures in the State of Alaska for civil and military aviation. They are:

Instrument Approach Procedure (IAP) Charts.
Standard Instrument Departure (SID) Charts.
Standard Terminal Arrival Route (STAR) Charts.
Airport Taxi Charts.
Radar Minimums.

All supplementary supporting data, i.e.; IFR Take-off and Departure Procedures, IFR Alternate Minimums, Rate of Descent Table, Inoperative Components Table etc., is also included.

The Alaska Terminal is published in a bound book 5¼" x 8¼", and is arranged alphabetically by airport name with all procedures appropriate to the airport following the airport name; STAR, IAP, TAXI, SID. The publication is issued every 56 days with provisions for an as required "Terminal Change" on the 28 day mid point.

624. RELATED PUBLICATIONS

a. The Airport Facility Directory

This directory is issued in seven volumes with each volume covering a specific geographic area of the conterminous U.S., including Puerto Rico and the U.S. Virgin Islands. The directory is 5 x 10 inches and is bound on the side. Each volume is reissued in its entirety each 56 days. Each volume is indexed alphabetically by state, airport, navigational aid, and ATC facility for the area of coverage. All pertinent information concerning each entry is included.

b. Alaska Supplement

This supplement is a joint Civil/Military Flight Information Publication (FLIP), published and distributed every 56 days by the National Ocean Survey. It is designed for use with the Flight Information Publication Enroute Charts, Alaska Terminal, WAC and Sectional Aeronautical Charts. This Supplement contains an Aerodrome/Facility Directory of all aerodromes shown on Enroute Charts and those requested by appropriate agencies, communications data, navigational facilities, special notices and procedures applicable to the area of chart coverage.

c. Pacific Supplement

This Chart Supplement is a Civil Flight Information Publication, published and distributed every 56 days by the National Ocean Survey. It is designed for use with the Flight Information Enroute Publication Charts and the Sectional Aeronautical Chart covering the State of Hawaii and that area of the Pacific served by U.S. facilities. An Amendment Notice is published 4 weeks after each issue of the Supplement. This chart Supplement contains an Aerodrome/Facility Directory of all aerodromes open to the public, and those requested by appropriate agencies, communications data, navigational facilities, special notices and procedures applicable to the Pacific area.

d. Defense Mapping Agency Aerospace Center (DMAAC) Publications

Pilotage Charts (PC/TPC)—Scale 1:5,000,000 used for detail pre-flight planning and mission analysis. Emphasis in design is on ground features significant in visual and radar, low-level high speed navigation.

Jet Navigation Charts (JNC–A)—Scale 1:3,000,000. Designed to provide greater coverage than the 1:2,000,000 scale Jet Navigation Charts described below. Uses include pre-flight planning and enroute navigation by long range jet aircraft with dead reckoning, radar, celestial and grid navigation capabilities.

Loran Navigation & Consol Loran Navigation Charts (LJC/CJC)—Scale 1:2,000,000. Use for pre-flight planning and in-flight navigation on long range flight in the Polar areas and adjacent regions utilizing Loran and Consol navigation aids.

Continental Entry Chart (CEC)—Scale 1:2,000,000. Used for consolan and loran navigation for entry into the United States when a high.degree of accuracy is required to comply with Air Defense identification and reporting procedures. Also suitable as a basic dead reckoning sheet and for celestial navigation.

Aerospace Planning Chart (ASC)—Scales 1:9,000,000 and 1:18,000,000. Six charts at each scale and with various projections, cover the world. Charts are useful for general planning, briefings, and studies.

Air Distance/Geography Chart (GH–2, 2a)—Scales 1:25,000,000 and 1:50,000,000. This chart shows great circle distances between major airports. It also shows major cities, international boundaries, shaded relief and gradient tints.

Loran C Navigation Chart (LCC)—Scale 1:3,000,000. Primarily designed for pre-flight and in-flight longe range navigation where Loran C is used as the basic navigation aid.

DOD Weather Plotting Chart (WPC)—Various scales. Designed as non-navigational outline charts which depict locations and identifications of meteorological observing stations. Primarily used to forecast and monitor weather and atmospheric conditions throughout the world.

Flight Information Publications (FLIP)—These include Enroute Low Altitude and High Altitude Charts, Enroute Supplements, Terminal (Instrument Approach Charts), and other informational publications for various areas of the world.

> NOTE.—FLIP. Terminal Publications do not necessarily include all instrument approach procedures for all airports. They include only those required for military operations."

More complete information and price may be obtained from National Ocean Survey, Distribution Division.

(1) World Aeronautical (WAC) and Operational Navigation Charts (ONC)

The Operational Navigation Charts (ONC) have the same purpose and contain essentially the same information as the WAC series except the terrain is portrayed by shaded relief as well as contours. The ONC series is replacing the WAC series and the WAC's will be available only where the ONC's have not been issued. ONC's are 42 x 57½ inches, WAC's are 22 x 30 inches. These charts are revised on a regular schedule.

(2) Jet Navigation Charts

These charts are designed to provide charts suitable for long range, high altitude, high speed navigation. They are produced at a scale of 1:2,000,000 (1 in=27.4 NM). Topographic features include large cities, roads, railroads, drainage and relief. The latter is indicated by contours, spot elevations and gradient tints. All aeronautical information necessary to conform to the purpose of the chart is shown. This includes restricted areas, L/MF and VOR ranges, radiobeacons and a selection of standard broadcasting stations and aerodromes. The runway patterns of the aerodromes are shown to exaggerated scale in order that they me be readily identified as visual landmarks. Universal Jet Navigation Charts are used as plotting charts in the training and practice of celestial and dead reckoning navigation. They may also be used for grid navigational training.

(3) Global Navigational Charts

These charts are designed to provide charts suitable for aeronautical planning, operations over long distances, and enroute navigation in long range, high altitude, high speed aircraft. They are produced at a scale of 1:5,000,000 (1 in=68.58 NM). Global Navigation Charts (GNC) are 42 by 57½ inches. They shown principal cities, towns and drainage, primary roads and railroads, prominent culture and shadient relief augmented with tints and spot elevations. Aeronautical data includes radio aids to navigation, aerodrome and restricted areas. Charts 1 and 26 have a polar navigation grid and charts 2 and 6 have sub-polar navigation grids.

Global Loran Navigation Charts (GLC) are the same size and scale and cover the same area as the GNC charts. They contain major cities only, coast lines, major lakes and rivers, and land tint. No relief or vegetation. Aeronautical Date includes radio aids to nagivation and Loran lines of position.

625. AUXILIARY CHARTS

a. Projections:

Equatorial Gnomonic. Scale 1:50,000,000. Size 21 x 22 inches.

Polar-Equatorial Gnomonic. Scale 1:50,000.000. Size 21 x 22 inches.

Equatorial Azimuthal Equidistant. Scale 1:52,670,165. Size 32 x 32 inches.

Aitoff's Equal Area Projection of the Sphere. Size 17 x 42 inches.

b. Outline Maps:

Conterminous United States on Lambert Conformal Conic Projectoin. Scale 1:5,000,00. Size 29 x 42 inches.

Conterminous United States on Lambert Zenithal Equal Area Projection. Scale 1:7,500,000. Size 22 x 48 inches.

Conterminous United States on Lambert Conformal Conic Projection (in two parts). Scale 1:3,000,000. Size 48 x 70 inches.

Conterminous United States. Scale 1:17,800,000. Size 9 x 13 inches.

Conterminous United States Murdoch's Projection on Intersecting Cone. Scale 1:7,000,000. Size 20 x 30 inches. World on Mercator Projection. Scale 1:38,000,000. Size 35 x 47 inches.

c. Miscellaneous Maps:

Chart of the World on Azimuthal Equidistant Projection Centered at New York City (in 4 colors). Scale 1:47,423,730. Size 36 x 42 inches. The projection on which this chart is constructed enables the user to determine true distances and azimuths from the point which the projection is centered to any other point within the area of the chart. A straight line drawn from the center to another point shows the shortest route, distance, and places traversed enroute.

Base map of the conterminous United States with gradient tints (2 parts). Scale 1:3,000,000. Size 36 x 47 inches.

Base map of Alaska on Lambert Conformal Conic Projection. Scale 1:5,000,000. Size 29 x 45 inches.

Great Circle Chart of the Conterminous United States on the Gnomonic Projection, showing the principal cities. Scale 1:5,094,000. Size 31 x 34 inches.

Outline maps for construction of a model of the world; produces a "Lambert Globe" 9 inches in diameter. Scale 1:55,800,000. Size 22 x 30 inches.

d. Airport Obstruction Charts (OC):

These large scale (1:12,000) charts of airports shows runways and flight paths for landing and take-off, together with the positions and elevations of the objects which are potential hazards to these operations. The charts are used in determining the maximum safe take-off and landing gross weight of civil aircraft, in determining airport instrument approach and landing procedures, and to provide data for engineering plans relative to clearing of obstructions and improvement of airport facilities.

e. Military Training Routes:

Charts and Booklet: The Defense Mapping Agency Aerospace Center (DMAAC) publishes a narrative description in booklet form and charts depicting the IFR and VFR Training Routes.

The charts and booklet are published every 12 weeks. Both the charts and narrative route description booklet are available to the general public as a brochure by single copy or annual subscription.

Subscription and single-copy requests should be for the "DOD Area Planning AP/1B, Military Training Routes".

NOTE.—The Department of Defense provides these booklets and charts to each airport and Flight Service Station for use in pre-flight pilot briefings. Pilots should review this information to acquaint themselves with those routes that are located along their route of flight and in the vicinity of the airports from which they operate.

626–999. RESERVED

AERONAUTICAL CHARTS AND RELATED PUBLICATIONS

INSTRUMENT APPROACH PROCEDURE CHARTS

AIRPORT/FACILITY DIRECTORY

AERONAUTICAL CHARTS AND RELATED PUBLICATIONS

ENROUTE LOW ALTITUDE CHARTS

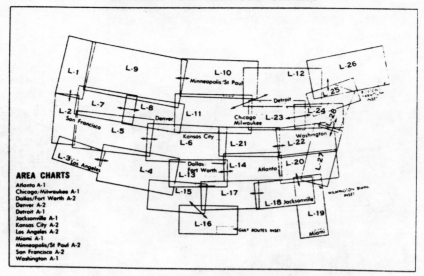

AREA CHARTS
Atlanta A-1
Chicago/Milwaukee A-1
Dallas/Fort Worth A-2
Denver A-2
Detroit A-1
Jacksonville A-1
Kansas City A-2
Los Angeles A-2
Miami A-1
Minneapolis/St Paul A-2
San Francisco A-2
Washington A-1

ENROUTE HIGH ALTITUDE AND RNAV CHARTS

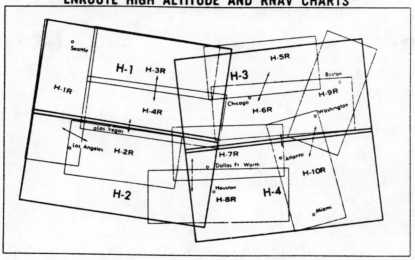

CARIBBEAN LOW ALTITUDE ENROUTE

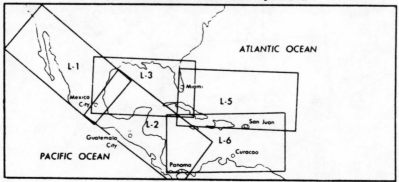

PLANNING CHARTS

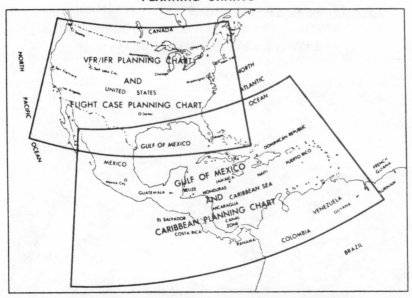

SECTIONAL AND VFR TERMINAL AREA CHARTS
CONTERMINOUS U.S. AND HAWAIIAN ISLANDS

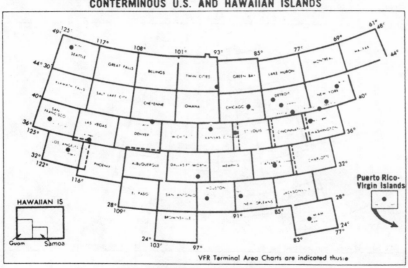

VFR Terminal Area Charts are indicated thus: ●

WORLD AERONAUTICAL CHARTS
CONTERMINOUS U.S., MEXICO, AND CARIBBEAN

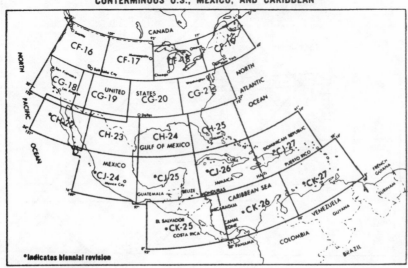

●indicates biennial revision

AERONAUTICAL CHARTS AND RELATED PUBLICATIONS
SECTIONAL AND VFR TERMINAL AREA CHARTS
ALASKA

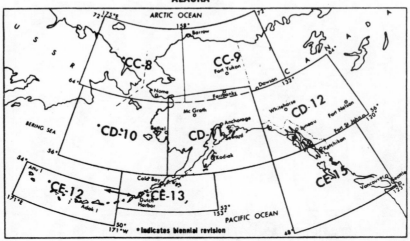

ALASKA

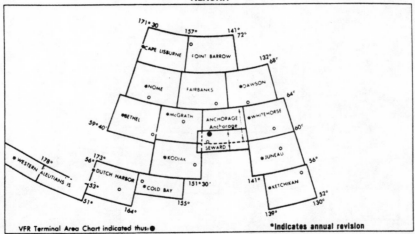

ALASKA ENROUTE CHARTS

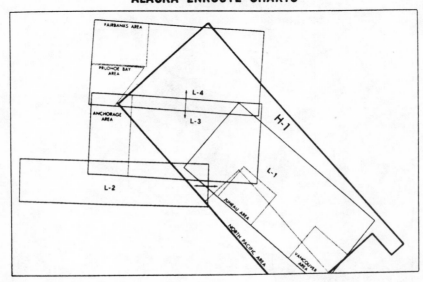

PILOT/CONTROLLER GLOSSARY

This Glossary was compiled to promote a common understanding of the terms used in the Air Traffic Control system. It includes those terms which are intended for pilot/controller communications. Those terms most frequently used in pilot/controller communications are printed in *bold italics*. The definitions are primarily defined in an operational sense applicable to both users and operators of the National Airspace System. Use of the Glossary will preclude any misunderstandings concerning the system's design, function, and purpose.

Because of the international nature of flying, terms used in the "Lexicon," published by the International Civil Aviation Organization (ICAO), are included when they differ from FAA definitions. These terms are *italicized*. For the reader's convenience, there are also cross references to related terms in other parts of the Glossary and to other documents, such as the Federal Aviation Regulations (FARs) and the Airman's Information Manual (AIM).

This Glossary will be revised as necessary to maintain a common understanding of the system.

ABBREVIATED IFR FLIGHT PLANS—An authorization by ATC requiring pilots to submit only that information needed for the purpose of ATC. It includesonly a small portion of the usual IFR flight plan information. In certain instances, this may be only aircraft identification, location, and pilot request. Other information may be requested if needed by ATC for separation/control purposes. It is frequently used by aircraft which are airborne, desire an instrument approach, or by aircraft on the ground which desire a climb to VFR on top (See VFR ON TOP) (Refer to AIM)

ABEAM—An aircraft is "abeam" a fix, point or object when that fix, point or object is approximately 90 degrees to the right or left of the aircraft track. Abeam indicates a general position rather than a precise point.

ABORT—To terminate a preplanned aircraft maneuver; e.g., an aborted takeoff.

ACKNOWLEDGE—Let me know that you have received and understand my message.

ACROBATIC FLIGHT—An intentional maneuver involving an abrupt change in an aircraft's attitude, an abnormal attitude, or abnormal acceleration, not necessary for normal flight. (Refer to FAR Part 91)

ICAO—ACROBATIC FLIGHT—Maneuvers intentionally performed by an aircraft involving an abrupt change in its attitude, an abnormal attitude, or an abnormal variation in speed.

ADDITIONAL SERVICES—Advisory information provided by ATC which includes but is not limited to the following.
1. Traffic advisories.
2. Vectors, when requested by the pilot, to assist aircraft receiving traffic advisories to avoid observed traffic.
3. Altitude deviation information of 300 feet or more from an assigned altitude as observed on a verified (reading correctly) automatic altitude readout (Mode C).
4. Advisories that traffic is no longer a factor.
5. Weather and chaff information.
6. Weather assistance.
7. Bird activity information.
8. Holding pattern surveillance.

Additional services are provided to the extent possible contingent only upon the controller's capability to fit them into the performance of higher priority duties and on the basis of limitations of the radar, volume of traffic, frequency congestion and controller workload. The controller has complete discretion for determining if he is able to provide or continue to provide a service in a particular case. The controller's reason not to provide or continue to provide a service in a particular case is not subject to question by the pilot and need not be made known to him. (See Traffic Advisories) (Refer to AIM)

ADMINISTRATOR—The Federal Aviation Administrator or any person to whom he has delegated his authority in the matter concerned.

ADVISE INTENTIONS—Tell me what you plan to do.

ADVISORY—Advice and information provided to assist pilots in the safe conduct of flight and aircraft movement. (See Advisory Service)

ADVISORY FREQUENCY—The appropriate frequency to be used for Airport Advisory Service. (See Airport Advisory Service and UNICOM) (Refer to Advisory Circular No. 90-42; AIM)

ADVISORY SERVICE—Advice and information provided by a facility to assist pilots in the safe conduct of flight and aircraft movement. (See Airport Advisory Service, Traffic Advisories, Safety Advisories, Additional Services, Radar Advisory, En Route Flight Advisory Service) (Refer to AIM)

AERIAL REFUELING/INFLIGHT REFUELING—A procedure used by the military to transfer fuel from one aircraft to another during flight. (Refer to Graphic Notices and Supplemental Data.

AERODROME—A defined area on land or water (including any buildings, installations, and equipment) intended to be used either wholly or in part for the arrival, departure, and movement of aircraft.

AERONAUTICAL BEACON—A visual navaid displaying flashes of white and/or colored light to indicate the location of an airport, a heliport, a landmark, a certain point of a Federal airway in mountainous terrain, or a hazard. (See Airport Rotating Beacon) (Refer to AIM)

AERONAUTICAL CHART—A map used in air navigation containing all or part of the following: topographic features, hazards and obstructions, navigation aids, navigation routes, designated airspace, and airports. Commonly used aeronautical charts are:
1. Sectional Charts—1:5000,000—Designated for visual navigation of slow or medium speed aircraft. Topographic information on these charts features the portrayal of relief, and a judicious selection of visual check points for VFR flight. Aeronautical information includes visual and radio aids to navigation, airports, controller airspace, restricted area, obstructions and related data.
2. VFR Terminal Area Charts—1:250,000 Depict Terminal Control Area (TCA) airspace which provides for the control or segregation of all the aircraft within the TCA. The chart depicts topographic information and aeronautical information which includes visual and radio aids to navigation, airports, controller airspace, restricted areas, obstructions, and related data.
3. World Aeronautical charts (WAC)—1:1,000,000—Provide a standard series of aeronautical charts covering land areas of the world at a size and scale convenient for navigation by moderate speed aircraft. Topographic information includes cities and towns, principal roads, railroads, distinctive landmarks, drainage, and relief. Aeronautical information includes visual and radio aids to navigation, airports, airways, restricted areas, obstructions, and other pertinent data.
4. En Route Low Altitude Charts—Provide aeronautical information for en route instrument navigation (IFR) in the low altitude stratum. Information includes the portrayal of airways, limits of controlled airspace, position identification and frequencies of radio aids, selected airports, minimum en route and minimum obstruction clearance altitudes, airway distances, reporting points, restricted areas, and related data. Area charts which are a part of this series furnish terminal data at a large scale in congested areas.
5. En Route High Altitude Charts—Provide aeronautical information for en route instrument navigation (IFR) in the high altitude stratum. Information includes the portrayal of jet routes, identification and frequencies of radio aids, selected airports, distances, time zones, special use airspace, and related information.
6. Area Navigation (RNAV) High Altitude Charts—Provide aeronautical information for en route IFR navigation for high altitude air routes established for aircraft equipped with RNAV systems. Information includes portrayal of RNAV routes, waypoints, track angles, changeover points, distances, selected navigational aids and airports, special use airspace, oceanic routes, and transitional information.
7. Instrument Approach Procedures (IAP) Charts—Portray the aeronautical data which is required to execute an instrument approach to an airport. These charts depict the procedures, including all related data, and the airport diagram. Each procedure is designated for use with a specific type of electronic navigation system including NDB, TACAN, VOR, ILS, and RNAV. These charts are identified by the type of navigational aid(s) which provide final approach guidance.
8. Standard Instrument Departure (SID) Charts—Designed to expedite clearance delivery and to facilitate transition between take-off and en route operations. Each SID procedure is presented as a separate chart and may serve a single airport or more than one airport in a given geographical location.
9. Standard Terminal Arrival (STAR) Charts—Designated to expedite air traffic control arrival route procedures and to facilitate transition between en route and instrument approach operations. Each STAR procedure is presented as a separate chart and may serve a single airport or more than one airport in a given geographical location.
10. Airport Taxi Charts—Designed to expedite the efficient and safe flow of ground traffic at an airport. These charts are identified by the official airport name, e.g., Washington National Airport.

ICAO-AERONAUTICAL CHART-A representation of a portion of the earth, its culture and relief, specifically designated to meet the requirements of air navigation.

AFFIRMATIVE—Yes.

AIR CARRIER DISTRICT OFFICE/ACDO—AN FAA field office serving an assigned geographical area, staffed with Flight Standards personnel serving the aviation industry and the general public, on matters related to the certification and operation of scheduled air carriers and other large aircraft operations.

AIRCRAFT—Device/s that are used or intended to be used for flight in the air and when used in air traffic control terminology may include the flight crew.

ICAO—AIRCRAFT—Any machine that can derive support in the atmosphere from the reactions of the air other than the reactions of the air against the earth's surface.

AIRCRAFT APPROACH CATEGORY—A grouping of aircraft based on a speed of 1.3 V_{SO} (at maximum certificated landing weight), or on maximum certificated landing weight. V_{SO} and the maximum certificated landing weight are those values as established for the aircraft by the certificating authority of the country of registry. If an aircraft falls into two categories, it is placed in the higher of the two. The categories are as follows:
1. Category A—Speed less than 91 knots; weight less than 30,001 pounds.
2. Category B—Speed 91 knots or more but less than

121 knots; weight 30,001 pounds or more but less than 60,001 pounds.

3. Category C—Speed 121 knots or more but less than 141 knots; weight 60,001 pounds or more but less than 150,001 pounds.

4. Category D—Speed 141 knots or more but less than 166 knots; weight 150,001 pounds or more.

5. Category E—Speed 166 knots or more; any weight.

(Refer to FAR Parts 1 and 97)

AIRCRAFT CLASSES—For the purposes of Wake Turbulence Separation Minima, ATC classifies aircraft as Heavy, Large and Small as follows:

1. Heavy—Aircraft capable of takeoff weights of 300,000 pounds or more whether or not they are operating at this weight during a particular phase of flight.

2. Large—Aircraft of more than 12,500 pounds, maximum certificated takeoff weight, up to 300,000 pounds.

3. Small—Aircraft of 12,500 pounds or less, maximum certificated takeoff weight. (Refer to AIM)

AIR DEFENSE EMERGENCY—A military emergency condition declared by a designated authority. This condition exists when an attack upon the continental U.S., Alaska, Canada, or U.S. installations in Greenland by hostile aircraft or missiles is considered probable, is imminent, or is taking place. (Refer to AIM)

AIR DEFENSE IDENTIFICATION ZONE/ADIZ—The area of airspace over land or water, extending upward from the surface, within which the ready identification, the location, and the control of aircraft are required in the interest of national security.

1. Domestic Air Defense Identification Zone—an ADIZ within the United States along an international boundary of the United States.

2. Coastal Air Defense Identification Zone—an ADIZ over the coastal waters of the United States.

3. Distant Early Warning Identification Zone (DEWIZ)—an ADIZ over the coastal waters of the State of Alaska.

ADIZ locations, and operating and flight plan requirements for civil aircraft operations are specified in FAR Part 99. (Refer to AIM)

AIRMAN'S INFORMATION MANUAL/AIM—A publication containing Basic Flight Information and ATC Procedures designed primarily as a pilot's instructional manual for use in the National Airspace System of the United States.

ICAO—AERONAUTICAL INFORMATION PUBLICATION—A publication issued by or with the authority of a state and containing aeronautical information of a lasting character essential to air navigation.

AIRMET/AIRMAN'S METEOROLOGICAL INFORMATION—Inflight weather advisories which cover moderate icing, moderate turbulence, sustained winds of 30 knots or more within 2,000 feet of the surface and the initial onset of phenomena producing extensive areas of visibilities below 3 miles or ceilings less than 1,000 feet. It concerns weather phenomena which are of operational interest to all aircraft and potentially hazardous to aircraft having limited capability because of lack of equipment, instrumentation or pilot qualifications. It concerns weather of less severity than SIGMETs or convective SIGMETs. (See Convective SIGMETs or SIGMETs) (Refer to AIM)

AIR NAVIGATION FACILITY—Any facility used in, available for use in, or designed for use in, aid of air navigation, including landing areas, lights, any apparatus or equipment for disseminating weather information, for signaling, for radio-directional finding, or for radio or other electrical communication, and any other structure or mechanism having a similar purpose for guiding or controlling flight in the air or the landing and takeoff of aircraft. (See Navigation Aid)

AIRPORT—An area of land or water that is used or intended to be used for the landing and takeoff of aircraft, and includes its buildings and facilities, if any.

AIRPORT ADVISORY AREA—The area within five statute miles of an airport not served by a control tower, i.e., there is no tower or the tower is not in operation, on which is located a Flight Service Station. (See Airport Advisory Service) (Refer to AIM)

AIRPORT ADVISORY SERVICE/AAS—A service provided by Flight Service Stations at airports not served by a control tower. This service consists of providing information to arriving and departing aircraft concerning wind direction and speed, favored runway, altimeter setting, pertinent known traffic, pertinent known field conditions, airport taxi routes and traffic patterns, and authorized instrument approach procedures. This information is advisory in nature and does not constitute an ATC clearance. (See Airport Advisory Area)

AIRPORT ELEVATION/FIELD ELEVATION—The highest point of an airport's usable runways measured in feet from mean sea level. (See Touchdown Zone Elevation)

ICAO—AERODROME ELEVATION—The elevation of the highest point of the landing area.

AIRPORT/FACILITY DIRECTORY—A publication designed primarily as a pilot's operational manual containing all airports, seaplane bases and heliports open to the public; including communications data, navigational facilities and certain special notices and procedures. This publication is issued in seven volumes according to geographical area.

AIRPORT INFORMATION DESK/AID—An airport unmanned facility designed for pilot self-service briefing, flight planning, and filing of flight plans. (Refer to AIM)

AIRPORT LIGHTING—Various lighting aids that may be installed on an airport. Types of airport lighting include:

1. Approach Light System/ALS—An airport lighting facility which provides visual guidance to landing aircraft by radiating light beams in a directional pattern by which the pilot aligns the aircraft with the extended centerline of the runway on his final approach for landing.

   Condenser-Discharge Sequential Flashing Lights/Sequenced Flashing Lights may be installed in conjunction with the ALS at some airports.

   Types of Approach Light Systems are:

   a. ALSF-I—Approach Light System with Sequenced Flashing Lights in ILS Cat-1 configuration,

   b. ALSF-II—Approach Light System with Sequenced Flashing Lights in ILS Cat-II configuration,

   c. SSALF—Simplified Short Approach Light System with Runway Alignment Indicator Lights,

   d. SSALR—Simplified Short Approach Light System with Runway Alignment Indicator Lights,

   e. MALSF—Medium Intensity Approach Light System with Sequenced Flashing Lights,

   f. MALSR—Medium Intensity Approach Light System with Runway Alignment Indicator Lights,

   g. LDIN—Sequenced Flashing Lead-in Lights,

   h. RAIL—Runway Alignment Indicator Lights (Sequenced Flashing Lights which are installed only in combination with other light systems).

2. Runway Lights/Runway Edge Lights—Lights having a prescribed angle of emission used to define the lateral limits of a runway. Runway lights are uniformly spaced at intervals of approximately 200 feet, and the intensity may be controlled or preset.

3. Touchdown Zone Lighting—Two rows of transverse light bars located symmetrically about the runway centerline normally at 100 foot intervals. The basic system extends 3,000 feet along the runway.

4. Runway Centerline Lighting—Flush centerline lights spaced at 50-foot intervals beginning 75 feet from the landing threshold and extending to within 75 feet of the opposite end of the runway.

5. Threshold Lights—Fixed green lights arranged symmetrically left and right of the runway centerline, identifying the runway threshold.

6. Runway End Identifier Lights/REIL—Two synchronized flashing lights, one on each side of the runway threshold, which provide rapid and positive identification of the approach end of a particular runway.

7. Visual Approach Slope Indicator/VASI—An airport lighting facility providing vertical visual approach slope guidance to aircraft during approach to landing by radiating a directional pattern of high intensity red and white focused light beams which indicate to the pilot that he is "on path" if he sees red/white, "above path" if white/white, and "below path" if red/red. Some airports serving large aircraft have three-bar VASIs which provide two visual glide paths to the same runway.

8. Boundary Lights—Lights defining the perimeter of an airport or landing area. (Refer to AIM)

AIRPORT ROTATING BEACON—A visual NAVAID operated at many airports. At civil airports aoternating white and green flashes indicate the location of the airport. At military airports, the beacons flash alternately white and green, but are differentiated from civil beacons by dualpeaked (two quick) white flashes between the green flashes. (See Special VFR Operations, Instrument Flight Rules) (Refer to AIM Rotating Beacons)

ICAO—AERODROME BEACON—Aeronautical beacon used to indicate the location of an aerodrome.

AIRPORT SURFACE DETECTION EQUIPMENT/ASDE—Radar equipment specifically designed to detect all principal features on the surface of an airport, including aircraft and vehicular traffic and to present the entire image on a radar indicator console in the control tower. Used to augment visual observation by tower personnel of aircraft and/or vehicular movements on runways and taxiways.

AIRPORT SURVEILLANCE RADAR/ASR—Approach control radar used to detect and display an aircraft's position in the terminal area. ASR provides range and azimuth information but does not provide elevation data. Coverage of the ASR can extend up to 60 miles.

AIRPORT TRAFFIC AREA—Unless otherwise specifically designated in FAR Part 93, that airspace within a horizontal radius of 5 statute miles from the geographical center of any airport at which a control tower is operating, extending from the surface up to, but not including, an altitude of 3,000 feet above the elevation of the airport. Unless otherwise authorized or required by ATC, no person may operate an aircraft within an airport traffic area except for the purpose of landing at, or taking off from, an airport within that area. ATC authorizations may be given as individual approval of specific operations or may be contained in written agreements between airport users and the tower concerned. (Refer to FAR Parts 1 and 91)

AIRPORT TRAFFIC CONTROL SERVICE—A service provided by a control tower for aircraft operating on the movement area and in the vicinity of an airport. (See Movement Area, Tower)

ICAO—AERODROME CONTROL SERVICE—Air traffic control service for aerodrome traffic.

AIR ROUTE SURVEILLANCE RADAR/ARSR—Air route traffic control center (ARTCC) radar, used primarily to detect and display an aircraft's position while en route between terminal areas. The ARSR enables controllers to provide radar air traffic control service when aircraft are within the ARSR coverage. In some instances, ARSR may enable an ARTCC to provide terminal radar services similar to, but usually more limited, than those provided by a radar approach control.

AIR ROUTE TRAFFIC CONTROL CENTER/ARTCC—A facility established to provide air traffic control service to aircraft operating on IFR flight plans within controlled airspace and principally during the en route phase of flight. When equipment capabilities and controller workload permit, certain advisory/assistance services may be provided to VFR aircraft. (See NAS Stage A, En Route Air Traffic Control Service) (Refer to AIM)

AIRSPEED—The speed of an aircraft relative to its surrounding air mass. The unqualified term "airspeed" means one of the following:

1. Indicated Airspeed—The speed shown on the aircraft airspeed indicator. This is the speed used in pilot/controller communications under the general term "airspeed." (Refer to FAR Part 1)

2. True Airspeed—The airspeed of an aircraft relative to undisturbed air. Used primarily in flight planning and en route portion of flight. When used in pilot/controller communications, it is referred to as "true airspeed" and not shortened to "airspeed."

AIRSTART—The starting of an aircraft engine while the aircraft is airborne, preceded by engine shutdown during training flights or by actual engine failure.

AIR TRAFFIC—Aircraft operating in the air or on an airport surface, exclusive of loading ramps and parking areas.

ICAO—AIR TRAFFIC—All aircraft in flight or operating on the maneuvering area of an aerodrome.

AIR TRAFFIC CLEARANCE/ATC CLEARANCE—An authorization by air traffic control, for the purpose of preventing collision between known aircraft, for an aircraft to proceed under specified traffic conditions within controlled airspace. (See ATC Instructions)

ICAO—AIR TRAFFIC CONTROL CLEARANCE—Authorization for an aircraft to proceed under conditions specified by an air traffic control unit.

AIR TRAFFIC CONTROL/ATC—A service operated by appropriate authority to promote the safe, orderly, and expeditious flow of air traffic.

ICAO—AIR TRAFFIC CONTROL SERVICE—A service provided for the purpose of:
1. Preventing collisions:
   a. Between aircraft, and
   b. On the maneuvering area between aircraft and obstructions, and
2. Expediting and maintaining an orderly flow of air traffic.

AIR TRAFFIC CONTROL SERVICE—(See Air Traffic Control)

AIR TRAFFIC CONTROL SPECIALIST/CONTROLLER—A person authorized to provide air traffic control service. (See Air Traffic Control Service, Flight Service Station)

ICAO—CONTROLLER—A person authorized to provide air traffic control service.

AIR TRAFFIC CONTROL SYSTEMS COMMAND CENTER/ATCSCC—An air traffic service facility consisting of four operational units.

1. Central Flow Control Function/CFCF—Responsible for coordination and approval of all major intercenter flow control restrictions on a system basis in order to obtain maximum utilization of the airspace. (See Quota Flow Control, Fuel Advisory Departure)

2. Central Altitude Reservation Function/CARF—Responsible for coordinating, planning, and approving special user requirements under the Altitude Reservation (ALTRV) concept. (See Altitude Reservation)

3. Airport Reservation Office/ARO—Responsible for approving IFR flights at designated high density traffic airports (John F. Kennedy, LaGuardia, O'Hare, and Washington National) during specified hours. (Refer to FAR Part 93; Airport/Facility Directory)

4. ATC Contingency Command Post—A facility which enables the FAA to manage the ATC system when significant portions of the system's capabilities have been lost or are threatened.

AIRWAY BEACON—Used to mark airway segments in remote mountain areas. The light flashes Morse Code to identify the beacon site. (Refer to AIM)

AIRWAY/FEDERAL AIRWAY—A control area or portion thereof established in the form of a corridor, the centerline of which is defined by radio navigational aids. (Refer to FAR Part 71; AIM)

ICAO—AIRWAY—A control area or portion thereof established in the form of corridor equipped with radio navigational aids.

ALERT AREA—(See Special Use Airspace)

ALERT NOTICE/ALNOT—A message sent by a flight Service Station (FSS) or Air Route Traffic Control Center (ARTCC) that requests an extensive communication search for overdue, unreported, or missing aircraft.

ALPHA-NUMERIC DISPLAY/DATA BLOCK—Letters and numerals used to show identification, altitude, beacon code, and other information concerning a target on a radar display. (See Automated Radar Terminal Systems, NAS Stage A)

ALTERNATE AIRPORT—An airport at which an aircraft may land if a landing at the intended airport becomes inadvisable.

ICAO—ALTERNATE AERODROME—An aerodrome specified in the flight plan to which a flight may proceed when it becomes inadvisable to land at the aerodrome of intended landing.

ALTIMETER SETTING—The barometric pressure reading used to adjust a pressure altimeter for variations in existing atmospheric pressure or to the standard altimeter setting (29.92) (Refer to FAR Part 91; AIM)

ALTITUDE—The height of a level, point, or object measured in feet Above Ground Level (AGL) or from Mean Sea Level (MSL). (See Flight Level)

1. MSL Altitude—Altitude, expressed in feet measured from mean sea level.

2. AGL Altitude—Altitude expressed in feet measured above ground level.

3. Indicated Altitude—The altitude as shown by an altimeter. On a pressure or barometric altimeter it is altitude as shown uncorrected for instrument error and uncompensated for variation from standard atmospheric conditions.

ICAO—ALTITUDE—The vertical distance of a level, a point, or an object considered as a point, measured from mean sea level.

ALTITUDE READOUT/AUTOMATIC ALTITUDE REPORT—An aircraft's altitude, transmitted via the Mode C transponder feature, that is visually displayed in 100-foot increments on a radar scope having readout capability. (See Automated Radar Terminal Systems, NAS Stage A, Alpha Numeric Display) (Refer to AIM)

ALTITUDE RESERVATION/ALTRV—Airspace utilization under prescribed conditions normally employed for the mass movement of aircraft or other special user requirements which cannot otherwise be accomplished. ALTRVs are approved by the appropriate FAA facility. (See Air Traffic Control Systems Command Center)

ALTITUDE RESTRICTION—An altitude or altitudes stated in the order flow, which are to be maintained until reaching a specific point or time. Altitude restrictions may be issued by ATC due to traffic, terrain or other airspace considerations.

ALTITUDE RESTRICTIONS ARE CANCELLED—Adherence to previously imposed altitude restrictions is no longer required during a climb or descent.

APPROACH CLEARANCE—Authorization by ATC for a pilot to conduct an instrument approach. The type of instrument approach for which clearance and other pertinent information is provided in the approach clearance when required. (See Instrument Approach Procedure, Cleared for Approach) (Refer to AIM FAR Part 91)

APPROACH CONTROL/APPROACH CONTROL FACILITY—A terminal air traffic control facility providing approach control service. (See Approach Control Service, Tower, Terminal Radar Approach Control, Radar Approach Control, Radar Air traffic Control Facility.)

APPROACH CONTROL SERVICE—Air traffic control service provided by an approach control facility for arriving and departing VFR/IFR aircraft and, on occasion, en route aircraft. At some airports not served by an approach control facility, the ARTCC provides limited approach control service. (Refer to AIM)

ICAO—APPROACH CONTROL SERVICE—Air Traffic service for arriving or departing controlled flights.

APPROACH GATE—The point on the final approach course which is 1 mile from the final approach fix on the side away from the airport or 5 miles from landing threshold, whichever is farther from the landing threshold. This is an imaginary point used within ATC as a basis for final approach course interception for aircraft being vectored to the final approach course.

APPROACH LIGHT SYSTEM—(See Airport Lighting)

APPROACH SEQUENCE—The order in which aircraft are positioned while on approach or awaiting approach clearance. (See Landing Sequence)

ICAO—APPROACH SEQUENCE—The order in which two or more aircraft are cleared to approach to land at the aerodrome.

APPROACH SPEED—The recommended speed contained in aircraft manuals used by pilots when making an approach to landing. This speed will vary for different segments of an approach as well as for aircraft weight and configuration.

APRON/RAMP—A defined area, on a land airport, intended to accommodate aircraft for purposes of loading or unloading passengers or cargo, refueling, parking or maintenance. With regard to seaplanes, a ramp is used for access to the apron from the water.

ICAO—APRON—A defined area, on a land aerodrome, intended to accommodate aircraft for purposes of loading or unloading passengers or cargo, refueling, parking or maintenance.

ARC—The track over the ground of an aircraft flying at a constant distance from a navigational aid by reference to distance measuring equipment (DME).

AREA NAVIGATION/RNAV—A method of navigation that permits aircraft operations on any desired course within the coverage of station-referenced navigation signals or within the limits of self-contained system capability. (Refer to AIM, FAR Part 71)

1. Area Navigation Low Route—An area navigation route within the airspace extending upward from 1,200 feet above the surface of the earth to, but not including 18,000 feet MSL.

2. Area Navigation High Route—An area navigation route within the airspace extending upward from and including 18,000 feet MLS to flight level 450.

3. Random Area Navigation Routes/Random RNAV Routes—Direct routes, based on area navigation capability, between waypoints defined in terms of degree/distance fixes or offset from published or established routes/airways at specified distance and direction.

4. RNAV Waypoint/W/P—A predetermined geographical position used for route or instrument approach definition or progress reporting purposes that is defined relative to a VORTAC station position.

ICAO—AREA NAVIGATION/RNAV—A method of navigation which permits aircraft operation on any desired flight path within the coverage of station-referenced navigation aids or within the limits of the capability of self-contained aids or a combination of these.

ARMY AVIATION FLIGHT INFORMATION BULLETIN/USAFIB—A bulletin that provides air operation data covering Army, National Guard, and Army Reserve aviation activities.

ARMY RADAR APPROACH CONTROL/ARAC—An air traffic control facility located at a U.S. Army Airport utilizing surveillance and normally precision approach radar and air/ground communications equipment to provide approach control services to aircraft, departing or transiting the airspace controlled by the facility. Service may be provided to both civil and military airports. Similar to TRACON (FAA), RAPCON (USAF) and RATCF (Navy). (See Approach Control, Approach Control Service, Departure Control)

ARRESTING SYSTEM—A safety device consisting of two major components, namely, engaging or catching devices, and energy absorption devices for the purpose of arresting both tail hook and/or non-tail hook equipped aircraft. It is used to prevent aircraft from overrunning runways when the aircraft cannot be stopped after landing or during aborted takeoff. Arresting systems have various names, e.g., arresting gear, hook, device, wire, barrier cable. (See Abort) (Refer to AIM)

ARRIVAL TIME—The time an aircraft touches down on arrival.

ARTCC—(See Air Route Traffic Control Center)

ASR APPROACH—(See Surveillance Approach)

ATC ADVISES—Used to prefix a message of noncontrol information when it is relayed to an aircraft by other than an air traffic controller. (See Advisory)

ATC ASSIGNED AIRSPACE/ATCAA—Airspace of defined vertical/lateral limits, assigned by ATC, for the purpose of providing air traffic segregation between the specified activities being conducted within the assigned airspace and other IFR air traffic. (See Military Operations Area, Alert Area)

ATC CLEARANCE—(See Air Traffic Clearance)

ATC CLEARS—Used to prefix an ATC clearance when it is relayed to an aircraft by other than an air traffic controller.

ATC INSTRUCTION—Directives issued by air traffic control for the purpose of requiring a pilot to take specific actions; e.g., "Turn left heading two five zero", "Go around," "Clear the runway." (Refer to FAR Part 91)

ATCRBS—(See Radar)

ATC REQUESTS—Used to prefix an ATC request when it is relayed to an aircraft by other than an air traffic controller.

AUTOMATED RADAR TERMINAL SYSTEMS/ARTS—The generic term of the ultimate in functional capability afforded by several automation systems. Each differs in functional capabilities and equipment. ARTS plus a suffix Roman Numeral denotes a specific system. A following letter indicates a major modification to that system. In general, an ARTS displays for the terminal controller aircraft identification, flight plan data, other flight associated information, e.g., altitude and speed, and aircraft position symbols in conjunction with his radar presentation. Normal radar co-exists with the alphanumeric display. In addition to enhancing visualization of the air traffic situation, ARTS facilitate intra/inter-facility transfer and coordination of flight information. These capabilities are enabled by specially designed computers and subsystems tailored to the radar and communications equipments and operational requirements of each automated facility. Modular design permits adoption of improvements in computer software and electronic technologies as they become available while retaining the characteristics unique to each system.

1. ARTS IA—The functional capabilities and equipment of the New York Common IFR Room Terminal Automation System. It tracks primary as well as secondary targets derived from two radar sources. The aircraft targets are displayed on a radar type console by means of an alphanumeric generator. Aircraft identity is depicted in association with the appropriate aircraft target. When the aircraft is equipped with an encoded altimeter (Mode C), its altitude is also displayed. The system can exchange flight plan information with the ARTCC.

2. ARTS II—A programmable non-tracking computer aided display subsystem capable of modular expansion. ARTS II systems provide a level of automated air traffic control capability at terminals having low to medium activity. Flight identification and altitude may be associated with the display of secondary radar targets. Also, flight plan information may be exchanged between the terminal and ARTCC.

3. ARTS III—The Beacon Tracking Level (BRL) of the modular programmable automated radar terminal system in use at medium to high activity terminals. ARTS III detects, tracks and predicts secondary radar derived aircraft targets. These are displayed by means of computer generated symbols and alphanumeric characters depicting flight identification, aircraft altitude, ground speed and flight plan data. Although it does not track primary targets, they are displayed coincident with the secondary radar as well as the symbols and alphanumerics. The system has the capability of communicating with ARTCCs and other ARTS III facilities.

4. ARTS IIIA—The Radar Tracking and Beacon Tracking Level (RT&BTL) of the modular, programmable automated radar terminal system. ARTS IIIA detects, tracks and predicts primary as well as secondary radar derived aircraft targets. An enhancement of the ARTS III, this more sophisticated computer driven system will eventually replace the ARTS IA system and upgrade about half of the existing ARTS III systems. The enhanced system will provide improved tracking, continuous data recording and fail-soft capabilities.

AUTOMATIC ALTITUDE REPORTING—That function of a transponder which responds to Mode C interrogations by transmitting the aircraft's altitude in 100-foot increments.

AUTOMATIC CARRIER LANDING SYSTEM/ACLS—U.S. Navy final approach equipment consisting of precision tracking radar coupled to a computer data link to provide continuous information to the aircraft, monitoring capability to the pilot and a backup approach system.

AUTOMATIC DIRECTION FINDER/ADF—An aircraft radio navigation system which senses and indicates the direction to a L/MF nondirectional radio beacon (NDB) ground transmitter. Direction is indicated to the pilot as a magnetic bearing or as a relative bearing to the longitudinal axis of the aircraft depending on the type of indicator installed in the aircraft. In certain applications, such as military, ADF operations may be based on airborne and ground transmitters in the VHF/UHF frequency spectrum. (See Bearing, Nondirectional Beacon)

AUTOMATIC TERMINAL INFORMATION SERVICE/ATIS—The continuous broadcast of recorded noncontrol information in selected terminal areas. Its purpose is to improve controller effectiveness and to relieve frequency congestion by automating the repetitive transmission of essential but routine information, e.g., "Los Angeles Information Alpha. 1300 Greenwich Weather, measured ceiling 2000 overcast, visibility three, haze, smoke, temperature seven one, wind two five zero at five, altimeter two niner niner six. ILS runway two five left approach in use, runway two five right closed, advise you have Alpha." (Refer to AIM)

ICAO—AUTOMATIC TERMINAL INFORMATION SERVICE—The provision of current, routine information to arriving and departing aircraft by means of continuous and repetitive broadcasts throughout the day or a specified portion of the day.

AUTOROTATION—A rotorcraft flight condition in which the lifting rotor is driven entirely by action of the air when the rotorcraft is in motion.

1. Autorotative Landing/Touchdown Autorotation—used by a pilot to indicate that he will be landing without applying power to the rotor.

2. Low Level Autorotation—Commences at an altitude well below the traffic pattern, usually below 100 feet AGL and is used primarily for tactical military training.

3. 180 degrees Autorotation—Initiated from a downwind heading and is commenced well inside the normal traffic pattern. "Go around" may not be possible during the latter part of this maneuver.

AVIATION WEATHER SERVICE—A service provided by the National Weather Service (NWS) and FAA which collects and disseminates pertinent weather information for pilots, aircraft operators and ATC. Available aviation weather reports and forecasts are displayed at each NWS office and FAA FSS. (See En Route Flight Advisory Service, Transcribed Weather Broadcasts, Scheduled Weather Broadcasts, Inflight Weather Advisories, Pilots Automatic Telephone Weather Answering Service) (Refer to AIM)

BASE LEG—(See Traffic Pattern)

BEACON—(See Radar, Non Directional Beacon, Marker Beacon, Airport Rotating Beacon, Aeronautical Beacon, Airway Beacon)

BEARING—The horizontal direction to or from any point, usually measured clockwise from true north, magnetic north or some other reference point, through 360 degrees. (See Nondirectional Beacon)

BELOW MINIMUMS—Weather conditions below the minimums prescribed by regulation for the particular action involved, e.g., landing minimums, takeoff minimums.

BLAST FENCE—A barrier that is used to divert or dissipate jet or propeller blast.

BLIND SPEED—The rate of departure or closing of a target relative to the radar antenna at which cancellation of the primary radar target by moving target indicator (MTI) circuits in the radar equipment causes a reduction or complete loss of signal.

ICAO—BLIND VELOCITY—The radial velocity of a moving target such that the target is not seen on primary radars fitted with certain forms of fixed echo suppression.

BLIND SPOT/BLIND ZONE—An area from which radio transmissions and/or radar echoes cannot be received. The term is also used to describe portions of the airport not visible from the control tower.

BOUNDARY LIGHTS—(See Airport Lighting)

BRAKING ACTION (GOOD, MEDIUM OR FAIR, POOR, NIL)—A report of conditions on the airport movement area providing a pilot with a degree/quality of braking that he might expect. Braking action is reported in terms of good, medium (or fair), poor or nil. (See Runway Condition Reading)

BROADCAST—Transmission of information for which an acknowledgement is not expected.

ICAO—BROADCAST—A transmission of information relating to air navigation that is not addressed to a specific station or stations.

CALL-UP—Initial voice contact between a facility and an aircraft, using the identification of the unit being called and the unit initiating the call. (Refer to AIM)

CARDINAL ALTITUDES OR FLIGHT LEVELS—"Odd" or "Even" thousand-foot altitudes or flight levels; e.g., 500, 6000, 7000, FL 250, FL 260, FL 270. (See Altitude, Flight Levels)

CEILING—The heights above the earth's surface of the lowest layer of clouds or obscuring phenomena that is reported as "broken," "overcast," or "obscuration," and not classified as "thin" or "partial".

ICAO—CEILING—The height above the ground or water of the base of the lowest layer of cloud below 6000 meters (20,000 feet) covering more than half the sky.

CELESTIAL NAVIGATION—The determination of geographical position by reference to celestial bodies. Normally used in aviation as a secondary means of position determination.

CENTER—(See Air Route Traffic Control Center)

CENTER'S AREA—The specified airspace within which an air route traffic control center (ARTCC) provides air traffic control and advisory service. (See Air Route Traffic Control Center) (Refer to AIM)

CHAFF—Thin, narrow metallic reflectors of various lengths and frequency responses, used to reflect radar energy. These reflectors when dropped from aircraft and allowed to drift downward result in large targets on the radar display.

CHASE/CHASE AIRCRAFT—An aircraft flown in proximity to another aircraft normally to observe its performance during training or testing.

CIRCLE TO LAND MANEUVER/CIRCLING MANEUVER—A maneuver initiated by the pilot to align the aircraft with a runway for landing when a straight-in landing from an instrument approach is not possible or is not desirable. This maneuver is made only after ATC authorization has been obtained and the pilot has established required visual reference to the airport (See Circle to Runway, Landing Minimums) (Refer to AIM)

CIRCLE TO RUNWAY (RUNWAY NUMBERED)—Used by ATC to inform the pilot that he must circle to land because the runway in use is other than the runway aligned with the instrument approach procedure. When the direction of the circling maneuver in relation to the airport/runways is required, the controller will state the direction (eight cardinal compass points) and specify a left or right downwind or base leg as appropriate, e.g., "Cleared VOR Runway three six approach circle to Runway two two" or "Circle northwest of the airport for a right downwind to Runway two two." (See Circle to Land maneuver, Landing Minimums) (Refer to AIM)

CIRCLING APPROACH—(See Circle-to-land Maneuver)

CIRCLING MINIMA—(See Landing Minimums)

CLEAR-AIR TURBULENCE/CAT—Turbulence encountered in air where no clouds are present. This term is commonly applied to high-level turbulence associated with wind shear. CAT is often encountered in the vicinity of the jet stream. (See Wind Shear, Jet Stream)

CLEARANCE—(See Air Traffic Clearance)

CLEARANCE LIMIT—The fix, point, or location to which an aircraft is cleared when issued an air traffic clearance.

ICAO—CLEARANCE LIMIT—The point of which an aircraft is granted an air traffic control clearance.

CLEARANCE VOID IF NOT OFF BY (TIME)—Used by ATC to advise an aircraft that the departure clearance is automatically cancelled if takeoff is not made prior to a specified time. The pilot must obtain a new clearance or cancel his IFR flight plan if not off by the specified time.

ICAO—CLEARANCE VOID TIME—A time specified by an air traffic control unit at which a clearance ceases to be valid unless the aircraft concerned has already taken action to comply therewith.

CLEARED AS FILED—Means the aircraft is cleared to proceed in accordance with the route of flight filed in the flight plan. This clearance does not include the altitude, SID, or SID Transition. (See Request Full Route Clearance) (Refer to AIM)

CLEARED FOR (Type Of) APPROACH—ATC authorization for an aircraft to execute a specific instrument approach procedure to an airport; e.g., "Cleared for ILS runway three six approach." (See Instrument Approach Procedure, Approach Clearance) (Refer to AIM; FAR Part 91)

CLEARED FOR APPROACH—ATC authorization for an aircraft to execute any standard or special instrument approach procedure for that airport. Normally, an aircraft will be cleared for a specific instrument approach procedure. (See Instrument Approach Procedure, Cleared for (type of) Approach) (Refer to AIM; FAR Part 91)

CLEARED FOR TAKE-OFF—ATC authorization for an aircraft to depart. It is predicated on known traffic and known physical airport conditions.

CLEARED FOR THE OPTION—ATC authorization for an aircraft to make a touch-and-go, low approach, missed approach, stop and go, or full stop landing at the discretion of the pilot. It is normally used in training so that an instructor can evaluate a student's performance under changing situations. (See Option Approach) (Refer to AIM)

CLEARED THROUGH—ATC authorization for an aircraft to make intermediate stops at specified airports without refiling a flight plan while en route to the clearance limit.

CLEARED TO LAND—ATC authorization for an aircraft to land. It is predicated on known traffic and known physical airport conditions.

CLEARWAY—An area beyond the takeoff runway under the control of airport authorities within which terrain or fixed obstacles may not extend above specified limits. These areas may be required for certain turbine powered operators and the size and upward slope of the clearway will differ depending on when the aircraft was certificated. (Refer to FAR Part 1)

CLIMBOUT—That portion of flight operation between takeoff and the initial cruising altitude.

CLIMB TO VFR—ATC authorization for an aircraft to climb to VFR conditions within a control zone when the only weather limitation is restricted visibility. The aircraft must remain clear of clouds while climbing to VFR. (See Special VFR) (Refer to AIM)

CLOSED RUNWAY—A runway that is unusable for aircraft operations. Only the airport management/military operations office can close a runway.

CLOSED TRAFFIC—Successive operations involving takeoffs and landings or low approaches where the aircraft does not exit the traffic pattern.

CLUTTER—In radar operations, clutter refers to the reception and visual display of radar returns caused by precipitation, chaff, terrain, numerous aircraft targets, or other phenomena. Such returns may limit or preclude ATC from providing services based on radar. (See Ground Clutter, Chaff, Precipitation, Target)

ICAO—Radar Clutter—The visual indication on a radar display of unwanted signals.

COASTAL FIX—A navigation aid or intersection where an aircraft transitions between the domestic route structure and the oceanic route structure.

CODES/TRANSPONDER CODES—The number assigned to a particular multiple pulse reply signal transmitted by the transponder. (See Discrete Code)

COMBINED CENTER-RAPCON/CERAP—An air traffic control facility which combines the functions of an ARTCC and a RAPCON. (See Air Route Traffic Control Center/ARTCC, Radar Approach Control/RAPCON).

COMBINED STATION/TOWER/CS/T—An air traffic control facility which combines the functions of a flight service station and an airport traffic control tower. (See Tower, Flight Service Station) (Refer to AIM)

COMMON ROUTE/COMMON PORTION—That segment of a North American route between the inland navigation facility and the coastal fix.

COMPASS LOCATOR—A low power, low or medium frequency (L/MF) radio beacon installed at the site of the outer or middle marker of an instrument landing system (ILS). It can be used for navigation at distances of approximately 15 miles or as authorized in the approach procedure.

1. Outer Compass Locator/LOM—A compass locator installed at the site of the outer marker of an instrument landing system. (See Outer Marker)
2. Middle Compass Locator/LMM—A compass locator installed at the site of the middle marker of an instrument landing system. (See Middle Marker)

ICAO—LOCATOR—An LM/MF NDB used as an aid to final approach.

COMPASS ROSE—A circle, graduated in degrees, printed on some charts or marked on the ground at an airport. It is used as a reference to either true or magnetic direction.

COMPOSITE FLIGHT PLAN—A flight plan which specifies VFR operation for one portion of flight and IFR for another portion. It is primarily used in military operations. (Refer to AIM)

COMPOSITE ROUTE SYSTEM—An organized oceanic route structure, incorporating reduced lateral spacing between routes, in which composite separation is authorized.

COMPOSITE SEPARATION—A method of separating aircraft in a composite route system where, by management of route and altitude assignments, a combination of half the lateral minimum specified for the area concerned and half the vertical minimum is applied.

COMPULSORY REPORTING POINTS—Reporting points which must be reported to ATC. They are designated on aeronautical charts by solid triangles or filed in a flight plan as fixes selected to define direct routes. These points are geographical locations which are defined by navigation aids/fixes. Pilots should discontinue position reporting over compulsory reporting points when informed by ATC that their aicraft is in "radar contact."

CONFLICT ALERT—A function of certain air traffic control automated systems designed to alert radar controllers to existing or pending situations recognized by the program parameters that require his immediate attention/action.

CONSOLAN—A low frequency, long-distance NAVAID used principally for transoceanic navigations.

CONTACT—
1. Establish communications with (followed by the name of the facility and, if appropriate, the frequency to be used).
2. A flight condition wherein the pilot ascertains the attitude of his aircraft and navigates by visual reference to the surface. (See Contact Approach, Radar Contact.)

CONTACT APPROACH—An approach wherein an aircraft on an IFR flight plan, operating clear of clouds with at least 1 mile flight visibility and having an air traffic control authorization, may deviate from the instrument approach procedure and proceed to the airport of destination by visual reference to the surface. This approach will only be authorized when requested by the pilot and the reported ground visibility at the destination is at least 1 statute mile. (Refer to AIM)

CONTERMINOUS U.S.—The forty-eight adjoining states and the District of Columbia.

CONTINENTAL CONTROL AREA—(See Controlled Airspace)

CONTINENTAL UNITED STATES—The 49 states located on the continent of North America and the District of Columbia.

CONTROL AREA—(See Controlled Airspace)

CONTROLLED AIRSPACE—Airspace designated as continental control area, control area, control zone, terminal control area, or transition area within which some or all aircraft may be subject to air traffic control. (Refer to AIM; FAR Part 71)

ICAO—CONTROLLED AIRSPACE—Airspace of defined dimensions within which air traffic control service is provided to controlled flights.

Types of U.S. Controlled Airspace:

1. Continental Control Area—The airspace of the 48 contiguous states, the District of Columbia, and Alaska, excluding the Alaska peninsula west of Long. 160°00'00"W, at and above 14,500 feet MSL, but does not include:
   a. The airspace less than 1,500 feet above the surface of the earth, or
   b. Prohibited and restricted areas, other than the restricted areas listed in FAR Part 71.

2. Control Area—Airspace designated as Colored Federal Airways, VOR Federal Airways, Terminal Control Areas, Additional Control Areas, and Control Area Extensions, but not including the Continental Control Area. Unless otherwise designated, control areas also include the airspace between a segment of a main VOR airway and its associated alternate segments. The vertical extent of the various categories of airspace contained in control areas are defined in FAR Part 71.

   ICAO— Control Area—A controlled airspace extending upward from a specified limit above the earth.

3. Control Zone—Controlled airspace which extends upward from the surface and terminates at the base of the continental control area. Control zones that do not underlie the continental control area have no upper limit. A control zone may include one or more airports and is normally a circular area within a radius of 5 statute miles and any extensions necessary to include instrument approach and departure paths.

   ICAO—Control Zone—A controlled airspace extending upwards from the surface of the earth to a specified upper limit.

4. Terminal Control Area/TCA—Controlled airspace extending upward from the surface or higher to specified altitudes, within which all aircraft are subject to operating rules and pilot and equipment requirements specified in FAR part 91. TCA's are depicted on Sectional, World Aeronautical, En Route Low Altitude, DOD FLIP, and TCA charts. (Refer to FAR Part 91; AIM)

   ICAO—Terminal Control Area— A control area normally established at the confluence of ATS routes in the vicinity of one or more major aerodromes.

5. Transition Area—Controlled airspace extending upward from 700 feet or more above the surface of the earth when designated in conjunction with an airport for which an approved instrument approach procedure has been prescribed or from 1,200 feet or more above the surface of the earth when designated in conjunction with airway route structures or segments. Unless otherwise limited, transition areas terminate at the base of the overlying controlled airspace. Transition areas are designed to contain IFR operations in controlled airspace during portions of the terminal operation and while transiting between the terminal and en route environment.

CONTROLLER—See Air Traffic Control Specialist)

CONTROL SECTOR—An airspace area of defined horizontal and vertical dimensions for which a controller, or group of controllers, has air traffic control responsibility, normally within an air route traffic control center or an approach control facility. Sectors are established based on predominant traffic flows, altitude visory concerning convective weather significant to the safety of all aircraft. Convective SIGMETs are issued for tornadoes, lines of thunderstorms, embedded thunstrata, and controller workload. Pilot-communications during operations within a sector are normally maintained on discrete frequencies assigned to the sector. (See Discrete Frequency)

CONTROL SLASH—A radar beacon slash representing the actual position of the associated aircraft. Normally, the control slash is the one closest to the interrogating radar beacon site. When ARTCC radar is operating in narrowband (digitized) mode, the control slash is converted to a target symbol.

CONTROL ZONE—(See Controlled Airspace)

CONVECTIVE SIGMET/CONVECTIVE SIGNIFICANT METEOROLIGICAL INFORMATION—A weather adderstorms of any intensity level, isolated thunderstorms for intensity level 5 and above, areas of thunderstorms containing intensity level 4 and above, and hail ¾ inch or greater. (See SIGMET and AIRMET) (Refer to AIM)

COORDINATES—The intersection of lines of reference, usually expressed in degrees/minutes/seconds of latitude and longitude, used to determine position or location.

COORDINATION FIX—The fix in relation to which facilities will handoff, transfer control of an aircraft, or coordinate flight progress data. For terminal facilities, it may also serve as a clearance for arriving aircraft.

CORRECTION—An error has been made in the transmission and the correct version follows:

COURSE—

1. The intended direction of flight in the horizontal plane measured in degrees from north.

2. The ILS localizer signal pattern usually specified as front course or back course. (See Bearing, Radial, Instrument Landing Systems)

CRITICAL ENGINE—The engine which, upon failure, would most adversely affect the performance or handling qualities of an aircraft.

CROSS (FIX) AT (ALTITUDE)—Used by ATC when a specific altitude restriction at a specified fix is required.

CROSS (FIX) AT OR ABOVE (ALTITUDE)—Used by ATC when an altitude restriction at a specified fix is required. It does not prohibit the aircraft from crossing the fix at a higher altitude than specified; however, the higher altitude may not be one that will violate a succeeding altitude restriction or altitude assignment. (See Altitude Assignment, Altitude Restriction) (Refer to AIM)

CROSS (FIX) AT OR BELOW (ALTITUDE)—Used by ATC when a maximum crossing altitude at a specific fix is required. It does not prohibit the aircraft from crossing the fix at a lower altitude; however, it must be at or above the minimum IFR altitude. (See Minimum IFR Altitude, Altitude Restriction) (Refer to FAR Part 91)

CROSSWIND—

1. When used concerning the traffic pattern, the word means "crosswind leg." (See Traffic Pattern)

2. When used concerning wind conditions, the word means a wind not parallel to the runway or the path of an aircraft. (See Crosswind Component)

CROSSWIND COMPONENT—The wind component measured in knots at 90 degrees to the longitudinal axis of the runway.

CRUISE—Used in an ATC clearance to authorize a pilot to conduct flight at any altitude from the minimum FIR altitude up to and including the altitude specified in the clearance. The pilot may level off at any intermediate altitude within this block of airspace. Climb/descent within the block may be made at the discretion of the pilot. However, once the pilot starts descent and reports leaving an altitude in the block he may not return to that altitude without additional ATC clearance. Further, it is approval for the pilot to proceed to and make an approach at destination airport and can be used in conjunction with:

1. An airport clearance limit at locations with a standard/special instrument approach procedure. The FARs require that if an instrument letdown to an

airport is necessary the pilot shall make the letdown in accordance with a stand/special instrument approach procedure for that airport, or

2. An airport clearance limit at locations that are within/below/outside controlled airspace and without a standard/special instrument approach procedure. Such a clearance is NOT AUTHORIZATION for the pilot to descend under IFR conditions below the applicable minimum IFR altitude nor does it imply that ATC is exercising control over aircraft in uncontrolled airspace; however, it provides a means for the aircraft to proceed to destination airport, descend, and land in accordance with applicable FARs governing VFR flight operations. Also, this provides search and rescue protection until such time as the IFR flight plan is closed. (See Instrument Approach Procedure)

CRUISING ALTITUDE/LEVEL—An altitude or flight level maintained during en route level flight. This is a constant altitude and should not be confused with a cruise clearance. (See Altitude)

ICAO—CRUISING LEVEL—A level maintained during a significant portion of a flight.

DECISION HEIGHT/DH—With respect to the operation of aircraft, means the height at which a decision must be made during an ILS or PAR instrument approach to either continue the approach or to execute a missed approach.

ICAO—DECISION HEIGHT—A specified height at which a missed approach must be initiated if the required visual reference to continue the approach to land has not been established.

DECODER—The device used to decipher signals received from ATCRBS transponders to effect their display as select codes. (See Codes, Radar)

DEFENSE VISUAL FLIGHT RULES/DVFR—Rules applicable to flights within an ADIZ conducted under the visual flight rules in FAR Part 91. (See Air Defense Identification Zone) (Refer to FAR Part 99)

DELAY INDEFINITE (REASON IF KNOWN) EXPECT APPROACH/FURTHER CLEARANCE (TIME)—Used by ATC to inform a pilot when an accurate estimate of the delay time and the reason for the delay cannot immediately be determined; e.g., a disabled aircraft on the runway, terminal or center area saturation, weather below landing minimums, etc. (See Expect Approach Clearance, Expect Further Clearance)

DEPARTURE CONTROL—A function of an approach control facility providing air traffic control service for departing IFR and, under certain conditions, VFR aircraft. (See Approach Control) (Refer to AIM)

DEPARTURE TIME—The time an aircraft becomes airborne.

DEVIATIONS—

1. A departure from a current clearance, such as an off course maneuver to avoid weather or turbulence.

2. Where specifically authorized in the FAR's and requested by the pilot, ATC may permit pilots to deviate from certain regulations. (Refer to AIM)

DF APPROACH PROCEDURE—used under emergency conditions where another instrument approach procedure cannot be executed. DF guidance for an instrument approach is given by ATC facilities with DF capability. (See DF Guidance, Direction Finder) (Refer to AIM)

DF FIX—The geographical location of an aircraft obtained by one or more direction finders. (See Direction Finder)

DF GUIDANCE/DF STEER—Headings provided to aircraft by facilities equipped with direction finding equipment. These headings, if followed, will lead the aircraft to a predetermined point such as the DF station or an airport. DF guidance is given to aircraft in distress or to other aircraft which request the service. Practice DF guidance is provided when workload permits. (See Direction Finder, DF Fix) (Refer to AIM)

DIRECT—Straight line flight between two navigational

aids, fixes, points or any combination thereof. When used by pilots in describing off-airway routes, points defining direct route segments become compulsory reporting points unless the aircraft is under radar contact.

DIRECTION FINDER/DF/UDF/VDF/UVDF—A radio receiver equipped with a directional sensing antenna used to take bearings on a radio transmitter. Specialized radio direction finders are used in aircraft as air navigation aids. Others are ground based primarily to obtain a "fix" on a pilot requesting orientation assistance or to locate downed aircraft. A location "fix" is established by the intersection of two or more bearing lines plotted on a navigational chart using either two separately located Direction Finders to obtain a fix on an aircraft or by a pilot plotting the bearing indications of his DF on two separately located ground based transmitters both of which can be identified on his chart. UDF's receive signals in the ultra high frequency radio broadcast band; VDFs in the very high frequency band; and UVDFs in both bands. ATC provides DF service at those air traffic control towers and flight service stations listed in Airport/Facility Directory and DOD FLIP IFR En Route Supplement. (See DF Guidance, DF Fix)

DISCRETE CODE/DISCRETE BEACON CODE—As used in the Air Traffic Control Radar Beacon System (ATCRBS), any one of the 4096 selectable Mode 3/A aircraft transponder codes except those ending in zero zero; e.g., discrete codes: 0010, 1201, 2317, 7777; non discrete codes: 0100, 1200, 7700. Non-discrete codes are normally reserved for radar facilities that are not equipped with discrete decoding capability and for other purposes such as emergencies (7700), VFR aircraft (1200), etc. (See Radar) (Refer to AIM)

DISCRETE FREQUENCY—A separate radio frequency for use in direct pilot-controller communications in air traffic control which reduces frequency congestion by controlling the number of aircraft operating on a particular frequency at one time. Discrete frequencies are normally designated for each control sector in en route/terminal ATC facilities. Discrete frequencies are listed in the Airport/Facility Directory, and DOD FLIP IFR En Route Supplement. (See Control Sector)

DISPLACED THRESHOLD—A threshold that is located at a point on the runway other than the designated beginning of the runway. (See Threshold) (Refer to AIM)

DISTANCE MEASURING EQUIPMENT/DME—Equipment (airborne and ground) used to measure, in nautical miles, the slant range distance of an aircraft from the DME navigational aid. (See TACAN, VORTAC)

DME FIX—A geographical position determined by reference to a navigational aid which provides distance and azimuth information. It is defined by a specific distance in nautical miles and a radial or course (i.e., localizer in degrees magnetic from that aid. (See Distance Measuring Equipment/DME, Fix)

DME SEPARATION—Spacing of aircraft in terms of distances (nautical miles) determined by reference to distance measuring equipment (DME) (See Distance Measuring Equipment/DME)

DOD FLIP—Department of Defense Flight Information Publications used for flight planning, en route, and terminal operations. FLIP is produced by the Defense Mapping Agency for world-wide use. United States Government Flight Information Publications (en route charts and instrument approach procedure charts) are incorporated in DOD FLIP for use in the National Airspace System (NAS).

DOWNWIND LEG—(See Traffic Pattern)

DRAG CHUTE—A parachute device installed on certain aircraft which is deployed on landing roll to assist in deceleration of the aircraft.

EMERGENCY LOCATOR TRANSMITTER/ELT—A radio transmitter attached to the aircraft structure which operates from its own power source on 121.5 MHz and 243.0 MHz. It aids in locating downed aircraft by radiating a downward sweeping audio tone, 2-4 times per second. It is designed to function without human action after an accident. (Refer to FAR Part 91; AIM)

EMERGENCY SAFE ALTITUDE—(See Minimum Safe Altitude)

EN ROUTE AIR TRAFFIC CONTROL SERVICES—Air traffic control service provided aircraft on an IFR flight plan, generally by centers, when these aircraft are operating between departure and destination terminal areas. When equipment capabilities and controller workload permit, certain advisory/assistance services may be provided to VFR aircraft. (See NAS Stage A, Air Route Traffic Control Center) (Refer to AIM)

EN ROUTE AUTOMATED RADAR TRACKING SYSTEM/EARTS—An automated radar and radar beacon tracking system. Its functional capabilities and design are essentially the same as the terminal ARTS IIIA system except for the EARTS capability of employing both short-range (ASR) and long-range (ARSR) radars, use of full digital radar displays, and fail-safe design. (See Automated Radar Terminal Systems/ARTS)

EN ROUTE CHARTS—(See Aeronautical Charts)

EN ROUTE DESCENT—Descent from the en route cruising altitude which takes place along the route of flight.

EN ROUTE FLIGHT ADVISORY SERVICE/FLIGHT WATCH—A service specifically designed to provide, upon pilot request, timely weather information pertinent to his type of flight, intended route of flight and altitude. The FSSs providing this service are listed in Airport/Facility Directory—See Flight Watch. (Refer to AIM)

EXECUTE MISSED APPROACH—Instructions issued to a pilot making an instrument approach which means continue inbound to the missed approach point and execute the missed approach procedure as described on the Instrument Approach Procedure Chart, or as previously assigned by ATC. The pilot may climb immediately to the altitude specified in the missed approach procedure upon making a missed approach. No turns should be initiated prior to reaching the missed approach point. When conducting an ASR or PAR approach, execute the assigned missed approach procedure immediately upon receiving instructions to "execute missed approach." (Refer to AIM)

EXPECT APPROACH CLEARANCE (TIME)/EAC—The time at which it is expected that an arriving aircraft will be cleared to commence an approach for landing. It is issued when the aircraft clearance limit is a designated Initial, Intermediate, or Final Approach Fix for the approach in use and the aircraft is to be held. If delay is anticipated, the pilot should be advised of his EAC at least 5 minutes before the aircraft is estimated to reach the clearance limit.

EXPECT (ALTITUDE) AT (TIME) or (FIX)—Used under certain conditions in a departure clearance to provide a pilot with an altitude to be used in the event of two-way communication failure. (Refer to AIM)

EXPECT DEPARTURE CLEARANCE (TIME)/EDCT—Used in Fuel Advisory Departure (FAD) program. The time the operator can expect a gate release. Excluding long distance flights, an EDCT will always be assigned even though it may be the same as the Estimated Time of Departure (ETC). The EDCT is calculated by adding the ground delay factor. (See Fuel Advisory Departure)

EXPECT FURTHER CLEARANCE (TIME)/EFC—The time at which it is expected that additional clearance will be issued to an aircraft. It is issued when the aircraft clearance limit is a fix not designated as part of the approach procedure to be executed and the aircraft will be held. If delay is anticipated the pilot should be advised of his EFC at least 5 minutes before the aircraft is estimated to reach the clearance limit.

EXPECT FURTHER CLEARANCE VIA (AIRWAYS, ROUTES OR FIXES)—Used to inform pilot of the routing he can expect if any part of the route beyond a short range clearance limit differs from that filed.

EXPEDITE—Used by ATC when prompt compliance is required to avoid the development of an imminent situation.

FAST FILE—A system whereby a pilot files a flight plan via telephone that is tape recorded and then transcribed for transmission to the appropriate air traffic facility. Locations having a fast file capability are contained in the Airport/Facility Directory. (Refer to AIM)

FEATHERED PROPELLER—A propeller whose blades have been rotated so that the leading and trailing edges are nearly parallel with the aircraft flight path to stop or minimize drag and engine rotation. Normally used to indicate shutdown of a reciprocating or turboprop engine due to malfunction.

FEEDER ROUTE—A route depicted on instrument approach procedure charts to designate routes for aircraft to proceed from the en route structure to the initial approach fix (IAF). (See Instrument Approach Procedure)

FERRY FLIGHT—A flight for the purpose of:

1. returning an aircraft to base;
2. delivering an aircraft from one location to another;
3. moving an aircraft to and from a maintenance base.

Ferry flights, under certain conditions may be conducted under terms of a special flight permit.

FILED—Normally used in conjunction with flight plans, meaning a flight plan has been submitted to ATC.

FINAL—Commonly used to mean that an aircraft is on the final approach course or is aligned with a landing area. (See Final Approach Course, Final Approach—IFR, Traffic pattern, Segments of an Instrument Approach Procedure)

FINAL APPROACH COURSE—A straight line extension of a localizer, a final approach radial/bearing, or a runway centerline, all without regard to distance. (See Final Approach—IFR, Traffic Pattern)

FINAL APPROACH FIX/FAF—The designated fix from or over which the final approach (IFR) to an airport is executed. The FAF identifies the beginning of the final approach segment of the instrument approach. (See Final Approach Point, Segments of an Instrument Approach Procedure, Glide Slope Intercept Altitude)

FINAL APPROACH-IFR—The flight path of an aircraft which is inbound to an airport on a final instrument approach course, beginning at the final approach fix or point and extending to the airport or the point where a circle to land maneuver or a missed approach is executed. (See Segments of an Instrument Approach Procedure, Final Approach Fix, Final Approach Course, Final Approach Point)

ICAO—FINAL APPROACH—That part of an instrument approach procedure from the time the aircraft has:

1. Completed the last procedure turn or base turn, where one is specified, or
2. Crossed a specified fix, or
3. Intercepted the last track specified for the procedures until it has crossed a point in the vicinity of an aerodrome from which:
   a. A landing can be made, or
   b. A missed approach procedure is initiated.

FINAL APPROACH POINT—The point, within prescribed limits of an instrument approach procedure, where the aircraft is established on the final approach course and final approach descent may be commenced. A final approach point is applicable only in non-precision approaches where a final approach fix has not been established. In such instances, the point identifies the beginning of the final approach segment of the instrument approach. (See Final Approach Fix, Segments of an Instrument Approach Procedure, Glide Slope Intercept Altitude)

FINAL APPROACH SEGMENT—(See Segments of an Instrument Approach Procedure)

FINAL APPROACH—VFR—(See Traffic Pattern)

FINAL CONTROLLER—The controller providing information and final approach guidance during PAR and ASR approaches utilizing radar equipment. (See Radar Approach)

FIX—A geographical position determined by visual reference to the surface, by reference to one or more radio NAVAIDs, by celestial plotting, or by another navigational device.

FIXED-WING SPECIAL IFR/FW/SIFR—Aircraft operating in accordance with a waiver and a Letter of Agreement within control zones specified in FAR 93.113. These operations are conducted by IFR qualified pilots in IFR equipped aircraft and by pilots of agricultural and industrial aircraft.

FLAG/FLAG ALARM—A warning device incorporated in certain airborne navigation and flight instruments indicating that:

1. Instruments are inoperative or otherwise not operating satisfactorily, or
2. Signal strength or quality of the received signal falls below acceptable values.

FLAMEOUT—Unintended loss of combustion in turbine engines resulting in the loss of engine power.

FLIGHT INFORMATION REGION/FIR—An airspace of defined dimensions within which Flight Information Service and Alerting Service are provided.

1. Flight Information Service—A service provided for the purpose of giving advice and information useful for the safe and efficient conduct of flights.
2. Alerting Service—A service provided to notify appropriate organizations regarding aircraft in need of search and rescue aid, and assist such organizations as required.

FLIGHT INSPECTION/FLIGHT CHECK—Inflight investigation and evaluation of a navigational aid to determine whether it meets established tolerances. (See Navigational Aid)

FLIGHT LEVEL—A level of constant atmospheric pressure related to a reference datum of 29.92 inches of mercury. Each is stated in three digits that represent hundreds of feet. For example, flight level 250 represents a barometric altimeter indication of 25,000 feet; flight level 255, an indication of 25,500 feet.

ICAO—FLIGHT LEVELS—Surfaces of constant atmospheric pressure which are related to a specific pressure datum. 1013.2 mb (29.92 inches) and are separated by specific pressure intervals.

FLIGHT PATH—A line, course, or track along which an aircraft is flying or intended to be flown. (See Track, Course)

FLIGHT PLAN—Specified information relating to the intended flight of an aircraft that is filed orally or in writing with an FSS or an ATC facility. (See Fast File, Filed) (Refer to AIM)

FLIGHT RECORDER—A general term applied to any instrument or device that records information about the performance of an aircraft in flight or about conditions encountered in flight. Flight recorders may make records of airspeed, outside air temperature, vertical acceleration, engine RPM, manifold pressure, and other pertinent variables for a given flight.

ICAO—FLIGHT RECORDER—Any type of recorder installed in the aircraft for the purpose of complementing accident/incident investigation.

FLIGHT SERVICE STATION/FSS—Air traffic facilities which provide pilot briefing, en route communications and VFR search and rescue services, assist lost aircraft and aircraft in emergency situations, relay ATC clearances, originate Notices to Airmen, broadcast aviation weather and NAS information, receive and process IFR flight plans, and monitor NAVAIDS. In addition, at selected locations FSSs provide Enroute Flight Advisory Service (Flight Watch), take weather observations, issue airport advisories, and advise Customs and Immigration of transborder flights. (Refer to AIM).

FLIGHT STANDARDS DISTRICT OFFICE/FSDO—An FAA field office serving an assigned geographical area, staffed with Flight Standards personnel who serve the aviation industry and the general public on matters relating to the certification and operation of air carrier and general aviation aircraft. Activities include general surveillance of operational safety, certification of airmen and aircraft, accident prevention, investigation, enforcement, etc.

FLIGHT TEST—A flight for the purpose of:

1. Investigating the operation/flight characteristics of an aircraft or aircraft component.
2. Evaluating an applicant for a pilot certificate or rating.

FLIGHT VISIBILITY—(See Visibility)

FLIGHT WATCH—A shortened term for use in air-ground contacts on frequency 122.0 MHz to identify the flight service station providing En Route Flight Advisory Service; e.g., "Oakland Flight Watch." (See En Route Flight Advisory Service)

FLIP—(See DOD FLIP)

FLOW CONTROL—Measures designed to adjust the flow of traffic into a given airspace, along a given route, or bound for a given aerodrome (airport) so as to ensure the most effective utilization of the airspace. (See Quota Flow Control) (Refer to Airport/Facility Directory)

FLY HEADING (DEGREES)—Informs the pilot of the heading he should fly. The pilot may have to turn to, or continue on, a specific compass direction in order to comply with the instructions. The pilot is expected to turn in the shorter direction to the heading, unless otherwise instructed by ATC.

FORMATION FLIGHT—More than one aircraft which, by prior arrangement between the pilots, operate as a single aircraft with regard to navigation and position reporting. Separation between aircraft within the formation is the responsibility of the flight leader and the pilots of the other aircraft in the flight. This includes transition periods when aircraft within the formation are maneuvering to attain separation from each other to effect individual control and during join-up and breakaway.

1. A standard formation is one in which a proximity of no more than 1 mile laterally or longitudinally and within 100 feet vertically from the flight leader is maintained by each wingman.
2. Nonstandard formations are those operating under any of the following conditions:
   a. When the flight leader has requested and ATC has approved other than standard formation dimensions.
   b. When operating within an authorized altitude reservation (ALTRV) or under the provisions of a Letter of Agreement.
   c. When the operations are conducted in airspace specifically designed for a special activity. See Altitude Reservation) (Refer to FAR Part 91)

FSS—(See Flight Service Station)

FUEL ADVISORY DEPARTURE/FAD—Procedures to minimize engine running time for aircraft destined for an airport experiencing prolonged arrival delays. (Refer to AIM)

FUEL DUMPING—Airborne release of usable fuel. This does not include the dropping of fuel tanks. (See Jettisoning of External Stores)

FUEL SIPHONING/FUEL VENTING—Unintentional release of fuel caused by overflow, puncture, loose cap, etc.

GATE HOLD PROCEDURES—Procedures at selected airports to hold aircraft at the gate or other ground location whenever departure delays exceed or are anticipated to exceed 5 minutes. The sequence for departure will be maintained in accordance with initial call up unless modified by Flow Control restrictions. Pilots should monitor the ground control/clearance delivery frequency for engine startup advisories or new proposed start time if the delay changes. (See Flow Control)

GENERAL AVIATION—That portion of civil aviation which encompasses all facets of aviation except air carriers holding a certificate of public convenience and necessity from the Civil Aeronautics Board, and large aircraft commercial operators.

ICAO—GENERAL AVIATION—All civil aviation operations other than scheduled air services and nonscheduled air transport operations for remuneration or hire.

GENERAL AVIATION DISTRICT OFFICE/GADO—An FAA field office serving a designated geographical area, staffed with Flight Standards personnel who have responsibility for serving the aviation industry and the general public on all matters relating to the certification and operation of general aviation aircraft.

GLIDE PATH (ON/ABOVE/BELOW)—Used by ATC to inform an aircraft making a PAR approach of its vertical position (elevation) relative to the descent profile. The terms "slightly" and "well" are used to describe the degree of deviation; e.g., "slightly above glidepath." Trend information is also issued with respect to the elevation of the aircraft and may be modified by the terms "rapidly" and "slowly," e.g., "well above glidepath, coming down rapidly." (See PAR Approach)

GLIDE SLOPE/GS—Provides vertical guidance for aircraft during approach and landing. The glide slope consists of the following:

1. Electronic components emitting signals which provide vertical guidance by reference to airborne instruments during instrument approaches such as ILS, or
2. Visual ground aids such as VASI which provides vertical guidance for VFR approach or for the visual portion of an instrument approach and landing.

ICAO—GLIDE PATH—A descent profile determined for vertical guidance during a final approach.

areas, and other data not requiring frequent change.

GROUND CLUTTER—A pattern produced on the radar scope by ground returns which may degrade other radar returns in the affected area. The effect of ground clutter is minimized by the use of moving target indicator (MTI) circuits in the radar equipment resulting in a radar presentation which displays only targets which are in motion. (See Clutter)

GROUND CONTROLLED APPROACH/GCA—A radar approach system operated from the ground by air traffic control personnel transmitting instructions to the pilot by radio. The approach may be conducted with surveillance radar (ASR) only or with both surveillance and precision approach radar (PAR). Usage of the term "GCA" by pilots is discouraged except when referring

GLIDE SLOPE INTERCEPT ALTITUDE—The minimum altitude of the intermediate approach segment prescribed for a precision approach which assures required obstacle clearance. It is depicted on instrument approach procedure charts. (See Segments of an Instrument Approach Procedure, Instrument Landing System)

GO AHEAD—Proceed with your message. Not to be used for any other purpose.

GO AROUND—Instructions for a pilot to abandon his approach to landing. Additional instructions may follow. Unless otherwise advised by ATC, a VFR aircraft or an aircraft conducting a visual approach should overfly the runway while climbing to traffic pattern altitude and enter the traffic pattern via the crosswind leg. A pilot on an IFR flight plan making an instrument approach should execute the published missed approach procedure or proceed as instructed by ATC, e.g., "Go around" (additional instructions, if required). (See Low Approach, Missed Approach)

GRAPHIC NOTICES AND SUPPLEMENTAL DATA—A publication designed primarily as a pilot's operational manual containing a tabulation of parachute jump areas, special notice area graphics, terminal radar service area graphics, civil flight test areas, military refueling tracks and to a GCA facility. Pilots should specifically request a "PAR" approach when a precision radar approach is desired, or request an "ASR" or "surveillance" approach when a nonprecision radar approach is desired. (See Radar Approach)

GROUND SPEED—The speed of an aircraft relative to the surface of the earth.

GROUND VISIBILITY—(See Visibility)

HANDOFF—Transfer of radar identification of an aircraft from one controller to another either within the same facility or interfacility. Actual transfer of control responsibility may occur at the time of the handoff, or at a specified time, point, or altitude.

HAVE NUMBERS—Used by pilots to inform ATC that they have received runway, wind, and altimeter information only.

HEAVY (AIRCRAFT)—(See Aircraft Classes)

HEIGHT ABOVE AIRPORT/HAA—The height of the Minimum Descent Altitude above the published airport elevation. This is published in conjunction with circling minimums. (See Minimum Descent Altitude)

HEIGHT ABOVE LANDING/HAL—The height above a designated helicopter landing area used for helicopter instrument approach procedures. (Refer to FAR Part 97)

HEIGHT ABOVE TOUCHDOWN/HAT—The height of the Decision Height or Minimum Descent Altitude above the highest runway elevation in the touchdown zone (first 3,000 feet of the runway). HAT is published on instrument approach charts in conjunction with all straight-in minimums. (See Decision Height, Minimum Descent Altitude)

HELICOPTER/COPTER—Rotorcraft that, for its horizontal motion, depends principally on its engine-driven rotors.

ICAO—HELICOPTER—A heavier-than-air aircraft supported in flight by the reactions of the air on one or more power-driven rotors on substantially vertical axes.

HELIPAD—That part of the landing and takeoff area designed for helicopters.

HELIPORT—An area of land, water, or structure used or intended to be used for the landing and takeoff of helicopters.

HERTZ/Hz—The standard radio equivalent of frequency in cycles per second of an electromagnetic wave. Kilohertz (kHz) is frequency of one thousand cycles per second. Megahertz (MHz) is a frequency of one million cycles per second.

HIGH FREQUENCY COMMUNICATIONS/HF COMMUNICATIONS—High radio frequencies (HF) between 3 and 30 MHz used for air-to-ground voice communication in overseas operations.

HIGH FREQUENCY/HF—The frequency band between 3 and 30 MHz. (See High Frequency Communications)

HIGH SPEED TAXIWAY/EXIT/TURNOFF—A long radius taxiway designed and provided with lighting or marking to define the path of aircraft, traveling at high speed (up to 60 knots), from the runway center to a point on the center of a taxiway. Also referred to as long radius exit or turn-off taxiway. The high speed taxiway is designed to expedite aircraft turning off the runway after landing, thus reducing runway occupancy time.

HOLD/HOLDING PROCEDURE—A predetermined maneuver which keeps aircraft within a specified airspace while awaiting further clearance from air traffic control. Also used during ground operations to keep aircraft within a specified area or at a specified point while awaiting further clearance from air traffic control. (See Holding Fix) (Refer to AIM)

HOLDING FIX—A specified fix identifiable to a pilot by NAVAIDS or visual reference to the ground used as a reference point in establishing and maintaining the position of an aircraft while holding. (See Fix, Holding, Visual Holding) (Refer to AIM)

ICAO—HOLDING POINT—A specified location, identified by visual or other means, in the vicinity of which the position of an aircraft in flight is maintained with air traffic control clearances.

HOMING—Flight toward a NAVAID, without correcting for wind, by adjusting the aircraft heading to maintain a relative bearing of zero degrees. (See Bearing)

ICAO—HOMING—The procedure of using the direction finding equipment of one radio station with the emission of another radio station, where at least one of the stations is mobile, and whereby the mobile station proceeds continuously towards the other station.

HOW DO YOU HEAR ME?—A question relating to the quality of the transmission or to determine how well the transmission is being received.

IDENT—A request for a pilot to activate the aircraft transponder identification feature. This will help the controller to confirm an aircraft identity or to identify an aircraft. (Refer to AIM)

IDENT FEATURE—The special feature in the Air Traffic Control Radar Beacon System (ATCRBS) equipment. It is used to immediately distinguish one display beacon target from other beacon targets. (See IDENT)

IF FEASIBLE, REDUCE SPEED TO (SPEED)—(See Speed Adjustment)

IF NO TRANSMISSION RECEIVED FOR (TIME)—Used by ATC in radar approaches to prefix procedures which should be followed by the pilot in event of lost communications. (See Lost Communications)

IFR AIRCRAFT/IFR FLIGHT—An aircraft conducting flight in accordance with instrument flight rules.

IFR CONDITIONS—Weather conditions below the minimum for flight under visual flight rules. (See Instrument Meteorological Conditions)

IFR DEPARTURE PROCEDURE—(See IFR Takeoff Minimums and Departure Procedures) (Refer to AIM)

IFR MILITARY TRAINING ROUTES (IR)—Routes used by the Department of Defense and associated Reserve and Air Guard units for the purpose of conducting low-altitude navigation and tactical training in both IFR and VFR weather conditions below 10,000 feet MSL at airspeeds in excess of 250 knots IAS.

IFR OVER THE TOP—The operation of an aircraft over the top on an IFR flight plan when cleared by air traffic control to maintain "VFR conditions" or "VFR conditions on top." (See VFR on Top)

IFR TAKEOFF MINIMUMS AND DEPARTURE PROCEDURES—FAR, Part 91, prescribes standard takeoff rules for certain civil users. At some airports, obstructions or other factors require the establishment of nonstandard takeoff minimums, departure procedures, or both, to assist pilots in avoiding obstacles during climb to the minimum en route altitude. Those airports are listed in NOS/DOD Instrument Approach Charts (IAPs) under a section entitled "IFR Takeoff Minimums and Departure Procedures." The NOS/DOD IAP chart legend illustrates the symbol used to alert the pilot to nonstandard takeoff minimums and departure procedures. When departing IFR from such airports, or from any airports where there are no departure procedures, SIDs, or ATC facilities available, pilots should advise ATC of any departure limitations. Controllers may query a pilot to determine acceptable departure directions, turns, or headings after takeoff. Pilots should be familiar with the departure procedures and must assure that their aircraft can meet or exceed any specified climb gradients.

ILS CATEGORIES

1. ILS Category I—An ILS approach procedure which provides for approach to a height above touchdown of not less than 200 feet and with runway visual range of not less than 1800 feet.
2. ILS Category II—An ILS approach procedure which provides for approach to a height above touchdown of not less than 100 feet and with runway visual range of not less than 1200 feet.
3. ILS Category III:
   a. IIIA—An ILS approach procedure which provides for approach without a decision height minimum and with runway visual range of not less than 700 feet.
   b. IIIB—An ILS approach procedure which provides for approach without a decision height minimum and with runway visual range of not less than 150 feet.
   c. IIIC—An ILS approach procedure which provides for approach without a decision height minimum and without runway visual range minimum.

IMMEDIATELY—Used by ATC when such action compliance is required to avoid an imminent situation.

INCREASE SPEED TO (SPEED)—(See Speed Adjustment)

INFORMATION REQUEST/INREQ—A request originated by an FSS for information concerning an overdue VFR aircraft.

INITIAL APPROACH FIX/IAF—The fixes depicted on instrument approach procedure charts that identifies the beginning of the initial approach segment(s). (See Fix, Segments of an Instrument Approach Procedure)

INITIAL APPROACH SEGMENT—(See Segments of an Instrument Approach Procedure)

INNER MARKER/IM/INNER MARKER BEACON—A marker beacon used with an ILS (CAT II) precision approach located between the middle marker and the end of the ILS runway, transmitting a radiation pattern keyed at six dots per second and indicating to the pilot, both aurally and visually, that he is at the designated decision height (DH), normally 100 feet above the touchdown zone elevation, on the ILS CAT II approach. It also marks progress during a CAT III approach. (See Instrument Landing System) (Refer to AIM)

INSTRUMENT APPROACH PROCEDURE/IAP/INSTRUMENT APPROACH—A series of predetermined maneuvers for the orderly transfer of an aircraft under instrument flight conditions from the beginning of the initial approach to a landing, or to a point from which a landing may be made visually. It is prescribed and approved for a specific airport by competent authority. (See Segments of an Instrument Approach Procedure)

(Refer to FAR Part 91, AIM)

1. U.S. civil standard instrument approach procedures are approved by the FAA as prescribed under FAR, Part 97, and are available for public use.
2. U.S. military standard instrument approach procedures are approved and published by the Department of Defense.
3. Special instrument approach procedures are approved by the FAA for individual operators, but are not published in FAR, Part 97, for public use.

ICAO—INSTRUMENT APPROACH PROCEDURE—A series of predetermined maneuvers for the orderly transfer of an aircraft under instrument flight conditions from the beginning of the initial approach to a landing, or to a point from which a landing may be made visually.

INSTRUMENT FLIGHT RULES/IFR—Rules governing the procedures for conducting instrument flight. Also a term used by pilots and controllers to indicate type of

flight plan. (See Visual Flight Rules, Instrument Meteorological Conditions, Visual Meteorological Conditions) (Refer to AIM)

ICAO—INSTRUMENT FLIGHT RULES—A set of rules governing the conduct of flight under instrument meteorological conditions.

INSTRUMENT LANDING SYSTEM/ILS—A precision instrument approach system which normally consists of the following electronic components and visual aids.

1. Localizer (See Localizer)
2. Glide Slope (See Glide Slope)
3. Outer Marker (See Outer Marker)
4. Middle Marker (See Middle Marker)
5. Approach Lights (See Airport Lighting)

(Refer to FAR Part 91, AIM)

INSTRUMENT METEOROLOGICAL CONDITIONS—IMC—Meteorological conditions expressed in terms of visibility, distance from cloud, and ceiling less than the minima specified for visual meteorological conditions. (See Visual Meteorological Conditions, Instrument Flight Rules, Visual Flight Rules)

INSTRUMENT RUNWAY—A runway equipped with electronic and visual navigation aids for which a precision or nonprecision approach procedure having straight-in landing minimums has been approved.

ICAO—INSTRUMENT RUNWAY—A runway intended for the operation of aircraft using nonvisual aids and comprising:

1. Instrument Approach Runway—An instrument runway served by a nonvisual aid providing at least directional guidance adequate for a straight-in approach.
2. Precision Approach Runway, Category I—An instrument runway served by ILS or GCA approach aids and visual aids intended for operations down to 60 metres (200 feet) decision height and down to an RVR of the order of 800 metres (2600 feet.)
3. Precision Approach Runway, Category II—An instrument runway served by ILS and visual aids intended for operations down to 30 metres (100 feet) decision height and down to an RVR of the order of 400 metres (1200 feet.)
4. Precision Approach Runway, Category III—An instrument runway served by ILS (no decision height being applicable) and:
   a. By visual aids intended for operations down to an RVR of the order of 200 metres (700 feet);
   b. By visual aids intended for operations down to an RVR of the order of 50 metres (150 feet);
   c. Intended for operations without reliance on external visual reference.

INTERMEDIATE APPROACH SEGMENT—(See Segments of an Instrument Approach Procedure)

INTERMEDIATE FIX/IF—The fix that identifies the beginning of the intermediate approach segment of an instrument approach procedure. The fix is not normally identified on the instrument approach chart as an intermediate fix (IF). (See Segments of an Instrument Approach Procedure)

INTERNATIONAL AIRPORT—Relating to international flight, it means:

1. An airport of entry which has been designated by the Secretary of Treasury or Commissioner of Customs as an international airport for customs service.
2. A landing rights airport at which specific permission to land must be obtained from customs authorities in advance of contemplated use.
3. Airports designated under the Convention on International Civil Aviation as an airport for use by international commercial air transport and/or international general aviation. (Refer to Airport/Facility Directory and IFIM)

ICAO—INTERNATIONAL AIRPORT—Any airport designated by the Contracting State in whose territory it is situated as an airport of entry and departure for international air traffic, where the formalities incident to customs, immigration, public health, animal and plant quarantine and similar procedures are carried out.

INTERNATIONAL CIVIL AVIATION ORGANIZATON/CAO—A specialized agency of the United Nations whose objective is to develop the principles and techniques of international air navigation and to foster planning and development of international civil air transport.

INTERNATIONAL FLIGHT INFORMATION MANUAL/IFIM—A publication designed primarily as a pilot's

preflight planning guide for flights into foreign airspace and for flights returning to the U.S. from foreign locations.

INTERROGATOR—The ground-based surveillance radar beacon transmitter-receiver which normally scans in synchronism with a primary radar, transmitting discrete radio signals which repetitiously requests all transponders, on the mode being used, to reply. The replies received are mixed with the primary radar returns and displayed on the same plan position indicator (radar scope). Also applied to the airborne element of the TACAN/DME system. (See Transponder) (Refer to AIM)

INTERSECTING RUNWAYS—Two or more runways which cross or meet within their lengths. (See Intersection)

INTERSECTION—

1. A point defined by any combination of courses, radials or bearings of two or more navigational aids.
2. Used to describe the point where two runways cross, a taxiway and a runway cross or, two taxiways cross.

INTERSECTION DEPARTURE/INTERSECTION TAKEOFF—A takeoff or proposed takeoff on a runway from an intersection. (See Intersection)

I SAY AGAIN—The message will be repeated.

JAMMING—Electronic or mechanical interference which may disrupt the display of aircraft on radar or the transmission/reception of radio communications/navigation.

JET BLAST—Jet engine exhaust (thrust stream turbulence). (See Wake Turbulence)

JET ROUTE—A route designed to serve aircraft operations from 18,000 feet MSL up to and including flight level 450. The routes are referred to as "J" routes with numbering to identify the designated route; e.g., J 105. (See Route) (Refer to FAR Part 71)

JET STREAM—A migrating stream of high-speed winds present at high altitudes.

JETTISONING OF EXTERNAL STORES—Airborne release of external stores; e.g., tiptanks, ordinances. (See Fuel Dumping) (Refer to FAR Part 91)

JOINT USE RESTRICTED AREA—(See Restricted Area)

KNOWN TRAFFIC—With respect to ATC clearances, means aircraft whose altitude, position and intentions are known to ATC.

LANDING AREA—Any locality either of land or water, including airports and intermediate landing fields, which is used, or intended to be used, for the landing and takeoff of aircraft, whether or not facilities are provided for the shelter, servicing, or for receiving or discharging passenger or cargo.

ICAO—LANDING AREA—That part of the movement area intended for the landing and takeoff of aircraft.

LANDING DIRECTION INDICATOR—A device which visually indicates the direction in which landings and takeoffs should be made. (See Tetrahedron) (Refer to AIM)

LANDING MINIMUMS/IFR LANDING MINIMUMS— The minimum visibility prescribed for landing a civil aircraft while using an instrument approach procedure. The minimum applies with other limitations set forth in FAR Part 91, with respect to the Minimum Descent Altitude (MDA) or Decision Height (DH) prescribed in the instrument approach procedures as follows:

1. Straight-in landing minimums—A statement of MDA and visibility, or DH and visibility, required for straight-in landing on a specified runway, or
2. Circling minimums—A statement of MDA and visibility required for the circle-to-land maneuver.

Descent below the established MDA or DH is not authorized during an approach unless the aircraft is in a position from which a normal approach to the runway of intended landing can be made, and adequate visual reference to required visual cues is maintained. (See Straight-in Landing, Circle-to-Land Maneuver, Decision Height, Minimum Descent Altitude, Visibility, Instrument Approach Procedure) (Refer to FAR Part 91)

LANDING ROLL—The distance from the point of touchdown to the point where the aircraft can be brought to a stop or exit the runway.

LANDING SEQUENCE—The order in which aircraft are positioned for landing. (See Approach Sequence)

LAST ASSIGNED ALTITUDE—The last altitude/flight level assigned by ATC and acknowledged by the pilot. (See Maintain) (Refer to FAR Part 91)

LATERAL SEPARATION—The lateral spacing of aircraft at the same altitude by requiring operation on different routes or in different geographical locatons. (See Separation)

LIGHTED AIRPORT—An airport where runway and obstruction lighting is available. (See Airport lighting) (Refer to AIM)

LIGHT GUN—A handheld directional light signaling device which emits a brilliant narrow beam of white, green, or red light as selected by the tower controller. The color and type of light transmitted can be used to approve or disapprove anticipated pilot actions where radio communications is not available. The light gun is used for controlling traffic operating in the vicinity of the airport and on the airport movement area. (Refer to AIM)

LIMITED REMOTE COMMUNICATIONS OUTLET/LRCO—An unmanned satellite air/ground communications facility which may be associated with a VOR. These outlets effectively extend the service range of the FSS and provide greater communications reliability. LRCO's are depicted on En Route Charts. (See Remote Communications Outlet)

LOCALIZER—The component of an ILS which provides course guidance to the runway. (See Instrument Landing System) (Refer to AIM)

ICAO—LOCALIZER COURSE (ILS)—The locus of points, in any given horizontal plane, at which the DDM (difference in depth of modulation) is zero.

LOCALIZER TYPE DIRECTIONAL AID/LDA—A NAVAID used for nonprecision instrument approaches with utility and accuracy comparable to a localizer but which is not a part of a complete ILS and is not aligned with the runway. (Refer to AIM)

LOCALIZER USABLE DISTANCE—The maximum distance from the localizer transmitter at a specified altitude, as verified by flight inspection, at which reliable course information is continuously received. (Refer to AIM)

LOCAL TRAFFIC—Aircraft operating in the traffic pattern or within sight of the tower, or aircraft known to be departing or arriving from flight in local practice areas, or aircraft executing practice instrument approaches at the airport. (See Traffic Pattern)

LONGITUDINAL SEPARATION—The longitudinal spacing of aircraft at the same altitude by a minimum distance expressed in units of time or miles. (See Separation) (Refer to AIM)

LORAN/LONG RANGE NAVIGATION—An electronic navigational system by which hyperbolic lines of position are determined by measuring the difference in the time of reception of synchronized pulse signals from two fixed transmitters. Loran A operates in the 1750–1950 kHz frequency band. Loran C and D operate in the 100–110 kHz frequency band. (Refer to AIM)

LOST COMMUNICATIONS/TWO-WAY RADIO COMMUNICATONS FAILURE—Loss of the ability to communicate by radio. Aircraft are sometimes referred to as NORDO (No Radio). Standard pilot procedures are specified in FAR Part 91. Radar controllers issue procedures for pilots to follow in the event of lost communications during a radar approach when weather reports indicate that an aircraft will likely encounter IFR weather conditions during the approach. (Refer to FAR Part 91; AIM)

LOW ALTITUDE AIRWAY STRUCTURE/FEDERAL AIRWAYS—The network of airways serving aircraft operations up to but not including 18,000 feet MSL. (See Airway) (Refer to AIM)

LOW ALTITUDE ALERT, CHECK YOUR ALTITUDE IMMEDIATELY—(See Safety Advisory)

LOW APPROACH—An approach over an airport or runway following an instrument approach or a VFR approach including the go-around maneuver where the pilot intentionally does not make contact with the runway. (Refer to AIM)

LOW FREQUENCY/LF—The frequency band between 30 and 300 kHz. (Refer to AIM)

MACH NUMBER—The ratio of true airspeed to the speed of sound, e.g., MACH .82, MACH 1.6. (See Airspeed)

MAINTAIN—

1. Concerning altitude/flight level, the term means to remain at the altitude/flight level specified. The phrase "climb and" or "descend and" normally precedes "maintain" and the altitude assignment, e.g., "descend and maintain 5000."
2. Concerning other ATC instructions, the term is used in its literal sense, e.g., maintain VFR.

MAKE SHORT APPROACH—Used by ATC to inform a pilot to alter his traffic pattern so as to make a short final approach. (See Traffic Pattern)

MANDATORY ALTITUDE—An altitude depicted on an Instrument Approach Procedure Chart requiring the aircraft to maintain altitude at the depicted value.

MARKER BEACON—An electronic navigation facility transmitting a 75 MHz vertical fan or boneshaped radiation pattern. Marker beacons are identified by their modulation frequency and keying code, and when received by compatible airborne equipment, indicate to the pilot, both aurally and visually, that he is passing over the facility. (See Outer Marker, Middle Marker, Inner Marker) (Refer to AIM)

MAXIMUM AUTHORIZED ALTITUDE/MAA—A published altitude representing the maximum usable altitude or flight level for an airspace structure or route segment. It is the highest altitude on a Federal airway, Jet route, area navigation low or high route, or other direct route for which an MEA is designated in FAR Part 95, at which adequate reception of navigation and signals is assured.

MAYDAY—The international radiotelephony distress signal. When repeated three times, it indicates imminent and grave danger and that immediate assistance is requested. (See PAN) (Refer to AIM)

METERING—A method of time regulating arrival traffic flow into a terminal area so as not to exceed a predetermined terminal acceptance rate.

METERING FIX—A fix along an established route from over which aircraft will be metered prior to entering terminal airspace. Normally, this fix should be established at a distance from the airport which will facilitate a profile descent 10,000 feet above airport elevation (AAE) or above.

MICROWAVE LANDING SYSTEM/MLS—An instrument landing system operating in the microwave spectrum which provides lateral and vertical guidance to aircraft having compatible avionics equipment. (See Instrument Landing System) (Refer to AIM)

MIDDLE COMPASS LOCATOR—(See Compass Locator)

MIDDLE MARKER/MM—A marker beacon that defines a point along the glide slope of an ILS normally located at or near the point of decision height (ILS Category I). It is keyed to transmit alternate dots and dashes, two per second, on 1300 HZ tone which is received aurally and visually by compatible airborne equipment. (See Marker Beacon, Instrument Landing System) (Refer to AIM)

MID RVR—(See Visibility)

MILITARY AUTHORITY ASSUMES RESPONSIBILITY FOR SEPARATION OF AIRCRAFT/MARSA—A condition whereby the military services involved assume responsibility for separation between participating military aircraft in the ATC system. It is used only for required IFR operations which are specified in Letters of Agreement or other appropriate FAA or military documents.

MILITARY OPERATIONS AREA/MOA—(See Special Use Airspace)

MILITARY TRAINING ROUTES/MTR—Airspace of defined vertical and lateral dimensions established for the conduct of military flight training at airspeeds in excess of 250 knots IAS. (See IFR (IR) and VFR (VR) Military Training Routes)

MINIMUM CROSSING ALTITUDE/MCA—The lowest altitude at certain fixes at which an aircraft must cross when proceeding in the direction of a higher minimum en route IFR altitude (MEA). (See Minimum En Route IFR Altitude)

MINIMUM DESCENT ALTITUDE/MDA—The lowest altitude, expressed in feet above mean sea level, to which descent is authorized on final approach or during circle-to-land maneuvering in execution of a standard instrument approach procedure where no electronic glide slope is provided. (See Nonprecision Approach Procedure)

MINIMUM EN ROUTE IFR ALTITUDE/MEA—The lowest published altitude between radio fixes which assures acceptable navigational signal coverage and meets obstacle clearance requirements between those fixes. The MEA prescribed for a Federal airway or segment thereof, area navigational low or high route, or other direct route applies to the entire width of the airway, segment, or route between the radio fixes defining the airway, segment, or route. (Refer to FAR Parts 91 and 95; AIM)

MINIMUM FUEL—Indicates that an aircraft's fuel supply has reached a state where, upon reaching the destination, it can accept little or no delay. This is not an emergency situation but merely indicates an emergency situation is possible should any undue delay occur.

MINIMUM HOLDING ALTITUDE/MHA—The lowest altitude prescribed for a holding pattern which assures navigational signal coverage, communications, and meets obstacle clearance requirements.

MINIMUM IFR ALTITUDES—Minimum altitudes for IFR operations as prescribed in FAR Part 91. These altitudes are published on aeronautical charts and prescribed in FAR Part 95 for airways and routes, and FAR Part 97 for standard instrument approach procedures. If no applicable minimum altitude is prescribed in FAR Parts 95 or 97, the following minimum IFR altitude applies:

1. In designated mountainous areas, 2000 feet above the highest obstacle within a horizontal distance of 5 statute miles from the course to be flown; or
2. Other than mountainous areas, 1000 feet above the highest obstacle within a horizontal distance of 5 statute miles from the course to be flown; or
3. As otherwise authorized by the Administrator or assigned by ATC. (See Minimum En Route IFR Altitude, Minimum Obstruction Clearance Altitude, Minimum Crossing Altitude, Minimum Safe Altitude, Minimum Vectoring Altitude) (Refer to FAR Part 91)

MINIMUM OBSTRUCTION CLEARANCE ALTITUDE/MOCA—The lowest published altitude in effect between radio fixes on VOR airways, off-airway routes, or route segments which meets obstacle clearance requirements for the entire route segment and which assures acceptable navigation signal coverage only within 25 nautical miles of a VOR. (Refer to FAR Part 91 and 95)

MINIMUM RECEPTION ALTITUDE/MRA—The lowest altitude at which an intersection can be determined. (Refer to FAR Part 95)

MINIMUM SAFE ALTITUDE/MSA—

1. The minimum altitude specified in FAR Part 91 for various aircraft operations.
2. Altitudes depicted on approach charts which provide at least 1,000 feet of obstacle clearance for emergency use within a specified distance from the navigation facility upon which a procedure is predicated. These altitudes will be identified as MINIMUM SECTOR ALTITUDES or EMERGENCY SAFE ALTITUDES and are established as follows:

MINIMUM SECTOR ALTITUDES—Altitudes depicted on approach charts which provide at least 1,000 feet of obstacle clearance within a 25-mile radius of the navigation facility upon which the procedure is predicated. Sectors depicted on approach charts must be at least 90 degrees in scope. These altitudes are for emergency use only and do not necessarily assure acceptable navigational signal coverage.

EMERGENCY SAFE ALTITUDES—Altitudes depicted on approach charts which provide at least 1,000 feet of obstacle clearance within a 100-mile radius of the navigation facility upon which the procedure is predicated and are normally used only in military procedures. These altitudes are identified on published procedures as "Emergency Safe Altitudes."

ICAO—MINIMUM SECTOR ALTITUDE—The lowest altitude which may be used under emergency conditions which will provide a minimum clearance of 300 meters (1000 feet) above all obstacles located in an area contained within a sector of a circle of 25 nautical miles radius centered on a radio aid to navigation.

MINIMUM SAFE ALTITUDE WARNING (MSAW)—A function of the ARTS III computer that aids the controller by alerting him when a tracked Mode C equipped aircraft is below or is predicted by the computer to go below a predetermined minimum safe altitude. (Refer to AIM)

MINIMUMS/MINIMA—Weather conditions requirements established for a particular operation or type of operation, e.g., IFR takeoff or landing, alternate airport for IFR flight plans, VFR flight, etc. (See Landing Minimums, IFR Takeoff Minimums, VFR Conditions, IFR Conditions) (Refer to FAR Part 91; AIM)

MINIMUM VECTORING ALTITUDE/MVA—The lowest MSL altitude at which an IFR aircraft will be vectored by a radar controller, except as otherwise authorized for radar approaches, departures, and missed approaches. The altitude meets IFR obstacle clearance criteria. It may be lower than the published MEA along an airway or J-route segment. It may be utilized for radar vectoring only upon the controllers' determination that an adequate radar return is being received from the aircraft being controlled. Charts depicting minimum vectoring altitudes are normally available only to the controllers and not to pilots. (Refer to AIM)

MISSED APPROACH—

1. A maneuver conducted by a pilot when an instrument approach cannot be completed to a landing. The route of flight and altitude are shown on instrument approach procedure charts. A pilot executing a missed approach prior to the Missed Approach Point (MAP) must continue along the final approach to the MAP. The pilot may climb immediately to the altitude specified in the missed approach procedure.

2. A term used by the pilot to inform ATC that he is executing the missed approach.

3. At locations where ATC radar service is provided, the pilot should conform to radar vectors, when provided by ATC, in lieu of the published missed approach procedure. (See Missed Approach Point) Refer to AIM

ICAO—MISSED APPROACH PROCEDURE—The procedure to be followed if, after an instrument approach, a landing is not effected, and occurring normally:

1. When the aircraft has descended to the decision height and has not established visual contact, or

2. When directed by air traffic control to pull up or to go around again.

MISSED APPROACH POINT/MAP—A point prescribed in each instrument approach procedure at which a missed approach procedure shall be executed if the required visual reference does not exist. (See Missed Approach, Segments of an Instrument Approach Procedure)

MISSED APPROACH SEGMENT—(See Segments of an Instrument Approach Procedure)

MODE—The letter or number assigned to a specific pulse spacing of radio signals transmitted or received by ground interrogator or airborne transponder components of the Air Traffic Control Radar Beacon System (ATCRBS). Mode A (military Mode 3) and Mode C (altitude reporting) are used in air traffic control. (See Transponder, Interrogator, Radar) (Refer to AIM)

ICAO—MODE (SSR MODE)—The letter or number assigned to a specific pulse spacing of the interrogation signals transmitted by an interrogator. There are four modes—A, B, C, and D—corresponding to four different interrogation pulse spacings.

MOVEMENT AREA—The runways, taxiways, and other areas of an airport which are utilized for taxiing, takeoff, and landing of aircraft, exclusive of loading ramp and parking areas. At those airports with a tower, specific approval for entry onto the movement area must be obtained from ATC.

ICAO—MOVEMENT AREA—That part of an aerodome intended for the surface movement of aircraft, including the maneuvering area and aprons.

MOVING TARGET INDICATOR/MTI—An electronic device which will permit radar scope presentation only from targets which are in motion. A partial remedy for ground clutter.

MSAW—(See Minimum Safe Altitude Warning)

NAS STAGE A—The en route ATC system's radar, computers and computer programs, controller plan view displays (PVDs/Radar Scopes), input/output devices, and the related communications equipment which are integrated to form the heart of the automated IFR air traffic control system. This equipment performs Flight Data Processing (FDP) and Radar Data Processing (RDP). It interfaces with automated terminal systems and is used in the control of en route IFR aircraft. (Refer to AIM)

NATIONAL AIRSPACE SYSTEM/NAS—The common network of U.S. airspace; air navigation facilities, equipment and services, airports or landing areas; aeronautical charts, information and services; rules, regulations and procedures, technical information, and manpower and material. Included are system components shared jointly with the military.

NATIONAL BEACON CODE ALLOCATION PLAN AIRSPACE/NBCAP AIRSPACE—Airspace over United States territory located within the North American continent between Canada and Mexico, including adjacent territorial waters outward to about boundaries of oceanic control areas (CTA)/Flight Information Regions (FIR). (See Flight Information Region)

NATIONAL FLIGHT DATA CENTER/NFDC—A facility in Washington, D.C., established by FAA to operate a central aeronautical information service for the collection, validation, and dissemination of aeronautical data in support of the activities of government, industry, and the aviation community. The information is published in the National Flight Data Digest. (See National Flight Data Digest)

NATIONAL FLIGHT DATA DIGEST/NFDD—A daily (except weekends and federal holidays) publication of flight information appropriate to aeronautical charts, aeronautical publications, Notices to Airmen, or other media serving the purpose of providing operational flight data essential to safe and efficient aircraft operations.

NATIONAL SEARCH AND RESCUE PLAN—An interagency agreement which provides for the effective utilization of all available facilities in all types of search and rescue missions.

NAVAID CLASSES—VOR, VORTAC, and TACAN aids are classed according to their operational use. The three classes of NAVAIDS are:

T—Terminal

L—Low altitude

H—High altitude

The normal service range for T, L, and H class aids is found in AIM. Certain operational requirements make it necessary to use some of these aids at greater service ranges than specified. Extended range is made possible through flight inspection determinations. Some aids also have lesser service range due to location, terrain, frequency protection, etc. Restrictions to service range are listed in Airport/Facility Directory.

NAVIGABLE AIRSPACE—Airspace at and above the minimum flight altitudes prescribed in the FARs including airspace needed for safe take-off and landing. (Refer to FAR Part 91)

NAVIGATIONAL AID/NAVAID—Any visual or electronic device airborne or on the surface which provides point to point guidance information or position data to aircraft in flight. (See Air Navigation Facility)

NDB—(See Nondirectional beacon)

NEGATIVE—"No," or "permission not granted," or "that is not correct."

NEGATIVE CONTACT—

Used by pilots to inform ATC that:

1. Previously issued traffic is not in sight. It may be followed by the pilot's request for the controller to provide assistance in avoiding the traffic.

2. They were unable to contact ATC on a particular frequency.

NIGHT—The time between the end of evening civil twilight and the beginning of morning civil twilight, as published in the American Air Almanac, converted to local time.

ICAO—NIGHT—The hours between the end of evening civil twilight an the beginning of morning civil twilight or such other period between sunset and sunrise as may be specified by the appropriate authority.

NO GYRO APPROACH/VECTOR—A radar approach/vector provided in case of a malfunctioning gyrocompass or directional gyro. Instead of providing the pilot with headings to be flown, the controller observes the radar track and issues control instructions "turn right/left" or "stop turn," as appropriate. (Refer to AIM)

NON-COMPOSITE SEPARATION—Separation in accordance with minima other than the composite separation minimum specified for the area concerned.

NONDIRECTIONAL BEACON/RADIO BEACON/NDB—An L/MF or UHF radio beacon transmitting nondirectional signals whereby the pilot of an aircraft equipped with direction finding equipment can determine his bearing to or from the radio beacon and "home" on or track to or from the station. When the radio beacon is installed in conjunction with the Instrument Landing System marker, it is normally called Compass Locator. (See Compass Locator, Automatic Direction Finder)

NONPRECISION APPROACH PROCEDURE/NONPRECISION APPROACH—A standard instrument approach procedure in which no electronic glide slope is provided; e.g., VOR, TACAN, NDB, LOC, ASR, LDA, or SDF approaches.

NONRADAR—Precedes other terms and generally means without the use of radar, such as:

1. Nonradar Route—A flight path or route over which the pilot is performing his own navigation. The pilot may be receiving radar separation, radar monitoring, or other ATC services while on a nonradar route. (See Radar Route)

2. Nonradar Approach—Used to describe instrument approaches for which course guidance on final approach is not provided by ground based precision or surveillance radar. Radar vectors to the final approach course may or may not be provided by ATC. Examples of nonradar approaches are VOR, ADF, TACAN, and ILS approaches. (See Final Approach—IFR, Final Approach Course, Radar Approach, Instrument Approach Procedure)

3. Nonradar Separation—The spacing of aircraft in accordance with established minima without the use of radar, e.g., vertical, lateral, or longitudinal separation. (See Radar Separation)

   ICAO—NON-RADAR SEPARATION—The separation used when aircraft position information is derived from sources other than radar.

4. Nonradar Arrival—An arriving aircraft that is not being vectored to the final approach course for an instrument approach or towards the airport for a visual approach. The aircraft may or may not be in a radar environment and may or may not be receiving radar separation, radar monitoring, or other services provided by ATC. (See Radar Arrival, Radar Environment)

NONRADAR APPROACH CONTROL—An ATC facility providing approach control service without the use of radar. (See Approach Control, Approach Control Service)

NORDO—(See Lost Communications)

NORTH AMERICAN ROUTE—A numerically coded route preplanned over existing airway and route systems to and from specific coastal fixes serving the North Atlantic. North American Routes consist of the following:

1. Common Route/Portion—That segment of a North American route between the inland navigation facility and the coastal fix.

2. Non-Common Route/Portion—That segment of a North American route between the inland navigation facility and a designated North American terminal.

3. Inland Navigation Facility—A navigation aid on a North American route at which the common route and/or the non-common route begins or ends.

4. Coastal Fix—A navigation aid or intersection where an aircraft transitions between the domestic route structure and the oceanic route structure.

NOTICES TO AIRMEN/PUBLICATION—A publication designed primarily as a pilot's operational manual containing current NOTAM information (see Notice to Airmen—NOTAM) considered essential to the safety of flight as well as supplemental data to other aeronautical publications.

NOTICE TO AIRMEN/NOTAM—A notice containing information (not known sufficiently in advance to publicize by other means) concerning the establishment, condition, or change in any component (facility, service, or procedure of, or hazard in the National Airspace System) the timely knowledge of which is essential to personnal concerned with flight operations.

1. NOTAM(D)—A NOTAM given (in addition to local dissemination) distant dissemination via teletypewriter beyond the area of responsibility of the Flight Service Station. These NOTAMS will be stored and repeated hourly until cancelled.
2. NOTAM(L)—A NOTAM given local dissemination by voice (teletypewriter where applicable), and a wide variety of means such as: TelAutograph, teleprinter, facsimile reproduction, hot line, telecopier, telegraph, and telephone to satisfy local user requirements.
3. FDC NOTAM—A notice to airmen, regulatory in nature, transmitted by NFDC and given all-circuit dissemination.

ICAO—NOTAM—A notice, containing information concerning the establishment, condition, or change in any aeronautical facility, service, procedure, or hazard, the timely knowledge of which is essential to personnel concerned with flight operations.

NUMEROUS TARGETS VICINITY (LOCATION)—A traffic advisory issued by ATC to advise pilots that targets on the radar scope are too numerous to issue individually. (See Traffic Advisories)

OBSTACLE—An existing object, object of natural growth, or terrain at a fixed geographical location, or which may be expected at a fixed location within a prescribed area, with reference to which vertical clearance is or must be provided during flight operation.

OBSTRUCTION—An object which penetrates an imaginary surface described in FAR Part 77. (Refer to FAR Part 77)

OBSTRUCTION LIGHT—A light, or one of a group of lights, usually red or white, frequently mounted on a surface structure or natural terrain to warn pilots of the presence of an obstruction.

OFF-ROUTE VECTOR—A vector by ATC which takes an aircraft off a previously assigned route. Altitudes assigned by ATC during such vectors provide required obstacle clearance.

OFFSET PARALLEL RUNWAYS—Staggered runways having centerlines which are parallel.

ON COURSE—
1. Used to indicate that an aircraft is established on the route centerline.
2. Used by ATC to advise a pilot making a radar approach that his aircraft is lined up on the final approach course. (See On-Course Indication)

ON-COURSE INDICATION—An indication on an instrument which provides the pilot a visual means of determining that the aircraft is located on the centerline of a given navigational track, or an indication on a radar scope that an aircraft is on a given track.

OPTION APPROACH—An approach requested and conducted by a pilot which will result in either a touch-and-go, missed approach, low approach, stop-and-go, or full stop landing. (See Cleared for the option) (Refer to AIM)

ORGANIZED TRACK SYSTEM—A moveable system of oceanic tracks that traverses the North Atlantic between Europe and North America the physical position of which is determined twice daily taking the best advantage of the winds aloft.

OUT—The conversation is ended and no response is expected.

OUTER COMPASS LOCATOR—(See Compass Locator)

OUTER FIX—A general term used within ATC to describe fixes in the terminal area, other than the final approach fix. Aircraft are normally cleared to these fixes by an Air Route Traffic Control Center or an Approach Control Facility. Aircraft are normally cleared from these fixes to the final approach fix or final approach course.

OUTER MARKER/OM—A marker beacon at or near the glide slope intercept altitude of an ILS approach. It is keyed to transmit two dashes per second on a 400

Hz tons which is received aurally and visually by compatible airborne equipment. The OM is normally located four to seven miles from the runway threshold on the extended centerline of the runway. (See Marker Beacon, Instrument Landing System) (Refer to AIM)

OVER—My transmission is ended; I expect a response.

OVERHEAD APPROACH/360 OVERHEAD—A series of predetermined maneuvers prescribed for VFR arrival of military aircraft (often in formation) for entry into the VFR traffic pattern and to proceed to a landing. The pattern usually specifies the following:
1. The radio contact required of the pilot.
2. The speed to be maintained.
3. An initial approach 3 to 5 miles in length.
4. An elliptical pattern consisting of two 180 degree turns.
5. A break point at which the first 180 degree turn is started.
6. The direction of turns.
7. Altitude (at least 500 feet above the conventional pattern).
8. A "Roll-out" on final approach not less than ¼ mile from the landing threshold and not less than 300 feet above the ground.

PAN—The international radio-telephony urgency signal. When repeated three times indicates uncertainty or alert, followed by nature of urgency. (See MAYDAY) (Refer to AIM)

PARALLEL ILS APPROACHES—ILS approaches to parallel runways by IFR aircraft which, when established inbound toward the airport on the adjacent localizer courses, are radar-separated by at least 2 miles. (See Simultaneous ILS Approaches)

PARALLEL OFFSET ROUTE—A parallel track to the left or right of the designated or established airway/route. Normally associated with Area Navigation (RNAV) operations. (See Area Navigation)

PARALLEL RUNWAYS—Two or more runways at the same airport whose centerlines are parallel. In additio to runway number, parallel runways are designated as L (left) and R (right) or, if three parallel runways exist, L (left), C (center), and R (right).

PAR APPROACH—A precision instrument approach wherein the air traffic controller issues guidance instructions, for pilot compliance, based on the aircraft's position in relation to the final approach course (azimuth), the glide slope (elevation), and the distance (range) from the touchdown point on the runway as displayed on the controller's radar scope. (See Precision Approach Radar, Glide Path) (Refer to AIM)

PERMANENT ECHO—Radar signals reflected from fixed objects on the earth's surface; e.g., buildings, towers, terrain. Permanent echoes are distinguished from "ground clutter" by being definable locations rather than large areas. Under certain conditions they may be used to check radar alignment.

PHOTO RECONNAISSANCE (PR)—Military activity that requires locating individual photo targets and navigating to the targets at a preplanned angle and altitude. The activity normally requires a lateral route width of 16NM and altitude range of 1,500 feet to 10,000 feet AGL.

PILOT BRIEFING/PRE-FLIGHT PILOT BRIEFING—A service provided by the FSS to assist pilots in flight planning. Briefing items may include weather information, NOTAMS, military activities, flow control information and other items as requested. (Refer to AIM)

PILOT IN COMMAND—The pilot responsible for the operation and safety of an aircraft during flight time. (Refer to FAR Part 91)

PILOTS AUTOMATIC TELEPHONE WEATHER ANSWERING SERVICE/PATWAS—A continuous telephone recording containing current and forecast weather information for pilots. (See Flight Service Station) (Refer to AIM)

PILOT'S DISCRETION—When used in conjunction with altitude assignments, means that ATC has offered the pilot the option of starting climb or descent whenever he wishes and conducting the climb or descent at any rate he wishes. He may temporarily level off at any intermediate altitude. However, once he has vacated an altitude he may not return to that altitude.

PILOT WEATHER REPORT/PIREP—A report of meteorological phenomena encountered by aircraft in flight. (Refer to AIM)

POSITION REPORT/PROGRESS REPORT—A report over a known location as transmitted by an aircraft to ATC. (Refer to AIM)

POSITION SYMBOL—A computer generated indication shown on a radar display to indicate the mode of tracking.

POSITIVE CONTROL—The separation of all air traffic, within designated airspace, by air traffic control. (See Positive Control Area.)

POSITIVE CONTROL AREA/PCA—Airspace designated in FAR Part 71 wherein aircraft are required to be operated under Instrument Flight Rules (IFR). Vertical extent of PCA is from 18,000 feet to and including flight level 600 throughout most of the conterminous United States. In Alaska, it includes the airspace over the State of Alaska from 18,000 feet to and inlcuding FL 600, but not including the airspace less than 1,500 feet above the surface of the earth and the Alaskan Peninsula west of longitude 160° 00′ W. Rules for operating in positive control area are found in FARs 91.97 and 91.24.

PRECIPITATION—Any or all forms of water particles (rain, sleet, hail, or snow), that fall from the atmosphere and reach the surface.

PRECISION APPROACH PROCEDURE/PRECISION APPROACH—A standard instrument approach procedure in which an electronic glide slope is provided; e.g., ILS and PAR. (See Instrument Landing System, Precision Approach Radar)

PRECISION APPROACH RADAR/PAR—Radar equipment in some ATC facilities serving military airports, which is used to detect and display the azimuth, range, and elevation of an aircraft on the final approach course to a runway. It is used by air traffic controllers to provide the pilot with a precision approach, or to monitor certain nonradar approaches. (See PAR Approach)

ICAO—PRECISION APPROACH RADAR/PAR—Primary radar equipment used to determine the position of an aircraft during final approach, in terms of lateral and vertical deviations relative to a nominal approach path, and in range relative to touchdown.

PREFERENTIAL ROUTES—Preferential routes (PDRs, PARs, and PDARs) are adapted in ARTCC computers to accomplish inter/intra-facility controller coordination and to assure that flight data is posted at the proper control positions. Locations having a need for these specific inbound and outbound routes normally publish such routes in local facility bulletins and their use by pilots minimizes flight plan route amendments. When the workload or traffic situation permits, controllers normally provide radar vectors or assign requested routes to minimize circuitous routing. Preferential routes are usually confined to one ARTCC's area and are referred to by the following names or acronyms:

1. Preferential Departure Route/PDR—A specific departure route from an airport or terminal area to an en route point where there is no further need for flow control. It may be included in a Standard Instrument Departure (SID) or a Preferred IFR Route.
2. Preferential Arrival Route/PAR—A specific arrival route from an appropriate en route point to an airport or terminal area. It may be included in a Standard Terminal Arrival Route (STAR) or a Preferred IFR Route. The abbreviation "PAR" is used primarily within the ARTCC and should not be confused with the abbreviation for Precision Approach Radar.
3. Preferential Departure and Arrival Route/PDR—A route between two terminals which are within or immediately adjacent to one ARTCC's area. PDARS are not synonomous with Preferred IFR Routes but may be listed as such as they do accomplish essentially the same purpose. (See Preferred IFR Routes, NAS Stage A)

PREFERRED IFR ROUTES—Routes established between busier airports to increase system efficiency and capacity. They normally extend through one or more ARTCC areas and are designed to achieve balanced traffic flows among high density terminals. IFR clearances are issued on the basis of these routes except when severe weather avoidance procedures or other factors dicate otherwise. Preferred IFR Routes are listed in the Airport/Facility Directory. If a flight is planned to or from an area having such routes but the departure or arrival point is not listed in the Airport/Facility Directory, pilots may use that part of a Preferred IFR Route which is appropriate for the departure or arrival point that is listed. Preferred IFR Routes are correlated with SIDs and STARs and may be defined by airways, jet routes, direct routes between NAVAIDS, Waypoints, NAVAID radials/DME, or any other combinations thereof. (See Standard Instrument Departure, Standard Terminal Arrival Route, Preferential Routes, Center's Area) (Refer to Airport/Facility Directory and Notices to Airmen)

PREVAILING VISIBILITY—(See Visibility)

PROCEDURE TURN INBOUND—That point of a procedure turn maneuver where course reversal has been completed and an aircraft is established inbound on the intermediate approach segment or final approach course. A report of "procedure turn inbound" is normally used by ATC as a position report for separation purposes. (See Final Approach Course, Procedure Turn, Segments of an Instrument Approach Procedure)

PROCEDURE TURN/PT—The maneuver prescribed when it is necessary to reverse direction to establish an aircraft on the intermediate approach segment or final approach course. The outbound course, direction of turn, distance within which the turn must be completed, and minimum altitude are specified in the procedure. However, unless otherwise restricted, the point at which the turn may be commenced, and the type and rate of turn, are left to the discretion of the pilot.

ICAO—PROCEDURE TURN—A maneuver in which a turn is made away from a designated track followed by a turn in the opposite direction, both turns being executed so as to permit the aircraft to intercept and proceed along the reciprocal of the designated track.

PROFILE DESCENT—An uninterrupted descent (except where level flight is required for speed adjustment, e.g., 250 knots at 10,000 feet MSL) from cruising altitude/level to interception of a glide slope or to a minimum altitude specified for the initial or intermediate approach segment of a non-precision instrument approach. The profile descent normally terminates at the approach gate or where the glide slope or other appropriate minimum altitude is intercepted.

PROHIBITED AREA—(See Special Use Airspace)

ICAO—PROHIBITED AREA—An airspace of defined dimensions, above the land areas or territorial waters of a state, within which the flight of aircraft is prohibited.

PROPOSED BOUNDARY CROSSING TIME/PBCT—Each center has a PBCT parameter for each internal airport. Proposed internal flight plans are transmitted to the adjacent center if the flight time along the proposed route from the departure airport to the center boundary is less than or equal to the value of PBCT or if airport adaptation specifies transmission regardless of PBCT.

PUBLISHED ROUTE—A route for which an IFR altitude has been established and published, e.g., Federal Airways, Jet Routes, Area Navigation Routes, Specified Direct Routes.

QUADRANT—A quarter part of a circle, centered on a NAVAID, oriented clockwise from magnetic north as follows: NE quadrant 000-089, SE quadrant 090-179, SW quadrant 180-269, NW quadrant 270-359.

QUICK LOOK—A feature of NAS Stage A and ARTS which provides the controller the capability to display full data blocks of tracked aircraft from other control positions.

QUOTA FLOW CONTROL/QFLOW—A flow control procedure by which the Central Flow Control Function (CFCF) restricts traffic to the ARTC Center area having an impacted airport thereby avoiding sector/area saturation. (See Air Traffic Control Systems Command Center) (Refer to Airport/Facility Directory)

RADAR ADVISORY—The provision of advice and information based on radar observations. (See Advisory Service)

RADAR AIR TRAFFIC CONTROL FACILITY/RATCF—An air traffic control facility, located at a U.S. Navy or Marine Corps Air Station, utilizing surveillance and, normally, precision approach radar and air/ground communications equipment to provide approach control services to aircraft arriving, departing, or transiting the airspace controlled by the facility. The facility may be operated by the FAA, USN, or USMC and service may be provided to both civil and military airports. Similar to TRACON (FAA), RAPCON (USAF), and ARAC (Army). (See Approach Control, Approach Control Service, Departure Control)

RADAR APPROACH—An instrument approach procedure which utilizes Precision Approach Radar (PAR) or Airport Surveillance Radar (ASR). (See PAR Approach, Surveillance Approach, Airport Surveillance Radar, Precision Approach Radar, Instrument Approach Procedure) (Refer to AIM)

ICAO—RADAR APPROACH—An approach, executed by an aircraft, under the direction of a radar controller.

RADAR APPROACH CONTROL/RAPCON—An air traffic control facility, located at a U.S. Air Force Base, utilizing surveillance and, normally, precision approach radar and air/ground communications equipment to provide approach control services to aircraft arriving, departing, or transiting the airspace controlled by the facility. The facility may be operated by the FAA or the USAF and service may be provided to both civil and military airports. Similar to TRACON (FAA), RATCF (Navy) and ARAC (Army). (See Approach Control, Approach Control Service, Departure Control)

RADAR ARRIVAL—An arriving aircraft which is being vectored to the final approach course for an instrument approach or for a visual approach to the airport. (See Radar Approach, Visual Approach)

RADAR BEACON—(See Radar)

RADAR CONTACT—

1. Used by ATC to inform an aircraft that it is identified on the radar display and radar flight following will be provided until radar identification is terminated. Radar service may also be provided within the limits of necessity and capability. When a pilot is informed of "radar contact," he automatically discontinues reporting over compulsory reporting points. (See Radar Flight Following, Radar Contact Lost, Radar Service, Radar Service Terminated) (Refer to AIM)

2. The term an air traffic controller uses to inform the transferring controller that the target being transferred is identified and on his radar display.

ICAO—RADAR CONTACT—The situation which exists when the radar blip of a particular aircraft is seen and identified on a radar display.

RADAR CONTACT LOST—Used by ATC to inform a pilot that radar identification of his aircraft has been lost. The loss may be attributed to several things including the aircraft merging with weather or ground clutter, the aircraft flying below radar line of sight, the aircraft entering an area of poor radar return, or a failure of the aircraft transponder or ground radar equipment. (See Clutter, Radar Contact)

RADAR ENVIRONMENT—An area in which radar service may be provided. (See Radar Contact, Radar Service, Additional Services, Traffic Advisories)

RADAR FLIGHT FOLLOWING—The observation of the progress of radar identified aircraft, whose primary navigation is being provided by the pilot, wherein the controller retains and correlates the aircraft identity with the appropriate target or target symbol displayed on the radar scope. (See Radar Contact, Radar Service) (Refer to AIM)

RADAR IDENTIFICATION—The process of ascertaining that an observed radar target is the radar return from a particular aircraft. (See Radar Contact, Radar Serivce)

ICAO—RADAR IDENTIFICATION—The process of correlating a particular radar blip with a specific aircraft.

RADAR IDENTIFIED AIRCRAFT—An aircraft, the position of which has been correlated with an observed target or symbol on the radar display. (See Radar Contact, Radar Contact Lost)

RADAR MONITORING—(See Radar Service)

RADAR NAVIGATIONAL GUIDANCE—(See Radar Service)

RADAR POINT OUT/POINT OUT—Used between controllers to indicate radar handoff action where the initiating controller plans to retain communications with an aircraft penetrating the other controller's airspace and additional coordination is required.

RADAR/RADIO DETECTING AND RANGING—A device which, by measuring the time interval between transmission and reception of radio pulses and correlating the angular orientation of the radiated antenna beam or beams in azimuth and/or elevation, provides information on range, azimuth and/or elevation of objects in the path of the transmitted pulses.

1. Primary Radar—A radar system in which a minute portion of a radio pulse transmitted from a site is reflected by an object and then received back at that site for processing and display at an air traffic control facility.

2. Secondary Radar/Radar Beacon/ATCRBS—A radar system in which the object to be detected is fitted with cooperative equipment in the form of a radio receiver/transmitter (transponder). Radar pulses transmitted from the searching transmitter/receiver (interrogator) site are received in the cooperative equipment and used to trigger a distinctive transmission from the transponder. This reply transmission, rather than a reflected signal, is then received back at the transmitter/receiver site for processing and display at an air traffic control facility. (See Transponder, Interrogator) (Refer to AIM)

ICAO—RADAR—A radio detection device which provides information on range, azimuth and/or elevation or objects.

1. *Primary Radar*—A radar system which uses reflected radio systems.

2. *Secondary Radar*—A radar system wherein a radio signal transmitted from a radar station initiates the transmission of a radio signal from another station.

RADAR ROUTE—A flight path or route over which an aircraft is vectored. Navigational guidance and altitude assignments are provided by ATC. (See Flight Path, Route)

RADAR SEPARATION—(See Radar Service)

RADAR SERVICE—A term which encompasses one or more of the following services based on the use of radar which can be provided by a controller to a pilot of a radar identifed aircraft.

1. Radar Separation—Radar spacing of aircraft in accordance with established minima.

2. Radar Navigational Guidance—Vectoring aircraft to provide course guidance.

3. Radar Monitoring—The radar flight following of aircraft, whose primary navigation is being performed by the pilot, to observe and note deviations from its authorized flight path, airway, or route.
   When being applied specifically to radar monitoring of instrument approaches, i.e., with precison approach radar (PAR) or radar monitoring of simultaneous ILS approaches, it includes advice and instructions whenever an aircraft nears or exceeds the prescribed PAR safety limit or simultaneous ILS no transgression zone. (See Additonal Services, Traffic Advisories, Duty Priority)

ICAO—RADAR SERVICE—Term used to indicate a service provided directly by means of radar.

ICAO—RADAR SEPARATION—The separation used when aircraft position information is derived from radar sources.

ICAO—RADAR MONITORING—The use of radar for the purpose of providing aircraft with information and advice relative to significant deviations from nominal flight path.

RADIO BEACON—(See Nondirectional Beacon)

RADIO MAGNETIC INDICATOR/RMI—An aircraft navigational instrument coupled with a gyro compass or similar compass that indicates the direction of a selected NAVAID and indicates bearing with respect to the heading of the aircraft.

RAMP—(See Apron)

READ BACK—Repeat my message back to me.

RECEIVING CONTROLLER/FACILITY—A controller/facility receiving control of an aircraft from another controller/facility.

REDUCE SPEED TO (SPEED)—(See Speed Adjustment)

RELEASE TIME—A departure time restriction issued to a pilot by ATC when necessary to separate a departing aircraft from the other traffic.

RADAR SERVICE TERMINATED—Used by ATC to inform a pilot that he will no longer be provided any of the services that could be received while under radar contact. Radar service is automatically terminated and the pilot is not advised in the following cases:

1. An aircraft cancels its IFR flight plan, except within a TCA, TRSA, or where Stage II service is provided.
2. At the completion of a radar approach.
3. When an arriving aircraft receiving Stage I, II, or III service is advised to contact the tower.
4. When an aircraft conducting a visual approach or contact approach is advised to contact the tower.
5. When an aircraft making an instrument approach has landed or the tower has the aircraft in sight, whichever occurs first.

RADAR SURVEILLANCE—The radar observation of a given geographical area for the purpose of performing some radar function.

RADAR TRAFFIC ADVISORIES—(See Traffic Advisories)

RADAR TRAFFIC INFORMATION SERVICE—(See Traffic Advisories)

RADAR WEATHER ECHO INTENSITY LEVELS—Existing radar systems cannot detect turbulence. However, there is a direct correlation between the degree of turbulence and other weather features associated with thunderstorms, and the radar weather echo intensity. The National Weather Service has categorized six (6) levels of radar weather echo intensity. The following list gives the weather features likely to be associated with these levels during thunderstorm weather situations:

1. Level 1 (WEAK) and Level 2 (MODERATE). Light to moderate turbulance is possible with lightning.
2. Level 3 (STRONG). Severe turbulence possible, lightning.
3. Level 4 (VERY STRONG). Severe turbulence likely, lightning.
4. Level 5 (INTENSE). Severe turbulence, lightning, organized wind gusts. Hail likely.
5. Level 6 (EXTREME). Severe turbulence, large hail, lightning, extensive wind gusts and turbulence.

RADIAL—A magnetic bearing extending from a VOR/VORTAC/TACAN navigation facility.

RADIO—

1. A device used for communication.
2. Used to refer to a Flight Service Station, e.g., "Seattle Radio" is used to call Seattle FSS.

RADIO ALTIMETER/RADAR ALTIMETER—Aircraft equipment which makes use of the reflection of radio waves from the ground to determine the height of the aircraft above the surface.

ICAO—RELEASE TIME—Time prior to which an aircraft should be given further clearance or prior to which it should not proceed in case of radio failure.

REMOTE COMMUNICATIONS AIR/GROUND FACILITY/RCAG—An unmanned VHF/UHF transmitter/receiver facility which is used to expand ARTCC air/ground communications coverage and to facilitate direct contact between pilots and controllers. RCAG facilities are sometimes not equipped with emergency frequencies 121.5 MHz and 243.0 MHz. (Refer to AIM)

REMOTE COMMUNICATIONS OUTLET/RCO—An unmanned air/ground communications station remotely controlled, providing UHF and VHF transmit and receive capability to extend the service range of the FSS.

REPORT—Used to instruct pilots to advise ATC of specified information, e.g., "Report passing Hamilton VOR."

REPORTING POINT—A geographical location in relation to which the position of an aircraft is reported. (See Compulsory Reporting Point) (Refer to AIM)

ICAO—REPORTING POINT—A specified geographical location in relation to which the position of an aircraft can be reported.

REQUEST FULL ROUTE CLEARANCE/FRC—Used by pilots to request that the entire route of flight be read verbatim in an ATC clearance. Such request should be made to preclude receiving an ATC clearance based on the original filed flight plan when a filed IFR flight plan has been revised by the pilot, company, or operations prior to departure.

RESCUE COORDINATION CENTER/RCC— A search and rescue (SAR) facility equipped and manned to coordinate and control SAR operations in an area designated by the SAR plan. The U.S. Coast Guard and the U.S. Air Force have responsibility for the operation of RCCs.

ICAO—RESCUE CO-ORDINATION CENTRE—A unit responsible for promoting efficient organization of search and rescue service and for co-ordinating the conduct of search and rescue region.

RESTRICTED AREA—(See Special Use Airspace)

ICAO—RESTRICTED AREA—Airspace of defined dimensions, above the land areas or territorial waters of a State, within which the flight of aircraft is restricted in accordance with certain specified conditions.

RESUME OWN NAVIGATION—Used by ATC to advise a pilot to resume his own navigational responsibility. It is issued after completion of a radar vector or when radar contact is lost while the aircraft is being radar vectored. (See Radar Contact Lost, Radar Service Terminated)

RNAV—(See Area Navigation)

RNAV APPROACH—An instrument approach procedure which relies on aircraft area navigation equipment for navigational guidance. (See Instrument Approach Procedure, Area Navigation)

ROAD RECONNAISSANCE (RC)—Military activity requiring navigation along roads, railroads and rivers. Reconnaissance route/route segments are seldom along a straight line and normally require a laterao route width of 10NM to 30NM and altitude range of 500 feet to 10,000 feet AGI.

ROGER—I have received all of your last transmission. It should not be used to answer a question requiring a yes or no answer. (See Affirmative, Negative)

ROLLOUT RVR—(See Visibility)

ROUTE—A defined path, consisting of one or more courses in a horizontal plane, which aircraft traverse over the surface of the earth. (See Jet Route, Airway, Published Route, Unpublished Route)

ROUTE SEGMENT—Us used in Air Traffic Control, a part of a route that can be defined by two navigational fixes, two NAVAIDs, or a fix and a NAVAID. (See Route, Fix)

ICAO—ROUTE SEGMENT—A portion of a route to be flown, as defined by two consecutive significant points specified in a flight plan.

RUNWAY—A defined rectangular area, on a land airport prepared for the landing and takeoff run of aircraft along its length. Runways are normally numbered in relation to their magnetic direction rounded off to the nearest 10 degrees, e.g., Runway 25, Runway 01. (See Parallel Runways)

ICAO—RUNWAY A defined rectangular area, on a land aerodrome prepared for the landing and takeoff run of aircraft along its length.

RUNWAY CENTERLINE LIGHTING—(See Airport Lighting)

RUNWAY CONDITION READING/RCR—Numerical decelerometer readings relayed by air traffic controllers at USAF and certain civil bases for use by the pilot in determining runway braking action. These readings are routinely relayed only to USAF and Air National Guard Aircraft. (See Braking Action)

RUNWAY END IDENTIFIER LIGHTS—(See Airport Lighting)

RUNWAY GRADIENT—The average slope, measured in percent, between two ends or points on a runway. Runway gradient is depicted on Government aerodrome sketches when total runway gradient exceeds 0.3%

RUNWAY IN USE/ACTIVE RUNWAY/DUTY RUNWAY—Any runway or runways currently being used for takeoff or landing. When multiple runways are used, they are all considered active runways.

RUNWAY LIGHTS—(See Airport Lighting)

RUNWAY MARKINGS—

1. Basic marking—Markings on runways used for operations under visual flight rules consisting of centerline marking and runway direction numbers and, if required, letters.
2. Instrument marking—Markings on runways served by nonvisual navigation aids and intended for landings under instrument weather conditions, consisting of basic marking plus threshold marking.
3. All-weather (precision instrument) marking—Markings on runways served by nonvisual precision approach aids and on runways having special operational requirements, consisting of instrument markings plus landing zone marking and side strips. (Refer to AIM)

RUNWAY PROFILE DESCENT—An instrument flight rules (IFR) air traffic control arrival procedure to a runway published for pilot use in graphic and/or textual form and may be associated with a STAR. RUNWAY PROFILE DESCENTs provide routing, and may depict crossing altitudes, speed restrictions, and headings to be flown from the en route structure to the point where the pilot will receive clearance for and execute an instrument approach procedure. A RUNWAY PROFILE DESCENT may apply to more than one runway if so stated on the chart. (Refer to AIM)

RUNWAY USE PROGRAM—Action initiated by the airport proprietor, with assistance from the users and FAA, to reduce the effect of noise on residents surrounding an airport through the use of specific runways when wind, weather, and other safety related factors permit.

RUNWAY VISIBILITY VALUE—(See Visibility)

RUNWAY VISUAL RANGE—(See Visibility)

SAFETY ADVISORY—A safety advisory issued by ATC to aircraft under their control if ATC is aware the aircraft is at an altitude which, in the controller's judgment, places the aircraft in unsafe proximity to terrain, obstructions or other aircraft. The controller may discontinue the issuance of further advisories if the pilot advises he is taking action to correct the situation or has the other aircraft in sight.

1. Terrain/Obstruction Advisory—A safety advisory issued by ATC to aircraft under their control if ATC is aware the aircraft is at an altitude which, in the controller's judgment, places the aircraft in unsafe proximity to terrain/obstructions; e.g., "Low Altitude Alert, check your altitude immediately."
2. Aircraft Conflict Advisory—A safety advisory issued by ATC to aircraft under their control if ATC is aware of an aircraft that is not under their control at an altitude which, in the controller's judgment, places both aircraft in unsafe proximity to each other. With the alert, ATC will offer the pilot an alternate course of action when feasible, e.g., "Traffic Alert, advise you turn right heading zero niner zero or climb to eight thousand immediately."

The issuance of a safety advisory is contingent upon the capability of the controller to have an awareness of an unsafe condition. The course of action provided will be predicated on other traffic under ATC control. Once the advisory is issued, it is solely the pilot's prerogative to determine what course of action, if any, he will take.

SAY AGAIN—Used to request a repeat of the last transmission. Usually specifies transmission or portion thereof not understood or received, e.g., "Say again all after ABRAM VOR."

SAY ALTITUDE—Used by ATC to ascertain an aircraft's specific altitude/flight level. When the aircraft is climbing or descending, the pilot should state the indicated altitude rounded to the nearest 100 feet.

SAY HEADING—Used by ATC to request an aircraft heading. The pilot should state the actual heading of the aircraft.

SEARCH AND RESCUE FACILITY—A facility responsible for msintaining and operating a search and rescue (SAR) service to render aid to persons and property in distress. It is any SAR unit, station, NET or other operational activity which can be usefully employed during an SAR Mission, e.g., a Civil Air Patrol Wing or a Coast Guard Station. (See Search and Rescue)

SEARCH AND RESCUE/SAR—A service which seeks missing aircraft and assists those found to be in need of assistance. It is a cooperative effort using the facilities and services of available Federal, state and local agencies. The U.S. Coast Guard is responsible for coordination of search and rescue for the Maritime Region and the U.S. Air Force is reponsible for search and rescue for the Inland Region. Information pertinent to search and rescue should be passed through any air traffic facility or be transmitted directly to the Rescue Coordination Center by telephone. (See Flight Service Station, rescue Coordination Center) (Refer to AIM)

SEE AND AVOID—A visual procedure wherein pilots of aircraft flying in visual meteorological conditions (VMC), regardless of type of flight plan, are charged with the responsibility to observe the presence of other aircraft and to maneuver their aircraft as required to avoid the other aircraft. Right-of-way rules are contained in FAR, Part 91. (See Instrument Flight Rules, Visual Flight Rules, Visual Meteorological Conditions, Instrument Meteorological Conditions)

SEGMENTED CIRCLE—A system of visual indicators designed to provide traffic pattern information at airports without operating control towers. (Refer to AIM)

SEGMENTS OF AN INSTRUMENT APPROACH PROCEDURE—An instrument approach procedure may have as many as four separate segments depending on how the approach procedure is structured.

1. Initial Approach—The segment between the initial approach fix and the intermediate fix or the point where the aircraft is established on the intermediate course or final approach course.
2. Intermediate Approach—The segment between the intermediate fix or point and the final approach fix.
3. Final Approach—The segment between the final approach fix or point and the runway, airport or missed approach point.
4. Missed Approach—The segment between the missed approach point, or point of arrival at decision height, and the missed approach fix at the prescribed altitude. (Refer to FAR Part 97)

ICAO

1. *Initial Approach*—That part of an instrument approach procedure consisting of the first approach to the first navigational facility associated with the procedure, or to a predetermined fix.
2. *Intermediate Approach*—That part of an instrument approach procedure from the first arrival at the first navigational facility or predetermined fix, to the beginning of the final approach.
3. *Final Approach*—That part of an instrument approach procedure from the time the aircraft has:
   a. Completed the last procedure turn or base turn where one is specified, or
   b. crossed a specified fix, or
   c. intercepted the last track specified for the procedures; until it has crossed a point in the vicinity of an aerodrome from which:
      (1) a landing can be made; or
      (2) a missed approach procedure is initiated.
4. *Missed Approach Procedure*—The procedure to be followed when, if after an instrument approach, a landing is not effected and occuring normally:
   a. When the aircraft has descended to the decision height and has not established visual contact, or
   b. When directed by air traffic control to pull up or to go around again.

SEPARATION—In air traffic control, the spacing of aircraft to achieve their safe and orderly movement in flight and while landing and taking off. (See Separation Minima)

ICAO—SEPARATION—Spacing between aircraft, levels or tracks.

SEPARATION MINIMA—The minimum longitudinal, lateral, or vertical distances by which aircraft are spaced through the application of air traffic control procedures. (See Separation)

SEVERE WEATHER AVOIDANCE PLAN/SWAP—A plan to reroute traffic to avoid severe weather in the New York ARTCC area to provide the least disruption to the ATC system when large portions of airspace are unusable due to severe weather. (Refer to Airport/Facility Directory)

SHORT RANGE CLEARANCE—A clearance issued to a departing IFR flight which authorizes IFR flight to a specific fix short of the destination while air traffic control facilities are coordinating and obtaining the complete clearance.

SHORT TAKEOFF AND LANDING AIRCRAFT/STOL AIRCRAFT—An aircraft which, at some weight within its approved operating weight, is capable of operating from a STOL runway in compliance with the applicable STOL characteristics, airworthiness, operations, noise, and pollution standards. (See Vertical Takeoff and Landing Aircraft)

SIDESTEP MANEUVER—A visual maneuver accomplished by a pilot at the completion of an instrument approach to permit a straight-in landing on a parallel runway not more than 1200 feet to either side of the runway to which the instrument approach was conducted. (Refer to AIM)

SIGMET/SIGNIFICANT METEOROLOGICAL INFORMATION—A weather advisory issued concerning weather significant to the safety of all aircraft. SIGMET advisories cover severe and extreme turbulence, severe icing, and widespread dust or sandstorms that reduce visibility to less than 3 miles. (See Convective SIGMET and AIRMET) (Refer to AIM)

ICAO—SIGMET INFORMATION—Information prepared by a meteorological watch office regarding the occurrence or expected occurrence of one or more of the following phenomena:

1. At subsonic cruising levels:
   Active thunderstorm area
   Tropical revolving storm
   Severe line squall
   Heavy hail
   Severe turbulence
   Severe icing
   Marked mountain waves
   Widespread sandstorm/duststorm
2. At transonic levels and supersonic cruising levels:
   Moderate or severe turbulence
   Cumulonimbus clouds
   Hail.

SIMPLIFIED DIRECTIONAL FACILITY/SDF—A NAVAID used for nonprecision instrument approaches. The final approach course is similar to that of an ILS localizer except that the SDF course may be offset from the runway, generally not more than 3 degrees, and the course may be wider than the localizer, resulting in a lower degree of accuracy. (Refer to AIM)

SIMULATED FLAMEOUT/SFO—A practice approach by jet aircraft (normally military) at idle thrust to a runway. The approach may start at a relatively high altitude over a runway (high key) and may continue on a relatively high and wide downwind leg with a high rate of descent and a continuous turn to final. It terminates in a landing or low approach. The purpose of this approach is to simulate a flameout. (See Flameout)

SIMULTANEOUS ILS APPROACHES—An approach system permitting simultaneous ILS approaches to airports having parallel runways separated by at least 4,300 feet between centerlines. Integral parts of a total system are ILS, radar, communications, ATC procedures, and appropriate airborne equipment. (See Parallel Runways) (Refer to AIM)

SINGLE DIRECTION ROUTES—Preferred IFR routes which are sometimes depicted on high altitude en route charts and which are normally flown in one direction only. (See Preferred IFR Route) (Refer to Airport/Facility Directory)

SINGLE FREQUENCY APPROACH/SFA—A service provided under a Letter of Agreement to military single-piloted turbojet aircraft which permits use of a single UHF frequency during approach for landing. Pilots will not normally be required to change frequency from the beginning of the approach to touchdown except that pilots conducting an en route descent are required to change frequency when control is transferred from the air route traffic control center to the terminal facility. The abbreviation "SFA" in the DOD FLIP IFR Supplement under "Communications" indicates this service is available at an aerodrome.

SINGLE FREQUENCY OUTLETS/SFO and SIMULTANEOUS SINGLE FREQUENCY OUTLETS/SSFO—Frequency Outlets commissioned at locations in Alaska not served by air traffic control facilities and remotely controlled by adjacent FSSs. They are subject to undetected and prolonged outages.

SINGLE-PILOTED AIRCRAFT—A military turbojet aircraft possessing one set of flight controls; tandem cockpits or two sets of flight controls but operated by one pilot is considered single-piloted by ATC when determining the appropriate air traffic service to be applied. (See Single Frequency Approach)

SLASH—A radar beacon reply displayed as an elongated target.

SPEAK SLOWER—Used in verbal communications as a request to reduce speech rate.

SPECIAL EMERGENCY—A condition of air piracy, or other hostile act by a person(s) aboard an aircraft which threatens the safety of the aircraft or its passengers.

SPECIAL IFR—(See Fixed-Wing Special IFR)

SPECIAL INSTRUMENT APPROACH PROCEDURE—(See Instrument Approach Procedure)

SPECIAL USE AIRSPACE—Airspace of defined dimensions identified by an area on the surface of the earth wherein activities must be confined because of their nature and/or wherein limitations may be imposed upon aircraft operations that are not a part of those activities.

TYPES OF SPECIAL USE AIRSPACE:

1. Alert Area—Airspace which may contain a high volume of pilot training activities or an unusual type of aerial activity, neither of which is hazardous to aircraft. Alert Areas are depicted on aeronautical charts for the information of nonparticipating pilots. All activities within an Alert Area are conducted in accordance with Federal Aviation Regulations and pilots of participating aircraft as well as pilots transiting the area are equally responsible for collision avoidance.
2. Controlled Firing Area—Airspace wherein activities are conducted under conditions so controlled as to eliminate hazards to nonparticipating aircraft and to ensure the safety of persons and property on the ground.
3. Military Operations Area (MOA)—An MOA is an airspace assignment of defined vertical and lateral dimensions established outside positive control areas to separate/segregate certain military activities from IFR traffic and to identify for VFR traffic where these activities are conducted. (Refer to AIM)
4. Prohibited Area—Designated airspace within which the flight of aircraft is prohibited. (Refer to En Route Charts; AIM)
5. Restricted Area—Airspace designated under FAR Part 73, within which the flight of aircraft, while not wholly prohibited, is subject to restriction. Most restricted areas are designated joint use, and IFR/VFR operations in the area may be authorized by the controlling ATC facility when it is not being utilized by the using agency. Restricted areas are depicted on en route charts. Where joint use is authorized, the name of the ATC controlling facility is also shown. (Refer to FAR Part 73; AIM)
6. Warning Area—Airspace which may contain hazards to nonparticipating aircraft in international airspace.

SPECIAL VFR CONDITIONS—Weather conditions in a control zone which are less than basic VFR and in which some aircraft are permitted flight under Visual Flight Rules. (See Special VFR Operations) (Refer to FAR Part 91)

SPECIAL VFR OPERATIONS—Aircraft operating in accordance with clearances within control zones in weather conditions less than the basic VFR weather minima. Such operations must be requested by the pilot and approved by ATC. (See Special VFR Conditions)

ICAO—SPECIAL VFR FLIGHT—A controlled VFR flight authorized by air traffic control to operate within a control zone under meteorological conditions below the visual meteorological conditions.

SPEED—(See Airspeed, Groundspeed)

SPEED ADJUSTMENT—An ATC procedure used to request pilots to adjust aircraft speed to a specific value for the purpose of providing desired spacing. Speed adjustments are expected to maintain a speed of plus or minus 10 knots of the specified speed.

Examples of Speed Adjustments are:

1. "Increase speed to (speed)," or "Increase speed (number of) knots"—Used by ATC to request a pilot to increase the indicated airspeed of the aircraft.
2. "Reduce speed to (speed)" or "Reduce speed (number of) knots"—Used by ATC to request a pilot to reduce the indicated airspeed of the aircraft.
3. "If feasible, reduce speed to (speed)," or "If feasible, reduce speed (number of) knots"—Used by ATC to request a pilot to reduce the indicated airspeed of the aircraft below specified speeds. (Refer to AIM; FAR Part 91)

SPEED BRAKES/DIVE BRAKES—Moveable aerodynamic devices on aircraft that reduce airspeed during descent and landing.

SQUAWK (Mode, Code, Function)—Activate specific modes/codes/functions on the aircraft transponder, e.g., "Squawk three/alpha, two one zero five, low." (See Transponder)

STAGE I/II/III SERVICE—(See Terminal Radar Program)

STANDARD INSTRUMENT APPROACH PROCEDURE—(See Instrument Approach Procedure)

STANDARD INSTRUMENT DEPARTURE/SID—A preplanned instrument flight rule (IFR) air traffic control departure procedure printed for pilot use in graphic and/or textual form. SIDs provide transition from the terminal to the appropriate en route structure. (See IFR Takeoff Minimums and Departure Procedures) (Refer to AIM)

STANDARD RATE TURN—A turn of three degrees per second.

STANDARD TERMINAL ARRIVAL/STAR—A preplanned instrument flight rule (IFR) air traffic control arrival procedure published for pilot use in graphic and/or textual form. STARs provide transition from the en route structure to an outer fix or an instrument approach fix/-arrival waypoint in the terminal area.

STAND BY—Means the controller or pilot must pause for a few seconds, usually to attend to other duties of a higher priority. Also means to wait as in "stand by for clearance." If a delay is lengthy, the caller should reestablish contact.

STATIONARY RESERVATIONS—Altitude reservations which encompass activities in a fixed area. Stationary reservations may include activities such as special test of weapons systems or equipment, certain U.S. Navy carrier, fleet and anti-submarine operations, rocket, missile and drone operations, and certain aerial refueling or similar operations.

STEPDOWN FIX—A fix permitting additional descent within a segment of an instrument approach procedure by identifying a point at which a controlling obstacle has been safely overflown.

STOP ALTITUDE SQUAWK—Used by ATC to inform an aircraft to turn-off the automatic altitude reporting feature of its transponder. It is issued when the verbally reported altitude varies 300 feet or more from the automatic altitude report. (See Altitude Readout, Transponder)

STOP AND GO—A procedure wherein an aircraft will land, make a complete stop on the runway, and then commence a takeoff from that point. (See Low Approach, Option Approach)

STOP-OVER FLIGHT PLAN—A flight plan which includes two or more separate en route flight segments with a stopover at one or more intermediate airports.

STOP SQUAWK (Mode or Code)—Used by ATC to tell the pilot to turn specified functions of the aircraft transponder off. (See Stop Altitude Squawk, Transponder)

STOP STREAM/BURST/BUZZER—Used by ATC to request a pilot to suspend electronic countermeasure activity. (See Jamming)

STOPWAY—An area beyond the takeoff runway designated by the airport authorities as able to support an airplane during an aborted takeoff. (Refer to FAR Part 1)

STRAIGHT-IN APPROACH—IFR—An instrument approach wherein final approach is begun without first having executed a procedure turn; not necessarily completed with a straight-in landing or made to straight-in landing minimums. (See Straight-in Landing, Landing Minimums, Straight-in Approach-VFR)

STRAIGHT-IN APPROACH—VFR—Entry into the traffic pattern by interception of the extended runway centerline (final approach course) without executing any other portion of the traffic pattern. (See Traffic Pattern)

STRAIGHT-IN LANDING—A landing made on a runway aligned within 30° of the final approach course following completion of an instrument approach. (See Straight-in Approach-IFR)

STRAIGHT-IN LANDING MINIMUMS/STRAIGHT-IN MINIMUMS—(See Landing Minimums)

SUBSTITUTE ROUTE—A route assigned to pilots when any part of an airway or route is unusable because of NAVAID status. These routes consist of:

1. Substitute routes which are shown on U.S. Government Charts.
2. Routes defined by ATC as specific NAVAID radials or courses.
3. Routes defined by ATC as direct to or between NAVAIDs.

SUNSET AND SUNRISE—The mean solar times of sunset and sunrise as published in the Nautical Almanac, converted to local standard time for the locality concerned. Within Alaska, the end of evening civil twilight and the beginning of morning civil twilight, as defined for each locality.

SURVEILLANCE APPROACH—An instrument approach wherein the air traffic controller issues instructions for pilot compliance based on aircraft position in relation to the final approach course (azimuth) and the distance (range) from the end of the runway as displayed on

the controller's radar scope. The controller will provide recommended altitudes on final approach if requested by the pilot. (See PAR Approach) (Refer to AIM)

SYSTEM STRATEGIC NAVIGATION (SN)—Military activity accomplished by navigating along a preplanned route using internal aircraft systems to maintain a desired track. This activity normally requires a lateral route width of 10NM and altitude range of 1,000 feet to 6,000 feet AGL with some route segments that permit terrain following.

TACAN ONLY AIRCRAFT—An aircraft, normally military, possessing TACAN with DME but no VOR navigational system capability. Clearances must specify TACAN or VORTAC fixes and approaches.

TACAN/TACTICAL AIR NAVIGATION—An ultra-high frequency electronic rho-theta air navigation aid which provides suitably equipped aircraft a continuous indication of bearing and distance to the TACAN station. (See VORTAC) (Refer to AIM)

TARGET—The indication shown on a radar display resulting from a primary radar return or a radar beacon reply. (See Target Symbol, Radar)

ICAO—TARGET—In radar:

1. Generally, any discrete object which reflects or retransmits energy back to the radar equipment.
2. Specifically, an object of radar search or surveillance.

TARGET SYMBOL—A computer generated indication shown on a radar display resulting from a primary radar return or a radar beacon reply.

TAXI INTO POSITION AND HOLD—Used by ATC to inform a pilot to taxi onto the departure runway in takeoff position and hold. It is not authorization for takeoff. It is used when takeoff clearance cannot immediately be issued because of traffic or other reasons. (See HOLD, CLEARED FOR TAKE-OFF)

TAXI PATTERNS—Patterns established to illustrate the desired flow of ground traffic for the different runways or airport areas available for use.

TERMINAL AREA—A general term used to describe airspace in which approach control service or airport traffic control service is provided.

TERMINAL AREA FACILITY—A facility providing air traffic control service for arriving and departing IFR, VFR, Special VFR, Special IFR aircraft and, on occasion, en route aircraft. (See Approach Control, Tower)

TERMINAL CONTROL AREA—(See Controlled Airspace)

TERMINAL RADAR APPROACH CONTROL/TRACON—An FAA air traffic control facility using radar and air/ground communications to provide approach control services to aircraft arriving, departing, or transiting the airspace controlled by the facility. Service may be provided to both civil and military airports. A TRACON is similar to a RAPCON (USAF), RATCF (Navy), and ARAC (Army). (See Approach Control, Approach Control Service, Departure Control)

TERMINAL RADAR PROGRAM—A national program instituted to extend the terminal radar services provided IFR aircraft to VFR aircraft. Pilot participation in the program is urged but is not mandatory. The progressive stages of the program are referred to as Stage I, Stage II and Stage III. The stage service provided at a particular location is contained in Airport/Facility Directory.

1. Stage I/Radar Advisory Service for VFR Aircraft—Provides traffic information and limited vectoring to VFR aircraft on a workload permitting basis.

2. Stage II/Radar Advisory and Sequencing for VFR Aircraft—Provides, in addition to Stage I service, vectoring and sequencing on a full-time basis to arriving VFR aircraft. The purpose is to adjust the flow of arriving IFR and VFR aircraft into the traffic pattern in a safe and orderly manner and to provide traffic advisory to departing VFR aircraft.

3. Stage III/Radar Sequencing and Separation Service for VFR Aircraft—Provides, in addition to Stage II services, separation between all participating aircraft. The purpose is to provide separation between all participating VFR aircraft and all IFR aircraft operating within the airspace defined as a Terminal Radar Service Area (TRSA) or Terminal Control Area (TCA). (See Terminal Radar Service Area, Controlled Airspace) (Refer to AIM; Airport/Facility Directory, and Graphic Notices and Supplemental Data)

TERMINAL RADAR SERVICE AREA/TRSA—Airspace surrounding designated airports wherein ATC provides radar vectoring, sequencing, and separation on a full-time basis for all IFR and participating VFR aircraft. Service provided in a TRSA is called Stage III Service. AIM contains an explanation of TRSA. Graphics depicting TRSA layout and communications frequencies are shown in Graphic Notices and Supplemental Data. Pilot participation is urged but is not mandatory. (See Terminal Radar Program) (Refer to AIM; Airport/Facility Directory, and Graphic Notices and Supplemental Data)

TERRAIN FOLLOWING (TF)—The flight of a military aircraft maintaining a constant AGL altitude above the terrain or the highest obstruction. The altitude of the aircraft will constantly change with the varying terrain and/or obstruction.

TETRAHEDRON—A device normally located on uncontrolled airports and used as a landing direction indicator. The small end of a tetrahedron points in the direction of landing. At controlled airports, the tetrahedron, if installed, should be disregarded because tower instructions supersede the indicator. (See Segmented Circle) (Refer to AIM)

THAT IS CORRECT—The understanding you have is right.

THRESHOLD—The beginning of that portion of the runway usable for landing. (See Airport Lighting, Displaced Threshold)

THRESHOLD CROSSING HEIGHT/TCH—The height of the glide slope above the runway threshold. (See Threshold, Glide Slope)

THRESHOLD LIGHTS—(See Airport Lighting)

TIME GROUP—Four digits representing the hour and minutes from the 24-hour clock. Time group without time zone indicators are understood to be GMT (Greenwich Mean Time), e.g., "0205." A time zone indicator is used to indicate local time, e.g., "0205M." The end and beginning of the day are shown by "2400" and "0000," respectively.

TORCHING—The burning of fuel at the end of an exhaust pipe or stack of a reciprocating aircraft engine, the result of an excessive richness in the fuel air mixture.

TOUCH AND GO/TOUCH AND GO LANDING—An operation by an aircraft that lands and departs on a runway without stopping or exiting the runway.

TOUCHDOWN—

1. The point at which an aircraft first makes contact with the landing surface.
2. Concerning a precision radar approach (PAR), it is the point where the glide path intercepts the landing surface.

ICAO—TOUCHDOWN—The point where the nominal glide path intercepts the runway.

TOUCHDOWN RVR—(See Visibility)

TOUCHDOWN ZONE—The first 3,000 feet of the runway beginning at the threshold. The area is used for determination of Touchdown Zone Elevation in the development of straight-in landing minimums for instrument approaches.

TOUCHDOWN ZONE ELEVATION/TDZE—The highest elevation in the first 3,000 feet of the landing surface. TDZE is indicated on the instrument approach procedure chart when straight-in landing minimums are authorized. (See Touchdown Zone)

TOUCHDOWN ZONE LIGHTING—(See Airport Lighting)

TOWER/AIRPORT TRAFFIC CONTROL TOWER—A terminal facility that uses air/ground radio communications, visual signaling, and other devices to provide ATC services to aircraft operating in the vicinity of an airport or on the movement area. Authorizes aircraft to land or takeoff at the airport controlled by the tower or to transit the airport traffic area regardless of flight plan or weather conditions (IFR or VFR). A tower may also provide approach control services (radar or nonradar). (See Airport

Traffic Area, Airport Traffic Control Service, Approach Control/Approach Control Facility, Approach Control Service, Movement Area, Tower En Route Control Service/Tower to Tower) (Refer to AIM)

ICAO—AERODROME CONTROL TOWER—A unit established to provide air traffic control service to aerodrome traffic.

TOWER EN ROUTE CONTROL SERVICE/TOWER TO TOWER—The control of IFR en route traffic within delegated airspace between two or more adjacent approach control facilities. This service is designed to expedite traffic and reduce control and pilot communication requirements.

TPX 42—A numeric beacon decoder equipment/system. It is designed to be added to terminal radar systems for beacon decoding. It provides rapid target identification, reinforcement of the primary radar target, and altitude information from Mode C. (See Automated Radar Terminal Systems, Transponder)

TRACK—The actual flight path of an aircraft over the surface of the earth. (See Course, Route, Flight Path)

ICAO—TRACK—The projection on the earth's surface of the path of an aircraft, the direction of which path at any point is usually expressed in degrees from north (true, magnetic or grid).

TRAFFIC ALERT, ADVICE YOU TURN RIGHT/LEFT HEADING (DEGREES) AND/OR CLIMB/DESCEND TO (ALTITUDE) IMMEDIATELY—See Safety Advisory)

TRAFFIC ADVISORIES—Advisories issued to alert a pilot to other known or observed air traffic which may be in such proximity to his aircraft's position or intended route of flight to warrant his attention. Such advisories may be based on:

1. Visual observation from a control tower.

2. Observation or radar identified and nonidentified aircraft targets on an ATC radar display, or

3. Verbal reports from pilots or other facilities.

Controllers use the word "traffic" followed by additional information, if known, to provide such advisories, e.g., "Traffic, 2 o'clock, one zero miles, southbound, fast moving, altitude readout seven thousand five hundred."

Traffic advisory service will be provided to the extent possible depending on higher priority duties of the controller or other limitations, e.g., radar limitations, volume of traffic, frequency congestion, or controller workload. Radar/nonradar traffic advisories do not relieve the pilot of his responsibility to see and avoid other aircraft. Pilots are cautioned that there are many times when the controller is not able to give traffic advisories concerning all traffic in the aircraft's proximity; in other words, when a pilot requests or is receiving traffic advisories, he should not assume that all traffic will be issued.

TRAFFIC INFORMATION—(See Traffic Advisories)

TRAFFIC IN SIGHT—Used by pilots to inform a controller that previously issued traffic is in sight. (See Negative Contact, Traffic Advisories)

TRAFFIC NO LONGER A FACTOR—Indicates that the traffic described in a previously issued traffic advisory is no longer a factor.

TRAFFIC PATTERN—The traffic flow that is prescribed for aircraft landing at, taxiing on, or taking off from an airport. The components of a typical traffic pattern are upwind leg, crosswind leg, downwind leg, base leg, and final approach.

1. Upwind Leg—A flight path parallel to the landing runway in the direction of landing.

2. Crosswind Leg—A flight path at right angles to the landing runway off its upwind end.

3. Downwind Leg—A flight path parallel to the landing runway in the direction opposite to landing. The downwind leg normally extends between the crosswind leg and the base leg.

4. Base Leg—A flight path at right angles to the landing runway off its approach end. The base leg normally extends from the downwind leg to the intersection of the extended runway centerline.

5. Final Approach—A flight path in the direction of landing along the extended runway centerline. The final approach normally extends from the base leg to the runway. An aircraft making a straight-in approach VFR is also considered to be on final approach.

(See Taxi Patterns, Straight-In Approach-VFR) (Refer to AIM, FAR Part 91)

ICAO—AERODROME TRAFFIC CIRCUIT—The specified path to be flown by aircraft operating in the vicinity of an aerodrome.

TRANSCRIBED WEATHER BROADCAST/TWEB—A continuous recording of meteorological and aeronautical information that is broadcast on L/MF and VOR facilities for pilots. (Refer to AIM)

TRANSFER OF CONTROL—That action whereby the responsibility for the separation of an aircraft is transferred from one controller to another.

ICAO—TRANSFER OF CONTROL—Transfer of responsibility for providing air traffic control service.

TRANSFERRING CONTROLLER/FACILITY— A controller/facility transferring control of an aircraft to another controller/facility.

ICAO—TRANSFERRING UNIT/CONTROLLER—Air Traffic Control Unit/Air Traffic Controller in the process of transferring the responsibility for providing air traffic control service to an aircraft to the next air traffic control unit/air traffic controller along the route of flight.

TRANSITION—

1. The general term that describes the change from one phase of flight or flight condition to another, e.g., transition from en route flight to the approach or transition from instrument flight to visual flight.

2. A published procedure (SID Transition) used to connect the basic SID to one of several en route airways/jet routes, or a published procedure (STAR Transition) used to connect one of several en route airways/jet routes to the basic STAR. (Refer to SID/STAR Charts)

TRANSITION AREA—(See Controlled Airspace)

TRANSMISSOMETER—An apparatus used to determine visibility by measuring the transmission of light through the atmosphere. It is the measurement source for determining runway visual range (RVR) and runway visibility value (RVV). (See Visibility)

TRANSMITTING IN THE BLIND/BLIND TRANSMISSION—A transmission from one station to other stations in circumstances where two-way communication cannot be established, but where it is believed that the called stations may be able to receive the transmission.

TRANSPONDER—The airborne radar beacon receiver/transmitter portion of the Air Traffic Control Radar Beacon System (ATCRBS) which automatically receives radio signals from interrogators on the ground, and selectively replies with a specific reply pulse or pulse group only to those interrogations being received on the mode to which it is set to respond. (See Interrogator) (Refer to AIM)

ICAO—TRANSPONDER—A receiver/transmitter which will generate a reply signal upon proper interrogation; the interrogation and reply being on different frequencies.

TURBOJET AIRCRAFT—An aircraft having a jet engine in which the energy of the jet operates a turbine which in turn operates the air compressor.

TURBOPROP AIRCRAFT—An aircraft having a jet engine in which the energy of the jet operates a turbine which drives the propeller.

T-VOR/TERMINAL-VERY HIGH FREQUENCY OMNIDIRECTIONAL RANGE STATION—A very high frequency terminal omnirange station located on or near an airport and used as an approach aid. (See VOR, Navigational Aid)

TWO WAY RADIO COMMUNICATIONS FAILURE—(See Lost Communications)

ULTRAHIGH FREQUENCY/UHF—The frequency band between 300 and 3,000 MHz. The bank of radio frequencies used for military air/ground voice communications. In some instances, this may go as low as 225 MHz and still be referred to as UHF.

UNABLE—Indicates inability to comply with a specific instruction, request, or clearance.

UNCONTROLLED AIRSPACE—Uncontrolled airspace is that portion of the airspace that has not been designated as continental control area, control area, control zone, terminal control area, or transition area and within which ATC has neither the authority nor the responsibility for exercising control over air traffic. (See Controlled Airspace)

UNDER THE HOOD—Indicates that the pilot is using a hood to restrict visibility outside the cockpit while simulating instrument flight. An appropriately rated pilot is required in the other control seat while this operation is being conducted. (Refer to FAR Part 91)

UNICOM—A non-government air/ground radio communication facility which may provide airport advisory service at certain airports. Locations and frequencies of UNICOMs are shown on aeronautical charts and publications. (Refer to AIM and Airport/Facility Directory)

UNPUBLISHED ROUTE—A route for which no minimum altitude is published or charted for pilot use. It may include a direct route between NAVAIDS, a radial, a radar vector, or a final approach course beyond the segments of an instrument approach procedure. (See Route, Published Route)

UNWIND LEG—(See Traffic Pattern)

VECTOR—A heading issued to an aircraft to provide navigational guidance by radar.

ICAO—RADAR VECTORING—Provision of navigational guidance to aircraft in the form of specific headings, based on the use of radar.

VERIFY—Request confirmation of information, e.g., "verify assigned altitude."

VERIFY SPECIFIC DIRECTION OF TAKEOFF (OR TURNS AFTER TAKEOFF)—Used by ATC to ascertain an aircraft's direction of takeoff and/or direction of turn after takeoff. It is normally used for IFR departures from an airport not having a control tower. When direct communication with the pilot is not possible, the request and information may be relayed through an FSS, dispatcher, or by other means. (See IFR Takeoff Minimums and Departure Procedures)

VERTICAL SEPARATION—Separation established by assignment of different altitudes or flight levels. (See Separation)

ICAO—VERTICAL SEPARATION—Separation between aircraft expressed in units of vertical distance.

VERTICAL TAKEOFF AND LANDING AIRCRAFT/VTOL AIRCRAFT—Aircraft capable of vertical climbs and/or descents and of using very short runways or small areas for takeoff and landings. These aircraft include, but are not limited to, helicopters. (See Short Takeoff and Landing Aircraft)

VERY HIGH FREQUENCY/VHF—The frequency band between 30 and 300 MHz. Portions of this band, 108 to 118 MHz, are used for certain NAVAIDS; 118 to 136 MHz are used for civil air/ground voice communications. Other frequencies in this band are used for purposes not related to air traffic control.

VERY LOW FREQUENCY/VLF—The frequency band between 3 and 30 kHz.

VFR AIRCRAFT/VFR FLIGHT—An aircraft conducting flight in accordance with visual flight rules. (See Visual Flight Rules)

VFR MILITARY TRAINING ROUTES (VR)—Routes used by the Department of Defense and associated Reserve and Air Guard units for the purpose of conducting low-altitude navigation and tactical training under VFR below 10,000 feet MSL at airspeeds in excess of 250 knots IAS.

VFR NOT RECOMMENDED.—An advisory provided by a flight service station to a pilot during a preflight or inflight weather briefing that flight under visual flight rules is not recommended. To be given when the current and/or forecasted weather conditions are at or below VFR minimums. It does not abrogate the pilot's authority to make his own decision.

VFR ON TOP/VFR CONDITIONS ON TOP—An IFR clearance term used in lieu of a specific altitude assignment upon pilot's request which authorizes the aircraft to be flown in VFR weather conditions at an appropriate VFR altitude which is not below the minimum IFR altitude. (Refer to FAR Part 91)

VFR OVER THE TOP—The operation of an aircraft above the clouds under VFR when it is not being operated on an IFR flight plan. (See VFR On Top)

VFR TOWER/NON-APPROACH CONTROL TOWER—(See Tower/Airport Traffic Control Tower)

VIDEO MAP—An electronically displayed map on the radar display that may depict data such as airports, heliports, runway centerline extensions, hospital emergency landing areas, NAVAIDS and fixes, reporting points, airway/route centerlines, boundaries, handoff points, special use tracks, obstructions, prominent geographic features, map alignment indicators, range accuracy marks, and minimum vectoring altitudes.

VISIBILITY—The ability, as determined by atmospheric conditions and expressed in units of distance, to see and identify prominent unlighted objects by day and prominent lighted objects by night. Visibility is reported as statute miles, hundreds of feet or meters. (Refer to FAR Part 91; AIM)

1. Flight Visibility—The average forward horizontal distance, from the cockpit of an aircraft in flight, at which prominent unlighted objects may be seen and identified by day and prominent lighted objects may be seen and identified by night.

   ICAO—Flight Visibility—The visibility forward from the cockpit of an aircraft in flight.

2. Ground Visibility Prevailing horizontal visibility near the earth's surface as reported by the United States National Weather Service or an accredited observer.

   ICAO—Ground Visibility—The visibility at an aerodrome as reported by an accredited observer.

3. Prevailing Visibility—The greatest horizontal visibility equaled or exceeded throughout at least half the horizon circle which need not necessarily be continuous.

4. Runway Visibility Value/RVV—The visibility determined for a particular runway by a transmissometer. A meter provides a continuous indication of the visibility (reported in miles or fraction of miles) for the runway. RVV is used in lieu of prevailing visibility in determining minimums for a particular runway.

5. Runway Visual Range/RVR—An instrumentally derived value, based on standard calibrations, that represents the horizontal distance a pilot will see down the runway from the approach end. It is based on the sighting of either high intensity runway lights or on the visual contrast of other targets, whichever yields the greater visual range. RVR, in contrast to prevailing or runway visibility, is based on what a pilot in a moving aircraft should see looking down the runway. RVR is horizontal visual range, not slant visual range. It is based on the measurement of a transmissometer made near the touchdown point of the instrument runway and is reported in hundreds of feet. RVR is used in lieu of RVV and/or prevailing visibility in determining minimums for a particular runway.

a. Touchdown RVR—The RVR visibility readout values obtained from RVR equipment serving the runway touchdown zone.

b. MID RVR—The RVR readout values obtained from RVR equipment located midfield of the runway.

c. Rollout RVR—The RVR readout values obtained from RVR equipment located nearest the rollout end of the runway.

ICAO—Runway Visual Range—The maximum distance in the direction of takeoff or landing at which the runway or the specified lights or markers delineating it can be seen from a position above a specified point on its centerline at a height corresponding to the average eye-level of pilots at touchdown.

VISUAL APPROACH—An approach wherein an aircraft on an IFR flight plan, operating in VFR conditions under the control of an air traffic control facility and having an air traffic control authorization, may proceed to the airport of destination in VFR conditions.

ICAO—VISUAL APPROACH—An approach by an IFR flight when either part or all of an instrument approach procedure is not completed and the approach is executed in visual reference to terrain.

VISUAL APPROACH SLOPE INDICATOR—(See Airport Lighting)

VISUAL DESCENT POINT/VDP—A defined point on the final approach course of a nonprecision straight-in approach procedure from which normal descent from the MDA to the runway touchdown point may be commenced, provided visual reference is established.

VISUAL FLIGHT RULES/VFR—Rules that govern the procedures for conducting flight under visual conditions. The term "VFR" is also used in the United States to indicate weather conditions that are equal to or greater than minimum VFR requirements. In addition, it is used by pilots and controllers to indicate type of flight plan. (See Instrument Flight Rules, Instrument Meteorological Conditions) (Refer to FAR Part 91; AIM)

VISUAL HOLDING—The holding of aircraft at selected, prominent, geographical fixes which can be easily recognized from the air. (See Hold, Holding Fixes)

VISUAL METEOROLOGICAL CONDITIONS/VMC—Meteorological conditions expressed in terms of visibility, distance from cloud, and ceiling equal to or better than specified minima. (See Instrument Meteorological Conditions, Visual Flight Rules, Instrument Flight Rules)

VISUAL SEPARATION—A means employed by ATC to separate aircraft in terminal areas. There are two ways to effect this separation:

1. The tower controller sees the aircraft involved and issues instructions, as necessary, to ensure that the aircraft avoid each other.

2. A pilot sees the other aircraft involved and upon instructions from the controller provides his own separation by maneuvering his aircraft, as necessary, to avoid it. This may involve following another aircraft or keeping it in sight until it is no longer a factor. (See See and Avoid) (Refer to FAR Part 91)

VORTAC/VHF OMNIDIRECTIONAL RANGE/TACTICAL AIR NAVIGATION—A navigation aid providing VOR azimuth, TACAN azimuth, and TACAN distance measuring equipment (DME) at one site. (See VOR, Distance Measuring Equipment, TACAN, Navigational Aid) (Refer to AIM)

VORTICES/WING TIP VORTICES—Circular patterns of air created by the movement of an airfoil through the air when generating lift. As an airfoil moves through the atmosphere in sustained flight, an area of high pressure is created above it. The air flowing from the high pressure area to the low pressure area around and about the tips of the airfoil tends to roll up into two rapidly rotating vortices, cylindrical in shape. These vortices are the most predominant parts of aircraft wake turbulence and their rotational force is dependent upon the wing loading, gross weight, and speed of the generating aircraft. The vortices from medium to heavy aircraft can be of extremely high velocity and hazardous to smaller aircraft. (See Wake Turbulence, Aircraft Classes) (Refer to AIM)

VOR/VERY HIGH FREQUENCY OMNIDIRECTIONAL RANGE STATION—A ground-based electronic navigation aid transmitting very high frequency navigation signals, 360 degrees in azimuth, oriented from magnetic north. Used as the basis for navigation in the national airspace system. The VOR periodically identifies itself by morse code and may have an additional voice identification feature. Voice features may be used by ATC or FSS for transmitting instructions/information to pilots. (See Navigational Aid) (Refer to AIM)

VOT/VOR TEST SIGNAL—A ground facility which emits a test signal to check VOR receiver accuracy. The system is limited to ground use only. (Refer to FAR Part 91, AIM, and Airport/Facility Directory)

WAKE TURBULENCE—Phenomena resulting from the passage of an aircraft through the atmosphere. The term includes vortices, thrust stream turbulence, jet blast, jet wash, propeller wash, and rotor wash both on the ground and in the air. (See Jet Blast, Aircraft Classes, Vortices) (Refer to AIM)

WARNING AREA—(See Special Use Airspace)

WAYPOINT—(See Area Navigation)

WEATHER ADVISORY/INFLIGHT WEATHER ADVISORY—(See SIGMET, AIRMET)

WEATHER ADVISORY/WS/WA—In aviation weather forecast practice, an expression of hazardous weather conditions not predicted in the area forecast as they affect the operation of air traffic and as prepared by the NWS.

WILCO—I have received your message, understand it, and will comply with it.

WIND SHEAR—A change in wind speed and/or wind direction in a short distance resulting in a tearing or shearing effect. It can exist in a horizontal or vertical direction and occasionally in both.

WORDS TWICE—

1. As a request, "Communication is difficult. Please say every phase twice."

2. As information, "Since communications are difficult, every phrase in this message will be spoken twice."

INDEX

THIS PUBLICATION IS DIVIDED INTO THREE PARTS: (1) THE FIRST PART CONSISTS OF NOTICES WHICH MEET THE CRITERIA FOR NOTAM (D) AND ARE EXPECTED TO REMAIN IN EFFECT FOR AN EXTENDED PERIOD. THESE NOTAMS ARE INCLUDED TO REDUCE CONGESTION ON THE TELETYPE CIRCUITS. NOTAM (L) AND, OCCASIONALLY, SPECIAL NOTICES ARE INCLUDED WHEN THEIR INCLUSION WILL CONTRIBUTE TO FLIGHT SAFETY. ALL INFORMATION CONTAINED IN THE PUBLICATION WILL BE CARRIED UNTIL THE INFORMATION BECOMES EXPIRED, IS CANCELLED OR, IN THE CASE OF PERMANENT INFRORMATION, IS PUBLISHED IN OTHER PERMANENT PUBLICATIONS, SUCH AS THE AIRPORT/FACILITY DIRECTORY. ALL NEW NOTICES ENTERED INTO THIS PART WILL BE INCLUDED ONLY IF THE INFORMATION CONTAINED IS EXPECTED TO REMAIN IN EFFECT FOR AT LEAST SEVEN DAYS AFTER THE EFFECTIVE DATE OF THE PUBLICATION. THE NUMBER IN PARENTHESIS AFTER EACH ENTRY IS THE MONTH AND YEAR THAT IT FIRST APPEARED IN THIS PUBLICATION. THE CUTOFF DATE FOR GETTING INFORMATION INCLUDED IN THIS SECTION IS TWO WEEKS PRIOR TO THE EFFECTIVE DATE OF THE PUBLICATION. (2) THE SECOND PART CONTAINS ALL FDC NOTAMS WHICH WERE CURRENT AT THE TIME OF PUBLICATION. THE NUMBER OF THE LAST FDC NOTAM INCLUDED IN THE PUBLICATION IS NOTED TO AID THE USER IN UPDATING THE LISTING WITH ANY FDC NOTAMS WHICH MAY HAVE BEEN ISSUED AFTER PUBLICATION. (3) THE THIRD PART CONTAINS NOTICES THAT, EITHER BECAUSE THEY ARE TOO LONG OR BECAUSE THEY CONCERN A WIDE OR UNSPECIFIED GEOGRAPHIC AREA, ARE NOT SUITABLE FOR INCLUSION IN THE FIRST PART OF THIS PUBLICATION. THE CONTENT OF THESE NOTICES VARY WIDELY AND THERE ARE NOT SPECIFIC CRITERIA FOR THEIR INCLUSION, OTHER THAN THEIR ENHANCEMENT OF FLIGHT SAFETY. TO BE INCLUDED IN THIS SECTION, ARTICLES MUST BE RECEIVED THREE WEEKS PRIOR TO THE EFFECTIVE DATE OF THE PUBLICATION (AN ADDITIONAL FOUR WEEKS IF GRAPHICS WILL BE REQUIRED).

NOTE: NOTICES ARE ARRANGED IN ALPHABETICAL ORDER BY STATE (AND WITHIN STATE BY CITY OR LOCALITY). NEW OR REVISED DATA ARE INDICATED BY BOLD ITALICIZING THE AIRPORT NAME.

NOTE: ALL TIMES ARE LOCAL UNLESS OTHERWISE INDICATED.

NOTICE: OBSTRUCTION LIGHT OUTAGES NO LONGER REQUIRE DISTANT DISSEMINATION (NOTAM(D) OR CLASS II). CHECK LOCAL NOTAMS FOR OUTAGES.

GENERAL

NOTICE: Due to the possibility of spot fuel shortages, pilots are advised to check enroute points for fuel availability.

ALABAMA

ALEXANDER CITY, THOMAS C. RUSSELL FLD: Rwy 18–36 3550 x 100 ft; thr rwy 18 dsplcd 620 ft. (10/79)

ANDALUSIA-OPP ARPT: Wt brg cpty S –30000 lbs. (11/79)

SELMA, CRAIG FLD ARPT: Apch/dep freq now 125.3. (11/79)

TALLASSEE MUNI ARPT: Apch/dep freq now 125.3. (11/79)

WETUMPKA MUNI ARPT: Apch/dep freq now 125.3. (11/79)

ALASKA

For information on Alaska other than FDC NOTAMS consult the Alaska Supplement.

ARIZONA

DOUGLAS BISBEE INTL ARPT: Rwy 12–30 and 17–35 and SW 2400 ft rwy 3–21 clsd. Thr 3 dsplcd 2550 ft until Dec. 15. (10/79)

FORT HUACHUCA: VOR "FHU" OTS thru OCT 17, 1980. (7/79)

NOGALES: NDB "OLS" OTS thru Oct 1981. (11/79)

ARKANSAS

ARKADELPHIA MUNI ARPT: M89 SW 200 FT. RWY 4–22 CLSD. (10/79)

BENTON, SALINE COUNTY ARPT: LIRL rwy 18–36 deleted. (10/79)

POCAHONTAS MUNI ARPT: VASI rwy 18 OTS. (5/78)

SILOAM SPRINGS, SMITH FLD ARPT: For MIRLS thr and twy lights key freq 122.8 3 times 5 sec low; 5 times 5 sec med; 7 times 5 sec high intst. (10/79)

STUTTGART MUNI ARPT: Rwy 14–32 clsd. (4/79)

CALIFORNIA

ARCATA-EUREKA ARPT: Rwy lights rwy 1–19 OTS. (6/78) (9/79)

CORONA MUNI ARPT: Wt brg cpty rwy 7–25 S –12000 lbs. (11/79)

EL MONTE ARPT: ATIS freq 118.75. (10/79)

SAN DIEGO INTL – LINDBERCH FLD: Arpt clsd tkof 2330–0630 excp emerg+ clsd landing excp emerg/FAR 36 Certified Acft 2330–0630+sked ACR dep/arr delays until 2345 permitted. (10/79)

SAN JOSE MUNI ARPT: Rwy 12R-30L clsd 0001–0630 excp Sun and Mon thru Nov 9. (8/79)

SAN LUIS OBISPO COUNTY ARPT: LOC rwy 11 unmon. (6/79) Thr rwy 11 dsplcd 400 ft. (7/79) Rwy 7–25 clsd.

VACAVILLE, NUT TREE ARPT: For rwy lights key freq 122.7 3 times in 5 secs stays on 15 min. Key 3 times to recycle timer eff 2200-sunrise. (11/79)

WESTOVER FIELD AMADOR COUNTY ARPT: Arpt clsd. (10/79)

COLORADO

LAMAR MUNI ARPT: Rwy 8–26 clsd. (10/79)

PUEBLO MEMORIAL ARPT: A/C freq 125.25. (10/79)

CONNECTICUT

BRADLEY INTL ARPT: The VICON System is operational for test and evaluation. VICON is not a control system. It is to be used only for confirmation of the voice takeoff clearance. Pilots should not taxi or takeoff upon seeing the green light from the VICON System without having received and understood the verbal takeoff clearance from the control tower. Additional information on the VICON System is contained in the publication Graphic Notices and Supplemental Data, Area Advisories Section, under Connecticut, Bradley Intl Arpt.

MARLBOROUGH, LESNEWSKI FLD: Arpt closed. (5/78)

NOTICE TO AIRMEN   PART II
F.A.A. NATIONAL FLIGHT DATA CENTER

FDC NOTAMS

EXCERPTS

THE LISTING BELOW INCLUDES, IN PART, CHANGES IN FLIGHT DATA, PARTICULARLY OF A REGULATORY NATURE, WHICH AFFECT STANDARD INSTRUMENT APPROACH PROCEDURES, AERONAUTICAL CHARTS AND SELECTED FLIGHT RESTRICTIONS, PRIOR TO THEIR NORMAL PUBLICATION CYCLE. THEREFORE, THEY SHOULD BE REVIEWED DURING PRE-FLIGHT PLANNING. THIS LISTING INCLUDES ALL FDC NOTAMS CURRENT THRU FDC NOTAM NUMBER SHOWN BELOW. TIMES ARE GMT OTHERWISE NOTED.

LEGEND

```
FDC ------- NATIONAL FLIGHT DATA CENTER
9/103 ----- ACCOUNTABILITY NUMBER ASSIGNED TO THE MESSAGE ORIGINATOR BY FDC
FI/T ------ FLIGHT INFORMATION/TEMPORARY
FI/P ------ FLIGHT INFORMATION/PERMANENT
#--------NEW NOTAM
```

THE FOLLOWING LISTING CONTAINS FDC NOTAMS
THRU FDC 9/1870 OCTOBER 18, 1979

EAST CENTRAL

ILLINOIS

FDC 9/1475 FI/T (3HA) LANSING MUNI CHICAGO IL. VOR-A AMDT 3 TAKEOFF MINIMUMS RWYS 9 18 27 AND 36 200FT CEILING AND 1 MILE VIS.

FDC 9/1582 FI/T (DNV) VERMILLION COUNTY, DANVILLE, IL. LOC RWY 21 ORIG ALTERNATE MINS NA.

FDC 9/1760 FI/P (PIA) GREATER PEORIA PEORIA IL. LOC (BC) RWY 12 AMDT 13 CANCELLED.

#FDC 9/1798 FI/T (UGN) WAUKEGAN MEMORIAL WAUKEGAN IL. NDB RWY 23 AMDT 3 LOC RWY 23 AMDT 3 CHANGE PROC DATA NOTES TO READ 3-STEP HIRL/REIL RWY 5–23 AND MIRL RWY 14–32 ON 123.0. OBTAIN LOCAL ALTIMETER SETTING ON UNICOM 123.0 WHEN NOT AVAILABLE USE CHICAGO OHARE ALTIMETER SETTING AND INCREASE ALL MDA 100 FT.

#FDC 9/1799 FI/T (SPI) CAPITAL, SPRINGFIELD IL. NDB RWY 4 AMDT 14 SI MDA 1100 FT/HAT 508 FT ALL CATS VIS CAT C RVR 5000 CAT D RVR 6000. CIRCLING CATS A, B AND C MDA 1100 FT HAA 503 FT CAT D MDA 1180 FT/HAA 583 FT. RNAV RWY 4 AMDT 3 SI MDA 1060 FT/HAT 468 FT ALL CATS VIS CAT C RVR 4000. CIRCLING CAT A MDA 1060 FT/HAA 463 FT. PROC DATA NOTE CHANGE TO READ; HORIZONTAL DIST MDA TO MAP ON GS 1.35 NM. RADAR-1 AMDT 2 ASR SI RWY 4 MIN ALT AT 2 MI RADAR FIX 1060 FT.

INDIANA

FDC 9/1204 FI/T (C39) MICHIGAN CITY MUNI MICHIGAN CITY IN. NDB RWY 23 AMDT 2. NA BETWEEN 2300 AND 0600 LOCAL TIME.

FDC 9/1205 FI/T (MGC) MICHIGAN CITY MICHIGAN CITY IN. NDB RWY 20 AMDT 9. NA BETWEEN 2300 AND 0600 LOCAL TIME.

#FDC 9/1835 FI/T (MIE) DELAWARE COUNTY JOHNSON FIELD MUNCIE IN ILS RWY 32 ORIG SI ILS VIS CAT A, B, C AND D 3/4 M SI LOC VIS CAT A, B AND C 3/4 MI. NDB RWY 32 AMDT 3 SI VI CAT A, B AND C 1 MI. VOR RWY 32 AMDT 8 VOR BASIC MINS S CAT A AND B 3/4 MI, VOR/NDB MINIMA SI VIS CAT A, B AND C 3/4 MI. TAKEOFF MINS RWY 32 STANDARD /FAR 135/.

MICHIGAN

FDC 9/1371 FI/T (RCT) MILLER FIELD, REED CITY, MI. VOR RWY 17 AMDT 4 PROC NA.

FDC 9/1376 FI/T (MKG) MUSKEGON COUNTY MUSKEGON MI LOC RWY 23 ORIG CHANGE TERMINAL ROUTE A FOLLOWS..MKG VORTAC (IAF) TO KLARE INT OM COURSE AND DISTANCE 316/4.9 MI ALTITUDE 2800 FT.

FDC 9/1439 FI/T (77D) ROBEN-HOOD BIG RAPIDS, MI. VOR-A AMDT 2 DME REQUIRED.

FDC 9/1583 FI/T (D98) ROMEO ARPT, ROMEO, MI VOR/DME-A AMDT 3 CHANGE PROC DATA NOTE TO READ PROC NA A NIGHT EXCEPT BY PRIOR ARRANGEMENTS FOR RWY LGTS.

FDC 9/1584 FI/T (BEH) ROSS FIELD, BENTON HARBOR, MI NDB RWY 27 AMDT 5, ILS RWY 27 AMDT 2 VOR RWY 27 AMDT 1 ADD PROC DATA NOTE WHEN CTLZ NOT IN EFFECT ACTIVATI 3 STEP MALSR RWY 27 ON 125.5.

#FDC 9/1787 FI/P (CIU) CHIPPEWA COUNTY INTNL SAULT STI MARIE MI. CORRECT US GOVT CHART AL-810 NDB RWY 1 AMDT 1 AND ILS RWY 15 AMDT 1 DELETE NOTE WHICH READ CAUTION POWER LINE 3000 FT FM THRESHOLD PENETRATE APCH LIGHT PLANE BY 30 FT. ILS RWY 15 AMDT 1 CHANGE S ILS RWY 15 DH TO 1028 FT/HAT 229 FT ALL CATS.

#FDC 9/1864 FI/T (DTW) DETROIT METROPOLITAN WAYNE COUNTY DETROIT MI. ILS RWY 3R AMDT 3 DUAL VOR/ RADAR MINIM NA.

180

NOTICE TO AIRMEN   PART III

EXCERPTS

Extended Demonstration of an Experimental Computer Generated Voice Response System (VRS) for Dissemination of Limited Preflight Weather Products

Since April 1978, the FAA has been conducting a Public Demonstration of a Computer Generated Voice Response System (VRS) in the Washington, D.C. area. This demonstration, including a survey of pilot response, was officially in operation for a six-month period and brought before pilots in the area, the first exposure to FSS weather data dissemination via a computer controlled voice. The system has been developed by FAA Research and Development to evaluate the concept for FSS applications. The current experimental system operates independently from the Washington Flight Service Station, however, the concept is planned for implementation as part of the FSS Automation Program.

As a result of substantial system utilization and excellent pilot response, the VRS will remain operational indefinitely and become a test-bed on which additional weather products and capabilities can be evaluated in the future. The system will undergo several months of intermittent operation in order that modifications can be made to accommodate the extended operational mode; however, after February 1979, the reconfigured system should be stablized thus improving availability and extending the hours of operation. Some additional weather products may become available by the Spring of 1979.

System Description

The system provides 3 preflight weather products: hourly surface observations, terminal forecasts and forecasts winds aloft. These products are intended to be used for early flight planning purposes, providing the pilot with "go" or "no-go to the airport" information. *The system does not contain all the weather and flight data products useful for complete preflight planning. It is therefore not intended to replace an FSS specialist briefing. Selected information will be checked against predescribed criteria to assure reasonableness of data. Reports which are not received, cannot be deciphered or do not meet predetermined criteria will be voiced as "not available".* A Dual Tone Multifrequency Touchtone ᴿ type 12-key phone or acoustically coupled adapter is required for system use and data entry by the pilot.

System operation is simple. Upon calling the assigned local telephone number, the pilot will have a choice of which products he will receive from the computer voice for the locations he enters. When prompted by the computer to specify a location, the pilot will enter on the keyset (technique described below) the unique 3-letter location identifier (LOCID) assigned to each weather reporting station and terminal forecast location. Three-letter identifiers are readily available from the Airport/Facility Directory.

Printed on most keys of the pushbutton pad are 3 letters and a number. To enter a letter, two keystrokes are required. First press the key that contains the desired letter, then press either the 1, 2 or 3 key to indicate if the desired letter is the first, second or third letter shown on the key. This procedure is followed for each of the 3 letters in the LOCID. When all 3 letters have been entered, press the # key *twice*. Two # depressions always alerts the computer that your entry is complete. Questions asked by the system regarding which reports are desired should be answered "yes" or "no" and are entered simply by depressing the "Y" or "N" key followed by 2 # keys. When forecasts winds aloft are selected, the system will query the pilot for a time and altitude. These entries, being numerical only, can be entered in a single keystroke, pressing the appropriate numbered key. Again when the time or altitude has been entered, 2 # keys tells the computer the entry is complete.

A Walk Through the System   P—pilot
                                  S—system

P—pilot dials 347–3222
S—"HELLO", Current Greenwich Time is 1831.
S—"Enter Location Identifier".
P—Desired location—Pittsburgh (PIT) P–1, I–3, T–1; # #
S—"PAPA", "INDIA", "TANGO"; "ENTER NEXT ID"
P—Desired location—Wilmington (ILG) I–3, L–3, G–1; # #
S—"INDIA"; "LIMA", "GULF"; "Enter next ID"
P—# # (If no additional entries, enter # #)
S—Do you want hourly surface observations, answer yes or no?"
P—Y; # #
S—reads hourlys for PIT and ILG
S—"Do you want terminal forecasts, answer yes or no?"
P—Y; # #
S—reads forecasts for PIT and ILG
S—Do you want forecast winds aloft, answer yes or no?"
P—Y; # #
S—"How many hours from now; maximum is 30?"
P—"Six"
S—"At what altitude?"
P—85; # # (or 8500; # #)
S—"eight five"
S—reads winds aloft at requested altitude, +4000 feet and −4000 feet for each location.
S—"Do you want more information, answer yes or no?"
P—Y; # #
S—"Enter location identifier" and so forth.

Two special case entries regarding location identifiers require additional comments. The first case occurs when the LOCID contains the letters Q or Z. These letters do not generally appear on pushbutton. The FAA system assigns these letters to the number 1 key in the sequence of Q, blank, Z in the 1, 2, 3 position respectively. Therefore Q would be entered as 1–1, Z as 1–3. The blank or second position is not used at this time. Secondly, when the LOCID contains both letters and numbers such as 6B2 (Greenville Maine) the numbers must be entered with two strokes such that the computer recognizes the sequence as a mixed alphanumeric entry. This is accomplished by preceding all numbers by O. The entry for 6B2 then becomes O6, B2, O2, # #.

Entry readback is a feature of this system which allows an accuracy check for each item entered. As each identifier, altitude, or time is entered a readback will be spoken, generally in the phonetic alphabet. For some predetermined locations, the actual names of the airport will be spoken such that pilots can evaluate which response is preferable. For example, Washington National Airport (DCA) will be voiced as "Washington National."

Pilot utilization of this new concept is encouraged. Pilots who desire additional information on the system operation or who have questions and comments regarding system use or future system designs, please mail a self-addressed and stamped request to:

VRS
DOT/FAA/NAFEC
ANA–250
Atlantic City, N.J. 08405

GRAPHIC NOTICES AND SUPPLEMENTAL DATA SECTION

FOREWORD

Graphic Notices and Supplemental Data is a publication containing aeronautical data, area notices or navigational route information which is supplemental to other operational areonautical publications and charts. Data contained in this publication is, generally, not subject to frequent change. Data of a more critical nature, such as the tabulation of North American Routes (NAR) or the graphic area notices (i.e., Terminal Radar Service Areas [TRSA] and Terminal Control Areas [TCA]), which may require revision prior to the next scheduled printing of this publication, will be revised in the publication *Notices to Airmen (Class II)*. These revisions will appear only once, so users are advised to tear them out of the *Notices to Airmen* and insert them in this publication until the next issue. *Graphic Notices and Supplemental Data* is a quarterly publication and is available through subscription from the Superintendent of Documents.

Graphic Notices and Supplemental Data also serves as the section RAC–9 in the *United States Aeronautical Information Publication*. The US AIP, issued in one volume, is the basic aeronautical information document published for international use and contains information of a lasting character, essential to international air navigation. It is available in English only and is maintained on a current basis by quarterly amendment service consisting of a checklist, reprinted pages and, in the case of minor amendments, manuscript corrections. This publication is a loose leaf publication made to fit a standard three ring binder. Subscriptions are available through the Superintendent of Documents. A subscription will consist of the basic issue (dated January, 1979) and seven amendments, as they are published. The next basic issue will be in January of 1981.

TABLE OF CONTENTS EXCERPTS

AREA ADVISORIES

THE FOLLOWING ADVISORIES CONTAIN AERONAUTICAL INFORMATION THAT DOES NOT CONCERN A SPECIFIC AIRPORT OR NAVAID, OR FAILS, FOR SOME OTHER REASON, TO MEET THE CRITERIA FOR INCLUSION OF OTHER PERMANENT BASE LINE PUBLICATIONS SUCH AS THE *AIRPORT/FACILITY DIRECTORY*. SUCH INFORMATION WILL BE AUTOMATICALLY TRANSFERRED TO THIS PUBLICATION FROM THE *NOTICES TO AIRMEN* (CLASS II) PUBLICATION WHEN THE ORIGINATOR INDICATES THAT THE ADVISORY IS EITHER PERMANENT OR EXPECTED TO REMAIN CURRENT LONG ENOUGH TO WARRANT PUBLICATION HERE. THESE ADVISORIES ARE GROUPED UNDER STATE HEADINGS, AND, WHERE APPROPRIATE, UNDER CITY OR GEOGRAPHIC LOCATIONS. ADVISORIES THAT PERTAIN TO MORE THAN ONE STATE OR REQUIRE A FULL PRINTED PAGE WILL BE INCLUDED UNDER THE *GENERAL* HEADING. THE NUMBER IN PARENTHESIS FOLLOWING EACH ENTRY IS THE MONTH AND YEAR THAT THE ADVISORY WAS ISSUED.

GENERAL

20 CHANNEL OPERATION: The implementation of 25 kHz channel communication assignments for high altitude en route sectors started on a case-by-case basis in 1977. Therefore, to insure unrestricted IFR operation, the use of 720 channel communications equipment (25 kHz channel spacing) is required.

LOW-LEVEL WIND SHEAR ALERT SYSTEM: This is a computerized system which detects the presence of a possible hazardous low-level wind shear by continuously comparing the winds measured by sensors installed around the periphery of an airport with the wind measured at the centerfield location. If the difference between the centerfield wind sensor and a peripheral wind sensor becomes excessive, a thunderstorm or thunderstorm gust front wind shear is probable. When this condition exists, the tower controller will provide arrival and departure aircraft with an advisory of the situation which includes the centerfield wind plus the remote site location and wind. Since the sensors are not all associated with specific runways, descriptions of the remote sites will be based on an eight point compass system. For example: "Delta one twenty four centerfield wind two seven zero at one zero. South boundary wind one four zero at three zero." Remote sensor wind information will be provided on an available basis and a local NOTAM will be issued when an outage occurs.

ARIZONA

THE GRAND CANYON CAVERNS AREA: Quarry located 3 miles west-southwest of Grand Canyon Caverns Landing Strip. Aircraft are cautioned to avoid this area during daylight hours, if necessary to fly over the area maintain a minimum altitude of 4000 feet AGL due to possible damage from flying rocks or turbulence caused by blasting. (3/78)

GRAND CANYON AND PETRIFIED FOREST NATIONAL PARKS: All pilots are requested to avoid flying below the canyon rim and to maintain a distance 1500 feet above and horizontally from all scenic overlooks, parks, and trails. (10/74)

CALIFORNIA

LOS ANGELES ARTCC: The use of 720 channel communication equipment is required for continued unrestricted IFR operations in the Los Angeles ARTCC high altitude sectors. (4/78)

OAKLAND ARTCC: The use of 720 communication equipment is required for continued unrestricted IFR operations in the Oakland ARTCC high altitude sectors. (4/78)

SALINAS RIVER AND OCEAN SHORELINE: Avoid flying below 1000 feet over a 400 acre Wildlife Refuge along the south side of the mouth of the Salinas River and ocean shoreline eastward. (1/76)

CONNECTICUT

BRADLEY INTERNATIONAL AIRPORT: Visual confirmation of voice takeoff clearance (VICON) test. During the period between August 1979 through March 1980, an operational evaluation will be conducted at the Bradley International Airport, of an experimental light system which is intended to enhance safety by providing a second stimulus (visual) which is used to "CONFIRM" the voice takeoff clearance. The nonstandard light system is installed at all departure points on all runways of the Bradley International Airport.

VISUAL CONFIRMATION OF VOICE TAKEOFF CLEARANCE
VICON

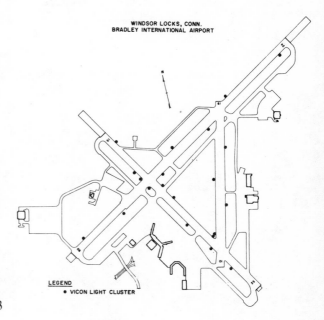

WINDSOR LOCKS, CONN.
BRADLEY INTERNATIONAL AIRPORT

LEGEND
● VICON LIGHT CLUSTER

AREA NAVIGATION ROUTES (RNAV)

Area navigation systems permit navigation via a selected course to a predefined point without having to fly directly toward or away from a navigational aid. Typical of such systems are doppler radar, inertial and course line computers.

Introduction of the area navigation capability into the National Airspace System provides a means of overcoming many of the constraints of the VOR system. Elimination of the requirement to fly along radials that lead directly to or from the ground station makes it possible to design routes and procedures that better facilitate the movement of traffic.

Guidelines for the implementation of area navigation within the National Airspace System were issued in the form of Advisory Circular 90–45A on 2 February 1975. Advisory Circular 90–45A contains standards and methods for obtaining approval for use of area navigation equipment in IFR operations. It also contains air traffic control procedures applicable to approved area navigation equipment.

Since the VOR system forms the basis for the existing airway and air traffic control systems, area navigation route definitions and air traffic control clearances will be in terms of, and referenced to, VOR ground stations. However, latitude/longitude descriptions of fixes forming area navigation routes are provided to facilitate the use of airborne systems that are not dependent on VOR input signals.

Area navigation routes are numbered in a manner similar to VOR airways and jet routes. The suffix "R" identifies the route as an area navigation route. When filing an IFR flight plan containing an area navigation route, the route number may be filed in the same manner as a VOR airway number. The filed route should clearly define the intended route during transition from the VOR structure to the area navigation structure.

Area navigation route numbering will be as follows:

(1) Series 700 (low) and 800, 900 (high) routes—Routes designated in Parts 71 and 75. Routes expected to be in frequent use by more than one user and published on appropriate U.S. Government Charts. MEA will be published in FAR 95.

(2) Series 500 (low) and 600 (high) routes—Routes published in the Graphic Notices and Supplemental Data. Routes planned for more than one user but their expected usage does not justify Government charting. MEA when not published in FAR 95 and the Graphic Notices and Supplemental Data, will be provided by ATC.

(3) Series 300 (low) and 400 (high) routes—Routes established primarily for one user. Not carried on Government charts. MEAs will be periodically published in the listing of non-95 routes.

The routes contained herein are those of the 500 and 600 Series.

Each area navigation route listed is based on a center line which extends between fixes, described by reference to VOR/DME, called waypoints, specified for that route. Each waypoint is listed by geographical name, followed by the VOR/DME fix description in the format: VOR STATION RADIAL/DME MILEAGE (example POR 033/010). Also included are the track to be flown (Mag track), the VOR changeover point (COP, with "MP" indicating Midpoint) the distance (DIST) between waypoints, and the latitude/longitude description.

HIGH ALTITUDE AREA NAVIGATION ROUTE
(UNCHARTED)

WAYPOINT NAME	DESCRIPTION VOR/DME	GEOGRAPHICAL COORDINATES

J620R
Hemlo (Pacific Ocean) to Dayah, Oregon

Hemlo .... ONP 216.0/137.0		43°18'08'',126°40'49''
MAG TRACK: 047.4/229.8		DIST: 158
COP: NOT REQUIRED		MEA: 18000
		MAA: 45000
Eugene .... ONP 105.8/45.2		44°07'16'',123°13'18''
MAG TRACK: 056.2/237.7		DIST: 95
MAG TRACK: 059.1/240.2		DIST: 70
COP: 95 E EUGENE		MEA: 18000
		MAA: 45000
Dayah .... PDT 178.3/69.4		44°33'58'',119°26'45''

LOW ALTITUDE AREA NAVIGATION ROUTE
(UNCHARTED)

WAYPOINT NAME	DESCRIPTION VOR/DME	GEOGRAPHICAL COORDINATES

V513R
Arcadia, Washington, to Cove, Washington

Arcadia .... SEA 212.4/27.2		47°10'13.0'',122°50'54
MAG TRACK: 017/197		DIST:
COP: NOT REQUIRED		MEA: 30
		MAA: 175
Cove .... SEA 255.3/8.3		47°27'11.0'',112°30'40.

V515R
Roy, Washington, to Meadowdale, Washington

Roy .... SEA 175.4/25.4		47°01'54.0'',122°29'36.
MAG TRACK: 020/200		DIST:
COP: NOT REQUIRED		MEA: 30
		MAA: 175

SPECIAL OPERATIONS
CIVIL FLIGHT TEST AREAS

The graphics on the following pages depict areas that have been designated as flight test areas for civil aircraft manufacturers. These flight tests shall be conducted under the following conditions.

Operations—Conducted by military jet type aircraft at indicated airspeeds above 250 knots when ceiling greater than 3,000 feet AGL and visibility five (5) miles or more.

Altitudes—10,000 feet to surface.

Hours of Operations—Check graphics or Flight Service Station for hours of operation.

BOEING LOW LEVEL ROUTE #1

HOURS OF OPERATION-CONTINUOUS

OPERATIONS-CONDUCTED BY B52
AIRCRAFT IN EXCESS OF 250 KTS WHEN
CEILING GREATER THAN 3000 AGL AND
VISIBILITY 5 MILES OR MORE.

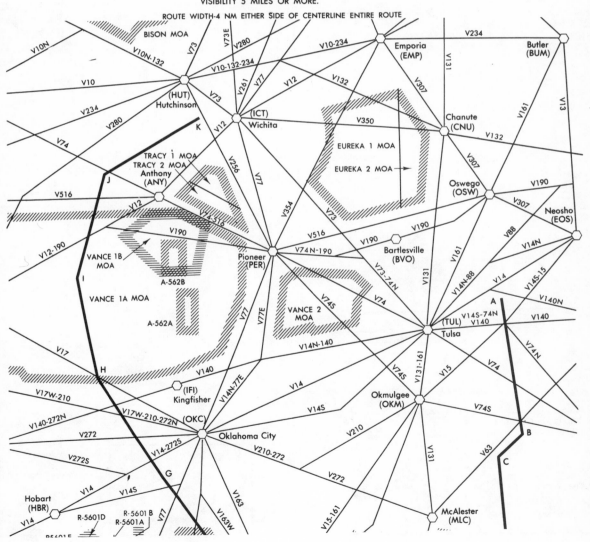

24 MAY 1979

NATIONAL WEATHER SERVICE (NWS) UPPER AIR OBSERVING STATIONS
EXCERPTS

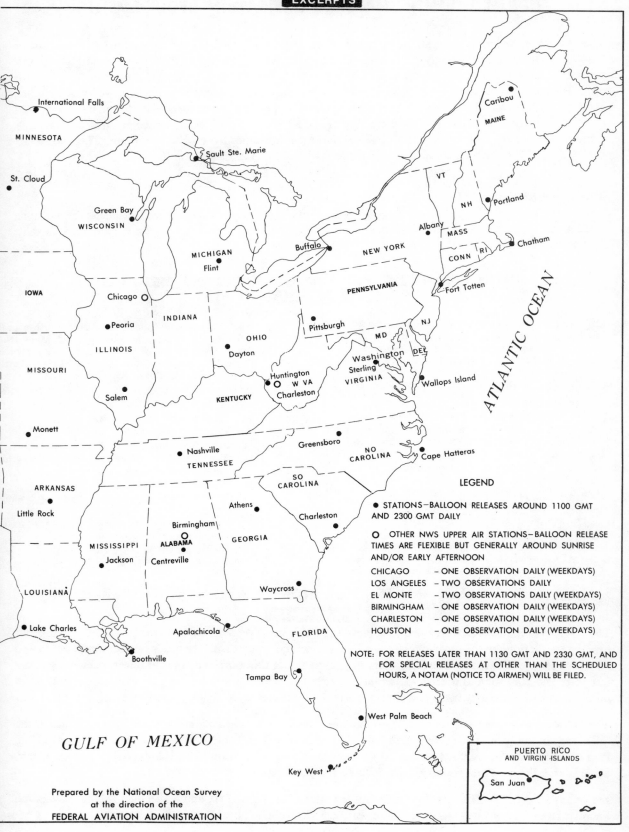

LEGEND

● STATIONS—BALLOON RELEASES AROUND 1100 GMT AND 2300 GMT DAILY

○ OTHER NWS UPPER AIR STATIONS—BALLOON RELEASE TIMES ARE FLEXIBLE BUT GENERALLY AROUND SUNRISE AND/OR EARLY AFTERNOON

CHICAGO	— ONE OBSERVATION DAILY (WEEKDAYS)
LOS ANGELES	— TWO OBSERVATIONS DAILY
EL MONTE	— TWO OBSERVATIONS DAILY (WEEKDAYS)
BIRMINGHAM	— ONE OBSERVATION DAILY (WEEKDAYS)
CHARLESTON	— ONE OBSERVATION DAILY (WEEKDAYS)
HOUSTON	— ONE OBSERVATION DAILY (WEEKDAYS)

NOTE: FOR RELEASES LATER THAN 1130 GMT AND 2330 GMT, AND FOR SPECIAL RELEASES AT OTHER THAN THE SCHEDULED HOURS, A NOTAM (NOTICE TO AIRMEN) WILL BE FILED.

Prepared by the National Ocean Survey
at the direction of the
FEDERAL AVIATION ADMINISTRATION

PUERTO RICO AND VIRGIN ISLANDS

San Juan

EXCERPTS
NORTH ATLANTIC MINIMUM NAVIGATION REQUIREMENTS

The concept of minimum Navigation Performance Specifications (MNPS) has been adopted on a world-wide basis by the International Civil Aviation Organization (ICAO). MNPS has the objective of ensuring both safe separation of aircraft and also to enable operators to derive maximum economic benefit from the improvement in accuracy of navigation equipment which has been demonstrated in recent years. An implicit condition of MNPS is that all operators must maintain the specified operating standards and be aware of the inherent obligations of the MNPS requirements. The MNPS concept will be implemented on a regional basis. Certain areas of the North Atlantic (NAT) region have introduced the MNPS concept. These areas are known as NAT MNPS airspace and include the following defined airspace boundaries:

(a) between FL275 and FL400;

(b) between latitudes 27°N and 67°N;

(c) in the East – the Eastern boundaries of CTAs Santa Maria Oceanic, Shanwick Oceanic and Reykjavik;

(d) in the West – the Western boundaries of CTAs Reykjavik and Gander Oceanic and New York Oceanic East of longitude 60°W.

NORTH ATLANTIC STANDARDIZED AIR/GROUND MESSAGES
EXCERPTS

1. *General*

1.1 In order to make an evaluation it is proposed that within the North Atlantic (NAT) Region all ATS Air/Ground messages should be categorized under one of the following headings:

    (a) Position report

    (b) Request Clearance

    (c) Revised estimate

    (d) Miscellaneous air/ground message

The purpose of the evaluation is to determine whether pilot/controller response times can be improved.

1.2 In order to enable the ground stations to process messages in the shortest possible time, it is requested that pilots should observe the following rules:

    1) use the correct type of message applicable to the data transmitted;

    2) state the message type on the contact call to the ground station or at the start of the message (except if it is a miscellaneous message);

3.1.2 REQUEST CLEARANCE

1) To be used in conjunction with a routine position report to obtain a change of Mach No. flight level or route and to obtain *Westbound* Oceanic clearance prior to entering Reykjavik Santa Maria or Shanwick CTAs.

CONTENT OF REQUEST CLEARANCE MESSAGE AND DATA SEQUENCE

    (a) "REQUEST CLEARANCE"

    (b) Flight identification

    (c) Present or last reported position

    (d) Time over present or last reported position (hours and minutes)

    (e) Present flight level

    (f) Next position on assigned route or oceanic entry point

    (g) Estimate for next position or oceanic entry point (hours and minutes)

    (h) Requested Mach No (if applicable)

    (i) Requested flight level (if applicable)

NORTH AMERICAN ROUTES FOR NORTH ATLANTIC TRAFFIC (NAR)
EXCERPTS

The NAR system has been developed to achieve the following objectives: (a) to organize the fluctuating and revising traffic flows in the most efficient possible manner, consistent with the needs of aircraft operators and air traffic services; (b) to expedite flight planning; (c) to reduce the complexity of route clearances and thereby minimize the confusion and error potential inherent in lengthy transmissions and readbacks; and (d) to minimize the time spent by pilots and controllers in the route clearance delivery function.

The NAR system comprises a series of pre-planned routes over existing airway/route systems from/to the following coastal fixes serving the North Atlantic traffic: Schefferville, Hopedale, Wabush, Waco, Lake Eon, Port Menier, Natashquan, St. Anthony, Dotty, Springdale, Gander, Ramea, St. John's (Nfld), Sydney, Color, Sable Island, Poggo. These routes are divided into two portions.

a. Common Portion – That portion of the route between the coastal fix and a specified Inland Navigation Facility. Example – Route NA108 common portion is "St. John's (Nfld) HL575 J575 Boston."

PARACHUTE JUMPING AREAS

The following tabulation lists all *reported* parachute jumping sites in the United States. Unless otherwise indicated, all activities are conducted during daylight hours and under VFR conditions. The busiest periods of activity are normally on weekends and holidays, but jumps can be expected at anytime during the week at the locations listed. Jumps within restricted airspace are not listed.

All times are local and altitudes MSL unless otherwise specified.

Refer to Federal Aviation Regulations Volume 6, Part 105 for required procedures relating to parachute jumping.

Organizations desiring listing of their jumping activites in this publication should contact the nearest FAA facility (FSS, tower, or ARTCC).

Qualified parachute jumping sites will be depicted on sectional charts.

Note: (c) in this publication indicates that the parachute jump area is charted.

To qualify for charting, a jump area must meet the following criteria:

(1) Been in operation for at least 1 year.

(2) Operate year round (at least on weekends).

(3) Log 4,000 or more jumps each year.

In addition, jump sites can be nominated by FAA Regions if special circumstances require charting.

LOCATION	DISTANCE AND RADIAL FROM NEAREST VOR/VORTAC	MAXIMUM ALTITUDE	REMARKS
ALABAMA			
Allen Army Heliport	11 NM; 253° Dothan	12,500	1 NM radius. SR–SS weekends and holidays
(c) Bayou La Batre, Roy E. Ray Arpt	12 NM; 217° Brookley	12,500	Daily **SR–SS**
Bessemer, Old Bessemer Arpt	16 NM; 057° Brookwood	10,000	1030–SS weekends
(c) Elberta, Horak Arpt	11 NM; 268° Saufley	12,500	Weekends and holidays 0800–½ hour after SS; Wed thru Fri 1000–½ hour after SS
Ellis Drop Zone	15 NM; 220° Decatur	1,500	0.4 NM radius. Occasional use
Eutaw Muni Arpt	30 NM; 200° Tuscaloosa	13,000 AGL	Weekends and holidays
Harvest, Epps Arpk	9 NM; 297° Huntsville	13,500	Daily SR–SS
Headland Muni Arpt	8 NM; 070° Dothan	15,000	Weekdays 1200–SS; Sat-Sun, and holidays SR–SS
Jacksonville Muni Arpt	18 NM; 126° Gadsden	12,500	SR–SS weekends

GRAPHIC NOTICES AND SUPPLEMENTAL DATA
TERMINAL AREA GRAPHIC NOTICES
EXCERPTS

Under this heading will be found a number of graphics showing areas of concentrated traffic for the information and guidance of pilots operating under VFR in the terminal areas depicted. The graphics are intended to assist VFR pilots planning flight in the areas and in many instances recommended or suggested VFR routes/corridors are shown. The information presented is in no way to be considered mandatory or "legal"; it is advisory only.

TABLE OF CONTENTS

TERMINAL AREA GRAPHIC NOTICE
(NOT TO BE USED FOR NAVIGATION)
EXCERPTS

ABILENE-DYESS, TEXAS

THIS GRAPHIC SHOWS THE PRINCIPAL IFR JET TRAFFIC FLOWS. AIRCRAFT LANDING ABILENE
MUNICIPAL ARE ENCOURAGED TO CONTACT ABILENE APPROACH CONTROL ON 121.3 MHz
APPROXIMATELY 25 MILES OUT FOR STAGE II SERVICES. RADAR TRAFFIC ADVISORY SERVICE
WILL BE PROVIDED VFR AIRCRAFT ON A TRAFFIC PERMITTING BASIS. THIS SERVICE DOES NOT RELIEVE
PILOTS OF THEIR RESPONSIBILITY TO SEE AND AVOID OTHER AIRCRAFT. STAGE II RADAR SERVICE
IS EXPLAINED IN THE AIM.

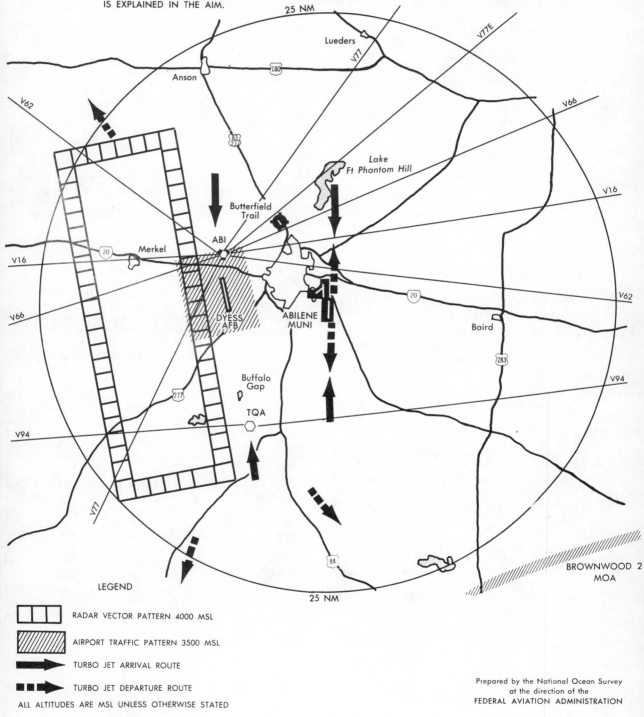

LEGEND

▢▢▢	RADAR VECTOR PATTERN 4000 MSL
▨	AIRPORT TRAFFIC PATTERN 3500 MSL
➤	TURBO JET ARRIVAL ROUTE
▪▪▪➤	TURBO JET DEPARTURE ROUTE

ALL ALTITUDES ARE MSL UNLESS OTHERWISE STATED

Prepared by the National Ocean Survey
at the direction of the
FEDERAL AVIATION ADMINISTRATION

TERMINAL RADAR SERVICE AREAS
(TRSA)

SERVICES PROVIDED

1. Services within a TRSA are provided on a voluntary pilot participation basis. ATC assumes that VFR aircraft entering or departing the TRSA want the service unless the pilot advises otherwise. If VFR pilots do not want the service, they should inform ground control or approach control, as appropriate, on initial contact by stating 'NEGATIVE STAGE III,' or by making a similar comment.

2. Radar vectoring and sequencing is provided on a full-time basis for all IFR and participating VFR aircraft landing at the primary airport, and at other airports if specifically advertised.

3. Separation between all participating VFR aircraft and all IFR aircraft operating within the TRSA is provided.

4. Radar advisories on all unidentified aircraft are provided on a workload permitting basis.

5. Service provided in a TRSA is also called Stage III Service and a more detailed explanation of the program is provided in the Airman's Information Manual, Part 1.

FLIGHT PROCEDURES

1. IFR Flights—Aircraft operating within the TRSA shall be operated in accordance with current IFR procedures.

2. VFR Flights

a. Airports within the TRSA:

(1) Arriving aircraft landing at airports within the TRSA are expected to contact Approach Control on specified frequencies in relation to geographical fixes depicted on the TRSA charts on the following pages. Initial contact should be made outside of the TRSA.

(2) Departing aircraft should inform ATC of their intended destination and/or route of flight and proposed cruising altitude. Departing aircraft will be advised by the tower when to contact departure control and given a frequency to be used.

b. Airports underlying the TRSA—Unless the flight will be conducted below the floor of the TRSA, arriving aircraft are expected to contact Approach Control on specified frequencies in relation to geographical fixes listed on the individual TRSA charts. Initial contact should be made outside of the TRSA.

c. Transiting aircraft—Aircraft desiring to transit the TRSA are expected to contact Departure/Approach Control on specified frequencies and in relation to geographical fixes listed on the individual TRSA charts.

ATC PROCEDURES

1. While operating within a TRSA, pilots are provided Stage III service and separation. In the event of a radar outage, separation and sequencing of VFR aircraft will be suspended as this service is depedent on radar. The pilot will be advised that the service is not available and issued wind, runway information, and the time or place to contact the tower. Traffic information will be provided on a workload-permitting basis.

2. To facilitate radar identification of arriving and transiting VFR aircraft, ATC may request such aircraft to report their position in relation to fixes (prominent geographical or radio).

3. Radar headings and, if required, altitude assignments may be given to VFR flights operating within the TRSA.

NOTE: Assignment of radar headings and/or altitudes are based on the provision that a pilot operating in accordance with VFR is expected to advise ATC if compliance with an assigned route, radar heading or altitude will cause the pilot to violate such rules.

4. Traffic information on observed but unidentified radar targets will be provided on a workload permitting basis.

5. When VFR aircraft are being held within the TRSA and control is based thereon, the ATC clearance will specify the distance (radius) and, if appropriate, the direction from the geographical fix within which holding is to be accomplished. In such cases, the pilot will be advised when to EXPECT FURTHER CLEARANCE.

6. During weather conditions equal to or better than basic VFR, 500 feet vertical separation may be employed between VFR flights and/or between VFR and IFR flights operating within the TRSA.

7. During weather conditions equal to or better than basic VFR, visual separation may be employed between VFR flights and/or between VFR and IFR flights operating within the TRSA.

8. When IFR flights, operating in VFR weather conditions, are being sequenced with other traffic and the pilot reports the aircraft he is to follow is in sight, the pilot may be advised to follow such traffic and may be cleared for a "visual approach."